SUGAR AND ALL THAT...

A History of TATE & LYLE

To that Royal Carbohydrate
SUCROSE
and its huge cousinhood,
and to those who sought it,
found it, produce it, and consume it
MANKIND*

*A technical term which, of course, embraces Personkind—if they so wish.

SUGAR AND ALL THAT...

A History of TATE & LYLE

Antony Hugill

GENTRY BOOKS · LONDON

First published 1978
© Antony Hugill
ISBN 0 85614 048 1

Published by Gentry Books Ltd.
Designed by Brian Roll
Filmset by Computer Photoset Ltd., Birmingham
Printed by William Clowes & Sons Ltd.,
London, Beccles and Colchester

Contents

	Author's Preface	9
	Introduction: Sugar is Here to Stay	11
1.	The Bee, the Reed and the Root	15
2.	First Beginnings	27
3.	'Before the War'	60
4.	1914–1918	67
5.	Tate and Lyle	74
6.	Between the Wars (1)	80
7.	The Beet Venture	87
8.	Between the Wars (2)	96
9.	The Greene Committee	102
10.	The Spanish Main (1)	108
11.	Before the Next War	126
12.	1939–1945	129
13.	'As If Nothing Had Happened'	138
14.	Mr. Cube and All That	145
15.	Post War	174
16.	Central Africa	201
17.	The Spanish Main (2)	209
18.	The 1950s and 1960s at Home	231
19.	West Africa	238
20.	Canada	240
21.	Towards the 1970s At Home	247
22.	Belize	251
23.	United Molasses	256
24.	A Foothold in Europe	269
25.	The Seventies and Change	277
26.	Research and All That	283
27.	The EEC and After: Manbré & Garton	297
28.	South Africa and All That	307
29.	Where Are We Now?	310
	Afterthoughts	314
	Bibliography	315
	Index	317

Illustrations

Colour Plates

frontispiece Mr. Cube
following page 32 Henry Tate's first enterprise–a grocer's shop in Liverpool.
following page 32 Address of thanks to Henry Tate from the Tate Institute, Silvertown.
following page 32 Thames Refinery in 1978, after 100 years.
following page 64 *Athel Monarch* at speed.
following page 64 Mechanical cane harvesting.
following page 64 Brechin Castle Factory, Trinidad.
following page 128 Belize–the new factory at Orange Walk (Liberdad).
following page 128 Unitank's installation at Gray's.
following page 160 One of the new generation of road tankers serving food manufacturers.
following page 160 Redpath Refinery, Toronto.
following page 224 Farrow–makers of irrigation equipment. Part of Tate & Lyle Engineering.
following page 224 Richards' Shipyard built this splendid craft.
following page 224 Berger and Plate grow peas and lentils–Springdale, Idaho.
following page 256 The Philip Lyle Memorial Research Laboratory, Reading.
following page 256 Yonkers Refinery, Albany, U.S.A.
following page 314 Mr. Cube.

Monochrome Illustrations

following page 31 John Kerr; James Fairrie; Robert MacFie; David Martineau.
following page 38 Handling 'wet char' the old way.
following page 38 The Gang's All Here. Outside Love Lane, 1897.
following page 40 A sugar baker and his loaves. Mid-nineteenth century.
following page 41 The Langen Cube Plant at Thames, 1890.
following page 49 A group at Henry Tate & Sons Ltd., Liverpool, 1881.
following page 49 A group at Abram Lyle & Sons Ltd., Plaistow Wharf, 1892.
following page 49 Plaistow Wharf before the Lyles.
following page 49 Ladies of the Bag Store, Thames Refinery.
following page 49 Dan Girdwood, Foreman of the Cooperage at Thames, 1878–1906.
following page 49 Miss L. Morgan in the Thames Laboratory, c. 1910.
following page 64 Thames Refinery from the river, c. 1908.
following page 70 King George V visits Thames Refinery.
following page 70 The old Plaistow chimney in 1907.
following page 108 Bobby Kirkwood and friends in the canepiece.
following page 129 'What's it like down there?' September 7th, 1940.
following page 129 The yard at Plaistow after a raid.
following page 146 Mr. Cube at work.
following page 146 Press cartoons from the Nationalization Campaign.
following page 177 Sir Ernest Tate; Sir Robert Park Lyle; Leonard Lyle; George Vernon Tate; Sir Ian Lyle; Sir Peter Runge; John Oliver Lyle; F. H. ('Tony') Tate.
following page 182 An early Lyle square-rigged vessel.
following page 182 An early Lyle Steamer
following page 183 One of the big 'uns, *Athel King*.
following page 183 Appropriately named *Sugar Carrier*.
following page 192 Before even steam lorries.
following page 192 A Tate 'Steamer'.
following page 232 Rig of the day for Hesser girls, 1925.
following page 232 Twenty-five years on. Hesser girls in 1950.
following page 264 *Athel King* (the first), 1926–1940.
following page 264 *Athel King*, sunk 1940–picture taken from her attacker.
following page 274 Dompierre, one of the beet factories owned by Raffineries Say.
following page 286 A.R.D.E.S.C.O.–home of Plaistow Wharf's Manager before the telephone.
following page 286 The first laboratory at Liverpool.

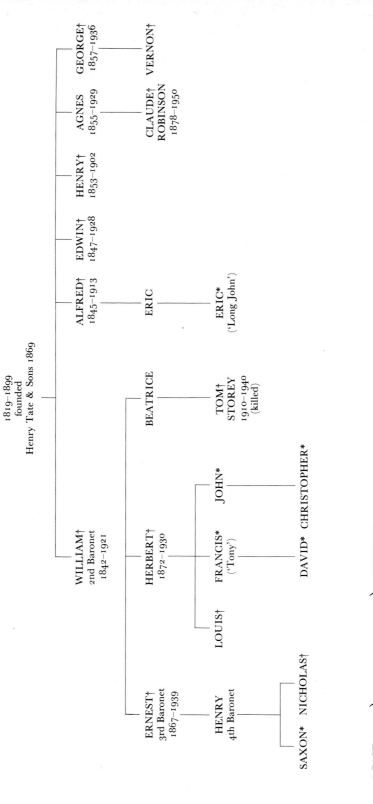

HENRY TATE
1st Baronet
1819–1899
founded
Henry Tate & Sons 1869

ALFRED† 1845–1913   EDWIN† 1847–1928   HENRY† 1853–1902   AGNES 1855–1929   GEORGE† 1857–1936

CLAUDE† ROBINSON 1878–1950   VERNON†

ERIC

ERIC* ('Long John')

WILLIAM† 2nd Baronet 1842–1921

BEATRICE

TOM† STOREY 1910–1940 (killed)

HERBERT† 1872–1930

JOHN*

FRANCIS* ('Tony')

LOUIS†

DAVID*   CHRISTOPHER*

ERNEST† 3rd Baronet 1867–1939

HENRY 4th Baronet

SAXON*   NICHOLAS†

1977

† PAST   } MEMBERS OF   } HENRY TATE & SONS
* PRESENT   TATE & LYLE LTD.

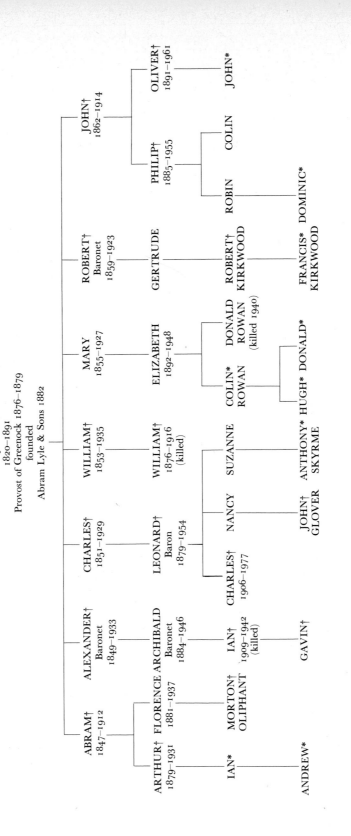

† PAST
* PRESENT
} MEMBERS OF {
ABRAM LYLE & SONS
TATE & LYLE LTD.

Author's Preface

'Memories are like mulligatawny soup in a cheap restaurant,
better not stirred.'
(P. G. Wodehouse, 1881–1977)

While admiring the late Master's works one does not have to accept everything he says as Gospel, and the above obiter dicta should – like the soup – be taken with a pinch. It is there merely to Lend Tone.

There have been numbers of histories of sugar, of Tate & Lyle, of some of its component parts, and of the major families involved in sugar refining in Britain and elsewhere. These have been ruthlessly pillaged for the present work, and acknowledgment is made to the authors, dead and alive. Most of them are listed in the Bibliography.

There has even been a brief history in verse, composed in 1971 by Mr. F. H. (Tony) Tate, at some distance from and with apologies to S. Holloway, Esq., from which certain immortal stanzas will be quoted in their place. Intended, if read aloud in a broad Lancashire accent, to give unabated pleasure to the reader, if not to his neighbours, this Opus begins:

> The history of Henry and Abram
> Has often been written in prose
> By many an eminent writer
> (For whom we have paid through the nose.)

The present writer is not eminent, but he has had the advantage of serving in the company at various levels, including that of director (and, what is more, being paid for it). He has thus had the luck to make friends with hundreds if not some thousands of his fellow employees, and other people involved in sugar. Retrospect, like absence, makes the heart grow fonder and they are remembered with affection even if only relatively few are mentioned by name.

North of the Border – the Ancient Habitat of Lyles and other Picts and Scots – there is a toast: 'Here's tae us. Wha's like us? Dom' few, an' they're a'deid.'

Fortunately, however, many are still around as this goes to press. To them and to those who are no longer with us, the author raises his glass.

Acknowledgments

So many people have helped with this book. First of all there was John Lyle who suggested it. Then Tony Tate and his Committee who guided it, Jimmy Somner, Martin Frizelle, Christopher Burness and Sheila Chisholm. Jimmy did most of the leg work and fishing out of documents, Sheila much of the typing – and soothing. Iris Dalton, Jackie Martin, Beryl Harris and Dorrie Brothers struggled successfully with my handwriting, and Sheila and Beryl put the manuscript together. I am very grateful to the Tate & Lyle Photographic Department, Eric Davey and Alan Smith, who produced most of the photographs and also copied a lot more.

Several determined men read the whole or large parts of the typescript and suggested improvements – John Lyle, Tony Tate, Morton Oliphant, Tony Wingate-Saul, Jimmy Somner, Fred Sudbury, Charles Runge, Bobby St. John Cooper and Martin Frizelle. Ann Alford read the proofs.

Others helped with the provision of information on different sections, and the very necessary checking for error: Sir Ian Lyle, Sir Henry Tate (Bt.), Saxon Tate, Jim Hobbs, John Ellyatt, Chuck Vlitos, Harold Powers, Bill North, Denis Dickinson; Fred Sudbury, Geoff Collard, Norman Kindon; Peter Nash, Gwilym Williams, Albert Casey, Malcolm Endersby and their colleagues at Plaistow, Thames Refinery and Liverpool; Neil Shaw, Clarence Coyle, Howarth Magee and Jack Wood; Bill Coupland and Frank Curtis; David Kerr, Harry Alexander, Miss Johnson; Alan Forster, Reg Gower, Peter Clark, Bill Bennett and Tim Duggan; Bill Meneight, Ted Tibbitts and Mike Gollin; Tom Williams.

Among living authors I am grateful to John Watson for his *Hundred Years of Sugar Refining,* Bill Meneight for letting me see the proofs of his *History of United Molasses,* Jeanne Stoddard for her *History of Manbré & Garton;* the anonymous author of the *History of Pease Transport;* John Orbell for letting me see his *History of the Lyle Shipping Company* in manuscript; John Beckett for permission to use as a source the *History of the British Sugar Corporation,* and Michael Gill and his young ladies for helping me go through *Tate & Lyle Times.*

Writing is a usually lonely business but the work of producing this book was made less lonely than most, thanks to the cloud of witnesses referred to above.

Introduction
Sugar is here to stay

Sugar is here to stay. It has been part of human diet for many millennia, an increasingly important part, occasionally a controversial one. It has been, if not the cause of, at least a major factor in arguments leading to and following wars. It has frequently been involved in politics, notably over the past two centuries. Disraeli, indeed, once observed–'Strange that a manufacture which charms infancy and soothes old age should so frequently occasion political disaster.'[1]   Yet what *is* sugar? It is one of an enormous family of naturally occurring substances, some much sweeter than others, all formed from carbon, hydrogen and oxygen and known to chemists as carbohydrates. The family includes celluloses at one end of the scale and the simplest member of the alcohols, methanol, at the other. The sweetening carbohydrates are relatively few in number and only two kinds need concern us here–sucrose, the sugar used most commonly in food and drink, and 'reducing sugars' or 'inverts' which are found in fruits and honey.

Sucrose occurs widely in the vegetable kingdom, in the roots and stems of all grasses, in numbers of other roots and in the sap of many trees. The juices of most fruits contain it, along with inverts, in quantities depending on the type of fruit and its ripeness.

Its presence is due to a complex natural chemical reaction not yet completely understood. This appears to take place in minute cells (called chloroplasts) in the leaves under the stimulus of sunlight in the presence of the green colouring matter of the plants (called chlorophyll) and results in carbon dioxide from the air combining with water to form sugar, the plant exhaling oxygen. The process is known as photosynthesis. The sugar, being water-soluble, travels in the sap of the plant from the leaves to other parts, where it is stored. In one major commercial source, sugar cane, the storage is in the stem, and in another, sugar beet, in the root. But the sugar is believed to move about in the growing plant under the influence of daylight.

Through no fault of his own, man cannot carry out this process himself and depends on plants to do it for him. When he consumes sugar, or any carbohydrate, his body inhales oxygen in order to convert his basic fuel, blood sugar in the form of glucose, into energy. While doing so his body exhales dioxide. Sugar consumption is thus the reverse of sugar formation. It is, therefore, correct to regard sugar as a totally natural food and it has, as we shall see, a long history.

[1] *Disraeli,* Lord George Bentinck (1852).

Just after the middle of the twentieth century it became a fashionable target for some dietitians and for certain scientists, as an alleged cause of numerous diseases to which every son or daughter of Adam and Eve must one day succumb. The success of medical science over a period of a century or so in finding single causal factors and cures for almost all infectious diseases had rid mankind of the chastening fear of smallpox, cholera, tuberculosis, measles, poliomyelitis and other complaints. But it had left a need for something else to worry about. 'Men fear death', said Francis Bacon, 'as children fear to go in the dark'.

Sugar can be obtained from the maple tree, from sorghum, from certain palm trees and from the carob tree. St. John, in the wilderness, is thought to have sustained himself on the 'locust' bean from the carob—known in German as *Johannesbrot*—St. John's bread. But the world's two main commercial sources are the sugar cane and the sugar beet. About 60 per cent of the world's sugar comes from cane and 40 per cent from beet. In Britain, by the 1980s it will be obtained in about equal quantities from these two plants.

The agricultural production of sugar is a major source of employment all round the world, but sugar differs from other crops in that it has to be extracted from the plants in which it occurs, and this generally involves science, technology and heavy capital investment. Since it occurs throughout the world, sugar is a commodity which lends itself to and impinges on world trade.

This book is an account of one of Britain's major companies, Tate & Lyle Limited, which has been engaged in the production, refining and trading of sugar together with all the many other activities which these involve for a very long time. The company will be seen over the years adapting itself to changes, changes brought about by wars and by the varying economic climate. It will be seen developing new activities in many different countries. It will be seen unwillingly but successfully fighting a political attack.

A company can only exist and prosper because it is served by men and women who tolerate the part of their day they spend at work and preferably enjoy it. It is they who provide its persona, its characteristics. One of those characteristics in Tate & Lyle is a strong development of parody, particularly over the last three decades. It is usually oral, but there is quite a collection—one almost said a respectable collection, but it is not that—of verse and prose sending up pomposity. Not by any means all of it is the product of more senior people. Though certain members of the Board have from time to time flourished as laureates, shift managers' logs are full of flippant rhyme and many a report on a technical meeting has blossomed out in ribald verse. The Hilaire Belloc quatrain quoted at the head of Chapter 2 is of the essence of this, but gentler.

It does not mean that the job is not taken seriously, merely that parody helps to make it more fun. Peter Fleming and his companions lightened an appalling journey on the Amazon in 1935, described in *Brazilian Adventure*, by referring to water as 'the precious fluid' or to some quite small and harmless insect as 'a creature whose slightest glance spells death'. So, the sometimes humdrum business of making sugar, varied as will appear from time to time by excitement, political, financial, or whatever, has been lightened by flippancy.

In the early 1960s, for example, there was a particularly gloomy Board Meeting. There had been strikes in Jamaica and insect havoc had reduced production in Trinidad. Freight rates had fallen and nobody wanted to buy engineering equipment. The then Chairman, Ian Lyle, picked up the sheet of figures which showed that the home market sales of refined sugar had fallen off, owing in part to the activities of subsidized competition from abroad. 'Ah', he said cheerfully, quoting an unprintable ballad, 'Home presents a dismal picture'.

At the Annual General Meeting that year the dismal picture had to be put over to some 500 people—i.e. that proportion of the many thousands of shareholders who come to such gatherings. They were not amused. Perhaps, however, they found comfort in the fact that some of the Directors could be seen writing notes, and frowning as they did so. 'Here', perhaps the shareholders said to themselves, 'are men who are taking their duties seriously'. If so, they were mistaken. The frowns were a sign of a visitation by Aganippe, the Muse of Poetry, resulting in a series of verses in the style of another Stanley Holloway monologue. The scene having been set, two couplets described the Chairman as giving his account to the owners:

> Ian's story was all about sugar
> And he told it like one of the best
> He said, 'Frankly, this year's been a booger'[2]
> And fingered his bullet-proof vest.

Or there was the time of Mr. Cube's campaign against nationalization in 1949/50, when Tony Tate produced a spoof scene from *Macbeth*.

Or, again, in 1972, because the company was involved in certain parts of Africa from which it is Received Wisdom among the Left to shy away, much as Jane Austen would have shied away from the mention of a W.C., a group of earnest young demonstrators collected outside the respectable venue of the Annual General Meeting, carrying banners and trying to read their lecture notes at the same time. Saxon Tate approached one of them, a girl (they were all what the U.S. passport authorities describe as 'Caucasian—white'), and asked what it was all about. She said actually she didn't know, but it was worth £1·50 for the day, and then, hearing who he

---

[2] There are, alas, very few words that rhyme with sugar.

was, added: 'Oh, do tell me, how's Nicola?[3] I haven't seen her since we left school.'

As this particular AGM proceeded, scribes on the rostrum were again seen to be at work, and an 'AGM Calypso' – not circulated to shareholders – was the result.

It is all highly reprehensible, of course, and it can be overdone, but, God knows, the world is far too solemn in the 1970s and it can't do any harm to take the mickey.

There will, in the course of this book, be occasional outbreaks of parody, but in fairness they will not be what the French call *esprit d'escalier*, the sort of thing it would afterwards be nice to have thought of saying. They will, as far as possible, be spontaneous and contemporarily composed.

The history of a sugar company can scarcely be undertaken, however, without a brief glance at the history of sugar itself and a brief account of how this most noble carbohydrate is made for man. Since these are entwined with the history, pre-history, and indeed in the life-work of mankind, they must be treated a little more seriously. But only a little.

---

[3] A second cousin of Saxon's.

CHAPTER ONE

The Bee, the Reed, and the Root

I
The Bee

Long before sugar became generally available, man learned to make use of honey, the fruit of the labours of the wild bee. In a cave at Arana, near Valencia, in Spain, there is a Neolithic wall-picture dating from about 20,000 years ago. It shows an androgynous, or as we now say, 'unisex' figure under attack from bees while robbing a store of wild honey.

A hieroglyph representing a bee occurs on ancient Egyptian tombs of 5,500 B.C., and by about 2,000 B.C. apiculture was being practised in Egypt.

Recorded history represents honey as the main source of sweetness to Western man until the mid-fifteenth century, when increased availability of cane sugar appears to have led to a change.

II
The Reed

Nobody knows quite where and when the cane first came to be used as a source of sugar, but its original home appears to have been in the South Pacific, where it occurs again and again in folklore. Indeed, in one Polynesian account of the origin of mankind, two fishermen, the only people on earth, found one day in their net a piece of cane. At first, thinking it useless, they threw it away, but having caught it by chance three days running, they planted it in the ground. It grew and after a while burst and a woman appeared from it. She cooked for the men by day and hid by night in the cane. From time to time she was taken by one or other of the men, and from these unions sprang the human race. How the two men got there in the first place is not explained. Many similar legends are found elsewhere, and Captain Cook saw indigenous cane still growing in Polynesia when he was there just over two hundred years ago. It was then being used for making a kind of beer.

Long before the Captain's day, however, the cane had begun its long migration, probably following a movement of peoples across the bridge of islands which stand between Australia and Asia. It was known in India a thousand years before the birth of Christ. In 510 B.C. a Persian military expedition found it in that sub-continent, and in his turn, Alexander the

Great came across it there. His Admiral, Nearchos, is on record as describing 'a reed which makes honey without bees'.

Nearly 1,000 years after this came its next migration, thanks to the Prophet Mohammed who, a few years before his death in 632 A.D., began a Holy War for the conversion of the world to Islam. His armies, apparently a rough, peasant lot, did not know of the cane themselves until they conquered Persia. Finding the plant useful, they adopted its cultivation and carried it with them, now calling it 'the Persian Reed', to Cyprus, Rhodes, Sicily, Spain and along the southern littoral of the Mediterranean, whence in time it reached the islands off the Atlantic coast of Africa.

Production of sugar was then a primitive process. A blindfold mule or ox treading in a circle, drove a vertical grinding mill or a pestle in a mortar to crush the cane, and the juice was evaporated by boiling to a sticky mixture of crystals and syrup. Such a method is still in use in India and elsewhere, and the product is called *gur* or *jaggery*. Although no doubt it tastes nice on bread, it does not keep well, in this unlike refined sugar.

In the Middle Ages similar equipment was used in Sicily, but was powered as a rule by men. There is a painting dating from about 1580 by one Hans van der Straat, of a factory near Palermo, and a contemporary description says that going into the place was like entering the Forge of Vulcan; 'the men who worked there being blackened by the smoke from the fires, dirty, sweaty, and scorched, more like demons than men'. It goes on to describe all the various jobs; cutting cane, crushing, boiling the juice, even the use of cane tops planted in manure as seed for the following year.

England, remote and on the outward fringe of Europe, saw very little sugar before the early fourteenth century. Indeed, its scarcity is indicated by an order, couched in the Norman French then in vogue, from King Henry III to the Mayor of Winchester in 1226, to provide 3 lb. of Alexandrian sugar for a banquet – 'if so much is to be had'. It is certain that the first regular seaborne trade to England began when in 1319 Venetian traders sold some 50 tons for £3,000 – the equivalent in late 1970s sterling of over £1 million.

From the mid-sixteenth century much of the sugar eaten in England was bought from 'Barbary', now called Morocco. The Barbary Company was 'invented' in 1551, one of its founders being Thomas Wyndham, a Vice-Admiral in King Henry VIII's Navy, who traded in a vessel called the *Lion* to Agadir.

Barbary sugar had a bad name for quality, Queen Elizabeth I's Secretary of State, Lord Burleigh, actually complaining to the Grocers' Company about it. Before it ceased to exist, the Barbary Company became the stepping stone to later British ventures further afield, pioneering the West Indian Trade which began to develop in the seventeenth century and became of immense importance in the eighteenth.

Sugar, in most people's minds, is associated with the New World, above all with the Caribbean, which our ancestors called the Spanish Main. Yet sugar cane was not indigenous to that area. It was first taken there by Christopher Columbus on his second transatlantic voyage in 1493, and the variety he took from the Canary Islands had as ancestor the Persian Reed.

Since Columbus had been supported by King Ferdinand and Queen Isabella of Aragon, Spain held most of the West Indian territories by right of discovery. For nearly a century, she carried out a long drawn out fight with England, for the area was reputed to be rich in gold and silver. Drake, when he died at Nombre de Dios Bay, was in fact engaged in legalized piracy, trying to capture Spanish silver. Raleigh's voyages to the Orinoco were made in search of Eldorado, the Golden One, the legendary figure whose clothes were made of that metal. On his last tragic voyage, for which he was released by King James I from the Tower, Sir Walter lost his son on the voyage and found no gold. When he returned he lost his head on Tower Hill.

While this often futile scramble for wealth was going on, wealth of another kind was slowly being developed in the West Indies and southwards into South America–sugar. The prime thrust in this came from the Spanish authorities. In the early years of British colonization in Barbados, for example, from 1620 to 1640 sugar was of no importance, only tobacco, indigo and cotton being planted. Then, after sugar had been introduced and although the population in 1700 was only 30,000, there were soon some 1,300 little plantations and nearly 500 factories driven by windmills or, as in India and Egypt, by animals, and Barbados was producing about 8,000 tons a year–15 tons per factory on average. Newer captures and acquisitions, like Antigua and Jamaica, became sources of sugar, and the French began to produce in their islands, Martinique and Guadeloupe.

British and French sea captains brought new varieties of cane to replace the original strains introduced by Columbus. One of these men, Captain Bligh, three years after the mutiny against him in H.M.S. *Bounty*, sailed into St. Vincent carrying cane plants and breadfruit from Oceania.

The reason for the breadfruit was a sinister one. It was intended as a form of food suited to Africans, for by the time the Captain arrived in the Caribbean there were many scores of thousands of these in the islands, living and working as slaves in the plantations. Earlier settlers had tried importing agricultural workers from England. As the demand for sugar grew so did the demand for labour, and it became the custom to 'transport' political dissidents, felons, and other undesirables as an alternative to hanging. Oliver Cromwell 'barbadoed' some hundreds, and these were later joined by the wretched remnants of the Army of the Duke of Monmouth, sent thither after the Battle of Sedgemoor by Judge Jeffreys in 1686. Not many survived in the climate, and although their few descendants can still be seen in Barbados, where they are called 'redlegs', some other source of labour had to be sought. It was found in Africa.

There was nothing new about this. Columbus is traditionally reported to have taken slaves with him, and by 1526 the use of slaves in Cuba was officially approved, a licence or *asiento* being granted by the King of Spain. This *asiento* became a British monopoly in 1713 after the Treaty of Utrecht, as one of the spoils of Marlborough's wars, and was finally abolished only in 1789.

A mass of literature and documentation covers the horrors of the middle passage and the evils of the slave trade, and this is not the place to stress them. It should perhaps, however, be remembered that in those days life for most of the world's population was nasty, brutish and short. A sailor in a King's ship was only marginally better off than a slave. He had usually been shanghai-ed or 'pressed' into the service, where his lot was a hammock space 14 inches wide, terrible food, and drinking water that was scummy; his pay was chronically in arrears and he was subject to appalling punishments. And on top of all this he had to fight the ship and set sail scores of dizzy feet up. Soldiers being transported by sea were even worse off, up to a third dying of exposure in a single voyage.

And who, in any case, is Twentieth Century Man, with his Belsens and Siberian Labour Camps, to be censorious about his ancestors two centuries ago?

If the growth of the sugar industry and that of the slave trade in the Caribbean were parallel in time, so was that of the anti-slavery movement, and there were many plantation owners who objected to the trade, partly for humanitarian reasons and partly because of fears that the importation of large numbers of Africans would upset the balance of the population. Yet, as the Council of the island of St. Kitts wrote to the House of Lords: 'It is as great a bondage for us to cultivate our plantations without negroes as for the Egyptians to make bricks without straw.' The sugar planter was only one link in a chain, and that not the most profitable, for he bore the risk of drought, heat, hurricane, insurrection, plague, and insect pests as well as isolation from home.

The trade in fact was triangular. Ships left Europe with goods such as textiles from Lancashire, hardware, and toys, which were bartered in West Africa for gold dust and slaves. The coastal tribes would supply the last from among their opposite numbers or enemies in the hinterland. On arrival in the West Indies, these would be sold and the money used to buy sugar and rum for Europe.

But quite early on there were stirrings, particularly in England, against the slave trade. John Locke, the philosopher, described it as early as 1689 as being 'opposed to the generous temper and courage of our nation', and Dr. Johnson in the 1730s was heard proposing a toast at Oxford 'to the success of the next revolt of negroes in the West Indies'. In 1772, Lord Mansfield declared in the case of a negro, James Summersett—was his name an echo of one of those prisoners sent to Barbados after

Sedgemoor? – that nothing could support the status of slavery in England. And, thanks to the efforts of William Wilberforce, begun in 1789, at length the Royal Assent was given to a Parliamentary Bill abolishing slavery in 1833.

Thereafter, affranchised slaves were unwilling to work on sugar and yet it was still in huge demand. So there was another search for labour, Portuguese, Chinese, labour of any kind. In the end, the major replacement became 'indentured' labour from India, imported in 'Companies' under regulated conditions. (The Portuguese and Chinese soon contrived to escape from sugar and set up shops and businesses.)

Slavery continued long after 1833 in the Far East for example, but this did not prevent a certain amount of humbug in the early nineteenth century. Sugar from Bengal was advertised in England, a Mrs. E. Henderson of Rye Lane, Peckham, respectfully informing the Friends of Africa that she had for sale an Assortment of Sugar Basins, handsomely labelled in gold letters 'East India sugar, not made by slaves'.

It is hard to exaggerate the importance of sugar in history two centuries ago. It was no longer a luxury as it had been in the Middle Ages, though it cost six or seven times as much as it does now, and it was then only readily available from the Caribbean. So, for a century, that area became the Cockpit of Neptune, a naval equivalent of Flanders. Here, among those islands, dark or sage green, or dried brown by drought, set in a sea varying in colour from Homer's wine-dark to turquoise, topped with white crests, and lapping the white beaches in such a way as to produce a colour which might be described as squashed peacock, the Navies of France and England fought and men died. Admiral John Benbow died of wounds in Port Royal in 1703 and his memorial is still there in the Parish Church of Kingston. Admiral Vernon, known as 'Old Grog' because he always wore a boat cloak of *grosgrain*, a French material anglicized as grogram, found while serving in the West Indies that sailors, issued with half a pint of neat rum every day were quite incapable of manning the ship. He therefore introduced a Fleet Order in 1740 that the rum must be diluted with three parts of water. (The word 'grog' has returned to use in France, where its true origin is not generally known.)

Admiral Sir George Rodney, whose statue, incongruous in the robes of a Roman Senator, stands in a pretty columned arcade in Spanish Town Square, Jamaica, fought there twice. The end of his first period of service in 1762 coincided with the end of the Seven Years War. England had won, capturing Cuba, Martinique, Guadeloupe and Canada.

When the terms of peace – the Treaty of Paris – were under discussion there was much argument about what should be retained as spoils of war. Lord Bute, the Prime Minister, said plaintively: 'Some want me to keep Guadeloupe and some Canada. No-one will tell me which I shall be hanged for *not* keeping.' (In those happy days Ministers resigned and sometimes were even impeached if their policies did not work out. If only . . . but let it pass.) In the end we kept the enormous land mass of Canada, not the tiny sugar island of Guadeloupe, and William Pitt the Elder thundered against the decision.

Nelson's involvement with the West Indies spanned most of his naval life. As a very young officer he was stationed at Port Royal in Jamaica and to this day on the wall of the little red-brick ruin of Fort Charles there is a plaque saying 'Horatio Nelson walked here. You who tread his footsteps remember his glory'.

As a Post Captain (twenty-seven years old) in 1785, based in H.M.S. *Boreas* at English Harbour, Antigua, he seized four American vessels flying the English flag nine years after the Declaration of Independence and carrying contraband. He was sued for £4,000 damages, won his case, but became unpopular with the local plantocracy who wished to trade with the States. This did not prevent him wooing and marrying Frances Nisbet, widow of a planter in neighbouring Nevis. The Duke of Clarence, afterwards King William IV, was his best man.

His apotheosis in the Spanish Main came just a few months before Trafalgar, when he chased the French fleet from the Mediterranean to the Caribbean but missed it. The French Admiral, Villeneuve, although a threat to the British sugar islands, was himself nervous and had sailed for Europe just before Nelson reached the Windwards. Otherwise, although it may sound Irish to say so, the Battle of Trafalgar would have been fought off Barbados.

The islands, though of major commercial interest, were by no means a paradise in those days, as is attested by the hundreds of plaques on church walls there, recording the names of twelve, twenty-five, forty, members of a ship's company or a regiment who died of yellow fever. This 'Yellow Jack' was more to be feared than the enemy. A British force of 15,000 sent to St. Domingue (now Haiti) in 1801 lost 11,000, dead of the disease, and more British troops succumbed to it in the first fifteen years of the nineteenth century than were killed at Waterloo.

> Their belts they girt about them
> In ships they crossed the sea
> They sought and found six feet of ground,
> And there they died – for me.

Or rather, in order that people might have sugar.

III
The Root

It was not long after Trafalgar – not quite six years in fact – and as a direct consequence of the destruction there of the combined fleets of France and Spain, that there came about the large scale development of the sugar beet as a source of sugar, and it was the Emperor Napoleon who must be given much of the credit for this.

It is difficult to be fair about the enigmatic Napoleon. He was only just over 5 foot 1 inch high (3 inches shorter than Nelson), but he dominated his era. During his exile in St. Helena, of course, he carefully constructed his legend, cooking the historical books where necessary. (There are many Frenchmen who find him repulsive if irresistible – he was a Corsican, not a Frenchman.) A liar – he once said: 'In this world one must appear friendly, make many promises, and keep none', an opportunist – he once said: 'When I need somebody, I am not squeamish, I'd kiss his ass',[1] he was nevertheless of a special mould. Perhaps he is kicking himself in the Elysian Fields for not having come up with the phrase 'A week is a long time in politics', and, of course, he would have loved appearing on The Box.

He also said that the word 'impossible' did not figure in his vocabulary, and certainly he had enormous capacity for getting things done. Although he did not originate the production of beet sugar, he certainly gave it the impetus it needed.

In 1806, in the Decrees of Berlin and Milan, he had reacted to Britain's blockade of Europe after Trafalgar by closing all Continental ports to British shipping. Britain had replied a year later in an Act 'fufpending the Counter Duties and Bounties on Sugar . . . in an Act for difcontinuing . . . etc'. And then, since Europe needed sugar and could not import it, on March 11th, 1811, Napoleon declared that commercial relations with England must cease. He went on:

'I am informed that from recent experiments France will be able to do without sugar from the two Indies. Chemistry has made such progress in this country that it will be possible to produce as great a change in our commercial relations as that produced by the discovery of the compass . . . The English will be obliged to throw into the Thames the sugars for which they have exchanged the objects of their industry, and which have afforded them such resources. . . .

'From January 1st, 1813 and after a report to be made to the Minister of the Interior, the sugar . . . from the two Indies shall be prohibited and considered as merchandise of English manufacture. . . .'

The timetable was kept. On January 2nd, 1813 Napoleon was told that one Benjamin Delessert had succeeded in making loaves of white sugar at a place called Plassy, using as labour Spanish prisoners of war who had worked in cane sugar factories. When the Emperor arrived to see the place Delessert was out. On his return he found the factory yard full of *Chasseurs* of the *Garde*. He had himself presented to the Emperor, who removed his own *Légion d'Honneur* sash and used it to decorate Delessert, also awarding a week's pay to the workforce, though history does not relate at whose expense. In a contemporary picture the Emperor and the Minister stand on either side of two large sugar loaves. Both are wearing the sashes of the

[1] *Buonaparte in Egypt* by J. Christopher Herald, Hamish Hamilton, 1943.

Légion, and Delessert, standing slightly shyly in the background in a white wig, has clearly not yet received the accolade.

As so often in his life, Napoleon had taken a major decision, scientifically sound, which, instead of being economically disastrous as it might have been, was justified. The industry nearly died after the first Treaty of Paris in 1814 when the blockade was lifted, but it recovered and by 1825 there were over 100 factories in France producing altogether 24,000 tons of sugar a year. Beet sugar production, the God-child of a state of war, in this like the use of lime-juice, aviation, radar and penicillin, had established itself in France.[2]

The beetroot has a long and honourable history. Temple drawings from Egypt in 2,000 B.C. show a plant which some Egyptologists believe to represent it. (Others think it a carrot.) In the catalogue of the kitchen garden of a Babylonian King of 722 B.C., it is given the name of Silga, the ancient name of Sicily. (It is still called *acelga* in Spain.) For hundreds of years it was used as a vegetable and as a cure for nose and throat ailments and constipation, but, although sweet, it had to wait until the eighteenth century until it was recognized as containing sucrose by Andreas Sigismund Marggraf, son of a royal apothecary in Berlin.

In a paper published in 1747 he described extracting sugar from beetroot using 'cannon-proof' brandy, the product being 'like the best yellow sugar of St. Thomas (West Indies)'. His process was clearly too expensive – and anyway what is brandy *for?* – and beet sugar remained a laboratory specimen until nineteen years later, when, also in Berlin, a Huguenot successor of Marggraf's, Franz Carl Achard, developed a pilot scale factory. It took him thirteen further years and a major fire in the factory before he was able to produce a sugar loaf. On January 11th, 1799, he wrote to King Frederick William IV of Prussia, asking for a monopoly in beet sugar production for ten years and a grant of land to carry on with his work.

The King was impressed and so were the Anti-Slavery Movement – there is a lampoon in the *Neuer Berliner Monatschrift* to prove this. And there also exists a contemporary picture of Achard presenting the King with a sugar loaf – unwrapped and therefore obviously not 'untouched by hand'. The tall young Monarch in enormous boots is accompanied by his wife in a high-bosomed dress, her arm round a small son in the kind of clothes associated for ever with Little Lord Fauntleroy. Achard looks as if he was going on talking too long.

Within three months, however, he had his grant, and quite a decent-sized gratuity, renewed every now and then by the King, for the Professor was not a practical man when it came to money. And in 1801 at Cunern in Silesia, the first-ever full-scale beet sugar factory was built on land obtained from a Baron Puckler. A picture shows what it looked like. It

---

[2] Benjamin Delessert is commemorated in the name of a scientific institute in France.

never made money but it did serve as a training school before being burned down in 1813 by Napoleon's armies.

Beet sugar is still produced in Silesia. In 1940, P. G. Wodehouse, picked up by the German Army at Le Touquet, was interned in Upper Silesia after several days' railway journey in a goods truck. On arrival, he looked round the vast expanse of flat land sown with sugar beet and asked himself: 'If this is *Upper* Silesia, what can *Lower* Silesia be like!'

Beet sugar production was often criticized in the years following 1815. The great German chemist, Liebig, said any fool could do it. Others said it used wood fuel which could be better employed. But it spread across the world to Austria, Russia, Denmark, Holland, the U.S.A. and Canada. In Europe, as we shall see, it was supported by fiscal arrangements which enabled it to compete against cane sugar when exported to Britain.

For Britain was one of the rare temperate-zone countries where beet sugar production made no progress until a century or more after Napoleon's Decree of 1811. One of the results of the Industrial Revolution was the need to keep a largely urban population which was employed in manufacture if not happy, at least fed as cheaply as possible. This policy meant bearing down on the farming community, as when Sir Robert Peel broke from the landed interests of the Conservative Party and repealed the Corn Laws in the 1840s. It went on for a century or more after that.

Sugar, like corn, was cheaper to buy from abroad than to produce at home, and moreover it was popular with the Treasury as a simple way of collecting customs duty with a mere handful of trusty men. So, what with the possession of an Empire and one thing and another, sugar continued to be imported into Britain. There were attempts at producing beet sugar, first by two Quakers, Reid and Marriage, at Utting, near Maldon, Essex, in 1830 – for anti-slavery reasons – then at Thames Bank, Chelsea in 1836, when beet was actually sown at Wandsworth. (A Dr. Bowring, M.P., was against all this – saying that 'beetroot should be plucked out by the roots'.) Both of these attempts failed.

In the 1870s a London sugar refiner, James Duncan, built a factory at Lavenham in Suffolk, but only went as far as producing a syrup which was sent to London for extraction. It only worked for one season, though the building was still there in 1900, and as recently as 1925 two tanks in the Refinery at Thames were called the 'Lavenham tanks'.

It was not until 1912 that, after prolonged pressure from the Earl of Denbigh and a well-known scientist, Sir William Crookes, who had travelled extensively in Europe and found that sugar beet cultivation had a beneficial effect on agricultural production generally, the first commercial beet sugar factory was established at Cantley in Norfolk.

Even so, it took a world war and some years of Treasury deliberation before 'the Root' became a proper native of Britain. But that is another story and will be taken up later.

IV
Refining

A Treatise on Sugar Refining (the dreariest subject I can think of . . .)
(Joseph Conrad. 'The Inn of the Three Witches')

Here, then, are the two sources of sugar – the cane and the beet. Cane is a tropical plant and needs strong sunlight and abundant water. It can only be successfully cultivated in the zone between 25° north and south of the Equator. Like a huge grass, it is a perennial, growing in eleven to eighteen months to a height of four to five metres during the well marked tropical wet seasons and ripening in the dry seasons. After cropping, the root is left in the ground and sprouts again for the following year. This practice is called 'ratooning', a technical term derived from the Spanish *retoño* or French *rejeton,* meaning, approximately, 'offspring'. In West Indian homes, the house guest, offered a ragout of the previous evening's joint may be told 'it's just ratoons'. Be that as it may, ratooning can be continued for six or seven years, or, if you are a farmer and feeling broke, for up to thirty, and it gives sugar cane an economic advantage over other crops. The yield of sugar per acre is from one to six tons, depending on soil, climate, and agricultural techniques. (As metres have been mentioned above, this can be metricated, if you will, as two and a bit to twelve and a bit tonnes per hectare.)

Much of the world's cane is still cut by hand, but rising costs, due to the cane cutter's new found and quite natural desire to turn up to work, if not in a Mercedes, at least on a Honda, began in the 1950s to result in the introduction of mechanical harvesting. This modernization – which has spread for example to Cuba – is quite understandable, for cane cutting by hand is a back-breaking job. Yet it might in its turn become uneconomical, if the price of oil were to rise too high.

After cropping, the cane, which deteriorates rapidly under the influence of bacteria, particularly one known as Leuconostoc, which sounds like some early Monarch of the Emerald Isle (Luke O'Nostock), is taken as rapidly as possible to the mill. Here it is cleaned of trash, stones, old inner tubes, assorted ironmongery, and undervests discarded by cane cutters (it is a *very* hot job, cutting cane), and passed through shredding knives to break up the hard rind and expose the inner core containing the sugar. It is then crushed between rollers under high pressure and sprayed with hot water to leach out the sugar.[3] The resulting juice is heated and lime is added. After filtration, which produces a clarified juice, this is concentrated by evaporation under a vacuum and then boiled in steam-heated pans, again under a vacuum to save destruction by heat. Boiling

[3] More recently diffusers have been introduced and a new process involving decortication is under trial.

forms a mix, *massecuite* or cooked mass – so many sugar terms are French – of crystals and mother syrup which is spun in centrifugal machines (large perforated tubs, rotated at high speed – like a spin drier in a washing machine) to separate the crystals from the residual syrup – known as 'molasses'.

The molasses is used for making into rum, or as cattle food. The residual fibre, called *bagasse* (French, once more) is used as fuel for making steam, thereby also providing electrical power; and the mud from the filter presses, containing phosphates and the like, is returned to the cane field as fertilizer. Bagasse – if there is a surplus – is sometimes made into building board, paper, or chemicals.

The 'campaign' lasts from five to eight months as a rule, until the rains come down. Some of the sugar is consumed locally, but many sugar-producing countries export the greater part of their product as 'raw cane sugar', *not* as cane, to metropolitan areas where the chief markets exist.

Sugar beet is an annual plant which grows in temperate zones, throughout Europe, in the U.S.A., Canada and the U.S.S.R. and other Iron Curtain countries. Planted in the spring, it is cropped in the same year in the autumn. About 65,000 beet seeds are usually planted per hectare (or 30,000 per acre, you dear, old-fashioned thing), and a new development, that of 'monogerm' seeds has enabled each seed to produce only a single plant, instead of several, thus doing away with the former expensive and arduous job of 'singling'. All operations, planting, weeding, fertilizing, and protection from pests are mechanized.

Beet is never planted two years running in the same field, but is rotated with cereals and other crops on whose yield it has a marked beneficial effect, as it breaks up the soil with its long thin rootlets.

By September (in the northern hemisphere) an average field yields about 16 tons an acre – equivalent to 2 to $2\frac{1}{2}$ tons of sugar, depending on the weather. (Aha! Back in acres again, you see. Well, it's 2·2 acres to the hectare. Work it out, chaps, in tonnes per hectare.) The beets are lifted, topped, and cleaned mechanically, the roots, which as you will remember contain the sugar, being loaded into trailers, or stored in clamps, and the tops fed to animals or ensiled.

After harvesting, the beets are transported to factories. Here they are washed free of earth and sliced by machines into thin fingers, or *cossettes* (Fr.). These are fed, together with hot water, into either a tower or a huge slowly rotating drum in which the sugar diffuses through the membrane of the plant into the water. The resultant juice is treated with lime and carbon dioxide gas is bubbled through it, forming a precipitate which is filtered off. Thereafter the process of extraction is similar to that used for cane sugar production. In earlier days much of the world's beet sugar was produced as 'raws' and required further treatment in a refinery, but modern technological improvements have now enabled the beet factory to produce a sugar virtually indistinguishable from refined cane sugar.

A beet sugar campaign lasts only 3 to 3½ months, as frost followed by a thaw has a deleterious effect on the root after lifting.

This brings us to the matter of sugar refining, which is the technique of converting a brown, sticky, impure crystalline substance, often accompanied by unwanted matter such as harmful bacilli, sugar lice, dead insects and other people's toenail clippings, into a reliable and consistent food which can be stored for ever. (Do *not* let the food-faddists deceive you, unless you are a toenail-fancier.)

A long time ago the separation of sugar from its accompanying 'goo' was accomplished by extremely primitive methods described briefly in the next chapter. The invention of new techniques – such as the use of lime and carbon dioxide, bone charcoal, resins, and the centrifugal machine – has made the whole thing more complicated. But basically it is still a fairly simple affair.

The raw sugar is washed to remove adhering syrup ('affined'), then dissolved in hot water, treated with lime and carbon dioxide gas (a process called 'carbonatation'), and filtered. The liquor emerging from the filter presses is a clear amber colour and is passed over bone charcoal ('char') or other newer, agents, to remove dissolved impurities, the resultant clear, colourless liquor then being boiled under a vacuum in large enclosed pans at low temperature. The crystals are separated by centrifuging, dried in a stream of warm pure air (in 'granulators') and graded before packing. Cubes are made by compressing moist crystals in moulds and then drying; icing by pulverizing; Golden Syrup by partial inversion of sugar liquor and passing over 'char' to produce something akin to honey.

Metropolitan refineries have no 'campaign' but work all year round, refining raw cane sugars from the northern hemisphere from January to June, from the southern from July to December, and beet raws, as required, from September to January or February.

This, and economy of scale, is what gives them their importance, together with their trading, storage and distribution facilities and their elaborate but smoothly running sales arrangements.

It is, of course, much more difficult than it looks, but Mr. Conrad was right, it is not a process to write treatises on for the general public.

CHAPTER TWO
First Beginnings

I

'From quiet homes and first beginning,
Out to the undiscovered ends.
There's nothing worth the wear of winning,
But laughter and the love of friends.'
(Hilaire Belloc 1870–1945)

By the late eighteenth century British sugar refining had become largely concentrated in three port areas; Greenock, on the Clyde, Liverpool, on the Mersey, and London. This is because supplies of raw sugar, largely, though not solely, from the Caribbean, were carried by ships registered in those ports, the two first-named being in the Western Approaches.

The first British sugar refineries were built in London in 1544 by Cornelius Bussine and four other 'adventurers' who put up two. Competition from Antwerp was strong until they were able to obtain a 'monopoly' from the Government of King Henry VIII.

Stow says in his chronicles of the time: 'there were but two sugar houses; and their profit was but little, by reason there was so many sugar bakers in Antwerp, and sugar came thence better and cheaper than it could be afforded in London. And for the space of twenty years together these two sugar houses served the whole realm, both to the commendation and profit of them that undertook the same.'

The reference to 'sugar bakers' is a reminder that refined sugar was then and long after sold in the form of 'loaves', whose manufacture will shortly be described.

By the 1650s there were fifty refineries in Britain, most of them in London. A century later there were eighty refineries in London, twenty in Bristol, 'and likewise refining houses at Chester, Liverpool, Lancaster, Whitehaven, Newcastle, Kingston-upon-Hull, and Southampton, and a number in Scotland', about 120 altogether in the United Kingdom. On average each gave work to six members of a family and nine 'yearly working servants'.

Refineries were very much a fire hazard. Allan Smith, a 'great sugar baker' of London, transferred his activities to Liverpool in 1666 after the Great Fire, which started in the area of his bakery – though not caused by him. Insurance companies charged very high premiums for refineries and the Phoenix Assurance Company was founded in 1782 by a number of

prominent refiners on a do-it-yourself basis. In its headquarters in King
William Street in the City was found in 1953 a box of papers referring to
meetings of the Sugar Refiners' Committee 1771–1834, from which some
of the following information has been obtained. The refiners had other
worries as well as fire, subject as they were to the cutting off of supplies of
raw material by war, and in 1753 an application was made for assistance to
the House of Commons. Ordered to be heard at the Bar of the House on
April 4th, it was eventually referred on May 14th to 'a Committee of the
Whole House to consider thereof.' Nothing resulted.

A Society of Sugar Refiners of London was formed in 1781, as the House
of Commons had done little. It was more a dining club than an association,
limited to forty, and it met in various pubs–the George & Vulture in
Cornhill, the Queen's Arms at St. Paul's and so forth. It tried to use the
London Tavern, but this was a somewhat upper-crust place and wouldn't
admit such base fellows as refiners,[1] so they retreated to a coffee house
instead.

On June 12th, 1781 there was a general meeting of the sugar refiners of
London this time at the Mermaid in Hackney. Parliament had again
failed to give assistance when supplies 'had been cut by the loss of some of
the islands, Grenada, St. Vincent and Dominica'. High prices of raw sugar
were caused by losses of cargoes captured by the enemy and when in return
the Royal Navy captured sugar vessels in prize these paid the same duty as
foreign sugar. The meeting decided to reduce production to three days a
week for twelve months. There were eighty-five signatures to this
agreement. Many of the names were German–Richter, Schröder,
Wagentrieber and so on, some with English Christian names and therefore
probably second-generation, others new immigrants like Mr. Diederich
Wackerbarth. It was a respectable enough trade for Mr. Wickham,
Under-Secretary at the Home Office, not to make any difficulties about
admitting foreign managers or labourers (at £14 a year all found).

But they were a quarrelsome lot and the Phoenix papers and others
contain violent recriminations between them and the West Indies planters
and the 'jobbers', who bought and resold imported sugar. By now, two-
thirds of the West Indies planters sent their sugar in 'in a white state,
getting in that way means to buy horses, cloth, provisions etc.' The jobbers
who bought such sugar were characterized by the refiners as persons 'of
very mean, base and infamous character (who) ought to be despised,
shunned, detested and excluded from all bodies of men whatsoever'.
Among these was Mr. Wackerbarth, who with others, was described as
'having deviated from the character of men of honour'.

In return when the refiners sought to get a duty of 5s. per cwt. placed on
West Indian molasses they were described as being unable 'to leave off

---

[1] Of course, they were not all base fellows. Sir John Vanbrugh, Captain of Marines,
playwright and architect of Blenheim Palace, was sired by a Dutch 'sugar baker' who had
married the daughter of Sir Dudley Carleton, British Ambassador to the Hague.

their griping monopolising humour . . .'. The planters stated that English refined sugar was of poor quality, to which the refiners replied that they 'clarified with eggs and afterwards strained through broadcloth'.

In 1787 William Pitt, the young Prime Minister, introduced a 'Consolidation Act' containing a set of complicated protective duties. This was not the end of the matter, for twelve years later, with a war on, Pitt told a deputation of refiners that he was thinking of putting an excise on refined sugar as an alternative to income tax, which did not yet exist. The refiners 'fought the monster manfully' and the excise was not imposed. It was no doubt thanks to his personal dealings with sugar refiners and the like that Pitt was moved one day during a debate in the House to raise his voice and say: 'Sugar, Mr. Speaker. Sugar! Who will laugh at Sugar now?'

By 1800 there were 100 refiners in London, and about 150 in Britain as a whole, importing on average 140,000 tons a year of raws. They were still bothered with supply problems and while they had prevented an excise duty being imposed they were still battling with the West Indies suppliers. Eleven years or so later they would be threatened by a new foe – beet sugar.

Although the first British sugar refineries had been built in London, primacy in the development of technology seems to have been on the Clyde, moving later to Liverpool, and later still back to London. The odious Mr. Slope in *Barchester Towers* having been understandably rejected by Eleanor Bold (née Harding) despite 'a clean handkerchief and a soupçon of not unnecessary scent', married 'the widow of a rich sugar refiner in London' (in the mid 1860s), and provides contemporary evidence that there was sometimes money in the business.

Sometimes, but not always. Family firms involved in sugar refining grew and prospered, then ran into hard times, either because of the vagaries of the market, because of over-investment, of trouble with the banks, or because the sons of the family were not interested.

In 1864 there were thirty-eight refineries in London and thirty-six in other parts of the country, of which fourteen were in Greenock. Fire was still a major hazard and the latter suffered no fewer than sixteen in thirty-five years. Among the London refineries was one owned by Mr. James Duncan of Greenock, who chose Clyde Wharf as a name for his venture. His works were situated about 200 yards from Plaistow Wharf where eighteen years later Abram Lyle would set up *his* refinery. Described as 'the prince of sugar refiners who never ceased to keep himself abreast of all that was going on . . . always at work, always thinking out some new scheme . . .' Duncan was the second Chairman of the British Sugar Refiners' Association, formed in 1872. We have noted his interest in beet sugar production at Lavenham in 1869–70. He was a Presbyterian and built churches in the Victoria Docks and Tidal Basin areas. The latter was destroyed by a bomb in 1940 and is now covered by the West Ham Corporation's Keir Hardie Estate. Mr. Duncan died in 1905.[2] He had had

[2] See *International Sugar Journal*, Vol. 7, 1905, p. 563: revised by F. C. Eastick.

to sell his Scottish estates and had tried to make a fresh start in Greenock and a further one at Goole in Yorkshire which he later sold to McFie's of Greenock. Clyde Wharf was bought by David Martineau in 1887 and was soon thereafter destroyed by fire.[3]

By 1882 there were only eight refineries in London including Henry Tate's newly established one and twenty-six elsewhere, of which ten were in Greenock and eight in Liverpool. By 1900 there were only four in London, including Tates' and Lyles', seven in Liverpool and five in Greenock. The others had all gone, although there were 'small houses' dealing with such charming materials as 'scrapings, drainings and scums'.

Imports in 1864 were 48 per cent from Germany and Austria (mostly refined), 28 per cent from France, 8 per cent from Holland and Belgium, and only 2½ per cent from the West Indies.

Companies surviving the stress of those times were relatively few even a generation ago. But the Tates and Lyles – much later amalgamating their two companies – managed to remain in the business and expanded (not without having from time to time to hang on by their bushy eyebrows) and are still involved; and there are members of some of the other old refining families still about – Fairries, Kerrs, Walkers, Martineaus – and happily still working in sugar.

When their ancestors began in the business it was still a fairly primitive affair. Their raw material came in hogsheads. Nominally it would be sugar which had been drained of molasses in the West Indies through holes in the bottom of the hogshead which were subsequently plugged before shipment. But forgetfulness is easy in a warm climate and often the hogshead contained a mixture of molasses and sugar. Whatever arrived, it was a sticky commodity. From it the old refiners produced a coarse yellowish-brown sugar called 'bastards' which was formed into loaves by cooling for days and by gravity, draining off the syrup in porous clay conical moulds through which water mixed with lime was percolated, the loaves weighing from 5 lb. to 35 lb. Crushed loaves and fragments were sold as 'pieces' and the drained-off syrup as 'treacle'. The prior removal of impurities was accomplished by simple means, a contemporary instruction reading: 'melt ye fugar to ye degree ye may defire and add lime and bullock's blood to clarify. . . .' The blood in the presence of lime acted as a flocculant and carried undesirable matter to the surface in a scum which was scraped off.[4]

A contemporary account, called 'A Day at a Sugar Refinery' was published in 1841 in *The Penny Magazine* of the Society for the Diffusion of Useful Knowledge.

It starts off with the words: 'Sugar refineries have certain peculiarities in their external appearance whereby they are distinguished from most other

[3] George Martineau, *Sugar*, 1910, pp. 9 and 78. (Pitman 1932).
[4] Sugar refineries were often built next to an abattoir, so that blood was easily obtainable. It was referred to by the 'refained' name of 'spice'.

factories; they are very lofty, consist of an unusual number of floors or storeys and are lighted by rather small windows. In the Sugar Refinery of Messrs. Fairrie[5] which we have just visited . . .' Then it proceeds to describe the whole process as it then was, in great detail, with black and white illustrations.

A more technical description of the same refinery, at Whitechapel, was quoted in the *International Sugar Journal* of June 1901, Vol. 3 No. 30, page 313 ff. This includes mention of the introduction of charcoal as a purifier instead of 'so offensive a substance as bullocks' blood', and of the use of the vacuum pan – invented by the Honourable Edward Charles Howard. Although this sprig of nobility had designed it in 1813 and the father of this Fairrie installed it in 1819, it was slow to be universally adopted. Another of his innovations was the whitening of sugar loaves by running a concentrated pure syrup through them. Between first quality loaves and 'bastards' there was now a second quality, called 'lumps', and the floor-sweepings etc. were all collected and the sugar extracted and sold. Remarking on the 'science, ingenuity, skill, and capital devoted to refined sugar production' the *I.S.J.* quotes a Dr. Prout who believed refined sugar to be 'inferior in nutritive properties to the raw sugar which furnishes it'. (So they existed then too, the food-faddists.)

This was hardly sugar refining as it is now carried out, but the old refiners were continuously on the look-out for improved methods and became increasingly bold in their introduction of these as time went by.

Let us have a look at these hard-working people in chronological order of families.

II
The MacFies

The MacFie family, starting in Sugar House Lane, Greenock in 1788 under Robert of that ilk, moved to Bogle Street in 1800 and set up refineries in 1804 in Leith, in 1829 in Edinburgh, and in 1838–1843 in Liverpool. The MacFies became connected by marriage with the Fairrie family in the 1850s and held an interest in Fairrie & Co's. refinery (q.v.). The old MacFie refinery at Batchelor Street in Liverpool (the others had closed) continued under family management until 1938. It was then bought by United Molasses[6] and its quota later transferred by them to Tate & Lyle. The buildings were sold and the company was wound up in 1946.

The original Robert MacFie, born the year after Bonnie Prince Charlie's débâcle, looks at you shrewdly from his portrait, as though about to say something like: 'Mony a mickle maks a muckle.'

[5] See page 33.
[6] See Chapter Twenty-three.

John Kerr 1823–1872

James Fairrie 1754–1815

Robert MacFie 1746–1827

David Martineau 1784–1840

Henry Tate's first enterprise – a grocers' shop in Liverpool.

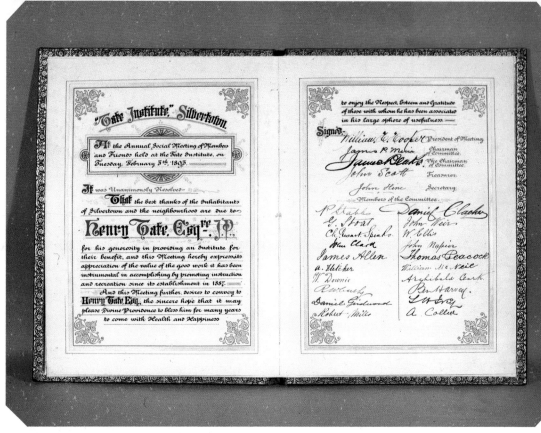

Address of thanks to Henry Tate from the Tate Institute, Silvertown.

Thames Refinery in 1978, after 100 years.

III
The Fairies

The first refining Fairrie, James (1754 to 1815), was a sea-faring man who by the age of forty-three had packed nearly thirty years of adventure into his life before deciding that things might be less risky ashore, even in sugar refining, and in 1797 he purchased a site and built a refinery at Cartsdyke Bridge, Greenock. Some of his sons continued in Scotland, but one, John, opened a refinery in Church Lane, Whitechapel in London, in 1830. He was the first to use animal bone charcoal in filters as a decolourizer and to revivify it by burning, and also the first to refine imported French raw beet sugar in 1856. The refinery closed when he died in 1864. His brothers, Adam, James and Thomas, went to Liverpool in 1847, building a refinery in Vauxhall Road. This continued in operation until 1937. In 1929 Fairrie & Company Limited had been amalgamated with Tate & Lyle, and the old Fairrie Refinery buildings now became part of the Love Lane Refinery of Tate & Lyle. (It was James the younger's daughter, Agnes, by the way, who married Robert MacFie.)

The Fairrie family are believed to be descended from a Spaniard named Fereira, a survivor of the Great Armada, whose ship was wrecked off the west coast of Scotland, having been driven north-about in 1588 by the winds that wrecked that expedition.

Although the Fairries' Greenock Refinery was burned down in 1846, it had also been the scene of innovation, being the first in Scotland to instal vacuum pans for crystallizing, instead of open pans. A second and later Fairrie refinery in Greenock, the Glebe, was sold in 1865 to Abram Lyle and John Kerr, of whom we shall shortly hear.

James Fairrie the First's face, above the white stock, is sad and reflective. Perhaps he had found sugar refining as perilous as sea-faring, and was wishing he was back on the briny.

Members of the Fairrie family, Tony and James, were serving with Tate & Lyle in the 1970s. It is pleasant to note that they are much more jovial than James (I).[7]

IV
The Martineaus

1797, the year of Nelson's victory in the Battle of the Nile, also saw two brothers, David and Peter Martineau, start sugar refining in London. They were the grandsons of Gaston Martineau, a French Huguenot surgeon who had come to London in 1686, when the Revocation of the Edict of Nantes in 1685 by Louis XIV, the 'Sun King', made life for a

[7] Tony, alas, died while this book was going to press after a painful illness, bravely borne.

Protestant in France impossible, and who had settled in Norwich. His two grandsons built their first refinery at Old Fish Street Hill in the City, almost on the spot where the Great Fire of 1666 had begun. Sugar refining was a fire hazard and new fire regulations in 1807 forced them to move out (the City Fathers were waking up) and they separated, David building his refinery in Christian Street and Peter his in Goulston Square, both in Whitechapel – then surrounded by fields. David's refinery later moved to Kingward Street,[8] and continued operating until 1961 when it was merged with Manbré & Garton. A descendent, William Martineau, works with Tate & Lyle in the late 1970s. Peter's refinery came to an end in 1873.

David Martineau's face, in his portrait, is high-coloured, with something still, after three generations, of a French look.

V
The Walkers

John Walker (1802–1866), son of a baker, was originally a ship-owner in partnership with his brother Hugh. The fleet consisted of three vessels, *Merlin* (364 tons), *Kilblain* (495 tons) and *Hugh Walker* (496 tons). The first named was lost at sea on the way to New York in 1847 and the other two sold in 1851. In 1849 he became interested in sugar refining, setting up his business at Upper Nicholson Street, Greenock in partnership with James Speir. (There were by now fourteen sugar refining firms in Greenock.) Like the Fairries an innovating family, the Walkers, although their refinery was burned down three times, introduced centrifugal machines for separating sugar crystals and were the first to bring electricity to a gas-lit Greenock in 1878. Walkers' remained an entirely family firm until 1928, when a fall in the market price of raw sugar landed it in difficulties and it became a limited company, associated with Tate & Lyle, who had come to the rescue. For many years after this, Hugh Walker, Barnhill Walker and Norman Walker ran the refinery, relieved of the worry of feeling rich on Friday only to wake on Monday to find that the price of sugar had fallen and they were paupers. Two Walkers – John Carmalt Walker and his son, also John, work in Tate & Lyle.

John Walker (I), born during a lull in the Napoleonic Wars, had a broad forehead, a prominent nose and a pair of kindly eyes. He was, like so many sugar refiners of the day, obviously and ineffably Scottish.

VI
The Kerrs

The Kerr family, like the Walkers, were ship-owners, carrying coal to and sugar from the West Indies. John, born in 1823, went into partnership

[8] In 1875 his company were joint licensees in Britain for the Langen cube-sugar patent with Henry Tate.

with Abram Lyle (III) (q.v.) in the 1850s, when they were both young men, salting and packing herrings for the West Indies, a venture which failed because the herrings arrived in Jamacia rotten. In 1865, together with the same A. Lyle, Kerr took over the Glebe Refinery from the Fairries, as mentioned above. The Lyles were later to sell out their interest in this undertaking. In 1896 the Kerrs erected the Westburn Refinery in Greenock – which still operates, having been acquired in 1962 by Manbré & Garton and, in 1976, by Tate & Lyle. Two members of the Kerr family serve in Tate & Lyle in the 1970s, having received their training there in the 1950s.

Slim and dark haired, in his black tie, stiff white shirt and dinner jacket, John Kerr seems in his portrait to be about to propose 'The Immorrtal Memory' on Burns Night.

VII
The Tates

The Tate interest in sugar dates from Henry, born at Chorley, Lancashire, in 1819, the seventh son of a Liverpool Unitarian clergyman, the Reverend William Tate, himself born in Newcastle in 1773. At thirteen the young Tate was apprenticed to a grocer – an older brother, Caleb – but at twenty he set up on his own and by thirty-six possessed a chain of six shops, of which at least one survived at Old Haymarket Street until recently. In 1859 he became the partner of John Wright, a sugar refiner, of Manesty Lane, Liverpool.

The present Director of Versification, Tony Tate, has put it all very succinctly:

Now back in the Georgian era
Up North was a parson named Tate.
He had raised up a Christian family
With Henry as child number eight.

Another son, probably Caleb,
Had gone into grocery trade.
Pa said: 'Better take Henry in with you,
–And mind that he's properly paid.'

For some years the family toiled on
And built up a nice chain of shops.
But Henry kept thinking of sugar
And learning of beet and cane crops.

He said: 'ee, all yon sugar looks scruffy
– Those loaves are all more grey than white'.
So he went to an aged Refiner
Well known as old Honest John Wright.

Tate said: 'I've a mind to be changing
I'll give all my shops to in-laws.
I've a bit of brass saved in wife's stocking
And I'd not mind a business like yours.'

So Henry and Wright set up business
And made quite an impact no doubt.
Till old man was called to his fathers
And Henry had business for nowt.

This is an almost factual summary of events except that it was Mrs. Tate who pushed her husband, no doubt offering the cash in the stocking as an inducement. A Scottish lady (née Hislop) she probably did the saving, too. Tate sold his shops on December 31st, 1861 and, forsaking the grocers' sugar choppers, opened another small refinery of his own in Earle Street in 1862. He thought of selling out to associates in Greenock, but nothing came of this and, on June 30th, 1869, the partnership with Wright was dissolved and Henry changed the name of the firm to Henry Tate and Sons, taking two of his sons, Alfred and Edwin, into partnership.

The Herkomer portrait of Henry Tate is well known. He was a handsome old man, and there is no mistaking the shrewd eyes, the straight nose, and, beneath the short white beard, the resolute chin of a founding father. He is reported to have been an indifferent public speaker but always to have put his point across economically.

Constantly on the look out for expansion, he built a new refinery on a site in Love Lane. Once upon a time the quarter where richer merchants lived, the area had become 'less desirable' for residences when the Leeds–Liverpool Canal was completed in 1774 and by 1870 the charmingly named Love Lane, Ladies' Walk and Maidens' Green had become coal yards and brick fields.

Building the refinery began in 1870 and operations in 1872. The techniques originally intended are thought, from the scanty evidence available, to have been those used in Scotland, including vacuum pan crystallization, but Henry Tate was an even keener innovator than most, and had bought the British rights of a new process for purifying sugar liquors patented in 1865 by two Frenchmen, Boivin and Loiseau. There is an undocumented story that in order to introduce this process, an early form of carbonatation, Tate scrapped his existing unused new plant, but as the refinery was working for four years before the new process was installed this seems unlikely. Nevertheless, this and other modern techniques (such as the centrifugal machine, invented by Penzoldt in 1837 for drying wool, first used for sugar in 1844 in Germany, and subsequently improved by Sir Henry Bessemer[9]) were included, the plant being supplied by Fives-Lille

---

[9] Bessemer, full of self-confidence, started refining himself. He lost £30,000 and stopped. Sugar is even more difficult than steel.

(a French machinery manufacturer still very prominent) and a now defunct Greenock engineering firm, Blake Barclay.

Henry Tate admired the Greenock system of refining and took on Greenock men in the early days as pan boilers and engineers. This was not always successful. A letter from him to his agents, dated August 14th, 1869, describes how one Davidson, sent by them, had not been satisfactory. His replacement, Alick McConnochie, turned out to be 'addicted to drink' and had been found, together with the engineer, Mitchell Hains, absolutely pie-eyed in the sugar house that Sunday evening. The letter, asking for another replacement at £4 or £5 a week, requested a reply by telephone by 2 o'clock *next day*. (The post obviously worked in those days.) Nobody knows if a suitable candidate was found.

In the first year, the refinery, drawing its supplies from Peru, Mauritius and the East and West Indies, 'melted' 400 tons. By 1881 the output was nearly three times as great – 1,146 tons to be precise. Sugar was packed in 2 cwt. hessian bags, in 10 cwt. casks and 3 cwt. barrels. (The use in refineries of barrels for sugar and, at Lyle's Refinery, for syrup, continued until the mid-twentieth century, and the coopers' shops with their magnificent tools and skilled craftsmen were a feature of all refineries. By 1945 there were only two or three elderly coopers about, repairing old barrels. Now, alas, there are no coopers' shops.)

The kind of difficulties which had to be surmounted and the amount of work and frustration involved in those days are indicated by the diary of James Blake. Born in 1849 and the son of the head of Blake Barclay from whom Henry Tate bought char kilns, he was sent to Liverpool in early 1875. Tate kept him on as Foreman Engineer, and he kept a diary which is a work of almost Pepysian candour.

'Friday, December 31st 1875. Breakdown in sugar house. Mr. E. Taite[10] (sic) said it was a d . . . shame nobody there to look after things.'

'Sunday, January 9th 1876. Of all the days I . . . love these the least. From early morning till 9 o'clock in the evening I toiled at the refinery amid dirt and disorder and went to bed weary and disgusted with my lot.'

Later, after a day when the pump wouldn't feed the boilers, and which included a rebuke from Mr. Muir, the Manager, for 'my men being untidy', and an endeavour to learn pan boiling, James Blake recorded:

'Sunday, March 26th 1876. Eight months in Tate's employ. Worry and disorder reigned supreme. Got home at 12 o'clock. Infernal!!'

But this sort of thing always happens in new operations, and James Blake was not all that to be pitied. He went to the opera, *La Traviata*, and the pantomime *Sinbad the Sailor*, took part in amateur theatricals and had 'psalmody rehearsals with Patterson and Dunlop', one of whom sang out of tune while the other could not read music. There are also dark references to 'promiscuous' activities, so he was probably a bit of a lad in his quiet way. But about now he wooed and won a Miss Jessie Miller who had been

[10] Probably, though not certainly, Edwin Tate.

brought up in Portugal but now lived in Scotland. They used to meet half-way, one taking the train from Glasgow, the other from Liverpool.

In the latter part of the year 1876 his diary is silent for a significant reason. Henry Tate had, sometime in 1874 or early 1875, gone to London to investigate the possible expansion of his business, and this would involve young Mr. Blake. But let us invite the Bard to introduce the next stage:

> Then he called seven sons into office
> And said 'Four up here will remain.
> But Edwin and two go to London'.
> Ted said 'Is the man really sane?
> 'He's bought up a marsh and a gasworks
> At least seven miles out of town.
> We'll either go down with swamp fever
> Or whole ruddy workforce will drown.'

Henry Tate's London purchase was a derelict shipyard owned by Messrs. Campbell & Johnston, which had operated for only ten years. It had produced several ships, including the fourth Ironclad, H.M.S. *Resistance* and a drydock capable of handling what were then thought vast vessels of up to 10,000 tons for Bermuda. It was, indeed, marshy, but it was near the London market, well placed for raw sugar supplies, and it had its own stone jetty extending 90 foot into the river and 40 foot wide.

James Blake was extracted from Love Lane, Liverpool, and sent as Chief Engineer to Silvertown to report back on what could be done with the site. Presumably surviving swamp fever, he produced a suggested layout for a refinery and was back within a few days. Henry Tate approved the scheme and Blake was sent once more to London to get on with it and to have a refinery built within twelve months.

He did so within nine months, with the help of a couple of draughtsmen from Blake Barclay, one of whom, Dan Clacher, was later to become works engineer. The first employee taken on at Thames was one Jimmy Allan, a foreman bricklayer, who employed a gang to install boilers and build the first chimney, which lasted until 1911; and subsequently a raw sugar warehouse to take sugar landed in baskets at the stone wharf.

The appointment of so young a man as Blake, so newly taken on, to undertake a new venture may have aroused jealousies, for Blake's diary for 1876 closes with a description of his time in Liverpool on his return: 'The intention of my visit (for I will call it so) to Liverpool is to gain information. Undoubtedly I have not come here in vain *but I am buying it at a high price*. Will hope to give an account of my stewardship next January.'

Possibly too, his selection of Greenock men for the work in London was unpopular in Liverpool. But there is no doubt that he made an excellent job of Thames Refinery and can be regarded as its architect. By June 1878 it was in production under the control of Edwin Tate and a Mr. J. P. Muir. Muir and J. W. MacDonald were two very successful Tate importations

The Gang's All Here. Outside Love Lane, 1897.

Handling 'wet char' – animal bone charcoal – the old way.

from Greenock to Liverpool. Muir came in 1875 as Manager and MacDonald in 1876 as Chief Chemist. MacDonald was the son of a sugar planter in St. Vincent, B.W.I., and was educated under a Dr. Wallace, presumably at a Greenock refinery. He introduced many new refinery techniques, was a prodigious worker, and a considerable statistician with a wide knowledge of commerce. He succeeded Muir as as General Manager in 1879 when the latter left Liverpool for Thames. There is a possibility that he was sent for a while to help commission the London Refinery in 1878, but the evidence is slight. J. W. eventually moved south in 1903, was made a Director, and took charge at Thames. He became Vice-Chairman of Tate & Lyle in 1921, dying in 1926 worth over £200,000.

In 1878, the first year of operation, 214 tons of raw sugar were melted and cubes produced by a new process. There were then 250 people employed. The cost of establishment was appalling and a major financial crisis resulted for the family, Henry even having to take his daughter Isolina away from boarding school as he couldn't afford the fees. However, by the end of the century the weekly Tates' melt both in London and Liverpool would be of the order of 2,000 tons.

Much of this expansion was due to the new Langen cube process – patented by Eugen Langen of Köln (the Langen family – ennobled since to von Langen were still very prominent in sugar in Germany in the firm of Pfeiffer und Langen in the 1970s). The patent agreement was signed in 1875[11] but Eugen Langen, having driven a hard bargain, permitted a delay in royalty payments until Thames was actually producing. When the agreement ran out in 1888, a renewed agreement was signed, reducing the royalty from 2 s. per ton to 6 d. In time the cube ousted the sugar loaf from the British scene. The latter is, however, still made in France and Belgium for export to North Africa, where people find it convenient for carrying on the backs of camels.

In 1882 Raffineries Say, of Paris, sued Henry Tate & Sons for infringing the patent for producing sugar cubes – or *morceaux* as they are called in France. They lost the case. Eighty-five years later Tate & Lyle were to be leading members of a Consortium which took over control of Say.[12]

Improvements continued at Thames under the leadership of Muir and Blake. Hessian bags were used instead of baskets for handling raw sugar, and in 1894 the Langen process was replaced by the Adant, which would last until 1961. Gustav Adant, its inventor, was foreman in a Brussels sugar refinery who assigned his patents to a Herr Richard Brockendorf of Köln, and Henry Tate & Sons purchased the exclusive British rights in 1892 for £12,000, with no royalties payable.

Thames at this time was in the overall control of Edwin and George Booth Tate, Muir and Blake providing day-to-day management. Blake himself was only there reluctantly. His father had died in 1882 and he was

[11] Jointly with David Martineau & Sons.
[12] See Chapter Twenty-four.

A sugar baker and his loaves. Mid-nineteenth century. Hygiene was not then important. Geese are no longer stuffed in sugar refineries.

The Langen Cube Plant at Thames – 1890.

thereupon required to return to his native Glasgow and take over running Blake Barclay. He did so, but Edwin Tate and Paddy Muir fell ill and Henry Tate (Senior) bombarded Blake with requests for his return to Thames, all of which were refused. Eventually he asked Blake by telephone to name his own terms. Blake records stating a figure so high that he was sure it would be turned down. It was not. So back he went to London accompanied by his wife, Jessie (whom he had married in 1878) and infants, and did not lose thereby.

The laboratory began to assume prominence in the affairs of Henry Tate[13] and in London three names figured among the chemists: Arthur Harrison and Hugh Main, one of them to be Manager and one Chief Chemist, and R. F. Wall, who would later be a Director. There was a fourth, Joe Yetman, who graduated to become a pan-boiler with a special grasp of this then highly idiosyncratic technique, and to pass on his skill to many. He would also pass on his name to many Yetmans at Thames in the generations to follow.

East London employers in the 1880s were a varied lot, but Tates like Lyles were thought of as good people to work for and there were queues of men outside the gate of Thames Refinery every day. Hours were long—about sixty a week—and there were early demands for more pay. Little is recorded of all this but there still exists a written wage demand entitled 'Applications from workmen for increased pay', dated September 25th, 1881, and containing a number of petitions from different departments. A covering letter, dated September 19th, 1881 and addressed, as are all the demands, to J. P. Muir, summarizes them, adding a clause to the effect that no departmental delegate should be dismissed for acting as spokesman. Some of the petitions are unsigned and one is in the form of a round-robin, a little like those of the seamen at the Spithead Mutiny in 1796. (We are at the very early stages of trade union organization.)

The demands amounted to: 1 d. an hour increase for men and $\frac{1}{2}$ d. for boys; work on Saturdays to stop at 1 p.m. instead of 4 p.m.; and overtime at time and a quarter for the first two hours and time and a half thereafter. The men in the Cube House worked in gangs of twenty-nine and got 15 s. 10 d. for every 1,000 moulds, out of which they had themselves to pay sundry ancillary workers. They seem to have been under-manned. There were also general demands for Good Friday and Christmas day to be paid holidays.

Pencil notes on the petitions are the only record of a final agreement at 2 s. per week increase for men and 1 s. for boys for a week ending on Saturday at 1 p.m., plus the paid holidays. Thereafter things seem to have settled down.

Occasionally, too, there was an outing. Once, on a Saturday in the mid-1890s, James Blake's son, John, recorded such an affair, everyone setting

13 See also Chapter Twenty-six.

off in horse-drawn drays for Rye House, Essex. Many of Tates' process workers were Orangemen from Liverpool, and as luck would have it, some of these, after a hearty nosh-up accompanied by ales, wines and spirits, fell in with a gathering of Irish Roman Catholics at a nearby fair ground. Many appeared at Waltham Abbey Police Court on the following Monday and the Refinery, short of process workers, was unable to start up until Tuesday.

Over the years both Tate Refineries began to thrive. The Tate policy was based on the idea that the public wanted and would pay for best quality sugar. Any grade or type the housewife wanted was produced. A particularly successful early product was 'yellows' sugar, made by crystallizing from the syrup resulting from washing raw sugar. By 1897 there were several grades of this—thirds, fourths, yellows and primrose, as crystals or as 'lumps'.

Henry Tate and his successors seem to have been very gifted at selecting good men once the early problems with the likes of Messrs. McConnochie and Hains had been overcome. Liverpool, in that last quarter of the nineteenth century, appears, like East London, to have been a moderately rough place. There were outbreaks of 'High Rippery' by groups like Teddy boys who, according to the Press, would 'jostle solitary females, insulting them with the coarsest ribaldry' or seize the top hats of respectable male citizens and squash them. Life was hard, too. Most of the children went barefoot. So did many employees when inside the refinery, for sugar is bad for shoes. Shiftworkers and dayworkers put in twelve hours at a stretch with two meal breaks. There were no canteen facilities and people brought in their own food. Leftovers were put on a ledge outside the Refinery on the way home and picked up by the neighbourhood children. One of the ways of getting a job was to be taken on as a beer boy, to provide for the thirst of the men who worked naked handling the 'char'—animal charcoal—in the cistern-filters. Some of these beer boys would later, like Steve Raymond, rise to senior positions.

The place must have looked like an Atkinson Grimshaw picture, the dark, misty, lanes and quays lit by an occasional gas lamp, or by yellow lamplight through a crack in a curtain. Electricity was, however, introduced into the Refinery in 1887, though candles and colza-oil flares were still in use thirty years later. The first telephone was installed in 1887. A primitive Small Packet Department was set up in 1898, in which sixteen Avery beam-scales were manned by sixty boys paid 10s. a week. But it was a characteristic of Tate's that the primitive was replaced as soon as possible by the up-to-date. Hence his success.

He was also interested, like many another successful Liverpool businessman such as Charles Booth, almost a contemporary, in South America, and took shares in the 1890s in the development of the railways of Argentina, which were then a-building, to the tune of £150,000.

Dying a Baronet in his eightieth year at his home at 'Park Hill',

Streatham, Henry Tate left a number of active descendants, and his name is forever associated with numerous educational, medical, and other endowments, of which the best known is the Tate Gallery for which he provided in 1896 the then huge sum of £150,000, by chance roughly the same as he had put into Argentine Railways. (A very balanced chap, Sir Henry.) An album of photographs of the paintings he bestowed on the Gallery exists. It is signed 'Henry Tate, Nov. 1897' and dedicated to Agnes Robinson, a daughter. The list is formidable, though naturally distinctly Victorian and a little serious. There is Millais' 'Ophelia' and 'The North West Passage', Orchardson's 'Her First Dance' and 'The First Cloud', Waterhouse's 'Lady of Shalott', and numerous Landseers and Tademas and Reids. (The taste for such works was beginning to revive, a century or so later.)

When Sir Henry died the Press were unanimous in their praise, every paper in the country carrying tributes to 'This venerable philanthropist', 'A national benefactor', 'A munificent donor', 'One of the munificent merchant princes whose names take an honourable place in the national record'.

'There are probably few things in the way of business that a shrewd Lancashire man with a pawky Scotch body for a wife cannot do', said one journal (*The Daily News*) a little condescendingly. After the grocers' shops, 'Mrs. Tate prompted her husband to the higher flight of sugar refining. He had doubts because he knew nothing of it'.

After the opening of the Tate Gallery on July 21st, 1897 by the Prince and Princess of Wales, Henry Tate was twice offered a Baronetcy and refused, only yielding to Lord Salisbury's personal explanation that his refusal seemed like a snub to his Sovereign. 'He was', said the Press 'as loyal as a subject as he was strict as a dissenter'.

With that Victorian optimism which was so notably absent eighty years later, the Press described how the Tate Gallery had been built on the site of the Old Millbank Prison–'which, thanks to the efforts of our moral teachers and the steady work of the Schoolmaster has become tenantless...'

'It is no exaggeration to say that all art lovers in this country owe Sir Henry Tate a debt of gratitude that can never be repaid.'

Some seventy-five years later one of the nest of songbirds at 21 Mincing Lane summed it all up:

> Sir Henry Tate, Bart.
> Was a lover of Art,
> Whom the Nation should still thank
> For his Gallery on Millbank.

A minor but still existent foundation of his is the Tate Institute, founded in 1887 in Silvertown. An illuminated presentation, dated February 5th, 1896, records 'The best thanks of the inhabitants of Silvertown and the neighbourhood due to Henry Tate Esquire, J.P. for his generosity in

providing an Institute for their benefit. . . .' Signed in the most beautiful
individual handwriting by the President, a Mr. William E. Cooper, and
twenty Committee members, it goes on to express their 'sincere hope that it
may please Divine Providence to bless him for many years to come with
Health and Happiness to enjoy the Respect, Esteem and Goodwill of those
with whom he has been associated'.

Alas, it was only three years, not 'many', after this that he died.

The total of his bequests is not known, but is believed to have been
many hundreds of thousands of pounds. One hopes that Isolina was able to
forgive Papa for taking her away from school.

VIII
The Lyles

The Lyles stem from Abram Lyle (I), a weaver, born in 1741, just five
years before Robert MacFie. A 'weaver' in those days need not have been
just a single working man, but, as probably in this case, a small-scale
capitalist employing up to a dozen people. But a connection postulated by
a descendant writing fifty years ago, with the family of Lyle, Barons of
Duchall, is probably tenuous in the extreme. On the other hand, there are
traces of the family as early as 1685 in the Parish records of Strathblane.
One John Key 'elopt' with a Jane Lyle. His sister, Jean Key was carried off
by Rob Roy, who was executed for this in 1748. (They were less permissive
then. One hopes Jean Key was worth the chop.)

Abram I's son, Abram II, 1783–1849, was a cooper and fishing-smack
owner who made £30,000 in a short while. He then appears to have
developed a taste for strong waters and to have lost his money in middle
age. His downfall was probably due to the drunkenness and dishonesty of a
Captain Shedden of the brig *Helen M'Gregor*. Abram himself appears to
have overcome his own failings. He died, as one of his descendants has
tersely put it, at the age of sixty-six at Gourock, in 'sanctity and debt' (to
the tune of £7,000) in 1849, having taken the pledge. (One of his early
descendants apparently acquired the same taste, for in a family record
it is noted laconically against his name: 'drank and went to
America'.)

Abram III, 1820–1891, is, however, the true founder of the firm.
(He has been mentioned in connection with John Kerr and the
herrings that went bad.) After a brief period in a lawyer's office he went
into his father's cooperage and later became a shipowner. By the time he
was forty-five he was earning the equivalent of £50,000 a year in present
day terms and during his lifetime he gave his sons £230,000 in mid-
nineteenth century sterling (multiply by fifteen or so). A rabid teetotaller,
he once told a public meeting he would sooner see his son carried home
dead than carried home drunk.

In youth and early middle age he was red-haired, and his face highly coloured. This led to occasional misunderstandings, as when a farmer from whom he had bought a horse suggested sealing the bargain with a dram. Abram refused, saying he was a teetotaller. The farmer, pointing to his red cheeks, said: 'Teetotaller are ye? Then, mon, ye shud tak doon the sign!'

About 5 ft. 7 in. tall and square in build, he began to go bald early in middle age. Although serious, he does not seem, according to his children, to have been a spoilsport. They did recall, however, being glad when their mother, born Mary Park, interposed between them and Papa. Certainly there was a strong Calvinist streak in the family, as Christian names like Gideon, Manasset and Abram bear witness. And he had a characteristic phrase to 'take a grip', which was accompanied by a clenching of his hand.[14]

He and John Kerr seem to have been admirable foils to each other, Kerr being intuitive and swift, Lyle bold but cautious. They were inseparable for twenty years, even taking their holidays together, but business was always uppermost in their minds. Kerr was once overheard saying to his companion as they sailed up the River Rhine, past the Drachenfels, 'I tell ye Lyle, raw sugars are *bound* tae rise'.

When John Kerr died in 1872 at the early age of forty, the partnership automatically ended, but, rather touchingly, Abram named his first individually purchased ship after his dead partner, *John Kerr*. The holdings in the Diamond K Line, as it was called, were amicably sorted out, Abram acquiring all the shares in four out of the eight vessels, and renaming three of them after Capes–Cormorin, Horn, and Wrath. (The Lyle Line would henceforth be nicknamed the Cape Line.) The fleet grew from four to ten between 1872 and 1880 but had its share of trouble, the flagship *John Kerr* and two others, *Cape Sable* and *Cape Cormorin* being lost with all hands between 1879 and 1882.

But, lovely as these vessels were to look at, with steel hulls and square-rigged sails, they were in effect the contemporary equivalent of tramp steamers, and financially the number of bad years exceeded the good by two to one. Worse still, the Line was almost entirely in sail. Abram III himself had been interested in ship design–some of his descendants would have a similar inventive streak. He liked his vessels to be solid and round at the fore and tail off. Once, going aboard one of these, the *Cape Finistère*, at Liverpool, after her maiden voyage, he was received by the Mate, the Captain being ashore. He asked the Mate, who had never before seen him, what he thought of the vessel. 'A fine ship, Sir, if the old bugger Lyle had not given her them bolster-bows.' He told that story against himself.

Late in the 1890s the Lyles decided to sell their sailing-vessels, getting out just in time and before the bottom dropped out of the market. They got £8 per ton.

Thereafter, Lyle Shipping and Abram Lyle & Sons went their separate

[14] A son, Robert Park Lyle, used to say in a similar way: 'It's time for a rrrow', and proceed to pick one.

ways. Alexander Park Lyle felt he was 'too Scottish' to go to London and, on his own admission, believed the shipping business, although less profitable, to be 'more noble'. Shipping was to continue, but refining, with all its problems, was to become the dominant family interest.

In a photograph taken later in life, Abram seems to exude strength and confidence. His eyes, under the high bald dome, are keen and appraising. The beard gives him a nautical look. Although referred to by his descendants as 'the Pirate King', he has more of the air of a Victorian Admiral. Definitely, however, a chap to have on your side. His expression seems to imply: 'What do ye mean, ye canna get to the worrks by sax-thirrrty?'

> The first Lyle known for our purpose
> Was Abram, 'the Pirate King'
> Who spent all his time up in Greenock
> At what's now called 'doing his thing'.
>
> His 'thing' was concerned with sea-faring
> And cargoes both arid and wet.
> Till one canny Scot paid in sugar
> And said 'juist tak that for ma debt'.
>
> Old Abe called his sons all around him
> And asked 'What's to do wi' yon muck?'
> Young Abe said 'Ye'd better refine it
> Or sides of that hold will get stuck'.
>
> So that was the start of his venture
> Which prospered and famously grew
> On sugar and Lyle's Golden Syrup
> (Which Tateses call 'that Devil's Brew').

This is more or less how it happened: Abram III, going into business with John Kerr at the Glebe, and accepting a cargo of distressed sugar in lieu of freight.

But after Kerr's death there had inevitably, however delayed, to be a change. The shipping belonged to the Lyles, but the Glebe refinery was a partnership, held jointly with the Grieve family and others, and Abram and his sons decided that they must either control it themselves or get out. Offered the choice of buying out the Lyles or being bought out by them, the Grieves opted for the former. Abram Lyle still wished to be a refiner, but where?

According to 'Sellers and Yeatman' Tate (another Tate persona, q.v.) he 'made the memorable decision to GO SOUTH AND MAKE GOLDEN SYRUP. This he and his Kith did, the Kin staying on the Clyde to look after the bawbees, or younger children'.

In fact it was a great deal more difficult than that to reach a decision.

Setting up in Greenock would be cheaper than elsewhere, labour costs would be lower, expertise was available, and to go anywhere else would deprive hundreds of folk on the Clyde of the chance of a job. As a former Provost, Abram had become deeply conscious of the misery and unemployment thereabouts, and had fostered and invested in such major works as the James Watt Harbour, a tidal basin, the fine municipal buildings, and the Lyle Road—later nicknamed The Heights of Abraham, in order to provide work. There is also a Lyle fountain.

Yet London presented a larger market for sugar than west Scotland, and there would perhaps be less competition. What appears to have brought about the final decision in 1880 was the refusal of the Greenock Harbour Trust to provide an exclusive discharging point for sugar, which Abram considered essential for the proper delivery of raw material.

This refusal in fact meant that henceforward the importance of the Clyde in sugar refining would disappear. In 1875 it was the second largest refining centre. By 1882, tonnages in round figures imported into Greenock, London and Liverpool were respectively: 250,000; 360,000; and 290,000. In 1881 Abram Lyle bought two adjacent sites on the north bank of the Thames, Odam's and Plaistow Wharves, together with a shed 'for storing petroleum and other hazardous goods', about $1\frac{1}{2}$ miles upstream from Henry Tate's refinery at Silvertown.

Like Henry Tate, Abram Lyle ran into difficulties. Before completion in 1882, there was a near disaster. The family resources were invested in sugar trading and shipping, and to build the refinery a Bank of Scotland loan of £100,000 had been obtained.

Abram IV (1847–1912) and his brother Charles (1851–1929) had been sent south to supervise the erection and commissioning. Some 400 men from Greenock (with their families) had been sent in a special train to work on the refinery erection and operation, housing having been found for them nearby. Alexander (1849–1933) and Robert (1853–1935) stayed with their father to control the Lyle shipping business.

Then there was a huge Continental beet sugar crop which knocked the bottom out of the raw sugar market, and the Lyles were forced to sell six cargoes of Java sugar at a thumping loss of £15,000 to £20,000 per cargo. In addition, by some deep and universal natural law, the cost of construction was well over estimate. (There was trouble in reaching gravel for the foundations beneath the muddy north bank of the Thames.) James Duncan, the London refiner—the one who had tried beet sugar production at Lavenham in 1870—had recently gone broke and his Clyde Wharf Refinery had fetched only £60,000 against a book value of £300,000. The Bank of Scotland took fright and demanded a reduction in the Lyle loan. Alexander was sent to see a Mr. Wenley at the Bank in Edinburgh and pointed out that, as a forced sale of the refinery as a non-going concern would bring in very little, certainly not enough to pay off the loan in full, it would be unwise not to give extra time. The Bank agreed,

A group at Abram Lyle & Sons Ltd., Plaistow Wharf, 1892. See six Lyles seated, second row from front.

A group at Henry Tate & Sons Ltd., Liverpool, 1881. Front row includes left to right: George Tate, Paddy Muir, James Blake and Dan Girdwood.

Plaistow Wharf before the Lyles.

Ladies of the Bag Store – Thames Refinery.

Dan Girdwood. Started at Love Lane
1871. Foreman of the Cooperage at
Thames Refinery 1878–1906.

Miss L. Morgan in the Thames
Laboratory – c. 1910.

one of the Lyle steamers was sold, the family barrel scraped, and the refinery was completed.

The corner was turned, but 1882[15] left a permanent scar. During this 'black year' the Directors took no fees and had to ask the staff and workforce to wait for a while before being paid in full. The grandfather (John) of the present Chairman would never thereafter buy an evening paper. A halfpenny was a bawbee (*not* a younger child, Tate!) and not to be frittered away on the *Evening News*.

The trade journal, *The Grocer*, printed on May 5th, 1883 a description of a visit to the 'new' refinery–'the sort of enterprise exactly suited to a Scotchman's power of achievement', it explains kindly. A little below the Victoria Docks and Clyde Wharf, the refinery stood in 'a commanding position'. The buildings consisted of ten stories and were of a total height of 110 feet. They had taken fifteen months to erect, the first sod having been cut on October 1st, 1881, and the foundations were of 'prepared concrete' fifteen feet below ground level. The buildings were of brick, with iron staircases and 'the whole process of refining was so arranged that it commences on the highest level and passes down through its different stages till the raw material is turned into the manufactured article.

'Everything is done with quickness and despatch . . . the whole operation does not occupy more than 10 or 12 hours, so that extra supplies can be had on the shortest notice, a fact of the utmost importance to the retail grocers who cannot always wait for useful raw sugars, that at this season [March–April] especially can come in only at the caprice of the wind.'

Lyle's policy was to produce a few types of sugar as cheaply as possible and to depend on one speciality, Golden Syrup, as his main source of earnings. The melt at Plaistow rose from 400 tons a week in 1883 to about 2,000[16] by 1900. The development of Lyle's Golden Syrup–the East-Enders engaged in its production usually called it 'surrip'–was a success. Abram III's strongly religious background left its impression when it came to the difficult matter of choosing a trade mark, and an illustration from the story of Samson was selected. Hence the appearance on the can of the lion killed by Samson, and surrounded by bees, and the quotation from Judges XIV. 'Out of the strong came forth sweetness (out of the eater came forth meat).'

In a history written in 1968, Tony Tate (masquerading again as Sellers and Yeatman) has another version: 'It is known today throughout the world wherever Socialists haul down the Union Jack. Abram III and his Kith, being utterly without Scruples (and the Bank having refused to lend any more), borrowed a lion who had just been having a Bath at Longleat, photographed him whilst sleeping it off surrounded by greenfly, and added

[15] Sir Alexander Park Lyle says it was 1883, the year of the Krakatoa eruption. Oliver Lyle's records show that the Refinery was already melting by January 18th that year, and this is confirmed by the article from *The Grocer* which is quoted below.

[16] Oliver Lyle gives the precise figure of 1,726 tons.

the immortal words "Honi soit qui mal y pense", which, of course, means "If you think this is honey, O.K." '

Two other sons of Abram III, William and John, followed Abram IV and Charles to London. Alexander and Robert stayed on with the shipping company, Robert coming south in 1900. The Lyle Shipping Company still exists as a separate entity.

A much less successful venture than Golden Syrup was the chocolate factory, built in 1897. This in fact was a disaster. No-one knows why the Lyles went into the business of confectionery and it was commercially unwise, for it involved competing with people who were themselves customers. Two French confectioners were engaged for the technical side of the affair and a magnificent building—later used as a works restaurant and still standing in 1977, was erected. The head Frenchman, a M. Auguste Jacoutot, was engaged at £400 a year, a high salary for those days—indeed after the Directors he was said to be the highest paid man in the firm. The local girls engaged were under the charge of Florence Maxey, whose one-eyed brother, Ernie, was chief shunter on the refinery railway.

Quality and design were superb, in fact too good; far too great a variety was produced—there were 170 recipes; the Lyle's had no goodwill in the confectionery business. And, after two years the factory was closed down.

The Lyles were generous benefactors, though on a more modest scale than Henry Tate, most of their donations, like those of the Walkers, Kerrs and MacFies, being made to local causes in Greenock.

By the 1890s the situation had become as it is described by the Bard:

> So Love Lane and Thameses Refineries
> Soon were biggest and best in the land.
> Till Abram brought Lyleses from Greenock.
> Tate said 'Well, this does beat the band.
>
> 'I've got ruddy Lyle on doorstep
> A thing that I always have feared.
> He's got lots of sons just as I have
> And he even has copied my beard.'

As far as is known, Henry Tate and Abram Lyle never met, and it was long before their descendants did so. But there was a tacit agreement not to poach on each other's speciality preserves. Lyle kept off cubes and Tate kept off syrup. Each conducted this part of his operations in total secrecy, the Lyles even going to the length of breaking up plant that was scrapped into unrecognizable fragments. When, in the 1890s the Lyles heard a rumour that the Tates were contemplating going into syrup production, they bought part of a cube plant and let it be widely known that they had done so. It remained unused and Tates made no syrup.

In the course of establishing these undertakings, many other people were involved. As has been mentioned, Abram Lyle sent not only his sons but a large contingent of people from the Clyde, Carmichaels, Mackays, Greenlaws, MacLeods, MacDonalds, McCullochs, MacMarths, McGlones, as plumbers, coopers, engineers and refinery operatives. Once in London, they were joined by English families, Oldfields, Tyzacks, Thompsons, Dunlops, Austins, Caulfields, Chambers, Gorsts, Graves, Bulls, Runeckles, Taylors. Irishmen joined, too, Fitzgeralds and Jamiesons, Flanagans and Kinsellas, and in the early years of the twentieth century these in turn were joined by immigrants from Germany and Austria, such as Lenz; from Italy, Migliori; and from Poland. The last used to sail from Danzig to Harwich on their way to the U.S.A., carrying a slip of paper on which was the word TATE. From Harwich this would in some magical way get them to Fenchurch Street and thence, via Canning Town to either a Tate or a Lyle refinery. Here, the gateman, finding their names impossible, would say: 'You Johnny Brown,' and the new employee would then be known, until he had saved enough money to Go West, as Johnny the Pole. Some, thank goodness, stayed on, too.

A similar patina of names was established at Thames Refinery, while in Liverpool the names are predominantly those of Jackson, Curtis, Mulhall, Neely, Gamble (some of these later came south), Bellman, Wilson, Begg, Galbraith, Hore, Raymond, Moretta, Lillicrap, Lycett, Armitage, Long, and many more, and the Clyde refineries continued to be manned by Scotsmen.

It is impossible to name them all, but–to run ahead of the story–one of the major strengths of the companies as they developed and amalgamated will be seen to be the continuing long service of so many employees and the frequency with which they obtained jobs for sons and daughters, grandsons and granddaughters in the same place. In the early 1950s, Oliver Lyle, then himself in his late sixties, recorded finding 750 out of the total workforce at Plaistow who had members of their families working there too. It was not, as sociologists and economists might deduce, simply a matter of 'having to' under social and economic pressure. The firms were known to be sound and in general remained continuously ahead of their times in humanity and fair treatment, even when they ran into difficulties.

Abram III died in 1891. Although only just seventy, he was vigorous and very much in command. One of his side interests was the Glasgow and South Western Railway, of which he had long been a conscientious Director. He caught influenza on a visit to London in the spring of 1891, but instead of taking to his bed on his return, insisted on going to Glasgow to chair a meeting of the Railway. Influenza developed into double pneumonia and in three days he was dead. Penicillin would have saved him, but perhaps he would have considered that he had reached the Biblical three score years and ten anyway.

He had had a successful, well-organized life and he left behind him six sons, two of whom, Alexander and Robert, were still in Greenock with his shipping business (though Robert was later to come south), while the other four, Abram, Charles, William and John, concentrated on the Refinery at Plaistow Wharf.

Thirty years later, on July 17th, 1923, there was an unsolicited tribute from a former employee, Charles McPhail, which deserves quoting in full, for it gives a contemporary view from an ordinary employee:

'As a Cooper, I wrought for a number of years with the firm of A. Lyle & Sons at Silvertown over 30 years ago, and what impressed me while there was the humane touch which seemed to pervade the whole factory. The consideration of the employers for their workers had in it a touch of the divine and this was reciprocated by every man who was worth calling a man.'

Mr. McPhail accompanied this with a short poem in memory of Robert Park Lyle, who had just died.

The Lyle characteristics were strong, and the facial resemblance between the portraits of a century ago and today is striking. So indeed are the likenesses in character between old Abram III and his great-grandchildren.

IX
An Electrical Interloper

Life in a refinery being hardly a bed of roses, it is not surprising that a New Method of Refining Sugar by Electricity should have had its attraction. It was, of course, a total swindle from beginning to end, but it fooled a lot of people at the time, for in 1889 the word 'electrical' had a sort of magic about it, and its perpetrator, 'Professor' Henry C. Friend, sometimes described as 'the wily Teuton', was a skilled racketeer. He knew that the bigger and bolder the lie the more likely it was to succeed.

He began it in 1883, with an experiment, at which those invited were shown two barrels of raw sugar and a complicated 'electric purifying machine'. They were then sent out of the room, and when they returned were shown an almost equal quantity of sugar said to have been refined by the machine. 'The Electric Sugar Refining Company' of New York was formed with a capital of 10,000 $100 shares, and these were readily bought by the gullible in New York (where, by 1889 the shares reached a value of $600) and Liverpool, where an agent called Mr. J. U. Robertson got as much as $580 a share. The 'Professor' had visited Liverpool in 1885 and had helped to fool some of the people there too. Nobody thought of checking on his past. If they had they would have discovered that he had done a year in gaol in Chicago in 1881 for a similar trick. As it was he collected about £80,000 towards building the plant and was to be paid a further £16,000 plus 3 shillings a ton royalty once he had produced 50 tons.

He never did, but he lived on the fat of the land until 1888 when he died without disclosing his secret to the Electric Sugar Company. He had not succeeded in fooling the sugar refiners, however, for James Fairrie (1861–1926), father of Geoffrey, had in 1887 asked a New York refiner, Thomas Havemeyer, what he thought and had been told it must be a fraud.

After the 'Professor's' death the Liverpool shareholders in the Electric Sugar Company sent a patent agent, Mr. W. P. Thompson of Brooklyn to see the 'Electric Refinery'. He found empty barrels of what had been refined sugar, some 36 tons of raw sugar ready for an experiment, and a locked strong-room containing the 'secret' plant. Against protests from the watchman, who said the strong-room was booby-trapped, he and two others, including a Mr. Cotterill, President of the Electric Sugar Company, broke in and found crushers of refined sugar and sieves. The enterprising 'Professor' and his associates had bought refined sugar in small lots at different groceries to provide the end product of the 'process'.

The 'Professor' was now out of reach but his Chief Engineer and other associates ended up in Sing Sing. Certain shrewd speculators must have made a killing but did not do time. Others, less shrewd, lost their shirts.

X

'When duty whispers low thou must, the youth
replies I will.'
(R. W. Emerson, 1803–1882)

To appreciate what an act of faith was required on the party of Henry Tate and Abram Lyle to found new refineries when they did, and the sheer determination needed to persist in the face of trouble and near-disaster, some understanding of the commercial position of sugar in the latter half of the nineteenth century and of the resultant difficulties is necessary. Those difficulties are involved with Customs duties, and the imagination boggles. However, it must be done, so hold my hand and take a deep breath.

Duty scales and 'Drawbacks' and 'Bounties' are among the least exciting of topics. Governments use Customs duties to enable them to help pay for the services they sometimes mistakenly inflict on those who vote them into power, and apply drawbacks and bounties to encourage those domestic industries which they wish to encourage while protecting them from external competition.

Sugar Bounties had existed in Continental Europe for many decades by the mid-1860s. In France a Bounty provided exported refined sugar with a drawback of the duty paid on the raw sugar from which it was made. The calculation of the amount of drawback assumed that a standard yield of refined sugar was obtained from raw and early on this was fixed at 44·4 per cent. If a refiner was able by technical improvements to get a higher yield, he pocketed the difference as a bonus, and although the authorities raised the 'official' yield figure from time to time, they always lagged behind technical developments.

When the domestic beet sugar industry grew in Europe a similar system was applied, a nominal duty being levied on the sugar produced from beets. So that, like the French refiners, the beet sugar producers received a concealed bonus on sugar exported. Holland and Belgium had similar systems. In Germany a fixed tax was paid on the weight of sugar beet produced and a drawback was allowed on all sugar exports based on a fixed yield from the sugar beet of 8·51 per cent. Sugar produced over and above that figure allowed the producer to sell abroad any surplus to home requirements, at less than the cost of production.

The Germans are a systematic, inventive people and they did much research into improving the varieties of sugar beet so as to obtain ever-increasing yields, and so did the producers in the Austro-Hungarian Empire. They profited, of course, from this.

In Britain there was no domestic beet sugar industry, and although the refiners received a drawback on sugar exported, the authorities frequently adjusted the drawback rate so as to conform with actual yields obtained. Moreover, sugar was refined 'in bond', i.e. under Customs supervision, and there was no laxity allowed. It was then British policy to buy food as cheaply as possible from wherever it could be obtained. This 'free breakfast table' policy lasted until the entry of the U.K. into the European Community and the adoption of E.E.C. agricultural policies. In the 1860s it led to the gradual disappearance of sugar duties, to the detriment of the British refiners.

In November 1864 a Convention was signed between England, France, Holland, and Belgium: 'to effect the abolition of all bounties which might be given to the refiners of any country in the amount of drawback allowed on the exportation of refined sugar'. Germany and Austria were not involved.

Despite attempts to standardize the various duty and drawback scales the Convention was only partly successful. The British refiners gained by being able to use a variety of raw cane sugars from all over the world, but meantime Continental refiners were using increasing amounts of raw beet sugars whose quality could not be established on the new scale of 'Dutch Standards'. In France, in particular, where the duty was very much larger, a refiner using beet raws could obtain a very large bonus on exported sugar. As a result, as early as August 1867 Henry Tate was writing:

'Our market is very flat and prices for our product seriously low. I really don't know what's to become of the trade. We hear that two or three of our manufacturers have almost stopped melting. . . .'

By 1872 the production of sugar loaves had almost ceased in Britain and firms were going out of business, or turning to other types of sugar – cubes and granulated. Firms in Liverpool such as Crosfield Barrow, Leitch, Jager and Heap disappeared

A Committee of refiners was set up to try to persuade the British

Government to take action and to obtain the co-operation of other governments; when it was established its members little knew that it had thirty years' work ahead of it. International Conferences were held in 1873, 1874 and 1875, but these, while establishing the use of the polarimeter as a means of measuring expected yields, did not otherwise result in agreement. In 1888 a further Conference suggested that countries should impose penal duties on imported 'Bounty-fed' sugar, but the House of Commons, under pressure from 'free breakfast table' supporters and the jam and other trades, would not permit this.

In 1896 Germany and Austria were in the lead, even doubling the rate of export Bounty, and people like Joseph Chamberlain were seriously worried by the effect of imports on the West Indies. (A Commission had reported on that region in December of that year.)

In June 1898 there was another Conference at Brussels and four years later in 1902, after much to-ing and fro-ing, all the major countries concerned agreed to suppress direct and indirect Bounties. Although the Convention of Brussels was ratified in 1903, this did not prevent Germany and Austria from allowing artificially high domestic prices to subsidize exports – with the result that Britain in 1914 was still importing 60 per cent of her sugar from these two countries – but it helped.

It was not until 1928 that the British Government modified its duty scale on imported refined sugar. In the meantime, however, it is clear that the new Tate and Lyle refineries had had to operate for the first thirty years of their existence against a daunting background of artificial competition.

All right; you can let go now. We've got to the other side. And so have those two bearded gentlemen and their progeny. One lifts one's hat to them and hopes the trumpets sounded.

CHAPTER THREE

'Before the War'

There'll be no War, as long as we've a
King like Good King Edward,
There'll be no War for he hates that sort
of thing,
Peace with Honour is his motto,
So God Save the King.
(Popular song. ca. 1903)

The nineteenth century was over and so was the Boer War and the Old Queen was dead. The new King (accompanied by Princess Alexandra) had as Prince of Wales opened the Tate Gallery six years earlier.

It was now 1903 and young Herbert Woodward came to work for Abram Lyle & Sons at 21 Mincing Lane as a sixteen-year-old for 10 s. a week. This would buy him all sorts of goodies: a fairly good shirt (2 s. 6 d.), a very good tie (1 s. 6 d.), half a bottle of Johnny Walker (1 s. 6 d.). a pint (1½ d.), an ounce of good tobacco (6 d.), a dozen boxes of matches (1½ d.). He could have an evening out for less than 1 s. including a seat at the Camberwell Palace (6 d.), five Woodbines (matches thrown in) (1 d.), and two half-pints (2 d.).

He was one of many millions who lived modestly but well, families often keeping a maid servant, taking a couple of weeks' holiday at Margate, and from time to time gladdened by a rise of £20 a year. There were also many millions living in squalor and poverty, spending half their earnings on food (as compared with under a quarter now). Seebohm Rowntree had just published a survey suggesting that people like this were badly under-nourished. Partly because of ignorance, partly from poverty they ate the wrong things. (Vitamins would not be known of for another 20 years.) Yet in 1911 the first universal old age pension would be introduced, largely because of the efforts of Charles Booth, like Henry Tate a successful Liverpool businessman.

It is difficult to capture the feel of those years. For one thing there was virtually no porn, certainly in public.

Letters were delivered six times a day and once on Sundays but–difficult to imagine–there was no radio or TV. Charles Booth's daughter, who had attended King Edward's Coronation as a girl of twenty-one (she died aged ninety-four in 1975) remembered meeting in 1906 'that nice Mr. Marconi' on a boat crossing to New York. He was experimenting with something called Wireless Waves and, using this and a system of dots and dashes invented earlier by a Mr. Morse, sent a message for Miss Booth to her younger sister, who was returning to London in another boat.

Within Britain there was tension between Conservatives and Liberals.

There was an embryonic Labour Party, whose members on principle wore cloth caps in the House. One of these, Ramsay MacDonald, spoke over and over again of the ideal socialist state which must come one day. There would be no tyranny and no crime and men would work, not for sordid gain, but for the sheer joy of labour. Some believed him. There was a kind of Lib-Lab pact in reverse and the Liberal Government passed the Trade Disputes Act in 1906, setting trade unions above the law.

There was about it all a mixture of innocence, insouciance, voluptuousness, vulgarity and propriety, of private vice and public virtue. There was certainly something uneasy there too, an instability like that of ageing gelignite, liable to go off at the drop of a top hat. Otherwise why the relief with which the mass of people everywhere were to welcome, four years after the death of Good King Edward (the popular song had been right), the outbreak of war in 1914? Why would Rupert Brooke, the gloriously handsome spokesman of a doomed generation write of them in 1914 as turning:

> Like swimmers into cleanness leaping,
> Glad from a world grown old and cold and weary?

But this is not yet and we are still back at Mincing Lane in 1903, and Henry Tate & Sons are going public. After the founder's death his eldest son, Sir William Henry (Bt.) was left in charge, assisted by Edwin, George, Alfred and Henry (Junior). William Henry was in London as Chairman, Alfred retired, and Liverpool was in the hands of William's sons, Ernest and Alfred Herbert (Bertie, father of Louis, F. H.–Tony, and Johnny). Henry Junior had died young, aged only forty-eight, in 1902. There is an oral tradition that the reason why the firm went public was that one of the Tate widows, perhaps his, wished to withdraw her investment. He had been made a director in 1896. A strong Unitarian and a keen amateur soldier, his last public appearance was a fortnight before his death when he and Sir John Brunner M.P. (son of Alfred) opened a Unitarian Church hall and cloisters built, in memory of their fathers, in Liverpool.

The issued capital was 30,000 5½ per cent cumulative preference shares of £10 each and 50,000 ordinary shares of £10 each, and the dividend book shows only seventeen shareholders at this time. Most were family, William Henry having 19,188 shares, Edwin 17,698. Ernest had nearly 4,000, Bertie 1,328, George Booth Tate (Vernon's father) 3,310, and there were a number of widows and in-laws. There were also a few non-family men such as John W. MacDonald who had just come south to manage the London Refinery, L. A. Martin who ran the sales, and John Patrick ('Paddy') Muir. These held each from 200 to 1,650 shares. James Blake the engineer, whose diary we have peeped at and who had finally settled in London, held 253 shares. The first year's dividend of the public company was 10 per cent. Income tax was 1 s. in the pound.

At Liverpool Ernest interested himself particularly in engineering,

Bertie in the people (who were very fond of him) and the horses (of which there were many). He liked all animals and was later to build a large aviary at his home in Surrey. Walking daily through the Refinery, wearing cloth caps and white coats to keep off the drips from pipes, Bertie talked to everybody and was much loved, while Ernest was more aloof. But he was a most capable and just negotiator in cases of grievance or wage claims. He would later be Chairman of Henry Tate & Sons and then the second Chairman of Tate & Lyle. Ernest at this time had a steam-driven automobile.

There was another chap, later to become well known, around in Liverpool at this time – Harry Tate. He was no relation, his real name being Ronald MacDonald Hutchinson. Nevertheless he worked for a time in Liverpool for Henry Tate and took his stage name from this.

The Tates like the Lyles, would no doubt then be looked down on, as being 'In Trade'. (In Rutland those who only turned out to hunt at weekends were known as the Early Closing Brigade.) But they and so many others were providing, all unrecognized, the financial and commercial muscle which furnished the wealth which would soon be poured away in war and the means whereby not only the very grand but the new office boy enjoyed meantime their *douceur de vivre*. Times changed and later they were looked down on by lefty intellectuals instead.

Abram Lyle & Sons was to remain a private firm until amalgamated with Tates'. Its capital of £287,000 consisted of 1,093 preference and 1,777 ordinary shares of £10 each. Early in the century one of the sons, William, reduced his holdings, and by 1911 the family held the following:

Abram	£41,400
Alexander	£57,300
Charles	£57,300
William	£16,300
Robert	£57,300
John	£57,300
plus – William Boyd (secretary)	£100

The Tates were extremely good technical sugar refiners, better, according to Oliver Lyle, than the Lyles, and had a more vigorous sales policy. But they did not take so much trouble over figures and statistics and only struck a balance half-yearly, when they would know their profits. The Lyles liked to work out the previous week's profits and the cumulative sugar loss every Tuesday and 'declared' an interim dividend every three weeks or so.

The Lyle Refinery was melting about 1,800 tons a week in 1903 and the Tate Refinery at Silvertown a little more. The name Silvertown, incidentally, comes from a Mr. Samuel Winkworth Silver. Born in 1791 and dying in 1855, he had been a pioneer in the rubber trade, and in 1852 had bought a site on a marsh in order to build the India Rubber, Gutta Percha and Telegraph Cable Works (now the Silvertown Rubber Company). He had persuaded the Stratford to Woolwich Branch Railway, part of Great Eastern, to erect a halt near his factory. It was called Silver's Halt, and later the area became Silver's Town, then Silvertown.

Henry Tate's site for his refinery had originally been that derelict shipyard and had an area of $7\frac{1}{2}$ acres plus a further $1\frac{3}{4}$ added by converting the foreshore to a wharf for receiving sugar barges. But melt was expanding rapidly, and in 1908 Tates bought a further $7\frac{1}{2}$ acres to the east. This had been the Silvertown Gas Works but had been taken over by the Gas Light & Coke Company. It provided another 584 feet of river frontage, some factory buildings, and a seven-bedroomed house which was split into two and occupied by a shift foreman and a shift engineer. The area is still called the Eastern Premises.

There was still then, beyond the railway, a view of green fields as far as the villages of Plaistow and East Ham, broken only by the Albert Dock, recently excavated. Much of the land was below high water level, and floods were frequent. At Thames the old wooden piles, sunk through the soft soil into shingle beds in the 1880s, were exposed as the water drained off to the new dock, and Tates' engineers became worried. The new chimney, built in 1911, was erected on concrete piles.

Rail trucks were drawn into the sidings by horses, raw sugar in barges was unloaded in baskets on to horse-drawn carts for the Melter House (where the Laboratory now is). The sugar, until the 1900s, was dissolved and treated with phosphoric acid and lime (bullock's blood was out). After passing through charcoal the liquor was evaporated and filled into cube moulds which were cooled for a day before being spun in centrifugal machines, dried, and cut. (This was the Langen process, now being replaced by the Adant.) Cubes were sold at first in barrels, later in wooden boxes (cases) holding one hundredweight net. The other product, as at Liverpool, was the yellow sugar called 'pieces' until the introduction of the water-driven centrifugal made affining more effective and carbonatation proper came in. By 1903 granulated sugar was being produced in increasing quantities. By 1903 there was electric light instead of gas.

Edwin Tate, 'Paddy' Muir and George Booth Tate, who had been running the Refinery had grown old and ill. Claude Robinson, a Tate son-in-law, Arthur Harrison and James Blake, replaced them.

Melts continued to rise, and so did profits. The Tate dividend book showed, except for 1908, a steady increase from 10 per cent to 25 per cent in 1911, and after a brief dip, to 25 per cent again in 1914. By then income tax had gone up to 1 s. 5 d. in the pound and the melt was at about 4,000 tons a week. The number of shareholders had grown to seventy-four.

In Liverpool the process was gradually modernized, the manufacture of 'primrose' and 'yellows' reduced, and by 1910 the techniques were in principle as they still are. By 1914 the melt there had reached 3,000 tons a week.

Abram Lyle & Sons Ltd. was managed by the second generation brothers. Abram IV, the eldest, had been until recently in charge of raw sugar purchases, always a ticklish business. He was regarded by the brokers as brilliant at it. William was in charge of sales. He, like his brother John, suffered from kidney stones, but after a couple of operations in 1903 recovered and lived to be eighty-two. Charles, father of Leonard, later the first Lord Lyle, and John (eleven years Charles' junior), grandfather of the present Chairman, ran the Refinery. They were tough, kindly, and sometimes a little over-strict in driving a bargain, forever arguing with each other, but bold in decision. Abram IV had retired in 1902 and brother Robert Park Lyle had taken over his job. Abram's son, Abram Arthur, refused to let himself be called Abram, preferring Arthur. He was in the firm from 1899 until the Tate amalgamation took place. (His son, Ian was elected President of Tate & Lyle in 1964 and another grandson of Abram IV, Morton Oliphant, was a Director from 1946 to 1974.) During the pre-war period Leonard joined the firm (in 1903) and by 1909 Charles felt that he could hand over to him. John's sons, Philip and Oliver, joined when they became twenty-one, Philip in 1906 and Oliver in 1912. Neither was to be made a Director until 1919, and Oliver was only permitted to join because of the departure of a cousin, 'young' Willie.

This all reads a little like one of the less inspired chapters in Chronicles II – and there will inevitably be other passages like it – but some of those mentioned above will emerge from the shadows and their personalities will be seen, individualistic, often memorable, sometimes quirky, always amusing.

There were some other Lyles, second cousins, who also came south to work at Plaistow Wharf, and one of their number would later become a Director. But let us leave them for the moment, merely recording that, with their help, by 1914 the Lyle Refinery was now melting just over 3,000 tons of sugar a week. On the granulated and other sugars produced it made, if lucky, a profit of about £1 5s. 0d. a ton, and about 500 tons a week was sent out as 'Goldie', Golden Syrup. On this the profit was considerably higher, about £6 a ton.

In the fourth year of the reign of King Edward's much less flamboyant son, King George V, therefore, the three Refineries, two Tate and one Lyle, were producing some 10,000 tons a week of various brands of sugar and syrup, against competition from Fairrie's and Walker's, Martineaus' and others, and in intense competition with one another and with imported sugar. Old Henry Tate and old Abram Lyle, now about twenty years in their graves, had not met. There had never been a meeting or discussion between their respective descendants, who only knew each other slightly from formal contacts on the Sugar Association or the Sugar Refiner's Association. They often travelled on the same Great Eastern

Athel Monarch at speed.

Mechanical cane harvesting.

Brechin Castle Factory–Trinidad. The canefield in the foreground has just been reaped–by hand in this case.

Thames Refinery from the river—c. 1908.

train from Fenchurch Street Station, but they avoided using the same compartment. Oliver Lyle records frequently walking behind 'old man MacDonald', a Director of Tate's, to the station. MacDonald went usually into the refreshment room and had a glass of sherry, while, said Oliver, 'I sidled along to the other end of the bar and had coffee (!) which I sipped until he left and had taken his seat, when I could be sure of getting into another compartment'.

For them, in their top hats and frock coats (to be changed on arrival at the refineries into something less formal – old trousers and a white coat plus a cloth cap or a bowler) it was often necessary to walk from Canning Town station, a mile or more away. This was also the general way to work for the less favoured. The road was muddy and at one point traversed a level-crossing which would from time to time be closed. The crossing keeper, tired of replying in kind to abuse flung at him by those who would arrive late to work, had, permanently, chalked on the crossing-gate the words: 'And you too.'

More significant than the competition between the British firms was that from foreign subsidized refined sugars, which still came in, despite the Brussels Convention of 1903. More important still was the fact that from 60 to over 90 per cent of the refineries' raw material was also coming in in the form of raw beet sugar, almost exclusively from Germany and Austria. Then, on a hot summer's day, August 4th, 1914, there began that watershed in time which splits us off forever from the days of Good King Edward and from all that had gone before him.

CHAPTER FOUR

1914–1918

'*Now God be thanked, Who has matched us with His hour*'
(Rupert Brooke, 1914)

Yes, people actually felt like that then.

On June 28th, 1914, at about 11.30 in the morning, in bright sunlight, at the Serbian town of Sarajevo a febrile nineteen-year-old Bosnian-Serb student called Gavril Princip administered the shock which set off the ageing gelignite. When the car carrying the heir apparent to the Austrian Empire on a state visit took a wrong turning and stopped, alongside where Princip was standing, he drew a revolver and fired twice, point blank, mortally wounding the Archduke and killing his wife, Sophie.

Gavril Princip was seized, beaten up, took an ineffective dose of poison, and ended up in jail. He was a consumptive and died soon afterwards of it, so the sentence of death was not carried out on him. Instead it was to be carried out vicariously on millions of his fellow-beings when, one after the other, Russia, Austria-Hungary, Germany, France, the British Empire, Italy, Portugal, Japan and finally the U.S.A. went to war. In London the Foreign Secretary, Sir Edward Grey, looking out of his windows at dusk on August 3rd, said miserably, in an echo of William Pitt after Austerlitz; 'The lamps are going out all over Europe; we shall not see them lit again in our lifetime.'

For Henry Tate & Sons Ltd., and Abram Lyle & Sons, Gavril Princip's act and its consequences meant changes, dislocation, problems, anxieties. For individuals at all levels in the companies, as for everyone else, it meant four and a quarter years of as yet unimagined grief and desperation, and–indeed Sir Edward was right–an indescribable darkness, for the lamps of civilization were put out. Those troops going into battle in the early days of the war as if it were some kind of tournament were, it was soon discovered, a tragic anachronism. Soon the men would be going away in their hundreds from the refineries, many of them never to be seen again. Most of them would spend months, even years, in close quarters in squalor it is hard to picture–boredom, fear, mud, fleas, rats, stink, extreme cold or great heat, and the ever-present hideous noise of the guns. The only consolation, and it was a curiously true one, was the discovery, as the hopes and ideals were leached into the slime of the trenches, of the value, the courage, the humour, and the humanity of other men, of their resourcefulness and loyalty, no matter where they came from. The good rose to the top in the front lines. Alas, they did not last long.

For those who waited at home there were the huge casualty lists, as Big Push followed *Grosser Drang*, the separation, the sight of the convalescent wounded in their blue, the apparently never-ending series of 'Great Victories' which turned out too often to be dead sea fruit, First and Second Ypres, Loos, the Somme, Cambrai, Vimy Ridge, the Chemin des Dames, Verdun, the Dogger Bank, Jutland and the rest. A woman working in a field hospital in France in 1917 summed it up for all women: 'The wind is in the N.E. and the guns go on and on. I shall be very, very old soon, like a grey moth that has lived in dust and darkness too long to remember that its underwings were orange.'

Then, too, there was the stranglehold of the U-Boat war and the resultant food shortages. It was this which in 1916 caused the setting up of a Committee under the Earl of Selborne: 'to consider and report upon the methods of effecting an increase in homegrown supplies having regard to the need for such an increase in the interest of national security'. As we shall see later,[1] this would, a few years hence, when the guns had fallen silent, have an effect lasting directly for fifteen years on the affairs of Tate & Lyle, and forever on the sugar pattern of Britain. For sugar was one of the commodities being lost by U-Boat attack, and it could be homegrown.

The Government had taken immediate control of sugar refining in 1914. They had to, for supplies had to be purchased from elsewhere than Germany and Austria. The Lyles had thought something was in the wind prior to August 1914 and had bought huge stocks of raw sugar. The Government took these over, and most of the profit accrued to them, not to the Lyles who nevertheless made £350,000. A Royal Sugar Commission was set up to ladle out supplies to the refiners. Robert Park Lyle served on this and was later awarded a baronetcy for his efforts. It was on this Commission that he got to know J. J. Runge (q.v.).

The change from anything up to 90 per cent beet to 100 per cent cane raws produced problems, for cane raws are more difficult to filter than beet. Plaistow's melt dropped by about 400 tons a week. Sugar losses rose by 1915 from an average 0·86 per cent to about 4 per cent. Plaistow eventually managed to raise the melt figure a little, thanks to a friendly gesture from old MacDonald of Tate's. Hearing of the filtration problem – due to choked passages in the filter presses – he provided details of a Tate strainer where air was bubbled through the perforations to keep them clear. It was the first example of co-operation between the companies, and it had taken a war to bring it about.

The staffs at the refineries were tiny, overworked and subject to fickle and arbitrary callings-up. Women came in to do many of the jobs done by men. Three girls at Plaistow, Maud Watson, Jennie Rogers and Emmy Jacques learned successfully to boil vacuum pans. Girls did 12-hour shifts on jobs unthinkable today, dealing with char cisterns, handling the char kilns, emptying centrifugal machines. (In those days this was done with hand paddles and the girls lay on their stomachs to do the work, their legs in the air.)

[1] See Chapter seven.

In common with the other young men in the firms, Oliver and Philip Lyle had joined up. Oliver got married in September 1914 by special licence. He had no money (his salary was £75 a year) and his best man was also broke, so he took a collection from the five members of the congregation in order to pay the parson. There was no time for a honeymoon. He served as a Captain in the Highland Light Infantry, was wounded at the Battle of Loos and twice mentioned in despatches – he wrote a long and fascinating account of trench life to his brother Philip. (Cousin Willie, whose departure had permitted Oliver to join the firm, was killed at the Somme in 1916.) From 1916 Oliver was sent to the Inventions Department of the Ministry of Munitions and was awarded an O.B.E. for his work there. Philip served in the East Surrey Regiment in the Middle East and India. A Tate whom we shall later meet, G. V. (Vernon) son of George Booth Tate, went from Winchester and Trinity, Cambridge into the Middlesex Regiment and won an M.C., only joining Henry Tate & Sons after the war was over.

They were like so many others that it seems unfair to single them out, but for Tate & Lyle they would be dominant figures after it was over. Leonard Lyle, in his late thirties, was too old to join up. He stayed on and his old father, Charles, came back temporarily in 1916 at the age of sixty-five to help, for there was a shortage of management strength. There could be no new work or modernization for all metals and other materials were needed for the war effort.

The Government, in controlling the refiners, permitted them to make the same profit as the average for the three years before the war, based on granulated sugar. This was technically demoralizing, for it was virtually a cost-plus arrangement based on a product which had never made much money, and losses and possible extravagances were not penalized. On this basis the Lyle profits overall rose from £1 7s. 0d. a ton in 1914 to £4 10s. in 1918. It is not clear why, except that their three-year profit average just before the war was luckily a relatively high figure and Golden Syrup was uncontrolled. But their actual war time melt was low. Thames Refinery, on the other hand, though melting much more, made only half the profits of Lyles'. Their (now) seventy-eight shareholders did however receive an average dividend of a little over 25 per cent until 1919 when it dropped. On the other hand income tax was increased to 2s. 1d. in the pound in 1915, to 4s. in 1916, and eventually to 5s. 6d. in 1918 and 6s. in 1919. But Tates' were, as a public company, on a depreciation basis and could allow for replacement and renewals of plant. Lyles' could not claim anything for the repairs and renewals they were unable to carry out in wartime but would one day need to do. They could not even replace their stock of bone charcoal. The Government, apprised of this by Charles Lyle and Walter Johnson, Lyle's chief technical man, soon to be a Director, ordered all suspended renewals to be listed. At the end of the war these amounted to £500,000 which was paid back in 1920 to the Company, having been previously removed from them in tax. Tates' received no such payment since they were allowed depreciation.

The basic wage in London had been 24 s. per week for nearly twenty years until 1912 when it was raised to 27 s.[2] During the war it rose to 30 s. 6 d., to 45 s. 4 d., to 59 s. 8 d. in 1918, and a melt bonus was paid on throughput in addition to normal wages. It was not grudged for inflation was there for all to see.

In that war London was the target for air raids by Zeppelins, but these attacks were puny affairs compared with what was to happen twenty-five years later. Public air raid shelters were made in the refineries by converting warehouses, and the local inhabitants came to these when the Zeppelins were overhead. But there was no air raid damage to the refineries, and only one man died, a complete stranger, who broke his neck by tripping down a step in the dark, in one of the shelters.

Although not damaged by enemy action the two London refineries were near neighbours of a man-made wartime catastrophe. This was the Silvertown explosion which took place at 7.00 p.m. on January 19th, 1917, at the Brunner-Mond (I.C.I.) factory about equidistant from the two refineries. Here TNT was being produced. A fire broke out there at about 6.40 p.m. and reached a vessel containing 17 tons of TNT which went off. The damage was enormous. The pressure wave went out in strange lines, one of which rolled right along the Edgware Road breaking windows as far as Maida Vale. At Plaistow Wharf many large windows were broken and every roof was lifted and dropped down out of position, with or without slates. It took only a few days to get going again for the process buildings were so strong that they withstood the blast and most of the windows so small that few were broken. There was for some freak reason little damage at Thames Refinery, although it was just as close to Brunner-Mond.

At the time of the explosion the refineries were working and the stalwarts present shut them down. One of these, George Bull, a giant of a man, then foreman of the Garret, saw the cables from the power house burning and ran down to stop the turbine and the four engines. There was at Plaistow a large ferro-concrete chimney, built in 1906, 250 feet high and 20 feet in diameter. In 1909 steel bands 3 inches wide and $\frac{3}{4}$ of an inch thick had been fitted every 3 feet because cracks had appeared. On the morning after the explosion it was found that all the bands had dropped evenly, by 3 inches. The passing explosion wave had compressed the chimney by closing the cracks enough to allow the bands to drop. The chimney survived until the late 1950s when demolishing it was a very difficult job. The same compression wave struck the big gas-holder at the South Metropolitan Gas Works at Blackwall, rolling up the top plating like a shaving from a carpenter's plane, and the heat from the tearing metal ignited the 12 million cubic feet of gas which burned in a few seconds, giving a glow that was seen for 20 miles. Much life was lost in the

[2] Oliver Lyle, as a Director designate, was only paid 30 s.

King George V visits Thames Refinery after the Silvertown explosion. Edwin Tate greets him.

The old Plaistow chimney in 1907 before being fitted with steel bands.

immediate district, but less than it might have been, for everyone knew what was going on inside Brunner-Mond and as soon as the alarm was given anybody who could move was away up the road as fast as his legs could carry him. Soon afterwards, King George V, in his quiet, undemonstrative way, visited the scene and also called at Thames Refinery.

There were still nearly two years more to come of black casualty lists, rationing, shortages and of the feeling that the war would *never* end; two years more of endless, raddled repetitions of 'Tipperary', 'Pack up your troubles in your old kit bag', 'Keep the home fires burning', 'There's a long, long trail a-winding', banal, but in their context heart-breaking. Then came Haig's 'Backs to the Wall' message, Hindenburg's 'Black Day for the German Army', April 21st, 1918, and, on November 11th at 11.00 a.m. the sudden silence over the battlefields as Armistice was declared and there was peace at last. For a bit. (A red-headed girl, christened Armistice[3] Poppy, used to serve lunch to directors at Plaistow in the 1940s and 1950s.)

The high-hearted clarion call of Rupert Brooke's words at the head of this chapter by now rang hollow – it had long since done so. Another poet, Wilfred Owen, himself killed a few days before the Armistice, was nearer to the true feelings of 1918. It had all been at once so apocalyptically awful and so squalid that men who had been directly involved preferred, at least at first, not to talk much about it. They were like the shocked survivors of Owen's 'Spring Offensive' who:

> Crawling slowly back, have by degrees,
> Regained cool, peaceful air in wonder,
> Why speak not they of comrades who went under?

---

[3] In the register it was 'Armatine'.

CHAPTER FIVE
Tate and Lyle

'1921. The Year of the Ampersand'
(R. St. John Cooper, 1906–   )

That's what it is, that thing that joins 'Tate' and 'Lyle',[1] but you could scarcely be blamed for not knowing, for lately it seems to have become Tate + Lyle, in order to be at home in a land fit for Logos to Live In.

After 1918, released soldiers and sailors were supposed to come back to a Home Fit For Heroes to Live In. It was far from that. Demobilization was badly handled and too many men came back in hordes to too few jobs. In the old days of the small professional army, Kipling had written:

> It's Tommy this, and Tommy that, and chuck him out the brute,
> But it's thank you, Mr. Atkins, when the guns begin to shoot.

But now the shooting was over, most men had been Tommy Atkins or Jack Tar, and the employment situation was out of control. Moreover far too many of them were permanently unfit to a greater or less degree from wounds, shell shock, or as a result of poison gas. Bill Migliori, the senior N.U.G.M.W. delegate at Plaistow in the 1940s and 1950s, for example, and one of the nicest men you could ever hope to know, still suffered greatly from his lungs in damp weather thirty years later.

Gradually and painfully things were sorted out, but never completely satisfactorily. At Henry Tate's and Abram Lyle's there was much to be done in the way of renewals and in order to find the money–much more than the Government would pay–the Lyles were considering selling part of their personal holdings. The Tates had other troubles.

Before the war both firms had been fighting each other so fiercely, instead of facing up to foreign subsidized sugar, that they made little or no profit at all on granulated sugar. This was no way in which to face post-war problems.

In 1918 Ernest Tate approached Charles and Robert Lyle. The Tates were anxious about their future because although their melt was twice that of the Lyles they were making a lower total profit and their profit per ton was less than half Lyles'. Oliver Lyle quotes figures prepared by a 'neutral', Mr. A. E. Cutforth of Deloitte Plender & Griffiths, on two bases, the years 1910 to 1913 and 1910 to 1917:

---

[1] The world is a corruption of 'and *per se*'–'and by itself'.

TATE

	Melt (tons)	*Profit £*	*Shilling/Ton*
4 years 1910–13	1,113,565	755,000	13·5
8 years 1910–17	2,496,359	2,055,000	16·5

LYLE

	Melt (tons)	*Profit £*	*Shilling /Ton*
4 years 1910–13	615,850	822,000	26·70
8 years 1910–17	1,204,800	2,094,000	34·95

But the principal reason for the Tate approach was that although Old Henry and Old Abram III had been the same age to within a year, the second and third Tate generations were much older than the Lyles and no young Tates had come into the firm. Vernon, then in his late twenties, was back from the war and was just about to leave a stockbroker's office and join Tates', but he was the only one. William, Edwin, Alfred, and Bertie wished to retire, leaving only Ernest. We have met Ernest before, at Liverpool. A man of strong character, he had a liking for Kümmel, and there were favourite haunts of his, the Savoy Grill in London, and outside the metropolis at sundry restaurants in Henley, Maidenhead and elsewhere, where a special bottle was kept for him. But he was overworked, was not in good health, and had leg trouble.

The Lyles, on the other hand, had Robert and Charles of the second generation. (John had died at fifty-two in 1914 from a bungled operation for stone in the kidneys, and William had retired.) There were also Arthur, Leonard, Philip and Oliver of the third generation, with from three to sixteen years' experience and aged between twenty-eight and thirty-nine.

Philip and Oliver were not at all happy to join with the Tates. Oliver in particular, although generally very nice to them, had some objection to Tates on principle, which he preserved to the end of his days.

The two companies were run on different lines. The Tates were directors, the Lyles managing directors. Tom Jenkinson bought raw sugar for Tates', Robert Lyle for Lyles'. Lionel Martin was in charge of sales for Tates in London, J. B. Crispin in Liverpool. The Lyles' salesman was Arthur Lyle. Thames Refinery was run by John W. MacDonald and R. F. Wall, with Charles Potter in Liverpool. Leonard Lyle and Philip ran Plaistow, with Oliver learning. It is however right to point out that since Arthur Lyle wanted to retire, and Leonard wanted to devote much of his time to public service there was soon to be no third generation 'commercial' Lyle. So Robert, who had got to know one Julius Joseph Runge on the Sugar Commission, invited him to come in. Julius Joseph sold his shirt[2], bought all the Lyle shares offered to him, and joined the Board of Abram Lyle & Sons in May 1921 when the Commission closed down. He was the father of Peter Runge, whom we shall meet later.

[2] i.e. his shares in Tolmé, Runge.

Tates' chief point in negotiation was that their refinery assets were twice those of Lyles'. But the Lyles argued that they made the same or more profit on half the melt, so that if amalgamation made granulated sugar profitable the gain to Tates' would be greater. Negotiations, conducted mainly by Ernest Tate and Charles Lyle, began in the autumn of 1918 and then hung fire from the spring of 1919 to the autumn of 1920. Conclusion was reached in the spring of 1921. Survivors could not, even twenty years ago, remember why the negotiations took so long, for the points of difference were minor, such as the fact that the Tates paid their directors four times as much as the Lyles.

Agreement was at length reached that the two concerns should join forces on a 50/50 basis with a Lyle (Charles) as first Chairman. As Tates' was a public company with by now about 100 shareholders the only practical way was for them to buy Lyles' but before this there had to be a complicated exchange of shares, Lyles' getting 325,000 £1 Tate shares, while Tates' received 625,000 £1 Lyle shares (they had been reduced from £10). The Lyle assets were written up as high as possible and £600,000 put in for goodwill. But even so, the agreed purchase price was not quite reached and Oliver calculated in 1959 that the Tates still owed the Lyles £18,000 or so.

Despite misgivings the amalgamation was a great success. One raw sugar buyer prevented Tates' from competing with Lyles' for the same lot and enabled bigger purchases to be made with considerable savings which could be passed on to the consumer. One saleroom enabled a reasonable profit to be made on granulated at last. Special sugars were virtually all made at Tates', Golden Syrup at Lyles'. Technical interchange was most beneficial. One of the first results was that Tates' cancelled a huge order for boilers, which the Lyles (who were good at steam and power) were able to demonstrate were unnecessary. Refining processes, such as carbonatation, long in use at Tates', were adopted by Lyles'.

The amalgamation has also been described in verse by Guess Who:

> Then Ernie and Robert Park Lyle
> With beards and dark glasses disguised
> Decided to form TATE & LYLE
> And the market were proper surprised!

Considering the fact that mergers on this scale were uncommon at the time, the market in fact, far from being surprised, took it very calmly, the only major comment being that of the *International Sugar Journal*, a stuffy old thing in those days, which spoke darkly of the possibility of a 'sugar refining trust' which should be deprecated both from the point of view of the raw sugar producer, and of the ultimate consumer. 'Any tendency in that direction' said the *I.S.J.*, shaking a severe admonitory finger, 'will need to be watched'.

But there was a great deal more to be watched than that in 1921. The Great War had just been officially declared over, for the Allies had now fixed a Reparations Bill to be paid by Germany over the next four years at £11·3 million pounds. By the standards of the 1970s this seems a relatively footling amount of money. Why was Hitler, thirteen years later, going to get so het up about a mere £11 million? Well, of course, for one thing the pound was different then. It bought less than it had done for Herbert Woodward in 1903 but you could still get a tailormade suit for £4 4 s. 0 d. (it's now about £200) or a half bottle of Johnny Walker for 7 s. For another, Hitler was Hitler.

The war was over, but there was a coal miner's strike, which certainly reduced the melt in the refineries, and which only ended after a State of Emergency had been proclaimed on March 31st. (The troops were called out, and bivouacked in Kensington Gardens in their bell tents. It took until July 1st to sort out.) King George V opened, appropriately enough, the King George V Dock near Plaistow Wharf on July 8th, arriving with Queen Mary by river and returning by road, close enough to the Tidal Basin bridge for Jim Atkinson and his wife-to-be to see them from 6 feet away.

There were other happenings, more deep-seated in their effect. The British Broadcasting Corporation was founded and there is a picture, to prove it, of Harry Tate, grey homburg hat in hand and every button doing its duty, singing into an enormous black box at Marconi House. This was the 1921 equivalent of the sort of thing those pretty girls in the 1970s clip into the cleavage when they are intending to deafen you with Rock.

And of even greater world significance, though at the time this was not generally realized, was a paper published in the Proceedings of the Royal Society, announcing demurely that a Professor Rutherford and a Dr. Chadwick had discovered a phenomenon which suggested that the atom might one day be split.

But what about the people working at the refineries, those who had come back from the war, those who were now starting? Unemployment was high – a million or so in a smaller population than we have now. 'Work was not easy to find and we were well aware of that,' said George Hildrup, fifty years later. Jim Freestone, who had started in the Thames Char House in 1919, was 'glad to have a job' for the same reason. People working in the two refineries in London and the one in Liverpool were understandably apprehensive about the amalgamation, though many, like Frank White in Liverpool, Miles Reynolds at Thames, and Mr. and Mrs. Hay and Mrs. Oldfield at Plaistow, were too busy getting over the war and settling down again to family life to worry much about it. Some thought that it was beneficial. Instead of being down to four days' work a week, said Charlie Mountjoy[3] and Harry Roof at Thames and Plaistow respectively, 'there

[3] Charlie, a great character, had started as a boy at Thames in 1906 and lived to be well over eighty.

was more work for the people in and around Silvertown and Canning Town'.

Tates' men in Liverpool heard that 'Lyles were very good people' although they liked their Tate Directors, particularly Mr. Bertie. The Fairrie employees, still twelve years away from another amalgamation, reckoned that their cubes were 'brighter' at Vauxhall Road than the Tates' version and should sell better. Some people felt that Lyles' had done well for themselves, others that the Tates 'had more pocket money than the Lyles and just bought them out'. There was a great deal of subterranean feeling. Some of the Tates' men felt that Lyles' men were enemies, and vice versa, although the more easy-going didn't make much of this. Methods of working were different. Conditions were different. Families had by then a second or third generation link with one or other company, and although a few occasionally switched, like Alf Lenz, these had a difficult time to begin with in the 'other' refinery.

For the people in Mincing Lane, looking after accounts, sales and so forth, the amalgamation brought chances of greater scope, although for many years afterwards deliveries of refined sugar were specified T.L.T. (Thames) or T.L.P. (Plaistow), and cargoes of raw sugar were similarly directed to Thames or Plaistow by Harry Hunt when he was allocating cargoes.

One of those who found a new future as a result of the amalgamation was Sidney Ellyatt (whose son, John, was twenty-seven years later to join the firm and would still be serving in 1977). Sidney (who had been in the H.A.C., served in a cavalry regiment and then in the R.F.C.) was demobbed in 1919. Robert Lyle asked for him to be attached to the Royal Commission on Sugar, as an assistant to Julius Joseph Runge. (Sidney had been with Tolmé, Runge before 1914.) When the Commission was dissolved he came, with J. J. R. to the Bosom of Abram, and eventually took over with success the purchase of raw sugars. The brokers always referred to him as 'The Curate'. J. J. Runge was known as 'The Vicar', perhaps because, when asked what was going to happen in the sugar market, he would give the advice: 'Watch and pray.'

Fraternization between those employed at the London refineries was a plant of slow growth and as late as 1938 Bill North, newly taken on at Thames, heard, when he visited Plaistow, the Manager, Alex Lyle ('young old Alex' q.v.) giving instructions that this interloper from Tates' was *not* to be shown the Golden Syrup process. *En revanche*, a trainee Plaistow shift manager, visiting Thames in 1947, would find the atmosphere, though polite, a trifle frigid.

Charles Lyle (Leonard's son) spent some years in the 1930s at Thames and Louis Tate spent some at Plaistow. They each had a difficult time, though gradually the Tates and Lyles came to discipline themselves to admit that the others might occasionally be right after all.

The scene at early meetings of the new joint Board of Tate & Lyle in

1921 was recorded in relentless verse almost certainly as accurate as that of Homer although in a different metre:

> The new Board first met at a party
> All done in the most lavish style,
> With plenty of Kümmel for Ernie,
> And Brose for Sir Robert Park Lyle.
>
> They say there were *some* fraternizing
> *Some* Tates and *some* Lyleses spoke.
> While some slid right under the table.
> (Young Phil told a rather rude joke).
>
> But most of the Board of Directors
> Sat and glared at each other in hate.
> The Runges were brought in by Lyle
> And Crispin, with others, by Tate.

However, in 1971, the same poet, this time under the guise of Albert Chevalier, would grudgingly admit in an address to 'My Old Scotch':

> We've been together now for fifty years
> And it does seem a damned long while.
> But compared with other people in the Trade
> I've come to prefer a Lyle.

CHAPTER SIX

Between the Wars (I)

We are now in that curious limbo between the First War to End All Wars and the Second Ditto, although the latter is not yet visible on the horizon. We are in a period of straight dresses, later becoming shorter, and apparently designed to suggest that the Flapper (1920s for Bird) was built on the same lines as the cigarette which she smoked through a long holder and her bright red mouth, under the Bob, Shingle or boyish Eton crop.

It is now 1922. Tates and Lyles are beginning to get used to being on speaking terms. Their sales are under pressure from white sugar imported from all over the place, even the U.S.A. Post-war shortages are forcing up the price of raws temporarily to over £100 a ton. The Government has just approved a subsidy to aid the home-grown production of beet sugar, and Tate & Lyle will be going in for this in 1924, while at the same time protesting at the competition home-grown beet sugar is forcing on refining.

At Liverpool, Charles Potter is still in charge–he had started as a boy in the Lab. in 1878–and long-held-up modernization is proceeding, new pans, new carbonatation and filtration plants are being introduced. The melt has increased to 4,000 tons a week and will be 5,000 by 1925, but the white sugar imports, which soon will amount to 600,000 tons a year, frequently cause short-time working. The Refinery has recently narrowly escaped being burned down by a fire in a disused oil works next door.

In London, the two Refineries are also boosting their capacities. At Plaistow Philip and Oliver Lyle are in charge as Refinery Directors. Bobby Kirkwood, in his early twenties, and the son of a Lyle mother (Robert Park Lyle's daughter), is learning the business after Harrow and a couple of years at school in Switzerland. With them is another Lyle, 'Young Old Alex'. He is the grandson of one of the three second cousins of Abram III whom we by-passed earlier, and also descended from the old Weaver. This one's grandfather Alex and a great uncle (John) had recruited the nucleus staff of Greenock Sugarhouse men and brought them south in that special train to Canning Town Station with their families at Christmas time in 1882, a wild and boisterous procession walking through the mud and under the leafless trees to the new Refinery. Another great-uncle, Jimmy, had helped erect the works and had managed it until 1913, but he had retired and his brother Jack had only done four years as his successor, because of ill health.

'Young Old Alex' was the last of the Victorian type of manager, tireless, a driver, a mimic and a male Malaprop. 'He had a bad mannerism', he would say of someone, 'and was excessively retycent', or 'His writing was not eligible', or 'that is just gasping at a straw and cuts both ices up to a certain hilt'.

Under these men, the Plaistow melt rose, gradually, to some 5,000 tons a week by the late 1920s. Golden Syrup production stayed at about the 500-ton-a-week level. Instead of buying syrup cans from outside the Lyles had begun in 1910 to make their own, and found it profitable, as well as enabling them to be sure that the inside of the can, where of course the syrup was put, was clean. During the war they had had to use cardboard cylinders for the can-bodies. Now they were able again to get tinplate. The can-making was staffed by girls, who were deft and rapid at their work. They were paid a bonus to use the minimum of solder, and one of them, Rose Dobson, seeing Oliver Lyle use a slide rule to check the bookwork for the bonus, taught herself to use one and became as quick as he. The can-making, perhaps because of the Hawthorne effect[1] of the interest taken in it by Oliver, was a proud department. It still is, although newer machines installed from 1934 onwards have mechanized much of the work. It is still the noisiest of places. Nothing rattles like cans. But the girls carry on conversations in a sign language of their own.

During the 1914/18 war girls had worked three eight-hour shifts in the can-making. Now they only worked two, preferring by eight to one in a secret ballot to do this rather than day work. Their views, as represented to a Government Committee by Oliver Lyle, and by three girls, one of them Bill Migliori's wife, Amelia Willmott, were largely responsible for the eventual specifications of the 1936 Women and Young Persons Act.

Delivery of syrup had been difficult during the war, and this had led to the firm doing its own deliveries in a 30 cwt. Vulcan. A Miss Victoria Hudson (later Mrs. King) was taught to drive it (men were scarce). After the war male lorry drivers were taken on. The first was one Sandy Wilson. The second had to be dismissed for delivering syrup not only to his customers but to himself.

At Thames, 'Paddy' Muir had retired through ill health by now, and the two Refinery Directors were John MacDonald (until 1926) and Colonel R. F. Wall, back from the 6th Essex Regiment at Gallipoli. One of his sons, Dudley, would become Refinery Manager there in 1925, while the other, Bob, went to Liverpool as Assistant Manager. Vernon Tate joined in this year of grace 1922, but had to learn the job. The General Manager was now Hugh Main, formerly Chief Chemist.[2] In this year too, Fred Sudbury came to Thames as a junior chemist, together with Claud, usually called Johnnie, Walker (in 1923), and John Dyke, who later went to the beet sugar factory at Allscott (his son is still with the British Sugar Corporation). The Chief Chemist was Alf Hornton, with Harold Powers on his staff. The

---

[1] See all those intense books about personnel management.
[2] See Chapter Twenty-six.

Chief Engineer was a chap called Leach and his assistant was 'Hoppy' Clark (who had a bad leg). 'Duke' Wellings was then a draughtsman and Walter King a checker on the Wharf.

Within the Refinery great secrecy still reigned. Junior chemists were not allowed into the Cube House, and when in 1925 Fred Sudbury was promoted to be assistant to Dudley Wall, Hugh Main showed him over the Raw Sugar Landing, the Melt House and the Filtration Plant and that was all. 'From now on', he said dismissively, 'you are in charge of *that*'. No question of being shown the Refinery or Cube House. One of the earliest of Sudbury's actions was to promote Walter King from checker to charge hand. Walter would in 1937 be the extremely dapper and effective Office Manager, having been Wharf Foreman (1928) and Warehouse Manager (1935).

Vernon Tate was by 1925 a full Director and spent much of each day at Thames. He had his cousin Bertie's knack with people and was genuinely liked for himself. Even when, on his becoming Chairman, his visits had to be less frequent, people's faces would always light up when they saw him, for there was so much genuine kindness in him.

In 1926–27 the increasing melt required the construction of a new refinery house. Walter Johnson, now a Director at Plaistow, and also a key figure in the beet sugar enterprise,[3] was brought in to direct the work. He, Leach and Clark did not hit it off and the latter two retired leaving the position open for Wellings, who had only just been promoted Chief Draughtsman. Over the next ten years or so, virtually until the Second World War, although nominally only Process Manager, Fred Sudbury seems to have held most of the reins in his hand. Vernon Tate thought well of him, and when Charles Lyle came to Thames as a trainee Director, he was made Fred Sudbury's assistant for a couple of years. (Charles became a Director in 1929.) He was succeeded by J. J. Runge's son Peter, who, after being what the French call a *stagiaire,* or trainee, at the Raffinerie Say in Paris, and putting in a campaign at Allscott, came to Thames in 1931. Ian Lyle had gone to Plaistow at the same time, and it was in 1935 that these two began a long and effective relationship, a little like that of Abram III and John Kerr. As young men they would start up a water pump in the basement of the old refinery building at Plaistow and race up the staircase to see if they could reach the roof tanks before the water did. More seriously, in 1937, they began to work out a standard method of recording product costs and profits which Peter would perfect during the long nights of 1939–45 and which was still in use with modifications thirty years later.

But this is to run ahead too far, and we should return to the 1920s. A Director of Tate & Lyle, although the Company was then less well-known, was a considerable personage and most of them were deservedly so in their own individual right. They did however, manage the affairs of the company in a collegiate manner, a system which still persists. The

[3] See Chapter seven.

Chairman was only *primus inter pares* by election from among his fellows. Individuals had considerable freedom of action in their own spheres, for example at a refinery, but they did not forget that they were, in the dictionary definition, part of 'a society of persons having common interests or corporate functions'. They all took the same pay after 1921. Votes were not taken, but arguments were carried through until there was agreement. When Leonard Lyle became Chairman, he would sometimes say plaintively: 'Do we *have* to decide that today?'

They worked hard and they enjoyed themselves, for even with the problems of the 1920s and 30s, they could generally afford to. They had their hobbies and their interests. Philip and Oliver invested their own money and a lot of time in the Invicta car. Philip took up statistics and also ran a successful farm. Oliver began the study of steam and heat use. He also built a new house looking over the Weald of Kent. The makers of the windows guaranteed them waterproof even in a tropical downpour and a wind of hurricane strength. Rigging up four fire hoses and an aeroplane engine, Oliver proved them wrong. Ernest Tate enjoyed lunching and dining – and the Kümmel. Vernon liked cricket and the races. Leonard Lyle became an M.P. and in 1928 was able to enlist the help of F. E. Smith (later Lord Birkenhead) in persuading the Chancellor of the Exchequer, Mr. Churchill, to safeguard the British sugar refining industry against the dumping of foreign subsidized sugar by imposing a duty differential of $\frac{1}{4}$d. in the lb. on white sugar as against raw. (Birkenhead joined the T. & L. Board after this, remaining a member until his death a year later.) In return the Chancellor demanded and received a written promise that the whole differential would be passed on to the consumer, and that the refiners would not increase their margins, but only increase prices by agreement with the Treasury and in accordance with overall indexed increases in wage-levels, coal price, etcetera. This arrangement was to last until Britain entered the E.E.C. in 1974.

Trainee directors were then in a curious limbo. They were treated with fair respect but expected to get on with everyone. Usually they were called 'Mr. Ian' or 'Mr. Vernon', not often Sir. They lunched with the established directors, and when, for example, Vernon and Charles arrived at Thames with a visitor for lunch, the man at the gate would telephone the Office Manager to say: 'Mr. Tate, Mr. Lyle and a *gentleman* have arrived.' Later the system of induction would become formalized.

Below director level the managers and foremen and chargehands at each refinery occupied fairly clearly defined positions but these varied somewhat from refinery to refinery for historical reasons.

We have noted the reaction of members of the workforce to the amalgamation. It is time to look more closely at the situation of the man on the shop floor now that the Ampersand has settled firmly into its place.

From the beginning the wages paid by both companies, and later by the amalgamated firm were, as a matter of policy, maintained at a level among the highest in the districts where the refineries were situated. Before the First War the standard rate had for long been, as we have seen, 24 s. a week. This sounds very little but was considerably above rates elsewhere.

There seems to be no recollection of when Tate & Lyle first recognized trade unions but when Oliver Lyle joined in 1912 they had certainly done so at Plaistow for some years while Thames appear only to have done so in the 20s. That well known, strange figure, Jack Jones (*not* the 1970s version), clever, witty, outrageous, but too often drunk, was a fairly frequent visitor. During the 1914/18 War the 'Whitley Council' had been invented as a device to bring about collaboration between employers and employees. The sugar refiners did not have a full-blown council. Instead, in 1919, an 'Interim Industrial Reconstruction Committee' was set up. This served only to embitter relations. No doubt there were faults on both sides, but the initial trouble seems to have been with the representative of a now defunct body, the Workers' Union, at that time the union with the largest representation at Thames, where, although still relatively small, it had been increasing its membership since 1910. Its leader put forward some highly extravagant claims at almost every meeting of the Committee, often simply in order to have a trade union item on the agenda. The employers reacted, went on the defensive, and put down unreasonable items as a counter-balance. The Committee was eventually disbanded in 1923.

Because of its intransigent leadership the Workers' Union came to be distrusted and disliked not only by the employers but by the other unions, and began to lose ground, eventually being absorbed by the Transport and General Workers' Union.

At Plaistow the main union has always been the same one. In 1889 Will Thorne had started the Gasworkers' Union, which gradually extended into other industries, changing its name in 1919 to the National Union of General Workers and then, after an amalgamation with two other unions (it was not only companies that were merging) to the National Union of General and Municipal Workers. (It is now the G.M.W.U. and one of the larger unions.)

Generally speaking, this union had good leadership. Mr. J. R. Clynes, M.P. was its head for a long spell, and had long championed moderation, avoidance of strikes where possible, the use of all possible means of conciliation, and the establishment of good relations with the employers. This certainly awakened the best in the Tate & Lyle Board. A succession of National Officers, Harry Harrison, Jim Matthews, Mark Hewitson, Fred Hayday, and others, and a series of equally straight but firm area and branch officers, usually enabled matters to be sorted out. There were few deadlocks. One in 1925 required the services of the National Arbitration Tribunal, but there would not be another such until 1948. And the good relationships would persist even when the Labour Party endeavoured to nationalize sugar refining. In the early 1920s the situation was a difficult one. The Industrial Reconstruction Committee met fruitlessly against a background of falling wages. There was considerable trouble in 1922 and long discussions over wages, piecework, melt bonuses and so forth. The Company felt it should follow the national downward trend but accepted the view of the mens' representatives that it was doing well enough to keep wages up. In the end a compromise reduction of 6 s. a week from 66 s. 11 d. to 60 s. 11 d. was agreed, against a national reduction of 16 s. 6 d. (It seems strange in the last quarter of the twentieth century that wages should actually be thought capable of *falling*. What about standards of living, which some trade unionists consider should be guaranteed as of right?)

In 1924 there were strikes in both London and Liverpool to back demands for higher wages. The men returned to work and the firm agreed to the demands. From talks years later with Oliver Lyle, one had the impression that he–and some of the younger members of the Board who had served in the War–always felt a strong sympathy for the mens' demands. (Philip, indeed, proposed a profit-sharing scheme in 1924, but it was found to be too complicated.) They were not, of course, in total control.

In 1925 the Arbitration Tribunal had awarded a rise of 1 s. 3 d. a week which was accepted by the union. Some 380 men on the raw sugar landing and in the Cube House at Thames refused to accept this and went on strike. The union backed the management in discharging the strikers, even though Mr. Will Thorne personally sought their reinstatement. There must have been some unrecorded animus here. Most of the men seem, however, to have returned in small groups later. During the General Strike of 1926 there was a brief 10 days exodus, but this was undertaken unwillingly and remained the only example of its kind in Tate & Lyle.

Over the next decade or so various forms of Christmas and Bank Holiday gifts were introduced, sometimes voluntarily, sometimes in response to trade union demand, together with long service grants, and later, after one or two false starts, an ex gratia pension scheme, based on $1\frac{1}{2}$ per cent of annual earnings for each year of service up to a maximum of 60 per cent. A scheme for building blocks of flats to replace the old cottages on the property opposite Plaistow Wharf was suggested by Oliver Lyle. It was not pursued for some reason, now no longer known, possibly because people preferred to live away from the area. There was a Knights' Castile soap factory on one side of the Refinery and a Fisons' fertilizer plant on the other and when the wind was in the south-east the smells in the block of flats would have been awful.

Although discipline was strict and life was hard–only to be solaced on pay day, according to men still working there twenty-five years later, by a far too convivial visit to a pub–there was a gradual, cautious build-up of good feeling. This was no doubt in large part due to the habit (already remarked on) that fathers and grandfathers had of sending their children and grandchildren to work at Tates' or Lyles'; Oldfields, McMartins, McKays, Tyzacks, Nottages, Thompsons, in London; Carsons, Lezemores, Fergusons, and others at Liverpool. Many a family might by 1930 have an aggregate service of a century and a half. (While this chapter was being written, a retired electrical engineer, Mr. C. N. McGlone wrote to the Chairman of Tate & Lyle. He himself had only stayed briefly with the Company from 1932–38 but his grandfather had started with Lyles' in Greenock in 1875, and his father, Mick McGlone, was Chief Plumber at Plaistow Wharf until his retirement in 1947. Mr. McGlone offered the two gold watches given to his ancestors and spanning 100 years' service, and a copy of a programme of a Grand Concert, chaired by Abram Lyle on January 4th, 1894, in the Plaistow Wharf library, to the Company's museum.)

But while the refineries adapt themselves to the amalgamation it seems appropriate to look at a venture undertaken by Tate & Lyle in the early 20s – into beet sugar production.

CHAPTER SEVEN

The Beet Venture

'My treasure, my darling, embowered in Beet.'
(Aristophanes, 440–380 B.C.)

Readers of Aristophanes will need no reminder that this is how the playwright described eels cooked in beet leaves. He would have been given the slow hand-clap, however, by the House of Commons in the nineteenth century, when John Bull's view of sugar beet was expressed by that Dr. Bowring M.P., who announced in Parliament that it should be 'plucked out by the roots'.

We have also seen the difficulties caused to the sugar refiners of Britain by Bounty-fed beet sugar from Europe until 1903, and even beyond. Uncle Matthew used to say: 'Abroad is unutterably bloody, and foreigners are fiends.' Yet those fiends across the Channel can sometimes be right, as had been strongly pressed in the early years of the twentieth century by the Earl of Denbigh and Sir William Crookes, F.R.S. who had actually been foolhardy enough to go and see what happened when sugar beet was grown in those outlandish places. To those who spoke warmly of the turnip and mangel-wurzel as a rotation root crop, Denbigh and Crookes were able to reply that while these were much appreciated no doubt by the pig population, sugar beet could actually feed *people.*

As a result of the advocacy of these two distinguished gents, some land-owners and farmers in East Anglia decided to try their hand at beet sugar production. They knew nothing about it, so they formed a Committee, which probably seemed the obvious thing to do. Called the Sugar Beet Committee, and formed in 1909, this was a group of aristos including Sir George Courthorpe Bt. (whose ancestor had been killed at Hastings trying to rescue King Harold's body after the Battle). They had the commonsense to invite the help of the Dutch. In particular they obtained not only the advice but the financial participation of Johannes Petrus Van Rossum, a remarkable and attractive figure. The descendant of a Dutch pirate of the sixteenth century whose two-handed sword is still preserved in Amsterdam, Van Rossum in his pictures looks a little like a buccaneering version of Edward VII. He had sugar interests in Germany and Holland, and he was a man who took risks. One year he'd be a millionaire, the next he'd be broke, the year after a millionaire again.

In 1912, when he was fifty-two, he and his English associates founded the Anglo-Netherlands Sugar Corporation and built the first small commercially active factory at Cantley in Norfolk. Later, this Corporation would be the 'Anglo-Dutch Group'. Van Rossum knew that sugar beet would grow in England. By 1910 there were in fact 100 acres under beet in Suffolk and 53 in Norfolk. By 1912 beet contracts were being signed with local farmers, a Mrs. King of Great Plumstead, Norfolk, for example, agreeing with the Anglo-Netherlands Sugar Corporation of 6 Throgmorton Avenue, E.C., to grow beet on not less than 6 acres and deliver the crop at '23 s. per ton of 20 cwt. net, of clean roots . . .' Mrs. King's land was, rather charmingly, to be 'dunged and plowed not later than April 1st'. In 1913 a group of eight agriculturalists formed the Sugar Beet Growers' Society and rented land from farmers. They obtained, a little surprisingly, £11,000 as a grant from Government, brought trained labour over from Holland, and from 3,000 acres produced 22,000 tons of beet. They made a thumping loss. So did the Cantley factory, and in 1915 it was closed down. Anglo-Netherlands, having lost over £250,000, was wound up in 1916.

Yet while this was going on, two other things were happening. An association of prominent public men, including those who had burnt their fingers already, formed the British Sugar Beet Society, a new body, and examined the possibility of large scale production of beet sugar, coming to the conclusion that risk capital in beet sugar factories must be put up by the State as well as by private investors (and who could blame them?). And simultaneously Britain's imported food, including cane sugar, was under severe U-boat attack.

> For the bread that you eat and the biscuits you nibble
> The sweets that you suck and the joints that you carve
> Are brought to you daily by all us Big Steamers
> And if anyone hinders our coming, you'll starve.

In August 1916, we were in fact starving because someone was hindering the coming of the Big Steamers, and a Government Committee under the Chairmanship of the Earl of Selborne was set up: 'to consider and report upon the methods of effecting an increase in the home grown food suppliers, having regard to the need of such an increase in the interest of national security.'

The Committee, reporting in March 1917, recommended the erection of an experimental beet factory, with Government in partnership with 'the business public', urging that this be done while our dependence on imports of sugar was so obvious. The Treasury put up about £130,000 to develop land at Kelham in Nottinghamshire but then took until February 1919 to make available its share for the construction of the factory. As the Government was determined to go ahead, this dithering is difficult to understand.

The British Sugar Beet Society thought of buying the Cantley factory to save time, for the world price of sugar was high just then, but the Government would not agree, and so missed the opportunity of carrying out an experiment that could have paid for itself. The price of sugar had fallen by 1922, and the chance disappeared. Cantley reopened in 1920, under the ownership of the 'English Beet Sugar Corporation Ltd.' Eventually, having held everything up for a year, and thus ensured that the erection cost would be greater than estimated, the Government gave the go-ahead for Kelham factory, but only so long as half the money was provided from private means because the Government must be able 'to justify its . . . contribution . . . on the grounds that the management would be in the hands of individuals with an interest in the enterprise'. (Well, two cheers for the Treasury, perhaps. It didn't then hold with nationalization.) Kelham factory (later called Newark) was begun.

But by 1922 it was clear that the infant industry could not survive if it had to pay excise duty of £19 18s. 10d. a ton. And at length, for one year only, excise was removed, giving home grown sugar an advantage of £25 13s. 4d. over foreign imported sugars and £21 6s. 11d. over Empire sugars. This was too late to save Kelham from making a loss, a good part of which was borne by the private investors. (One must admire the tenacity of these now forgotten men. It was their own *personal* money.) Now there was pressure to restore the excise duty, though meantime another factory, Colwick (later called Nottingham), had been built in hopes by the Anglo-Scottish Beet Sugar Corporation, who vociferously demanded freedom from excise.

At length, on July 30th, 1924, the Chancellor, Philip Snowden (it was now a Labour Government) announced a subsidy for the beet sugar industry for ten years from the 1924–25 crop. This decision, embodied in The British Sugar (Subsidy) Act of March 1925, affectionately known in Whitehall by the nickname '15 Geo. 5 Ch. 12', granted a subsidy on home grown sugar of £19 10s. 0d. for the first four years, £13 10s. 0d. for the next three, and £6 10s. 0d. for the rest. A minimum price for farmers' beet of £2 4s. 0d. per ton of beet of $15\frac{1}{2}$ per cent sugar content was also fixed for the first four years.

It was the signal for a rapid expansion in beet sugar production in Britain. The Anglo-Dutch Group controlling Cantley and the Anglo-Scottish Group controlling Colwick, gave an assurance that they would each build two new factories in time for the 1925 campaign, with more to follow. Tate & Lyle, hard hit as they were at this time by imports of white sugar from the Continent – up to 760,000 tons in 1925 – decided to go in for beet sugar themselves on a substantial basis, on the principle of 'if you can't beat 'em, join 'em'.

Oliver Lyle, in *Technology for Sugar Refiners*, still the standard work on this subject, says: 'From 1924 to 1928 the assistance received from the Government by the Beet Sugar Industry amounted to twice the value of the sugar. The result was that there were some eighteen factories to share this golden gift.' The Labour Government had, as such administrations tend to do, over-egged the pudding. But it had for once done the right thing from a long-term strategic point of view. In so doing it had also understandably been to some extent motivated by the very high unemployment figures of 1924–25.

The effects were remarkable. In 1923 there were 16,000 acres under beet. By 1930 there were nearly 350,000. In 1923 there were two factories limping along. By 1930 there were eighteen, most of them doing well. In 1924 the total daily 'slice' of beet was 2,190 tons. By 1930 it was 22,000. In 1923 13,000 tons of home grown beet sugar were produced, in 1930 420,000. The number of factory workers in 1923 was 1,160. In 1930 it was 10,000. And from a small unquantified number of agricultural workers in 1923, work was available in 1930 for over 40,000. Britain had at long last begun to become a big-scale producer of home grown beet sugar.

Five Groups were involved in the construction of the eighteen factories. First in the field were the Anglo-Dutch Group, with the 'aristos' and the redoubtable Van Rossum. They constructed five factories–Cantley (rebuilt), Newark, Ely, Ipswich, and King's Lynn. Thanks to Dutch expertise and the importation of Dutch engineers, Wijnberg and Wilhelmstijn, Van der Burg and Korsmit, de Vos and Van Heel, and of Dutch farmers and labourers, they had a head start. Apart from anything else, a century of acquired knowhow ensured that at least they selected areas where sugar beet would grow well.

Among the directors of the Group was Albert Palache, who would be associated with Tate & Lyle throughout his life. A Dutchman, he was then a partner in the merchant bank, Helbert Wagg & Co. An unusual, generous, admirable man, he was married four times and used to relate how once, waiting at Calais for the boat train, he found himself being kissed by an apparently strange lady.

'Madam,' he said stiffly, 'Have we had the pleasure . . . ?'

'But Albert, I am your first wife.'

Alas he died in 1958.

The next group chronologically was largely the creation of Lord Weir of Eastwood, whose family firm G. & J. Weir owned Duncan Stewart Ltd. (now as Stewart, Fletcher of Derby, part of Booker McConnell). His photograph suggests, unlike that of Abram Lyle, a certain pawky Caledonian self-satisfaction. Later commentators suggest that the chief reason for Anglo-Scottish entering the beet sugar industry was the praiseworthy desire of finding work for people in their engineering works. They also appear to have selected for the most part areas which would be near the markets for sugar rather than those where the beet would grow best. They were the only major Group to build a factory north of the border, at Cupar in Fife. Their six factories were Colwick (now Nottingham), Spalding (Lincs.), Kidderminster, Cupar, Felsted and Poppleton (now York).

Two smaller Groups, the Lincolnshire Group and Wissington, joined the band wagon. The Lincolnshire Group built Bardney and Brigg in that bracing county, its prime movers being McAlpines, the building firm, who also attracted equity from Dyers', the U.S. construction company. Perhaps even more importantly they obtained the services of Walter Blanchard, a young American engineer. Born in New Orleans of French-speaking parents, Walter spoke no English until he was seven. By the time he came to England he had forgotten his French. His factory designs had a fine basic simplicity and Gallic elegance. (When in 1936 the Government appropriated beet sugar production, Walter would join Tate & Lyle and design the new cane sugar factories they were to erect in Jamaica and Trinidad.) The two factories of the Lincolnshire Group were built by A. & W. Smith Ltd. of Glasgow – later (in 1953) to become part of the Tate & Lyle Group.

The other small Group was financially backed to a considerable extent by the commodity broking firm of Golodetz (also involved in the Tate & Lyle Group). Their factory at Wissington, Stoke Ferry, in Norfolk has since become one of the most modern in the world.

For the purposes of this account we are, however, really only interested in the third of the larger Groups – the Bury Group, for this is where Tate & Lyle came in. They had no beet expertise of their own, so Oliver and Philip Lyle went in 1924 to Hungary, a country with a long history of beet sugar production. While looking round a factory there, Oliver stepped backwards into a tank of juice. He was hauled out, but his suit – the only one he had with him – crystallized out, on cooling, into a fair representation of armour plate. Responsible for rescuing him was Robert Jorisch, who later became senior technical adviser to the Group and, in time, to the British Sugar Corporation. He retired in East Anglia where he and his wife, the novelist Norah Lofts still live. Three other Hungarian experts were brought over from the Szolnoker Zucker Fabrik: Dr. Aczel, Dr. Hirsch and Baron Hatvani. All spoke excellent though idiosyncratic English, which was just as well, for who in Tate & Lyle speaks Magyar? Once, watching with Leonard Lyle a demonstration in East Anglia of some early form of mechanical cultivator, Dr. Aczel turned to his companion with the helpful comment: 'In 'Oongaree, ve call 'im a boogah.'

Two things favoured the Bury Group's activities; first, Hungarian knowhow, not merely in factory techniques but also in selection of sites where beet would grow well, and secondly the ability to draw on the staff of the refineries who were of course trained in sugar technology.

First and foremost was Bobby Kirkwood. Robert Lucian Morrison Kirkwood, later Sir Robert Kirkwood K.C.M.G., was a Lyle on his mother's side. After Harrow and a period at school in Switzerland he joined Tate & Lyle at a tender age, becoming a Director in his early twenties. He learned the ropes at Plaistow, and while there used to have a private arrangement with certain of the foremen which enabled him to slip away across the Thames by boat and woo the lady he eventually married. His seniors were blissfully unaware of this, their enquiries as to his whereabouts being met with: 'Mr. Kirkwood? Oh, 'e was in the Wharf House 'arf an hour ago, Sir. 'Aven't seen 'im since.' (There was no loudspeaker call-system then.) Sybil Kirkwood, much mourned, died early in 1977.

When Bury was built, Bobby went there as Manager, taking with him a number of Tate & Lyle men, among them John Carmichael, Arthur Greene, Vernon Potter, Henry Austin, Bill Wetherall and Charlie Watson. Most of them were to return to T & L and some were still alive in the 1970s.

Another innovation – though this came three or four years later – was the employment of university graduates. Of the first four, Jo Whitmee, Kenneth Brown, C. L. ('Andie') Anderson, and Norman Adams, the first two became, in due time, Shift Managers at Plaistow, and the third joined Thames. Only Norman Adams remained in beet sugar, to become eventually a Director of the British Sugar Corporation. Jo and Kenneth later became Directors of Tate & Lyle. Jo recalled that the only time in his career when he had to ask for a rise was at Bury. After the first campaign he and the others had been promised an increase from £3 to £4 per week. When this did not occur, he was deputed by the others to mention the matter, not too diffidently, to Bobby Kirkwood who said: 'By God. Sorry. I forgot. You'd better have £5 to make up for that.'

Other Tate & Lyle men involved were Walter Johnson and Charles Newstead. Johnson had begun as a draughtsman at Plaistow in 1893 and had become a Director of Abram Lyle & Sons in 1920. (His grandson, John Graham, is in Tate & Lyle.) He was asked to take over technical supervision of the Bury Group of factories and remained associated with beet sugar production until 1950. Charles Newstead was Secretary to the four companies holding shares in the factories, later returning to Tate & Lyle. Another Tate & Lyle man, Peter Runge (later Sir Peter and a Vice-Chairman of Tate & Lyle), went for a campaign to Allscott factory, after Oxford and a brief time in Paris. To the end of his life Peter carried with him as a talisman a five shilling piece from his first week's wages at Allscott. That end was to come, too soon, in 1970.

A stipulation of the Sugar Subsidy Act and the Trade Facilities Act of the same period was that 75 per cent of the plant and machinery installed must be of British manufacture, in order to provide employment in Britain. Some competition from abroad was allowed, but this was later stopped except for special circumstances, and by 1930 less than 5 per cent came from overseas. This resulted in a high capital cost for British factories compared with those built abroad which had in any case for the most part been constructed before the 1914/18 War when costs were much lower.

Nevertheless, this does not seem to have hampered the Bury Group. Oliver Lyle later wrote that they, and Anglo-Dutch, were making 'almost indecent profits' and were inclined not to accept the subsidy. But other factories, notably the Anglo-Scottish Group, were much less profitable and required the subsidy. Its payment was under strict control of the Minister of Agriculture and Fisheries, who each year was given audited figures of profit and loss.

By 1930 the aggregate physical assets for the eighteen factories were £10·5 million and gross trading profits were up from £200,000 a year in 1924/25 to about £1·75 million. During the previous 6 years the State had paid £16 million to the factories, and these in turn paid £18 million to the farmers who had also had the use of beet-tops as cattle feed, valued at £1·7 million. Other enthusiasts were endeavouring to get permission and subsidies to build factories in Bedfordshire, Kent and Hampshire. They never did, for the subsidy was under criticism from many quarters. The refiners, notably Tate & Lyle, were regarded by Anglo-Scottish as the main promoters of this criticism. They certainly insisted that beet factories should produce raw, not white, sugar – a bone of contention between them and the other beet factory owners. But in fact the bulk of the criticism was from elsewhere. The Liberals, as supporters of free trade, and Labour, being a largely urban phenomenon and, therefore, usually unsympathetic to the farming community, were against the subsidy. (They had forgotten their acceptance of Selborne's reasoning, it seems.) The Conservatives were lukewarm. When, however, it was debated annually in Parliament, the Minister of Agriculture of the day insisted that the Subsidy Act had been introduced for a total period of ten years, and ten years it would be.

Anglo-Dutch, and in their turn, Tate & Lyle, introduced new types of contracts with the farmers which gave the growers a share in profits and made them more enthusiastic about sugar beet. Anglo-Scottish and the other two Groups were unable to do this for they were earning too little. They and their friends carried on quite an effective propaganda war, however, in favour of the retention of the subsidy. The refiners, they said, had received more protection under Winston Churchill's Budget of 1928[1] than even the beet sugar producers. Foreign sugar was now no longer a competitor – indeed, the Czech and other producers regarded the duty scale introduced in 1928 as a dirty trick, and sorrowfully said so. It was now a quarrel between the refiners, one of whom – Tate & Lyle – also had beet interests, and the beet sugar factory owners.

After eight years of sugar subsidy and with two still to go, the position was that it cost £24 15 s. 0 d. to produce a ton of white sugar from home grown beet, and only £11 15 s. 0 d. to do the same from imported raws. Thus the amount needed to maintain the home-grown industry and the farmers' beet price was £13 0 s. 0 d. per ton. But, it was said, the home-grown factory distributes *all* its revenue in Britain, while the refiners paid most of their revenue to 'foreigners' and spent only £4 3 s. 0 d. per ton in England. So the arguments went on.

Caught in the cross current of abuse the Minister of Agriculture tried various expedients to reconcile the different parties. He introduced in March 1933 an Agricultural Marketing Bill 'to regulate home production and imports', and set up a Committee to investigate the beet sugar position. The battle continued. Leslie Fairrie, of that well-known family

[1] See page 83.

but not involved in refining, wrote an article saying that while there were 'serious' beet factories in England, as good as any in the world, there were also a number of 'comic' factories. It was, he said, 'the Thespians who run these comic factories without recognizable diminution of their debentures and without dividends to their shareholders', who were causing all the fuss. (He meant Anglo-Scottish.) And the *Daily Herald* printed an attack on Tate & Lyle for making agreements with factories which would lead to a monopoly and to a withdrawal of the 1925 subsidy.

At length the Committee, probably thanks to Albert Palache and Walter Johnson who had a foot in both camps, hammered out an 'Industrial Agreement' in 1933, by which definite quotas were allocated to the competing units. Of a total domestic consumption of 1·9 million tons, 500,000 were allocated to the beet factories, 70 per cent of this to be produced as white during the campaign, and 30 per cent being refined after the campaign. Any surplus must be produced as raws and sent to refineries. If a factory could not fulfil its quota, a refiner might buy it from him.

As this was legally unenforceable, although it was an improvement on the previous dog-fight, the Minister introduced on February 7th, 1934 a sugar marketing scheme, to be operated by a very large Board. On the factories' side were names like Kirkwood, Talbot-Crosbie, Van Rossum, Palache, B. N. Forster, and Lord Weir; on the refineries' side, among others, Sir Leonard Lyle, J. J. Runge, G. V. Tate, J. B. Crispin and J. S. Wingate.

Numbering twenty-one and composed, it would appear, under undeviating pressure from every quarter that Buggins must be included, it is difficult to resist the feeling that, had the Board been called on to move it would have done so *very* slowly, and in a series of ever-decreasing circles. It is, therefore, perhaps fortunate that it was overtaken by events and never operated.

For criticism in Parliament was mounting, and a Public Inquiry was demanded. Mr. A. V. Alexander (Labour) said the scheme would raise prices to the consumer, and Sir Herbert Samuel, a Liberal free trader, said scornfully that rather than continue the sugar subsidies and have such a scheme as this, it would cost the Government less to pay all the workers on the farms £2 a week, and all the factory workers £3 to do nothing, to pay the dividends of all the beet sugar companies, and that this would leave ample money to buy the equivalent quantity of sugar elsewhere and give it free to the public, charging only customs duties. The *Economist*, quoting this with glee, called the situation: 'The Beet Sugar Scandal.'

Yet the situation was not as simple as that. Hitler had seized power in 1934 and it is possible, though there is no evidence for this, that Major Walter Elliott, the Minister of Agriculture, may have had strategic considerations in mind. At any rate, it is known, and not only from his subsequent actions, that he was determined that Britain should continue to have a home grown sugar industry.

When Governments don't know quite what to do next they usually appoint a Committee of Inquiry, not so much with a view to making any sense out of the situation as to lowering the temperature. And this is what happened in April 1934 when a Mr. Wilfrid Greene, K.C. was appointed to chair the Committee which bears his name. And a pretty futile Committee it proved to be, split down the middle, the Chairman changing his mind half-way through the hearings, and seeking for a solution that would please those who appointed him. It might just as well never have sat for all the attention paid to its advice.

But before briefly examining the Greene Committee's report let us see what was happening at the refineries.

CHAPTER EIGHT

Between the Wars (2)

The inter-war period at the refineries was one of innovations. Many of these look simple, viewed from fifty years later, but they took time, trouble and many a muttered oath to bring about.

Until the mid 1920s, for example, sugar was normally delivered in Russian bags, sewn up by hand on primitive machines. At Plaistow, from the very early days 7 lb. cotton bags printed in red and blue were also filled and hand-sewn. They were available to staff at the gate for 10½ d. Tate & Lyle seem to have been pioneers in the distribution of goods packeted on a large scale with a brand-name. Apart from these 7 lb. cotton bags the housewife up to the present had bought the familiar blue paper bag, parcel or poke, filled with a small shovel by a not necessarily accurate grocers' assistant. In 1922, however, Plaistow installed their first machine for packeting in a place called the Glass House. It did not work and subsequent variants still had to be hand-sealed, a job which was very hard on the fingers. They only turned out 8 tons a week. Then almost simultaneously all three refineries adopted machines for producing 1 lb. and 2 lb. paper-wrapped cardboard packets and delivering them in parcels of 28 lb. – an entirely new concept, for up to then small bags had been sent out in cases. Strangely enough the fact that the parcel looked flimsy meant that it received less rough treatment than cases of wood or cardboard, and loss by damage was very slight. Tate & Lyle were probably the first in sugar to introduce this form of machinery.

The type of packeting machine eventually adopted was one manufactured by Hesser of Stuttgart, a firm whose product has the mixture of imagination and solidity to be found in B.M.W. and Mercedes cars, and although British-made machines have since then been introduced, the Hesser is still predominant, much modified and improved, and much faster than the early models. But most machinery at this time was of British manufacture. It was early discovered that the Southall & Smith scale by which the net weight was put into the packet was a beautiful and accurate machine at high speed. Weights are most important. Either your customer may receive too little, in which case you are defrauding him and the law will be on your tail, or he may get too much, which is also illegal and any way you will soon be out of business. Set to a minute tolerance Southall & Smith weighers could be relied on to be consistently accurate.

The first Hesser machine to be installed gave trouble even though fitters like Wally Thomas and Bill Dillon had been sent to Stuttgart to learn the techniques, and progress was slow. Eventually, after only three machines had been installed and although they were still by no means satisfactory,

Plaistow decided to go in for Hessers on the grand scale, until there were eventually twenty-two of them. Equivalent numbers were put in at the other two refineries. The early Hesser machine turned out 19 tons of packets a week, $2\frac{1}{2}$ times its predecessors' production. 'Driving' the machines, which involved a sensitivity to mechanical things and the control of a team of four who served it, avoiding losses and a shambles following a breakdown in the grabbing, folding, filling, and packing of numerous bits of angry-looking ironmongery, demanded special qualities in the girls who were doing it, and these could only be selected after a long trial. Seeing a driver at work, listening for any minor fault in the machine and often better at judging where it is than any fitter, is like watching a skilled oboeist.

An attempt was once made by two long-haired gents from some work-study outfit to devise aptitude tests for the selection of drivers. After many weeks of playing with charts and coloured beads they announced that they had a completely reliable technique. Alas, the results of its application bore no relation to the skills of girls who were actually driving machines, and their two chaps sorrowfully departed with their beads, charts, and of course the hair. Oliver Lyle, who was automatically switched off by psychologists, returned with joy to the original method of selection.

Small Packets were not at first fully accepted by the Board, and Sir Ernest Tate, then Chairman, reacted vigorously against the first sample packet to be exhibited at a Board meeting. Jabbing it irritably with his walking stick, he said: '*I* think it's a bugger', and stalked out of the room until it had been removed.

At Liverpool the Small Packets Department was usually known by that name. At Plaistow and Thames they were referred to by male process workers as 'The Hessers', and the young women who worked them as 'them tarts up the 'essers'. This implied no slur. To a cockney a tart is a generic name for a girl and many of the girls in the Hessers would be sisters or cousins or nieces of the male chauvinist pigs in the process or the fitters' shop.

Small Packets Departments, when working well, which was 99 per cent of the time, were a pleasure to see. The physical effort varied, and there was therefore a mixture of the calm, smooth concentration of the drivers and the more rapid movement of parcellers and filling-wheel girls. The effect was almost that of a ballet and the good-humour was infectious. They and their sisters in the other girls' departments always seemed glad to see you. It wasn't just that old sex thing, $\male$ and $\female$ or whatever it is. They were just very nice people, doing a job well and glad to be seen doing so.

The Syrup-filling Department at Plaistow was also a pleasant place. Here, until the invention of a machine in the 1950s, the cans were neatly, precisely and rapidly hand-filled by girls who had taken some weeks to acquire the knack. The sale of syrup in casks was dropping rapidly by then. It had for long been the only pack, and by 1939 it would have gone for ever, and with it the splendid craftsmanship of the coopers' shops. Piece work was for many years paid to the girls on syrup filling, but as demand for Golden Syrup fell in the summer months, just when they were saving up for a holiday, and their earnings fell with it, a flat year-round rate was agreed. Output surprisingly fell off very little—less than 5 per cent.

In the girls' departments, numbering some hundreds, it was essential to have a senior woman in charge as well as a Foreman, and there were a succession of delightful people, Florrie Smith, Lil Williams, Nell Arnold, Rose Hale, and their sisters at Love Lane and Thames.

Following the 1928 sugar duties charge, Tate & Lyle were able, like other refiners, to build on a sure foundation, and output was to rise even more rapidly. By 1929 Liverpool was up to 7,000 tons a week, Thames to about the same, and Plaistow to 5,671. The precision of this last figure can be guaranteed by the existence of Oliver Lyle's pocket book. In this slim volume, which he carried everywhere, he recorded figures for melt, costs per ton, raw sugar prices, char used per cent of melt, Golden Syrup produced, and many other statistics. A small magnifying glass in one corner of his spectacles enabled him to write these with a mapping pen in a tiny, neat hand writing, year in year out. (It still exists, though he died in 1961). He not only noted refinery statistics but could be relied on for exact information on a number of esoteric subjects—e.g. the increase in the number of public lavatories in London from 1880 to 1920, and their location. And he had a habit of noting something you said and then, with a delighted cackle, facing you with it two or three years later, in order to show you that you were contradicting yourself.

Our Pocket Historian records of 1929 that: 'The Importance of Being Ernest began to wane and this gave rise to the memorable reign of Leonardanvernon. It was during this era that the Doctrine of Cash In and Cash Out gained credence and eventually acceptance by the Board. It was also now that the descendants, collaterals and cousins of Chap. II began to be subjected to a "wave of Lyles", which has been likened by some historians to Manna from Heaven and by others to the Eighth Plague of Egypt.'

Translated, this means that Sir Ernest Tate retired in 1929, to be succeeded as Chairman by Sir Leonard Lyle, who some six years later became President, then handing over the Chairmanship to Vernon Tate. It was Vernon who, liking to simplify the complex by a rule of thumb, referred to it as Cash In and Cash Out, and very effective it was. (Twenty years later, maddened by the complications of coping with post-war taxation, and by the even more complicated defensive evolutions of auditors and the like, he was to say with feeling: 'What we need is a good Jewish accountant from Whitechapel.' All right, all right. This was meant as a compliment, not an expression of racism.)

It is also true that sundry Lyles came in. Ian Lyle was soon to join, followed by Morton Oliphant, a little later by Ian Archie Lyle, and still later by Colin and Donald Rowan, whose grandmother was a Lyle.

In 1929, too, the other large Liverpool sugar firm, Fairrie & Co., ran into difficulties and was amalgamated with Tate & Lyle, the Fairrie plant operating independently until 1937 when Love Lane Refinery was rebuilt and was able to absorb the whole of the throughput.

With this amalgamation, Geoffrey Fairrie, then in his early forties, joined the Board of Tate & Lyle. An able engineer and an articulate man, with a strong personality and plenty of drive, he had written, on his return from the war, a standard book on sugar. He was something of a loner and was more at home in Liverpool than in London, where instead of the cloth cap favoured by Ernest and Bertie Tate, he used to tour the refinery daily in a bowler and later in a Homburg. He master-minded the reconstruction in Liverpool in 1936/37 and it was for long a model refinery. The reconstruction involved a large reduction in numbers of employees, the effect of which was softened by the introduction of an ex gratia and rather more ad hoc precursor of the pension scheme mentioned above.

Housekeeping at Liverpool was impeccable, for when Geoffrey himself was unable to cast an eye over the place, he made use of a triumvirate composed of C. V. Potter (son of Charles, the Tate Manager), Alf Potter the Chief Chemist[1] (no relation), who came to Tate & Lyle with Geoffrey, and D. W. Sutherland, a wartime army acquaintance of Geoffrey's.

It was unkindly said that they were chiefly busy watching each other but the Refinery itself was carefully and beautifully kept. Its condition was certainly the envy of London refinery men who called from time to time to see what the scouses were up to.

In 1931 the U.S. slump had hit Europe with its wake, and an ineffective Labour Goverment split, Ramsay MacDonald taking some of his colleagues with him to form a National Government with Mr. Baldwin and his Tories and the Liberal rump. Unemployment was appalling. But for Tate & Lyle, or more particularly for Plaistow Wharf, it witnessed a new departure in management.

Hitherto the Refinery had been run, under the manager and assistant managers, by the refinery foremen. But techniques were becoming more complicated, science was creeping up on the process, and by 1929 it had been decided that management should have a more sophisticated technical background.

Tate & Lyle were by this time deeply involved in beet sugar production, and Bobby Kirkwood, who was in charge at the Bury St. Edmunds factory, had been asked to take on a few science graduates from universities and teach them sugar, so that they should have a mixture of good scientific knowledge and practical experience. The first two, Jo Whitmee and Kenneth Brown, had now served two campaigns at Bury and came to Plaistow in 1931.

Henceforward shift managership was to be the route whereby new

---

[1] See also under Research, Chapter Twenty-six.

technical intakes and well-tried foremen would approach more senior jobs in the firm. Over the next three decades there would be some thirty at Plaistow, of whom just over a third were promoted foremen. Some six, including the present Chairman, would eventually become Directors. For a new boy, being a Trainee shift manager was demanding. You knew about some things, you knew nothing about others. You were not in charge, then suddenly you were. Jo Whitmee, arriving to take over his first shift on a Sunday evening, was greeted by the vast, slightly suspicious figure of George Bull, Refinery Shift Foreman—we saw him, as Foreman of the Garret in 1917 helping to shut down after the Silvertown explosion. Jo was short in stature, though not in character. 'Well', said George, looking down from his great height, 'I don't know what *you're* going to do but *I* shall be very busy for the next four hours starting up the Refinery'. George later became a Shift Manager himself, and a trainer, along with George Rutty, of many others.

To begin with, the employee in the process was suspicious of shift managers. Years later, men like Bob Gilbey, Harry Auger, and Dan Darlow, would say reflectively to a newcomer over a cup of tea at 2.00 a.m., 'Things were hard in the thirties but we reckoned we could get on with the old lot. Then, when they brought in those undergrads, as we called them, we thought it was some plan to make things more difficult for us. But we soon found different'. This was perhaps due to the light-heartedness this new brand of animal exhibited in addition to competence. Kenneth Brown, for instance, found a lad in the warehouse amusing himself by trying to run up the gravity rollers down which the sacks descended, a highly dangerous exercise. He cautioned the boy in the hearing of the Fill House B shift, who then went off to their tea break. On their return, according to Harry Auger, they heard the gravity rollers rattling below them and thought it was the boy, being defiant. 'Silly little bastard', they said to themselves, 'He's for it'. Then they looked down and saw who was trying to run up the rollers. It was Kenneth Brown.

It was fun in a way being a shift manager, but it cut you off from your usual friends, for you did 6.00 a.m. to 2.00 p.m. one week, 2.00 to 10.00 p.m. the next, and 10.00 p.m. to 6.00 a.m. the next, month in month out. Your friends couldn't make out why you couldn't meet them, your wife, if you had one, found you edgy at odd times of the day, and you might be on shifts for three, four or more years. But it was like being sent away to a public school. Nothing in life was ever so difficult afterwards, and you made friends with so many people. Moreover you could give vent to your feelings in the shift managers' log.

Liverpool adopted a similar but less developed system, two well known Shift Managers being the brothers Len and Bob Pullen; but Thames did not do so until after the 1939/45 war, continuing to run shifts under foremen. Each however had its own innovations. At Thames, for example, a fullblown personnel department was instituted in the mid 1930s, and a works medical service under a remarkable Belgian, Dr. de Bouk. Works canteens or restaurants for the most part had to wait until after 1939 when war conditions made it essential to provide proper meals as people could no longer bring in their own without difficulty. At Plaistow Wharf there was a primitive canteen from 1905 to 1940 in No. 28 shed for most of the time, run by Matt Carr. Matt was a concessionaire and liked to make a profit and it was said that all doors and windows in the canteen – it was called The Lobby – had to kept shut while he carved the ham, or the slices would be blown away.

After the change in duties in the 1928 Budget, then, the Refineries prospered. Their wellbeing was in fact to be more lasting for Tate & Lyle than the investment in beet sugar. For this, assailed by Liberal free-traders and by the Left, was now the subject of the Greene Committee of Inquiry, whose Report it is now time to examine.

CHAPTER NINE
The Greene Committee

I

'If you go down to the woods today, you'd better not go alone'
(Nursery song of the 1940s)

Committees of Inquiry appointed by Government bear some resemblance to visitors to the Teddy-Bears' Picnic. That is why they are usually Committees, not single individuals. Anyone fool enough to take on the job of Chairman is selected from a list called The Good and the Great. He – no, sorry, he/she – is usually either a Professor of something like Non-Applied Teleology, a retired Prime Minister, or a Lawyer. It doesn't matter who does it as long as he/she is prepared to accept that the result of two years' (paid) work will lead to three weeks' correspondence in *The Times* and then eventual consignment to an oubliette, or Cabinet filing-cabinet. Chairmen are usually appointed either because they know too much or, more commonly, too little of the matter in hand, let us say: 'The Effect of Multinational Companies on land tenure in the Outer Hebrides.' Or, alternatively, because they have to keep up their average weekly score of T.V. appearances. The only certainty is that, once outside its normal sphere of action, the Law is as big an Ass as the rest. The Greene Committee, although operating long before the arrival of T.V., was no exception to this.

Mr. Wilfrid Green, K.C., was fifty-three in 1934. Apart from War service in 1914/18 (he did very well), he had been in the Law all his life and his only experience of industry was in lawsuits such as one he was then conducting on patents for Courtaulds against British Celanese in the House of Lords, and which seems to have occupied his mind a great deal. He may have been used to mastering complex issues and his mind was no doubt a finely tuned instrument but he seems to have had difficulty in deciding which key to play it in. His two fellow members were Sir Kenneth Lee and Mr. Cyril Lloyd. Both were businessmen and both had been at Uppingham, where they may have known Philip Lyle. Apart from that they differed widely. Whatever else their Alma Mater had done for them it had left them with totally divergent views on economics, Lee being a 'Treasury' man and a free trader, Lloyd a Chamberlainite protectionist.

None of the three had any background in agriculture. The Secretary was only appointed after a tussle between the Treasury, who would not have a man from the Ministry of Agriculture, and the Ministry, who would not have a Treasury man. They compromised on Mr. Sydney Caine[1] of the Colonial Office, who had been Secretary to the Olivier Committee on the

[1] Later Sir Sydney Caine, Director of the L.S.E.

West Indies in 1929 and was well aware of Major Elliott's determination to keep the beet subsidy going.

The copy of the Report used in preparing this chapter belonged to Philip Lyle who made his own index and underlined in red pencil (if it was anti-refiners), green (if anti-beet), blue if neutral. If irked beyond bearing – and he was sometimes impatient – he would occasionally give vent to his feelings in black ink.

This is a great help in going through a hybrid and unreadable document whose only positive quality is that of being a *somnifère*. The Committee held fifty-five formal and informal meetings and heard representations from just about everyone it could think of. (Had they existed at the time it would not have been surprising if the Dagenham Girl Pipers had been asked for their views.) The only body which either was not asked or did not condescend to appear was the Committee for Imperial Defence. This is a little strange since it was for strategic purposes that home-grown sugar had been introduced following the Selborne Committee's findings in 1917.

By page 80 of this closely printed opus it becomes clear that Lee wants to get rid of the beet sugar industry and Lloyd to keep it. Christmas 1934 came and Greene went on holiday to North Africa taking the drafts of two conflicting reports. Up to now he had sided with Lloyd but on his return from Morocco he said he had changed his mind, and the Majority Report became Greene and Lee, the Minority Report Lloyd.

The Majority Report sets up all the possible advantages of keeping the industry in being and then knocks them down. It even states that the strategic value of home-grown sugar in time of war is 'not a very large advantage'. (Selborne is forgotten, it seems, and Hitler as yet no bigger than a man's hand.)

Then, having havered and wavered and finally come to the conclusion that the industry should not continue, the Majority proceeds to examine ways in which perhaps after all it might do so, only to dash back again to 'the disadvantageous effects of the industry' and to come down in favour of scrapping it.

If this is done 'we cannot feel the factory owners would have any claim for compensation or special consideration. . . . The farmers on the other hand would be subject to very considerable dislocation and should all receive compensation'.

But what about the workers? No way. 'Though it is possible that a system of Unemployment Allowance for Agricultural Workers may by that time be in operation.'

Oh, and by the way, 'there is a prima facie case for a revision of the 1928 Customs Duty Scales'. (Philip Lyle's pencil point appears here to have snapped under the impact of half a dozen red exclamation marks.)

Yet, was such a recommendation as scrapping the industry within his terms of reference? Greene was not sure. What did the Government *really* want? Better leave a loophole or two. The Majority Report was so framed, letting I dare not wait upon I would. (As Wodehouse reminds us somewhere, Lady Macbeth observes that cats do this in adages.)

The Minority Report is, by contrast, robust and fairly easy reading. No doubts assail Mr. Lloyd as he briskly traverses his colleagues' arguments, dealing out cracks of the whip in all directions as though in charge of a coach and four.

How can they be so emphatic, in the current state of world sugar, about the permanence of the need for assistance to beet? If beet is not grown, farmers will return to the mangel-wurzel, which, while popular in pig-styes, is otherwise uneconomic. There are tremendous indirect agricultural benefits from beet growing, and the strategic importance of home-grown beet-sugar is pivotal. The Majority Report says the sugar subsidy is extravagant and inequitable. Balderdash, or words to the effect. The State has spent £45 million on building up the industry. It would be crazy—he calls it mildly 'an error of judgement'—to abandon it.

He is clearly shocked, as well he might be, at his colleagues' cavalier attitude to factory-owners and labour. (One warms to the chap.) The consumers of Britain, he remarks shrewdly, have for long benefited at the expense of the producer and the taxpayer. Let them contribute towards the cost.

Having carried out a thorough whip-behind, he then shakes the reins again and makes recommendations. Excise Duty must be remitted. Growers of beet should organize themselves. A permanent Sugar Commission should be set up to exercise surveillance over the industry as a whole. And—'*The manufacturers of sugar from home-grown beet should be required to unify their interests in a single Corporation.*' (Multi-coloured queries and sidelines from Philip Lyle.)

Having sprinkled these, Mr. Lloyd has 'The Honour to be, Sir, Your Obedient Servant'. Then he disappears to the tune, perhaps, of a faint, derisive tantivy or toot on the coach horn.

II

The home-grown sugar industry waited until April 1935 for the Greene Committee's report, delayed in presentation by its Chairman's change of mind. It must have been a little like sitting in a capacity audience in a pre-war Gaumont Cinema, chewing peanuts and sweets and being entertained by Mr. Sandy MacPherson at the Mighty Wurlitzer.

When at length the Big Picture came on it was thoroughly panned by those who knew anything of the subject, and by those who did not. Farmers in their cars and trucks organized anti-Greene rallies. The beet sugar factory owners frothed like thin juice without sufficient lime. The

Production was a total flop but the Producer was knighted, made a Privy Councillor and later became Master of the Rolls.

That was a reward of a kind for a complete disregard of the Majority's recommendations. Bows and smirks, of course, but 'The Government have reached the conclusion that it is desirable on agricultural grounds to continue to assist the beet sugar industry without any specific limitation of the period . . .'

An independent Sugar Commission was to be appointed with powers in relation to the sugar beet industry. The volume of assisted production was to be limited to 500,000 tons per annum.

For Tate & Lyle the sting was in the tail: 'The existing sugar factory companies are to be amalgamated into a single Corporation under the supervision of the Sugar Commission.' This was an extension of the intent of both Majority and Minority Reports, and it was probably due to the presence at the Ministry of Agriculture as Deputy Under Secretary of Mr. A. W. Street.[2] A man of Socialist views—he would later be Deputy Chairman of the nationalized Coal Board—he was described as something of a bully and accustomed to getting his own way. It seems that he did so now.

The detailed proposals can be omitted. But for Tate & Lyle, the end result was forced acquisition of their beet assets, part of the payment being in fixed-interest shares in the new British Sugar Corporation, and an arrangement by which they would have to 'buy' at 1s. 4½d. per cwt. any surplus beet sugar over 500,000 tons a year, thus contributing £350,000 a year by way of concealed assistance to a Corporation from whose operations they were excluded for ever by law.

It is, however, only fair to say, some forty years later, that, in the decades following the 1939/45 War, the British Sugar Corporation, under successive Chairmen and Chief Executives, has made great strides and is well-placed in E.E.C. conditions.

III

As the terms of the White Paper: 'Sugar Policy. Proposals of His Majesty's Government' of July 1935 were implemented, feelings ran high. The beet growers complained of reduced acreages. Those factory owners who had been making a loss and would be relieved of their debentures kept quiet. Those who had made sense and a profit—Anglo-Dutch and Tate & Lyle—were unhappy.

A Tribunal appointed by Government to acquire the factories seems to have worn jack-boots. It is difficult to discover exactly what went on, for

[2] Later Sir Arthur Street.

Board minutes were brief and uninformative. Leonard Lyle's public comments, however, bear witness to what was clearly a struggle.

'The Government put forward projects which were . . . not only in our opinion monstrously unfair. They were unworkable. They must have emanated from people insufficiently acquainted with all the intricacies of the situation, or from enemies whose desire was to strike us a mortal blow . . . Later a greatly modified scheme was produced. It is still very unfair, but if we accept it we shall work loyally to make it a success.'

A Tate & Lyle survivor of those times later spoke of 'the *enforced* amalgamation of efficient factories and inefficient ones', of Tate & Lyle fighting 'like kicking steers' but getting no sympathy from the Conservatives since the whole matter was in the hands of the bureaucrats of the Ministry of Agriculture. 'It was', he reports, 'during these negotiations that I came to the conclusion that the average official negotiating on behalf of Government is entirely without scruples'.

Certainly – lest this should be thought biased – when the Sugar Industry (Reorganization) Bill was debated – it was one of the few to be enacted under King Edward VIII, who abdicated later in 1936 – members of both major parties gave voice to doubts about the fairness of the proceedings. And a further White Paper – Cmd. 5139 – in reporting on the 'negotiations' suggests something of the atmosphere of a shotgun wedding when it came to valuation of assets.

It is all a long time ago, but bureaucrats are still about. And in order to provide a non-Tate & Lyle reaction it is worth recalling the feelings of J. P. van Rossum, who died in Holland during the war in 1943 at the age of eighty-three. He had, with his colleagues, made an exceptional contribution to British agriculture. He had risked, and sometimes lost, his own money. He had had the courage to send Dutch farmers to teach the British how to grow beet. He had rented and bought land at his own expense.

He received not one word of praise or thanks from the British Government, or in the British Press. After years of effort the Anglo-Dutch Group, whose creation was due so much to him, was forcibly sequestered in the most overbearing manner, and this was all.

It is melancholy to record that his feelings towards this country when he died in 1943, separated from Britain by the War, were understandably anything but cordial.

The Bury Group received in return for their assets £1·4 million in British Sugar Corporation Shares, which they had to retain until 1956, and £1·7 million in cash which they returned to their shareholders, among them Tate & Lyle.

Kirkwood cut all connection with beet sugar in October 1936. He had refused an offer of a Managing Directorship in the B.S.C. Still only in his thirties, he was to begin a new phase in his own life and in the development of Tate & Lyle.

For Tate & Lyle it was farewell to those factories; Bury St. Edmunds near the ruins of the great Abbey; Selby near another Abbey church; Peterborough looking over towards the huge Cathedral where Katharine of Aragon lies buried; and Allscott in the Shropshire Lad's country. Henceforth, the company was excluded from home-grown beet sugar production, for this was to be a Government-controlled monopoly.

It was therefore a matter of looking for a new field for enterprise and endeavour.

CHAPTER TEN

The Spanish Main (1)

(I)
'Westward the course of Empire takes its way.'
(George Berkeley, 1681–1753)

Don't you believe it. Bishop George Berkeley was a philosopher, responsible for the helpful advice that 'tar water is of a nature to cheer but not to inebriate', and for a belief that matter did not exist. Dr. Johnson, kicking a stone, said of this: 'Sir, I refute him thus'.

In the West Indies in 1936 the course of Empire had been a downward one for a century, since the emancipation had finally taken effect. Freeing the slaves had cost the Government of Britain £20 million (in real pounds, based on gold), but King Sugar, on whom the economy of the area had for so long depended, had by now pawned his crown. Affranchised slaves had roamed the islands, no longer caring to work in the sugar mills or on the estates. Some, the more industrious, made a livelihood in the hills by following what had been a permitted hobby under slavery, growing vegetables, and had become rather better than subsistence peasant farmers. They and their friends and families would carry provisions and fruits (usually on their heads) to markets in town and village, as they had always done on their day off a week as slaves. Here the goods would be 'higgled' for a 'quattee' (quarter of a sixpence). Others fished or did odd jobs when it suited them.

The picture drawn in the opening chapters of Richard Hughes' *A High Wind in Jamacia* of derelict sugar factories and estates in the 1840s did not change for the better thereafter. One of the long-term results of slave labour was indolence in the plantation owner and his family, each generation tending, unless motivated by strong consciences, to produce children who were spoiled from birth, who spoke the same creole English as their slave attendants and who were lazy. It was perhaps, in a way, Ashanti's revenge for the Middle Passage.

As we have seen in Chapter I there were attempts to replace slave labour by Lebanese, Syrians, Chinese, Portuguese, and – notably in Trinidad and British Guiana – by the introduction of indentured workers from India. Planters went on living in reasonable comfort, rearing cattle and fishing or shooting 'bald pate' pigeons to take their minds off the miserable prospect of the sugar market. The price of sugar fell and stayed down. Gladstone's father was glad to get out of British Guiana at a loss. Wise estate management, particularly in Barbados where there were few absentee landlords, kept heads above water – just. But then there was the Navigation

Bobby Kirkwood and friends in the canepiece. The friends are Cedric Titus (left) and Farmer Brown.

Act of 1849 and the reduction in protective sugar duties on 'foreign' sugars. So down went the price again. Then down went wages, from 2 s. 6 d. per day in 1839 to 1 s. per day in 1862.

Anthony Trollope was sent to the Caribbean in 1859/60, to introduce a postal system. A compulsive writer, he used this talent as a moonlighting job to pay for his hobby of hunting. His basic salary was paid by the Post Office, on whose behalf he introduced the pillar box. He found the travelling in Jamaica hard, as it had been for decades—Sir George and Lady Nugent, travelling as Governor and wife, had taken forty-eight days to get round the island fifty years earlier, stopping only a night at a time—but Mr. Trollope enjoyed staying with the planters in Great Houses. (The name Great House is still used. Then it meant a modest edifice, never more than two storeys high, because of earthquakes, and usually flimsily built, without much privacy.) There was generous hospitality, and the visitor, as recorded by Trollope, enjoyed the leisure, the sherry and bitters, and the huge mid-day 'breakfast' of fish, steak, yams, plantains and eggs, with tea, coffee, claret, beer, rum, and brandy to help it down. Women drank little and often ate separately from the menfolk, who for the most part were heavy 'takers'. He left a vivid picture, conversations and all, in *The West Indies and the Spanish Main,* published in 1862 and now one of his least obtainable works.

But beneath the apparently placid surface all was not well. There were often riots particularly in Jamacia. Some, such as the Gordon Rebellion in Jamaica in 1865, four years after Trollope's visit and caused by the American Civil War which had forced prices of imports up and closed the market for exports, were put down with a severity which caused criticism in England. Shortages and poverty led to a deeper dependence on that importation of Captain Bligh, the breadfruit, and on those from Africa like the ackee and the mango. There was also widespread 'predial larceny', or theft of growing crops, an offence still punishable, together with the public use of certain four letter and five letter words, in Jamaica in the 1960s.

Yet in Barbados in 1860, according to Trollope, an agricultural labourer was better off than his opposite number in England, and even in slavery days, the cost of a slave, at £10 a year in wages plus full board and quarters, was probably the same as that of a field labourer in England at £18.

But this is not a social history of the Caribbean. There are too many of them, so let us move on. There were Commissions of Enquiry. One of these in 1896 had caused Joseph Chamberlain to react against Bounty-fed imports of beet sugar. The First War led to a brief period of wild prosperity. Sugar was for a time short in the world and the price rose in 1921 to over £100 per ton (multiply by about four for 1977). This did not last long and was succeeded by a long period when it fell as low as £3 12 s. 6 d. Estate owners lost their feverish euphoria and put their affairs into receivership or had to hand them over to the banks. Among the latter was the Colonial Bank, which had opened its doors in 1836 and later became Barclays Bank

D.C.O. Ltd. well known in the region for its reasonableness. But bankers have to be realists, and even imperial preference on sugar, when introduced, did little to help.

Lord Olivier's Commission of Inquiry in 1929 found the situation little altered since the Commission of 1896. If the British Government would guarantee to accept fixed quantities of sugar each year at a reasonable price it would help. But the 'Free Breakfast Table' policy still applied and anyway Britain was in the midst of a slump herself.

The West Indies, by 1936 then, were not in the best of conditions. Life was short and usually plagued by poverty, malaria, yellow fever, tropical yaws and venereal disease. Planters could not afford to take proper care of their estates or buy even replacements for their factory equipment let alone new machinery. It was a world where the natural beauty of the scene and the outwardly idyllic though circumscribed existence of a few was contrasted with grinding poverty and a general sullen hopelessness occasionally lightened by outbreaks of cheerfulness at 'John Canoe' or carnival time in some of the islands.

II

*'There are few ways in which a man can be more
innocently employed than in getting money.'*
(Dr. Samuel Johnson, 1709–1784)

The genesis of Tate and Lyle's interest in the Caribbean sprang directly from the forced purchase by the British Government of the Company's investments in domestic production of beet sugar and the introduction of a Government monopoly in that activity in Britain in the year 1936. There is therefore no history of Tate and Lyle involvement in the slave trade, for slavery had been abolished a century earlier.

It is characteristic of men of enterprise to seek ways and means of employing their money profitably and this besides being according to Dr. Johnson 'innocent', is usually not only to their benefit but to that of people in general. In 1936 Tate & Lyle had money available, not as much perhaps as it should in equity have been had their beet factories been paid for at a fair figure, but money nevertheless. As supplies of raw beet sugar might in future be affected by Government action there was an attraction in seeking a secure source of raw cane sugar supplies in what were then the Colonies.

There were also available men of vigour and experience. Two of these were Robert Kirkwood[1] and Fred Sudbury.[2] The latter went to Java to study raw sugar production with a view to possibly taking on the

[1] See page 91.
[2] See page 81.

management of some future investment in the field of cane sugar. The former, being as it were a spare wheel on the Board now that the beet sugar companies were no more, proposed that he should go to the West Indies and see if there were any possible acquisitions to be found there.

Kirkwood took with him Walter Blanchard who had also been involved with beet sugar in Tate & Lyle's East Anglian venture. They found possibilities in both Jamaica and Trinidad.

Kirkwood returned to London and recommended the purchase in Trinidad of Caroni Sugar Estates (Trinidad) Ltd. (whose chief proprietors were in London) and Waterloo Sugar Estates (Trinidad) Ltd. In Jamaica he recommended two groups of estates and factories in the county of Westmoreland at the western tip of the island, and another group in the county of Claredon, in the middle of the south coast. All would need heavy capital investment and considerable management effort. He suggested that he should undertake the job of bringing the new acquisitions into sound condition, and this was agreed. It was unfortunate for Fred Sudbury, for whom the Company found other activities in which to exercise his considerable abilities.

Tate & Lyle also found a partner prepared to invest in the area, the United Molasses Company Ltd., who were then expanding their world-wide system for purchasing, storing and shipping this by-product of sugar. An investment of the kind contemplated suited their policy, too.

III

'De new broom sweep clean but de old broom know de corners'
(Anon.)

This Jamaican proverb underlines the need for adaptability in anyone dealing with the island. Bobby Kirkwood had this quality and he needed it.

'Xaymaca', the Land of Woods and Streams, was discovered by Columbus on May 3rd, 1494. It is a mountainous island with peaks rising to over 7,000 feet and broad plains where sugar, citrus and banana grow. Its original inhabitants, the gentle Arawaks–who had given it its name–died off within two generations when forced by the Spaniards to work and have left little trace. The Spaniards made little use of Jamaica except as a base. The island was captured from them in 1655 by a British force under Admiral Penn and General Venables after they had made, at the order of Lord Protector Cromwell, an unsuccessful attempt on Hispaniola (now Haiti and San Domingo). The slaves freed from the Spaniards fled to the interior where they became known as Maroons and carried on a successful guerilla war against Britain for eighty-five years.

Meantime French attacks had been beaten off and Port Royal, on the tip of the Palisadoes, a coral reef which makes Kingston one of the finest natural harbours in the world, had become a nest of pirates, one of whom, Henry Morgan, turning from poacher to gamekeeper in the 1670s, had become Deputy Governor for a while before retiring to estates he had bought. It was a lawless part of the world, preoccupied with plunder, whoring and of course the Demon Rum. A former Poet Laureate, John Masefield, wrote a ditty, 'Captain Stratton's Fancy' which captures the atmosphere:

> 'Some are for the Spanish wine, and some are for the French,
> And some there are drink tay and stuff fit only for a wench.
> But I'm for ripe Jamaica till I roll beneath the bench',
> Said the old, bold, mate of Henry Morgan.

Port Royal was largely destroyed by an earthquake in 1692 but its shell remained one of the Navy's major bases in the area until after 1945. The capital of the island for a long time was Spanish Town–Sant'Iago de las Vegas. Later Kingston took over.

The island was administered under a Governor by *Custodes Rotulorum*–a seventeenth century English form of junior Lords Lieutenant, and her history is enshrined in her place names; Spanish names like Ocho Rios, Savanna-la-Mar and Oracabessa; English county names like Cornwall and Westmoreland; the names of prominent English families, like Clarendon, Manchester, Trelawny and other familiar English names like Blackheath and Barham; African names like Accompong. In churches one may see the names of regicides like Blagrove and Whitlocke; and the Barretts of Wimpole Street once had an estate in Jamaica.[3]

One of the two Tate & Lyle acquisitions was centred round a factory and estate called Monymusk which is the name of the ancestral home in Scotland of the Grant family, who are said by oral tradition to have lost their Jamaican possessions by gambling.

Its acquisition, together with the other groups of estates centred in Westmoreland, was completed during 1937. It is situated in Vere, a part of Clarendon, where it is said sugar cane was first cultivated in Jamaica before the Grants got there. At the time of the first invasion by the French in 1694 fifty sugar estates were destroyed between the sea and Alley Road, where St. Peter's Church, built in 1671, still stands, the oldest church in Jamaica though it had to be restored in 1715 after earthquake damage.

'Old Monymusk' comprised the Grants' Estates plus Greenwich, Carlisle, Knights and several others. During the period of the decline of sugar since 1833 it had had many owners. It had recently absorbed the small central factories of Vere Estates and Amity Hall and, by the time Tate & Lyle arrived it represented the amalgamation of several other

---

[3] Mr. Barrett's misanthropy is believed to be due to the fact that instead of an anticipated £140,000 he got only £20,000 in compensation from the British Government for the emancipation of his slaves.

sugar factories some of which had still been operating in the memory of people still living – Morelands, Pusey Hall, Hillside, Dry River, Raymonds, Suttons, Perrins and Chesterfield.

It is bounded to the north by low limestone hills and to the south by mangrove swamps and dry salinas. To the south and east lies the Caribbean Sea. The area is flat and not much above sea level, and through it flows the Rio Minho, a trickling stream in the dry season, occasionally a torrent in the wet. The crop is largely dependent on irrigation with water pumped from wells, for Vere is a harsh dry area and rainfall is usually sparse for most of the year.

It was to this area and heritage that the newly formed Tate & Lyle subsidiary, The West Indies Sugar Company known usually as W.I.S.Co., came on November 10th, 1937. They found living in districts in villages and in estate houses, a community of some 20,000 people almost entirely dependent on the Company for any cash wages. They found a policy of employment which sought to spread the available work among as many people as possible, with resulting high labour turnover and a pattern of part-time work. This had led many workers to regard their work on the estate as a means of supplementing their main occupation of cultivating their own holdings in the neighbouring Manchester hills.

With the advent for the first time in 1938 of a trade union, which developed as a result of events on the other W.I.S.Co. estate, Frome, as will be described below, there was a gradual and, from the Company's view point as well as the employees', welcome change to more regular employment.

For the first twelve years the Company continued to use the old Monymusk factory, gradually increasing production from about 18,000 tons a year to 25,000.

The other Tate & Lyle acquisition was 100 miles away to the west, and to reach it meant a long and dicey drive up into the hills, through Mandeville, down the hairpin bends of Flagstaff Hill to the long dry plain, then savanna but, since 1946, eroded for ever by the excavation of bauxite.

In Westmoreland the purchase consisted of James Charley's eleven estates and their factories, Frome and Masemure in that county and Prospect, in neighbouring Hanover, also the Morris Group consisting of five estates and three factories – Shrewsbury, Friendship and Blue Castle; and Mint Factory belonging to John Charley. The Charleys were among those who had had to go into receivership in the 1920s. (The name Charley still persists as a trade name for a certain brand of Rum.) Much of the area had once belonged to the Ricketts family, who were related to Admiral Sir John Jervis, later Earl St. Vincent, Nelson's 'Dear Lord'. The Ricketts and Jervises were absentee landlords. This usually meant that workers on the estate were either allowed to be idle or brutally treated for being so, depending on the 'Attorney', 'Manager' or 'Overseer'. The term 'driver', applied to a junior foreman, was still used in the 1930s and was abolished by Kirkwood. He was, however, unable to do away with the Jamaican term for a white man – 'buckra' – which is perhaps a derivation of flogging – 'back raw'. If so, it is an interesting social survival, particularly in a Jamaican proverb going back over the centuries: 'Two t'ings don't business 'pon Sugar Estate: buckra woman an' goat.'

Letters from the attorneys of the Jervis and Rickett families between 1780 and 1830 show that running an estate then was exactly parallel to the same job 150 years later: late deliveries of machinery, obstinate engineers, occasionally alcoholic overseers, extravagant young men on a visit, insect pests, floods, difficulties with labour – even slave labour. But in those days there was isolation too. There was no airmail and letters took three months to arrive.

W.I.S.Co. built in 1938 a new central factory at Frome to a design by Walter Blanchard, big, but simple and foolproof, and the seven small factories, with an aggregate production of some 22,000 tons a year, were demolished or allowed to tumble down.

Frome, unlike Monymusk, was blessed with a high rainfall and clearly marked wet and dry seasons. Westmoreland, by comparison with Vere, is a lush green park where all kinds of vegetation flourish and cattle do well. Seen from the air the Westmoreland and Hanover cane pieces look like velvet pin cushions. Water gushes up in 'blue holes', or artesian springs, and one of these near Frome, pictured in a coloured engraving of 1778 dedicated to the father of William Beckford (Esq.), still looks exactly the same two centuries later, with palm trees sprouting in the midst of the water. From the earliest days the chunky Darliston, Williamsfield and Dolphin Hills, 600 feet high in a semicircle rounded the plains, supplied delicious clear water. Relics of the watermills which powered the little factories still remain as reminders of a simpler age.

When the new Central at Frome was finished in 1939 there was not enough cane to feed it and both Company and farmers' cultivation had to be increased. Free technical advice and new varieties of cane were supplied to the farmers who, although at first suspicious ('What de men do? Dem crazy?') responded favourably at length.

Paradoxically, it was the building of this factory, creating new job opportunities for large numbers of unemployed, at wages higher than those available elsewhere in the island, which sparked off major troubles in 1938. People converged on Frome from all over Jamaica, and in a very short time there were thousands of strangers in the area. Some had no skills and had come on the desperate off-chance of getting work. Others were men who lived by their wits and had come in search of any pickings that might occur. Obviously not all could be hired. Those who were turned away incited others. The unhappy conditions of the times – a little like those of 1865 and the Gordon Rebellion – did the rest. The frustration, poverty and sense of hopelessness spilled over into violence on the morning of May 25th, 1938 and with the unreason of desperation, men set about smashing the buildings and equipment and burning the cane fields, which could and later did supply greater opportunities and greater hopes of livelihood.

The local police were overwhelmed – they were a tiny force anyway – the staff had to be armed, and the Army called in. (There was always a British Regiment in Jamaica in those days.) Inevitably there were casualties, though very few, and a Government Inquiry, while deprecating the situation, found little for which to blame the Company. After so long a period of depression the appearance of even a modest ability to invest and spend money was too rich for the island's digestion.

After the affair at Port Morant in 1865, its leader George William Gordon had been hanged. By all accounts he was a good man, and 100 years later he was virtually beatified by his fellow-countrymen. A more fortunate figure emerged as a result of the Frome disturbances of 1938, William Alexander Bustamante – 'Busta' as he will forever be known in Jamaica.[4]

In 1938 he was in his early fifties and had already packed a lot into his life. A first cousin of the almost equally legendary Norman Manley, whose son is Prime Minister of Jamaica in the 1970s, Busta's true surname was Clarke. He is worthy of a book on his own, but it will be difficult for its writer to separate fact from legend. He certainly went to Cuba as a mere youth and adopted somewhere along the line the Spanish-sounding name by which he is known. Some say that he became a police inspector in Cuba. He would talk of serving in the Spanish Cavalry in Tangier as a young man. He certainly lived for a time in New York thereafter, either working as a dietician (he favoured raw carrot juice as an item of diet) or as a hospital orderly (some say) or as a waiter (others say). During the 1929–31 slump he seems to have bought shares cheap in various businesses which later recovered, and by 1938 he was back in Jamaica and in business as a money-lender, but lonely, for his wife, whom he married in 1912, was a permanent invalid.

His appearance, with a shock of hair going grey, and a strongly-featured ruddy-coloured complexion, was that of an Irishman. (He admitted to being Irish in extraction.) He was in no way a typical Jamaican of mixed ancestry, yet suddenly he was fired with a genuine compassion for his fellow-Jamaicans, particularly the poorer negroes, and proceeded to Westmoreland, where he instinctively took on the leadership of those who were engaged in violent protest against – what, they were not sure, perhaps life in general.

His cousin, Norman Manley, was part negro, wholly intelligent, wholly articulate. He had been an outstanding pupil at Jamaica College, a first rate athlete, and a Rhodes Scholar at Oxford. He had served gallantly as a gunner in the 1914 war and won the M.M. He was a brilliant barrister, and remained one for the whole of his practising life. He also remained a

[4] He died on August 6th, 1977, aged ninety-three.

charming cool man, an easy though ascetic dinner companion, totally unflamboyant.

Busta was behaving like a Napoleon at Toulon in the front line. Twenty years later, he would rise from the dinner table in the middle of a meal to re-enact the scene when he walked up to a line of soldiers in Westmoreland, tearing open his shirt, and shouting: 'Shoot me, you murderers.' ('Of course', he would add dreamily, 'They were English, I knew they wouldn't'.)

But somehow in that turbulence, Busta seemed to ride the whirlwind. It was then that he met a young woman, Gladys Longbridge, a trained secretary, who at eighteen years of age, said to him simply: 'Chief I want to help you.' She did so, calming him, smoothing down the frequent difficulties which his impetuousness would cause, and became his true right hand. (It was to be most moving when in 1962, he was able, being widowed, to marry her on the eve of Jamaica's independence.) He conceived the idea of a trade union, and called it the Bustamante Industrial Trade Union, for he was not one to hide his light. And later, on that foundation he would build the Jamaica Labour Party—which was not to be at all like the British Labour Party.

For all his courage and masculinity, he was almost feminine in his intuitive reactions and for the next ten years he somehow came to represent instinctively the slowly burgeoning desire, fertilized by the cataclysmic changes which the Second War brought to world politics, of the people of Jamaica as a whole for some form of emancipation from Colonial rule.

Sixteen months after these riots at Frome, that war began. Cradled in the middle of the Caribbean, Jamaica saw only the fringe of things. In time American air bases were built. Allied flotillas were based on Kingston. The world outside was using Jamaica and in doing so fostering change. For W.I.S.Co. and for the sugar industry of the island as a whole, it was a strange limbo in time. No new machinery could be bought. Expansion of production was limited. Foodstuffs had to be grown in the cane piece to save imports—Jamaica is lucky that so many fruits and vegetables grow there with such rude vigour. Even though sugar was needed, its shipment had to be fitted in with convoy arrangements, for German U-boats were active in the area.

In 1943 an attempt was made under Colonial Office pressure to develop a cheap protein food in the form of edible yeast made from molasses. The process had been developed on a laboratory scale at the Research Laboratory of the D.S.I.R. at Teddington under the direction of Dr. A. L. Thayssen. Frome was selected as the site for the plant and much money, time, and effort went into the project. Technical problems were overcome but it failed. Being Government sponsored, the scheme had been put forward without any clear idea as to how the product could be made attractive. It might be cheap but it looked and tasted nasty. Jamaicans stuck to their traditional saltfish and ackee, and a pipe-dreamer's idea for feeding the masses in the Colonies dissolved. The Colonial Food Yeast Company, owned by H.M.G., was liquidated in 1948.

At the outset of the war, Bobby Kirkwood flew back to England. He had been too young for the First War. He was thirty-five, but was fit and active, and – as anyone who knows him would agree – he would have been an admirable battalion commander, if sometimes almost too dashing. He could not get into the Army – too old and with no peacetime T.A. experience. He joined the only outfit that would take him, the Balloon Barrage Section of the R.A.F. But he was extracted from this by the Chairman of Tate & Lyle, Leonard Lyle, and sent firmly back to Jamaica as one in a reserved occupation. Others, younger than himself, were able to leave and join up. He tried again and again, begging Leonard to let him go. It was very hard on him.

Jamaica was slowly stirring even if W.I.S.Co. had to stand still. Busta was learning, but rather erratically, to curb his impatience. In March 1943 his union had achieved the first ever collective bargaining agreement for workers in the sugar industry. But 'the Chief' as Miss Longbridge called him, began to be suspected of sedition, for he was inclined, when faced by a large audience, to be carried away by his own oratorical enthusiasm. The Governor, Sir Arthur Richards (later Lord Milverton), had him locked up for the best part of a year. Then, convinced that Busta was a patriotic Jamaican but not seditious, he let him out, first warning Gladys Longbridge to get his little house ready. She was the only person given advance notice, for like everyone else, Richards recognized how intensely reliable and trustworthy she was. And then Busta began to build his political party under fairly lenient supervision from King's House.

By now he and his cousin Manley were no longer comrades in arms. Busta felt that Cousin Norman had been insufficiently helpful during the recent time in prison, and in any case there was a difference in political approach. Manley leaned towards dogmatic socialism, Busta towards pragmatic capitalism coupled with an eye to the main chance for members of his union.

Richards retired,[5] probably the last of those splendid, self-reliant Governors of Colonies who did what they thought best and told Whitehall afterwards.

One policy fostered during this time largely by Bobby Kirkwood, was the 'Jamaicanization' of the staff on W.I.S.Co. estates. Gradually it became the practice for every job which could be done by a Jamaican to be filled by a Jamaican, however exalted the level. Certain posts, such as that of an accountant, or qualified engineer, could not at first be treated in this way but over the years men were to be trained for these. Soon after the end of the war the top general managers' jobs were to be filled by Jamaicans too. It was a farsighted measure.

At length the peace came and the world was short of sugar. And the Tate

[5] He later became Lord Milverton.

& Lyle investment in Jamaica, which amounted to about one-third of the island's production, was, although its development had been delayed by events beyond the control of anyone except perhaps the Four Horsemen of the Apocalypse, poised to move forward into a situation very different from the one in which it had begun.

IV

'Oh it's Westward Ho! for Trinidad
And Eastward Ho! for Spain.
And it's Ship Ahoy! a hundred times a day'
(Sir Henry Newbolt, 1862–1935)

No Newbolt, sorry. But no. Westward Ho for Trinidad, O.K. Eastward Ho to Spain if you must. But all that ship ahoy stuff, no. A *hundred* times a day? You must be joking. It's more like:

It's Westward Ho! for Trinidad
    And hey for Port of Spain
Where ten thousand men are thumping
    old tin cans.

Yet the name Trinidad, one must admit, has a splendid romantic resonance to it which lends dignity to doggerel. It is, of course, the Spanish for Trinity, and the island takes its name from the fact that Columbus on his third voyage, coming upon it from the south-east, thought he saw three hills. Like a good Catholic, he may also have been aware that it was the Umpteenth Sunday after Trinity.

It is geographically almost a part of Venezuela in South America, stretching out two partially submerged arms towards the mainland, cut in the north by the Dragon's Mouth, in the south by the Soldiers' Channel, and between them lies the Gulf of Paria. On the south and east are long brown-sanded beaches. On the north, for the most part a rocky coast falls sheer into the water. Thirty miles or so to the north-east is Tobago, which gave its name to smoking and provided Daniel Defoe with topography for *Robinson Crusoe.*

But do not be fooled. Trinidad may be small, 60 by 40 miles, and have only about a million inhabitants, but is possesses a character of its own. It is no mere appendage to South America. Until 1798, it was Spanish, but Spain had joined Revolutionary France, and General Sir Ralph Abercromby, on his way to Argentina, captured it. (There is an Abercromby Street in the capital, Port of Spain.) When it become officially British in 1802 the population was under 30,000, and there were relatively few slaves. As the emancipation came thirty years later there was almost no tradition of slavery under British rule, and the population is now about 40 per cent of African and 30 per cent of East Indian origin, both Hindu and Moslem. There are also French, Spanish, Portuguese and Chinese Trinidadians. (The first Governor-General of independent Trinidad in 1962 was Chinese, Sir Solomon Hochoy.) Somehow beneath the tropical languor there is almost always an air of gaiety and euphoria. Of course there have been clashes and explosions, for a mixed population is a tinder box. But Trinidad not only seems but is richer than the other islands. For there is oil underground and although this was expensive to recover until the recent discovery of huge deposits offshore, it meant that there has been, since oil fuel became a fact of life in 1911, an underlying economic strength. Even in 1960, before the offshore fields were known, sugar represented only 10 per cent or so of the island's earnings, much of the money coming from a huge oil refinery, once Trinidad Leaseholds Ltd., but after 1956 belonging to Texaco.

Nevertheless, sugar has always been the largest provider of jobs. The cane is grown in the broad plain which faces the Gulf of Paria and on the gentle hills to the east of San Fernando. And, since most of the farmers and agricultural labourers are East Indian, the rural scene has something about it of India – little houses with deep eaves to keep the rain from entering open windows, water buffaloes to pull the ploughs and carts, and, in the misty, pink, dawn light when the men are off to the canefields and the women are cooking, a truly Indian aroma. Rice is dried on the side roads, and you must be careful not to drive over it, or you will be told your fortune in vivid language. Little temples stand by the roadside, and flags on bamboo staffs indicate that the local Swami has been 'makin' pujah'.

Like Jamaica, Trinidad reflects her history in her place names: Carib names like Carapichaima, Naparima, Guayaguayare, Chacachacare; Spanish names like San Fernando, Manzanilla, La Gloria and Buen'Intento; French names like Ste Madeleine and Malgré Tout (pronounced Malgrytoot); English names like Monkey Point, Waterloo, Cross Crossing, and – after Wellington's General killed at Waterloo in his shining top hat – Picton; East Indian names like Hindustan, Golconda and Bejucal; Scottish names like Ben Lomond, Craignish and Brechin Castle. It is a name-collector's paradise.

It is also a historian's. Raleigh was there in 1595, sampling the delicious little oysters which 'grew' on mangrove trees (as they still do), caulking his ships with pitch from the Pitch Lake, at La Brea, which still provides material for many a road, and sacking the little town of San José, now St. Joseph.

It has been said that Trinidad has two seasons, the dry one which is wet, and the wet one which is wetter. Sometimes, because it is so damp, Trinidad seems drowsy, the immortelle trees lazing pink above the cocoa, the 'keskadee' birds aimlessly chattering, the little green parakeets fluttering in the shrubs. But there are occasional vicious outbreaks of violence, part 'anti-Colonial', part anti-business, part inter-religious or inter-ethnic. And in the days before the 1939/45 war it was sometimes necessary to send in the Royal Navy. The ships were described by local politicians as cruisers, but were in fact normally sloops. There are still occasional outbreaks against authority, even when that authority is indigenous.

This is not a travelogue, but one cannot think of Trinidad without Carnival in February, when for the days just before Mardi Gras and Lent, particularly in the towns, people of all ethnic origins 'Play Masque' going round the streets in *bandes* (the French influence) dressed in costumes which have taken much money and hard work to make. It is one of the fundamental links which bind Trinidadians together in huge numbers. New calypsos are sung each year, having been selected in competitions judged by critical audiences in 'tents'. Calypso is Trinidadian. The words of a calypso, usually satirical, are reminiscent in scansion of McGonagle, and full of *piquant* – Trinidad French for 'wit'. The tunes are lilting and rhythmic, and some are taken up as 'road marches' for the *bandes*, and played by Steel Bands. This, the newest form of music until the Moog synthesiser, is enchanting. The tunes are beaten out on the flat portions of steel oil drums which are cut off at different lengths to give variation of depth. There is apparently no conductor. It all just happens, producing a liquid, sensuous sound, but only after much cacophonous tuning and rehearsal. The instrumentation dates from the time when oil drums became plentiful, when in 1941 Churchill and Roosevelt exchanged bases in the Empire (one of those being at Guadarama in Trinidad) for forty destroyers and other assorted ironmongery in order to win the war.

Evenings in Trinidad are usually warm, which makes it less than ideal as a home for sugar cane, for the cane prefers for ripening cool nights and dry days. This piece of scientific fact was, however unknown in earlier days. There are few records from that time but such as there are disclose the presence of over 300 sugar mills in 1807, operated by mule, wind or water-power and each producing an average of 35 tons of sugar a year (measured and shipped in hogsheads). In 1830 Mr. Gregor Turnbull, a Glasgow merchant, was among those who considered the possibility of installing a steam engine at Harmony Hall factory, not far from San Fernando. Mr. Turnbull also established a small fleet of vessels, possibly in competition with Abram Lyle & Sons, sailing under the 'Turnbull' flag and carrying coal and manufactured goods to Trinidad and hogsheads of sugar back. (Until May 10/11, 1941, when the late Hitler destroyed the London Office of Tate & Lyle, a bust of Turnbull was to be seen in the basement of the West Indies section, adorned by the office boy with red and blue ink, as a relaxation from filling inkwells.)

Turnbulls' had associates in Trinidad and New York, and together they founded The Trinidad Shipping & Trading Co. Ltd., in 1895. Among other things they owned the Queen's Park Hotel in Port of Spain, and their

New York branch, at 29 Broadway, had a contract for the carriage of asphalt from the Pitch Lake in Trinidad to New York. This arrangement lasted until 1932.

It was T.S.T. which in 1902 acquired Caroni (the name comes from the River Caroni), Brechin Castle and Lothians, three sugar estates which had been in the hands of the banks. The sugar business was run from West George Street, Glasgow. By 1924 T.S.T. had run into its own problems, and was taken over in part by Furness Withy & Co. who floated a new company, Caroni Sugar Estates (Trinidad) Ltd., with offices in London and it was this Company, together with Waterloo Sugar Estates (Trinidad) Ltd., the two being almost contiguous north to south, which was acquired by Tate & Lyle, with equity participation by United Molasses Ltd. From 1903 to 1936, production by the Caroni Estates had varied from about 7,000 tons a year to 20,000.

After that technological breakthrough at Harmony Hall (such a good name for a pleasant spot) there was no immediate swing to that new source of power, steam, and by 1840 only 40 out of the 300 mills had adopted it. For some time also Tobago had been a successful exporter of sugar, and an expression in the London of the early nineteenth century was 'as rich as a Tobago planter'. But by 1900 Tobago was out of sugar.

Like Jamaica, Trinidad was badly hit by competition during the years following 1838 from beet sugar, but it was a smaller place, then less vociferous, less populated, and only recently British, and was less heard of. Owners of estates grew citrus or cocoa instead of cane. Small factories disappeared or were amalgamated. In 1870 The Colonial Company Ltd. of London built a large central called by the French name 'Usine Ste. Madeleine', near Princes' Town – so named after a visit by Prince Albert Edward (later King Edward VII) in 1871 – which first came into operation in 1874. Although Trinidad's sugar production was by now double that of Jamaica, there are few records of its early days. In 1886, a Mr. J. H. Collins, in his *Guide to Trinidad* stated of U.S.M.: 'it is the finest factory in the West Indies and I believe I am not wrong in asserting that, with one exception, it is the largest central factory of its kind in the world'. However, by 1895 the Company had gone bust. 'The New Colonial Company Ltd.' took over and operated it until 1913 when this Company, in its turn, went into liquidation. Then the Ste. Madeleine Sugar Company was created under the leadership of a century-old partnership, Henckell du Buisson, which still exists, and floated up on the tide of rising prices into the 1920s, absorbing little factories like La Fortunée and Malgré Tout.

Meantime other estates and factories grew and flourished or failed: Caroni, Brechin Castle, Waterloo and Esperanza – the last-named owned and operated by a Scottish firm based in Trinidad, Gordon Grant Ltd. together with Brontë, romantically named after Nelson's Sicilian Dukedom; Woodford Lodge, named after an early and popular Governor, James Woodford; Forres Park (note the persistent Scottish influence),

Trinidad Sugar Estates at Orange Grove and so on.

There is little written evidence, but the inquisitive visitor can stub his toes on bricks which mark, under bush vegetation, the sites of long-forgotten sugar-mills. On one site even in the 1950s he could once also stub them on a large and choice collection of empty 'squareface' bottles of Holland's gin, for the former manager, one of many Dutchmen who worked in Trinidad and neighbouring British Guiana, had spent a lifetime solacing his loneliness with 'Genever' and discarding the empties through the window.

But Trinidad's sugar, like early sugar refining in Britain, was more beholden to Scotland than to anywhere else. As recently as 1969 there died one Harold Gilbert, a tall, sardonic, delightful man of Glasgow origin. His father had gone to Trinidad in 1892. His mother, who lived until the 1950s had sailed (to be married) in 1894 with a third-class single ticket from Greenock to Monkey Point, Trinidad, including the rowing boat fare from the steamer to the shore. We shall meet Harold Gilbert again. Born in Trinidad, he was nevertheless very Scottish.

When Tate & Lyle arrived, they found a desolate place. Caroni was in financial difficulties and Waterloo Estates was in the hands of the bank. It was managed by Captain Willy Watson, a spry military-looking man in his fifties, with a liking for horseflesh. The engineers were usually Scottish and inclined to be nomadic. The overseers and book-keepers were usually young Scotsmen, Englishmen or Irishmen with some family background and no particular ambitions, who found the idea of a job in the Colonies better than one at home. They were not paid much and during their first three years were not permitted to marry. This embargo, long since dropped by Caroni Ltd., which soon followed the W.I.S.Co. process of 'localization', still continued at Ste. Madeleine until the late 1950s with many a rugger game having to be organized in the hopes of keeping the chaps' minds from straying to other more reproductive sources of entertainment. Occasionally the overseers and sometimes, when later they married, their wives, were eccentrics, but mostly they were harmlessly so.

Among those who had recently gone to Caroni Ltd. when Tate & Lyle arrived was Alan Walker. He was there as Office Manager and had just married Melissa de Pass, daughter of the Chief of Trinidad Police, when he was picked to return to England to become one of the small London Office staff which would look after the affairs of the two new West Indies companies. As communications were difficult between Jamaica and Trinidad, Bobby Kirkwood concentrated on the former and the latter was left in the control of Captain Watson. Immediately, the construction was begun of a new central factory, similar to that at Frome, at Brechin Castle, south of the old Waterloo Factory. The old Caroni factory in the far north of the estate was demolished, only the rum distillery remaining. Sugar cane was brought the 25 miles south by railway. The new Brechin Castle factory was just completed in time for the sugar crop of 1940.

There are two other aspects of Trinidad sugar which need mention, one good, the other bad. They are the cane farmer (good) and the frog-hopper (bad).

Well in advance of the situation in many another cane-growing island, an English Governor of Trinidad, Sir Neville Lubbock, had in the 1870s decided that cane-growing by small peasant farmers would, even though less efficient in terms of productivity, be politically more acceptable in the long term than estates' cane grown and cropped by landless labourers, and he gave encouragement, particularly in southern Trinidad, to the small peasant, living on half an acre or so, growing sugar cane as a cash crop and feeding his family on vegetables grown in the yard around his house. This edifice would be built on stilts in order to catch what breeze there was, and in the covered area beneath it the laundry would be hung, the cart stowed, the chickens would peck, and the children play.

It was an excellent idea, but soon after its introduction, an insect enemy, the frog-hopper – *aenulemia varia saccharis* – appeared. This little brute, looking like a striped housefly, has a life-cycle of eleven weeks. It lays its eggs in the soil near the cane roots, emerges as a larva in what looks like cuckoo spit, and, when adult, settles on the growing cane-leaves to draw nourishment. In doing so it injects an enzyme which poisons the leaf, turning it brown, and the cane plant begins to fade away. Starting in early July, there are three broods of frog-hoppers by the end of the year, the last brood leaving its eggs in the soil for next year. They breed by the hundreds of millions and if the cane is left unprotected, the crop of sugar per acre is reduced by 50 to 75 per cent. In most cane growing areas, it is controlled by natural predators, but not in Trinidad. Control measures took a long time to find. Indeed it was in Tate & Lyle's subsidiary, Caroni Ltd., that they were first to be effective in the late 1940s. But they require precise and careful application which is difficult for the small farmer to achieve. Originally in the 1890s the frog-hopper browning of the cane was thought of as a minor blight, but it contributed in no small measure to Trinidad's difficulties. It was still active in 1938, and became more so, although quite how seriously was not at the time realized. A venture, new for Tate & Lyle, was under way, and there must, it was thought, be a way of coping with blight.

To provide services for the two new West Indies Companies a small London Office was established, close to Tate & Lyle, in Market Building, Mark Lane. Walter Blanchard was there as Chief Technical Adviser. From the old Caroni, there were George Chalmers, the Secretary who had begun his life's work aged fourteen in Glasgow in 1907, and is still alive and alert at eighty-four in 1977, and David Andrews, Chief Purchasing Officer. There was also Leonard Carter, who started as an office boy in 1935. Walter Blanchard imported his old sparring partner, Archibald Gillies, from A. & W. Smith Ltd., and Jack Morris as draughtsman. The Chairman of Caroni Ltd. was Gordon Miller, who had come along with the old Company, and had brought over from Trinidad, now as London Manager of Caroni, Alan Walker, who was soon to become a Director.

The technical and purchasing affairs of the two West Indies Companies, and their central accounting were from henceforth undertaken by this small team which was joined in 1937 by a newly qualified Chartered Accountant, Bill Coupland. It was a small, lean, effective organization, and even when, some twenty-six years later, it had to handle the complications of producing about half a million tons of sugar a year in eight factories, separated by over 1,000 miles, it never comprised more than about fifty.

Like Jamaica, Trinidad was changed by the events of 1939–45. There was then of course, no air-conditioning. Clothes and boots collected a green mould in the cupboard within days. And sugar production in what was then a by no means over-populated island was seriously affected by the advent of American bases, which drew much of the unskilled and most of the skilled labour to them because of the higher wages paid.

One of the prettiest of Calypso tunes, 'Rum and Coca Cola', which was even picked up and recorded in Germany in 1944 as anti-Allied propaganda, is evidence of this:

> Rum and Coca-Cola,
> Down on Point Cumana
> De mother an' de little daughta'
> Working for de Yankee dollar.

Trinidad *piquant,* half-cynical, half-permissive, and graced by a captivating rhythm, was commenting on life in wartime Trinidad. But away from the American Naval Base and the huge concrete airfields, in the sugar belt, life went on much as before.

At Caroni there was a change. Captain Watson retired and Harold Gilbert became General Manager. Alan Walker, who flew out in 1943 to make the change, always used to call Harold 'The Great Sullivan'. He himself was now Managing Director.

Before he left, Captain Watson had built an attractive General Manager's house in Spanish style, called Sevilla, with materials he had collected before war broke out. Although there was some criticism of this as a wartime activity, later General Managers and their house guests came to appreciate the charm of the place. And, of course, it cost much less in 1942 than it would have in 1945.

The war, inevitably, would one day be over, and if the frog-hopper blight could be controlled, the new Caroni Ltd., like W.I.S.Co. would be a useful source of cane sugar, if not exclusively for Tate & Lyle, at any rate for a sugar-hungry post-war world.

CHAPTER ELEVEN

Before the Next War

It is now time to step back in both time and place and look at the Refineries as the Second World War loomed, and to follow their experiences through that war.

The last two or three years before 1939 had a certain brittle charm about them for some, although they were still difficult times for far too many. At the Refineries considerable efforts were being made to make life easier and more rewarding for those who worked in them, and many improvements in amenities were introduced. At the time, clean and well-kept changing rooms were regarded by some as something a little faddy. Nevertheless, in a food factory there was a need for proper hygiene and this was increasingly recognized. So was that of providing proper recreation facilities. A sports centre was founded for each of the London Refineries in 1937. Thames was the earliest to do so, and Fred Sudbury was the founder President, later resigning so that Vernon Tate could take on the post. Soon after this the clubs combined – they were financially strong – to buy a playing field at Manor Way. It was a great success and became a major asset, not only as a builder of morale and understanding but financially as well.

New faces came in. Jim Hobbs and Bill North from Oxford became trainee Process Managers at Thames. Sam Gee, grandson of Isolina Tate, whom old Henry had had to take away from school in the 1880s, started work at Liverpool in the laboratory and then came to Thames in 1934 to work in the Process. And Ian Archie Lyle, grandson of Sir Alexander, now arrived at Plaistow to learn about refining. Twenty years later he was still spoken of with affection there by men in their fifties. 'Lovely feller he was. Used to take a pint with us up at Canning Town. And then we'd go to one of them stalls and he'd say: Come on, what about a couple of saveloys and two o'drip?' (two pieces of bread and dripping). He went in 1937 as a Director to Liverpool but joined the army in 1939, to be killed at Alamein in 1942.

The war was now surely on its way. Hitler had moved into the Rhineland in March 1936 and not a dog had barked. Up in Liverpool the new Refinery was a-building. At Thames a new system of employing boys was introduced. Prior to this lads were taken on at eighteen and were then discharged at twenty, to hang about. Under the new scheme they were switched to departments where they could be employed at a special rate until they were twenty-four to twenty-seven and eventually were able to be put in a permanent job. Hiring and firing, which had affected a third of the workforce was cut to less than 5 per cent.

Unemployment was high, hence the in-and-out system, for grown men needed the work. Oliver Lyle proposed to the Board that in order to offer more jobs the working-week should be reduced from forty-seven to thirty-nine hours for the same pay, thus making more places available. The Board approved but nothing came of it, for the Government would not permit it. The Plaistow head gate-keeper, Bill Tyzack,[1] recalled a man asking him if there were any jobs going. 'No. sorry, they're turning them off at present.' The man gave a little laugh. 'Oh', he said, 'I 'ope they're not shootin' them too'.

Although we are only two generations away from those days it is difficult to recapture what it all felt like. There were many personalities about; in the laboratory at Thames names like De 'Ath, Lodge, Snelling, Gandell, Hunt; there was a senior day-work foreman, Henry Bennet, whose physical structure, being spherical, earned him the nickname of 'Sorbo'. There was another Bennett (two 't's), whose son Bill, was later to become a pillar of the Raw Sugar Purchasing Department.

But, although unsung and in many cases unrecorded, for when things go well it is not news, they were extremely effective at what they doing. And if this account seems light-hearted and trivial it should not disguise the fact that they were all involved in raising the production–and productivity–of the Refineries to a peak which was hitherto unheard of. By 1939, Thames would be the largest Refinery in the world, turning out 14,000 tons a week, with an occasional summit of 16,000. Liverpool would be producing 10,000 tons a week and Plaistow 8,575 (thank you, O.L.). At Plaistow a brand new Refinery building, called the Pan House, had just been completed.

Towering 180 feet up, resplendent with huge glass windows–soon to be blacked out–set in its white concrete walls, and only over-topped by the chimneys of the new boilers installed simultaneously with it and operating at the then uncommonly high pressure of 400 lb. a square inch (O.L. was a steam expert and a daring innovator), this great edifice would soon be a land-mark for the Luftwaffe. Yet at the same time, because of its indestructibility it would also be a symbol of hope to the district. (And, indeed, the top of the Pan House, where the air raid watch would be kept, although it felt a bit close to the Luftwaffe, was probably one of the safest places to be during an attack.) Within, the principle used in the first refinery of 1882 was adopted. Everything must start at the top and then descend by gravity in order to avoid wasteful use of power in pumping up again.

Four new shift managers joined Plaistow in 1939–the two Rowan brothers, Donald and Colin, and a little later Christopher King and Jimmie Boyle. They were all Territorials and would soon be in the Army. Christopher King and Donald Rowan would be killed and Jimmie Boyle would contract some obscure illness in India and die of it. Only Colin would come back.

[1] His niece, Margaret, is that marvellous actress.

Hitler had by now long since carried out the rape of Austria, and it is nine months after the Munich crisis of September 1938. There was an impalpable menace in the air everywhere, paralysing the will of some politicians, making all activities – a Cambridge May Week Ball, a summer holiday, a visit to a musical (Doing the Lambeth Walk – Oy!), earning a living at sugar refining – seem brittle and unreal. (An Oxford don, dining in Hall after correcting examination papers, was heard to say: 'The standard of marking is going to have to be lowered this year. After all, if a man is going to be some corner of a Foreign Field, one hesitates to plough him.' . . .)

'If only', many people felt, 'they'd get *on* with it. We *can't* go on like this.'

The I.R.A. selected this period to introduce their own insidious form of activity, aiming at industrial targets but also harming innocent individuals, particularly in Liverpool. Some damage was done, some I.R.A. men caught and executed. At Love Lane mobile patrols were set up, armed only with faith and blunt instruments, to keep watch on the perimeter of the Refinery. Fortunately it was not attacked.

Then it was September 3rd, 1939 and the lamps went out again all over Europe, much more completely than they ever had in 1914, for the blackout was something to be taken much more seriously this time, since the Luftwaffe was known to have those huge fleets of bombers . . .

But Winston Churchill expressed not for the last time the feelings of Britain when he said in the House of Commons as that first accidental air raid alert was given and people looked fearfully at the skies: 'There is peace in our hearts this Sunday morning.'

Belize–the new factory at Orange Walk (Liberdad).

CHAPTER TWELVE

1939–1945

*'And, Lord, bestow Thy special care
On One-Eight-Nine Cadogan Square.'*
('Westminister Abbey, September 1938': anon but probably John Betjeman.)

It would in fact be 52 not 189 Cadogan Square when the time came. For now, as Sellers Tate explains: 'The Germans had defaulted on some blank Czechs who had been filled in by Neville Chamberlain and anybody who *was* anybody went to war . . .' This included Tate & Lyle. During the first six months of this clash of arms, people probably wondered as they went in and out of Refinery gates whether the place would still look like this tomorrow or next week. For rather a long time it did, but not for ever.

The call-up was better managed than it had been in 1914. Territorials like Morton Oliphant, the Rowans, Nibs Hiscocks and lots more, went at once. Ian Lyle, Kenneth Brown, and others were in the R.N.V.R. so they also went.

'Name's Lyle? What do you do in peacetime?' a Captain R.N. asked Ian. 'Make sugar with a fellow called Tate' said Ian economically. 'What d'you mean?–Oh, you actually *do*.'

Many were not allowed to join up. Jo Whitmee, Peter Runge, Jim Hobbs, Bill North and a host of others. They were in nationally important jobs and could not be spared. Fred Sudbury had quite a struggle getting Vernon Tate to agree to release him to join the Royal Engineers.

A special war bonus was paid to the work force from December 1939, 4 s. a week for men, 3 s. for women–it would be increased at intervals during the war. The Refineries at first worked continuously from 10.00 p.m. on Sunday till 7.00 p.m. the following Saturday. Shift changes were now made at 7.00 a.m., 1.00 p.m. and 7.00 p.m. so as to be carried out as far as possible during daylight. (There were variations in Liverpool.)

In order to compensate for loss of earnings to those who were called up, special allowances were paid, starting in 1940, to men who had been in the firm before the war, of the rate they had been earning less 45 s. a week (the average Service pay). (Tate & Lyle are believed to be one of the first companies to do this.) Key workers were discouraged from volunteering and if they did so and were under thirty they were warned that they might forfeit the special allowance. Quite a number did volunteer. They were not docked when the time came.

The respite between the Munich crisis and the declaration of War, and then the six months of Phoney War were useful in enabling the refineries

E   H

D

A

C

B

'What's it like down there?' September 7th, 1940. Taken from one of the second of three waves of 182 German bombers which came in from the S.S.E. Bombing continued all night.
A: Burt Boulton of Heywoods Oil Tanks. B: Thames Refinery, West Premises, Raw Sugar Yard C: Smoke cloud over Silvertown Rubber Factory. D: End of Silvertown Way, Plaistow Wharf Refinery. E: Silvertown Way. F: Beckton Gas Works. G: Junction of Sewer Road and Tilbury by-pass. H: Sewer Outfall Road.

This is what it was like. Th
yard at Plaistow after a rai

to become fully prepared against air attack. Arrangements had been extremely sketchy in September 1938, but thereafter a great deal was done. Glass windows were replaced with tinplate or board or bricked in, air raid shelters built, headquarter centres established with emergency communications. Key areas were given steel shelters for those who had to be there after the imminent danger signal sounded. Emergency systems for supplying electricity and water to fight fires, were installed. Senior men like Bill Theakston and Bill Bartlett at Plaistow, Tommy Taylor at Thames, were trained in air raid precautions and then themselves trained the squads in the Refineries. At each Refinery there were between 800 and 1,000 men and women volunteers, trained in fire-fighting, rescue, first aid, and decontamination. Some were wardens. The cost was of the order of £500 per week at each place. The drill for a crash shut-down was first elaborated and then simplified and speeded up, until it took only seven minutes from full melt to shut down, without blowing off tell-tale steam. Meantime all those not needed at key points, some 500 men and 1,000 girls in each refinery, could be got into shelter in under four minutes. By the spring of 1940 there were those who wondered if all this was really necessary. It was still *la drôle de guerre*.

Meantime sugar had been placed on ration from mid-February 1940. The measure was introduced by Alan Lennox-Boyd, M.P., Parliamentary Under-secretary at the Ministry of Food. Twenty-five years later, as Viscount Boyd of Merton and after a distinguished political career, he would become a part-time director of Tate & Lyle. Now, however, he was determined to join the Navy. It took time but, after something of a row with Mr. Churchill in May 1940, he persuaded the new Prime Minister to let him go. He served in Coastal Forces like Ian Lyle.

Rationing, accompanied by a total stop to any export trade, meant a huge reduction in melt. By the middle years of the war, Thames would be doing only 5,500 tons a week against 14,000 and Plaistow 3,200 compared with 8,575. There was much discussion about concentrating on one Refinery only, to save steam, coal and manpower. In the end both were kept going, efforts being made to reduce steam and coal consumption, because only Plaistow made Golden Syrup, the most economical 'preserve' in the shops and under heavy demand, and only Thames made cubes. Just in case, either Refinery could have temporarily taken over had the other been badly damaged. Types of pack were drastically reduced in number from over 120 to 50, for grocers could not, with rationing, stock a large variety. The demand for cubes fell, and from 6,500 moulds a week in 1939 production fell to a mere 800 in 1940, only justifying the use of one shift. Thames converted much of its plant in order to dehydrate potatoes, cabbages and carrots for the Ministry of Food, and its fitting-shops produced gun parts, spares, shuttering for gun emplacements and gas producers for motor vehicles for the Ministry of Supply.

What Oliver Lyle called the 'technical demoralization' of the First War

was less evident in the Second, but despite all efforts, sugar loss rose from
0·98 per cent to 2·25 per cent, and water and steam consumption
increased. Since Golden Syrup was in such demand, an unintentional lowering
of standards came about gradually, the colour becoming darker and
the 'ash', which is what decides the taste, becoming less. At Thames and
Liverpool, under encouragement from the authorities, a syrup was
produced by a different process, using an enzyme called invertase. The
Lyles insisted that it be called Tates' Syrup, not Lyles' Golden Syrup, and
a few years after the war ended and sugar became more available, it was
rapidly dropped because of its quality.

The sugar ration at first was $\frac{3}{4}$ lb., later $\frac{1}{2}$ lb. a week. Packing these
quantities by hand was costly and slow, so in the end only 1 lb. and 2 lb.
packets were produced, and the ration was made fortnightly. Paper
became short and the packets went out without a wrapper. They leaked,
and were generally unsatisfactory. A local food controller – typical of the
petite bureaucratie – tried to insist that sugar should be rationed in the refinery
canteens as it was in ordinary catering establishments. It took a long time
to persuade him that people in the refineries need only fill their pockets
before coming to eat. Golden Syrup was on a 'points' rationing system – i.e.
it was a can of Syrup or a pair of socks or half a shirt. Employees were
allowed to buy one damaged tin a month.

The Phoney War ended abruptly and maps in the newspapers showed
those broad, curving arrows of the pincer movements scourging Europe.
Early in June there was the miracle of Dunkirk but Mr. Churchill made
the sobering point that wars are not won by evacuations, and then went on
to add that we would fight on the beaches or anywhere else and with
anything that came to hand, and people were cheered by the fact that we
were on our own and playing this one at home. It was, indeed, as the Prime
Minister put it, a little like the old days when the Armada came sweeping
up the Channel. Nobody who was not then alive can imagine what it really
felt like. General Sir Edward Spears says of those days:[1] 'Our generation
has suffered much and endured a good deal but we are to be envied by the
world, for we once passed through an intense fire and light that burnt out
everything mean and selfish in us, leaving only a common purpose and a
common unity . . .'

It was a sign of this when a girl employee, Doris Martineau, in the staff
mess at Thames, suggested opening a collection in the firm to buy a
bomber for the R.A.F. The fund ran from July 12th, 1940 to September
28th. Shareholders, employees, everyone contributed. There were fun fairs
and raffles. People had voluntary stoppages made in their pay. The ex-
Premier of Canada, Mr. Bennett, addressed a mass-meeting of employees.
By October 31st, £20,247 5s. 10d. had come in, much of it from
employees, and a Whitley Bomber called 'Golden Lion' was presented to
the R.A.F. A plaque was set up at Thames by the Ministry of Aircraft

[1] *Assignment to Catastrophe*, Vol. II, p. 4 (Heinemann, 1954).

Production, by way of thanks. On it were the words: 'They shall mount up with wings as eagles.'

Tate & Lyle had their own Home Guard units in Liverpool under Sergeant-Major Geoff Gough, in London under Jim Cary, a phenomenal character. He had joined the Queen's Bays as a boy soldier in the South African war and become a member of their Rough-Riding Squad. Commissioned as a Lieutenant-Quarter-Master in the Welsh Regiment in 1914 he had later transferred to the Denbigh Yeomanry, where he was noticed by Sir Ernest Tate, Honorary Colonel of that Regiment. He came to Thames as Foreman of Raw Sugar Landing. In 1940, now in his late fifties, he commanded the London Refineries' Home Guard, rising by 1945 to Lieut-Colonel and being awarded an O.B.E. There is extant a picture of him with his officers and N.C.O.s, who included Majors Tappin, Machon, Arthur Green, Captains Whitmee, Hobbs, Taylor, Lieutenants Howlett and Gee, Louis Tate, and 2nd Lieutenants Hayman, North, Alf and Cecil Caulfield, Ian Rose, Sid Hutchins and many others. Pensioned off after the war he would be unable to bear idleness and would insist on returning to a variety of jobs until finally, at eighty and rather deaf, he sounded the retreat. He died in his ninety-ninth year in 1976.

The 'intense fire and light' came to London, Greenock and Liverpool in September 1940, and lasted at this stage for well over six months on and off. Thames was hit many times with high explosives and incendiary bombs, one of the worst raids being an all night one on September 7th, 1940, the heaviest of all being on April 19th, again all night. The air raid precautions were most effective and only two minor casualties were reported. The sites and numbers of the bombs were meticulously recorded on a map.

Plaistow, too, was severely attacked, six H.E. bombs and one parachute mine exploding in the refinery and sixty-one incendiary bombs landing on it. London had sixty-nine days and seventy-nine nights with raids. Oliver Lyle remarked laconically: 'It was not pleasant but we got used to it.' Unexploded parachute mines were defused by the Navy. On one occasion Siegfried de Whalley,[2] who had recently bought a new car, drove it out before the Navy got to work, just in case. On another occasion some 300 girls in the Syrup Filling were unable to get to shelter because the route was accidentally blocked. It was lucky, because the bridge they had to cross was destroyed just as they would have been traversing it. On yet another, little Mark O'Connell was observed dancing round an incendiary bomb, muttering imprecations about Hitler.

Only one man was actually killed at Plaistow, W. Kinnison who ran straight into a bomb while on his way to shelter, but thirteen Plaistow men and women were killed at home and in the streets and a similar number from Thames. Mr. J. Burns of the Thames first aid team was awarded the B.E.M. for rescuing people when houses opposite the Refinery were hit.

[2] See Chapter Twenty-six.

Walkers Refinery was severely hit and put out of action for six weeks.

Liverpool Refinery was comparatively little damaged, even during the May 1941 blitz. The only occasion when it was actually hit was the night of Sunday, December 22nd, 1940 when three H.E. bombs, apparently intended for Manchester, which was that night's target, landed instead at Love Lane.

There were, of course, occasional laughs to compensate for the involuntary shivers caused by the wail of the syren or the whistle and thud of the bombs. An official from the Ministry of Labour rang Plaistow during a very heavy raid, demanded to speak to the manager, and when Alex Lyle came on, asked: 'How many men work in your factory?' Alex already had enough to think about. 'About half', he said briskly and ended the conversation.[3]

On the night of May 9/10th 1941 there was a fire-bomb raid on the City of London. On three occasions 21 Mincing Lane was hit, but the caretaker, W. H. Lessware and his family put out the fires. Three fires at the north end of the Lane got out of control and by now the watermains were empty. 21 Mincing Lane was burnt out, and with it all papers and documents except those which had been earlier evacuated to Pangbourne and the contents of the safes. These, sent to Thames, were easily opened by the fitters there, though the contents were scorched and the Secretary's gramophone records melted. (What were they doing there?) Oliver Lyle commented: 'Footnote to burglars. Don't fool around with nitro-glycerine on the front of a safe. Take a tin-opener to its back.'

Vernon Tate, who had for some time lived at 52 Cadogan Square, S.W.1, had arranged to put this house at the Company's disposal in the event of damage to Mincing Lane. Now he did so, continuing to camp out on the top floor. (He always resolutely refused to go anywhere near an air raid shelter.) Early in the war his residence had been the cause of a meeting with a relative, F. H. Tate, poet in the making, who at that time was stationed with his Army unit at No. 54. Vernon had complained to the C.O. at 54 about noise and probably language as well and the C.O. sent Tony in to see 'this old Tate chap' whom Tony had in fact met only once or twice. Blood was thicker than bad language, however. There was a rather good lunch at the Savoy and no further complaints from Vernon who had insisted on being host to the C.O.

52 Cadogan Square is reputed to have been built by a De la Rue, who as a maker of playing cards had a fancy for the number, and caused thereby some inconvenience to the other occupants of the Square. At some time its ground floor, main staircase and ballroom had been heavily panelled. Admired by some, this is looked on by others as in faultless bad taste. The Lord obliging with his special care, it was now a welcome port in a storm and became the Head Office of Tate & Lyle. It would remain so until

---

[3] Pope John XXIII later made the same reply when asked how many people worked in the Vatican.

1949, thereafter becoming a perching place for visitors to the firm from abroad, and later a conference centre with sleeping accommodation for the many senior members of overseas staff when in London.

On the morning of May 10th, 1941 those assembling there found they had no papers, no files, no books. Someone wanted to write a letter, so the first file was born. The bank was telephoned, to establish the state of the account; then the customers to see who owed money to whom. About a couple of weeks later all was running smoothly and there were no arguments as to the figures with either creditor or debtor. After all, there was a war on, and people helped each other.

By mid-1941, of the 3,600 people employed at Thames and Plaistow together, 17 per cent or so had had their homes destroyed or made uninhabitable, 15 per cent had been evacuated, and for those who found it impossible to go home each day – 8 per cent – arrangements had been made for dormitories, and a couple of hundred men and girls slept at each refinery, separated of course for propriety's sake. Buses were difficult, and a fleet of twenty-four coaches was hired for months to bring in people who had had to be evacuated from their homes. This cost about £500 a week between the two refineries. People whose houses were damaged had their furniture removed free by the Company's vans. Not only did people help each other, they took a pride in turning up for work. Coming from homes without gas, light, or sometimes even water, they would arrive on time, the men spruce and clean-shaven and the girls with hair tidy and nails varnished. As they had trouble getting to a hairdresser the Company started a girls' hairdressing department and beauty parlour, the one at Plaistow being run by Jessie Wiltshire, daughter of a Shift Manager, who commented that there were just as many nits in the hair in Bond Street, where she had worked, as at Plaistow. A girl who remembered those days reported to the *Tate & Lyle Times* fifteen years later that the place was like a beauty chorus. People worked hard, played hard, and were proud to look nice.

Across the water, 22 miles from England was Hitler's *Festungs-Europa,* and although the raids stopped in June 1941 – Hitler turned on Russia on the 22nd of that month, calling the operation 'Barbarossa', and Uncle Joe became at once a grasping, curmudgeonly, difficult ally – the onrush of the Nazis seemed irresistible. The black, menacing arrows had passed through Yugoslavia, Greece, Albania, Crete. They were now deep into Russia. Minor successes such as Wavell's in the desert against the Italians were countered by the German Afrika Korps. Rastafari's Ethiopia, over-run in 1935 by Mussolini, was freed, the first victim then the first to be liberated. But the sinkings of ships went on – it was 4 million tons each year in 1940 and 1941 and when the U.S.A. was brought in as an ally by the Japanese attack on Pearl Harbour this figure would be doubled.

More and more men were required for the forces or for armament production. At first this had corresponded to the reduction in melt, but within eighteen months it became essential to fill men's jobs with girls. Some, like Amelia Migliori, had done this in the First War and did so again. There were at first plenty of volunteers, for example, at Plaistow, two girls on each shift boiling vacuum pans in the Pan House, and each pair of centrifugal machines was worked by girls. In the can-making, one girl became brilliant as a fitter and in the packets two sisters became dabs at adjusting sensitive Southall & Smith's weighing machines. Their names are worth mentioning. (There were so many like them elsewhere in the firm). Here they are: Ada Arnold, Ivy Guile, Lottie Johnson, Daisy Lewis, Ivy Sands, Tilly Willis, Rose Hale, Peggy Burrows, Mable Kebbell, Gladys Lewis, Ivy Lewis . . . Rose Hale and Tilly Willis starred in a film of girls doing men's jobs. The unions were a little cagey about the girls' rates of pay, making it clear that while they were apparently doing the same work as men in fact this was only so until something went wrong, when men had to be brought in. In the end the unions agreed to 75 per cent of men's rates and the girls did not appear to have any sense of grievance. (There was one thing that they *always* had difficulty mastering and that was which way to turn a valve.)

By 1942 over half of each Refinery was 'manned' by girls, trim in their boiler suits and shirts. They would be there until 1946. The volunteer girls of the earlier war days however became hard to replace until women were registered, when they came to work from nearby, apparently to avoid being sent away from home.

As in most wars there were good things as well as bad. There was the improvement in the Company's medical facilities. A doctor all day, and two part-time nurses on each shift became the normal rule. Canteen facilities improved. Make-do-and-mend led to the improvement of various processes, to the formation of pig clubs (rabbits were not a success owing to a high 'unexplained mortality'), to the introduction of long service certificates. Wages increased, and so did war bonuses. (The unions objected to the use of the Cost of Living Index as a guide because it was not realistic and insisted on more than could be justified by reference to it.) Coal went up to £2 3s. 0d. per ton (before the war it had been 18s. 3d.). Entry to the Refineries required a pass for security reasons. Holidays were a mockery, for travel was a nightmare in rare, slow, crowded trains, petrol was strictly rationed and soon the seaside was one continuous restricted area. To reduce journeys to work, people went on a new shift system, twelve hours on and twenty-four off, and three long week-ends counted as a week's holiday.

Men would come back occasionally in khaki, in dark blue or light blue, feeling a little strange and out of place, perhaps finding the changes uncomfortable. Some men, an increasing number, would never come back, as Alamein was followed by 'Torch', Sicily by Salerno and Anzio, the preparations surged forward for 'Overlord', and – unknown to all but a few in Britain – the V1 and the V2 were being developed. The Emergency Work

Order was introduced. This made it difficult to fire or otherwise penalize anyone. It also made it difficult for anyone to leave of his own free will. In effect discipline was handed over to the local National Service Officer. It was a little like serving in some country behind the Iron Curtain, although that phrase had not yet been coined.

For long, air raids were so scarce that when the new *Vergeltungs-Waffene* began to arrive in 1944 it came as an unpleasant shock. From June 18th to August 31st, 1944, the V1 period, none of these little brutes actually landed near the Refineries, although roof spotters on the Pan House recorded sighting three-quarters of all that reached the London area. They themselves are remembered as urging the V1's to move on further. 'Go *on*! Go *on*! Whitechapel Road's only another couple of miles', they would shout. V1's upset the girls more than the bombs did. Jack Couzens, in the Hesser Department, coaxed them to courageous acceptance of these phenomena, which, as one of them put it: 'seemed so un-human like'. Sometimes in the early morning, people on the Pan House roof could see the vapour trails of V2's launched 150 miles away in Holland. None of these landed on the Refineries, but one day Peter Runge and Ian Lyle, driving in separate cars through Poplar, each thought the other had been hit when a V2 landed between them.

Then, suddenly, it was May 8th, 1945, and the Refineries' loud-speaker systems, so often used to carry the news of air raid alerts, to announce this, that or the other message from outside, to convey a Christmas or New Year greeting from the resident Refinery Director, broadcast the words: 'Tomorrow will be V.E. Day. The Refinery will now shut down as soon as possible.'

The Second War to End All Wars was almost over. V.J. Day would follow three months later thanks in no small measure to the discovery announced by Rutherford and Chadwick in the Year of the Ampersand that the atom could be split.

CHAPTER THIRTEEN
'As if Nothing Had Happened'

'Let not concealment, like a worm i'the bud feed on thy damask cheek'
(William Shakespeare, *Twelfth Night*, ca. 1601)

Demobilization after the Second War like the Call-up when it began, was better managed than in the First. Men and women were 'phased out' of the Forces according to a system. Mind you, the authorities were glad to see you go and doctors seemed delighted to pass you fit unless you were an obvious case of G.P.I. They (the authorities I mean) sent you to Wembley Stadium with a special ration card which entitled you to one suit, shirt, tie, underclothes (a bit scratchy) socks and shoes–or, if you were (F) rather than (M), with a coat and skirt, stockings, shoes, blouse and a Ministry of Supply two-way stretch. It was a little like 1984 before its time but all quite fair and you were used to doing things by numbers.

There had been a change in the political situation. In July 1945 the people of Britain, with their customary sense of gratitude had slung out Mr. Churchill a few weeks after V.E. Day. (They had done much the same 214 years earlier to his ancestor the first Duke of Marlborough.) And now, it seemed, politicians were divided into two kinds, the Guilty Men who had started the War and the Blameless Men who had won it with a little help from Mr. Churchill. From now on, Britain, said the B.M.'s, would bask in the Broad Sunny Uplands which had been promised to them when peace should break out again. (The Army Education Corps and the like had long been giving lectures on Post Hostilities Britain.)

Was this a good time to be looking for a job in industry? What did Tate & Lyle, for example, seem like to a demobbed chap who had gone from Oxford into the Navy? Let us say that he had by chance during the war met Lieut.-Commander Kenneth Brown, D.S.C., R.N.V.R., who had said casually: 'Well, when the war's over, if ever it is, why not come and see us?' So, still waiting for demob, and therefore in uniform and feeling a bit of a Charlie, you Went and Saw Them, wondering whether on arrival you might be torn apart by an angry mob shouting the London E.16 equivalent of '*À la lanterne*.' Not a bit of it. Tube, trolley-bus and Bob's your uncle. To the right of the gate there were temporary wooden shacks–the office had been demolished by the Luftwaffe. There was a pervasive smell of old bones. Can sugar refining *really* pong like this? you wondered. Later you learned that it was the aroma involved in the production of Knights' Castile soap next door.

A very smart commissionaire, Wally Galloway, saluted. You were shown up into a gloomy office in a converted warehouse, whose low head room was reminiscent of one of H.M. ships. Kenneth, looking strangely undressed in a gents' natty (also from Wembley?) handed you over to a middle-aged chap called George Rutty who took you at a smart gallop round the *vast* premises. George had been in the Army in Mesopotamia in the First War and was full of tales about what they got up to there–mostly, it seemed, No Good. People said 'Hullo, George' and grinned at you too. After this, by now relatively at ease, you were asked to stay for lunch. Good, homely food it was and no nonsense. (One day the pretty blonde waitress was to say to Ian Lyle: 'You can't have roast potatoes. Cook says it's *boiled* with cold dinner, see?')

There was a short chap of about sixty with a husky voice–Oliver Lyle, and a taller, deceptively casual one (Ian Lyle). They were informal but very sharp.

'You were a chemist', said O.L. 'so you must know a bit of maths. Ever played around with tensors?' (What a hell of a question! But, ah! Wait.)

'Only the Riemann-Christopherson tensor, sir, actually.' (It had been mentioned in some classy whodunit read by chance a week earlier. But what *was* it anyway? Take a deep breath.)

Ah. All's well.

'Ian', said Oliver abruptly, 'Have you any questions'?

There was a lot of probing of a general sort, and you felt you were being given a thorough work-over. At the end of it, Ian said: 'I should know, but what sort of degree did you get? Oh, really? Well, it couldn't have mattered less. *I* was sent down.'

Then, they said, you must come back again to lunch. And, each time you did, you met different people: Peter Runge, dark, amusing and clever; Jo Whitmee–there was a photograph of him sitting astride a landmine ('Actually it had been defused', he explained helpfully); John Carmichael, Alex Laurie, George Payne, Charlie Allen, Jim Hobbs and many others. Later you gathered that each time you had been carefully scrutinized. If more than a very few expressed doubts you were not taken on. But the atmosphere was so agreeable, they were so much nicer than all those other industrial chaps you'd been interviewed by, that you wanted to join, even if it meant shift work, even if for your trial year you would be paid less than others had offered.[1] ('While you're learning,' they said soberly, 'you're a Costly Item'.) At one of these interviews, a very senior chap (Philip Lyle) spoke of the great future for Research. Another (Walter Johnson) disagreed. 'You must remember, young man, that business means making money', he said sharply.

'But', said many of them, 'we're a bit tired. And we welcome chaps with fresh ideas'. And they *were* tired, people like that nice Arthur Greene, who had served in the First War and, during the Second, while Ian and

[1] Tim Duggan, some years later, felt the same way. He later became the Legal Eagle of Tate & Lyle.

Kenneth and others had been away in the Forces, had kept things going, doing A.R.P. and Home Guard in his spare time. They meant what they said. They did welcome new ideas.

You learned your way about. You spent weeks in each department doing–a bit ham-handedly–the various jobs, getting to know how tedious they can be, or how messy and sweaty. Tom Willis, union delegate in the Char House watched you get hot and filthy in a char cistern and then offered a bath. 'Those were put in twenty-five years ago', someone said, 'And at first people tore the taps off and took them home for a lark'.

You met a whole bunch of new people, who showed you the ropes most generously; diminutive Mark Connell, vast Albert Reed, silent Joe Tyrell, plump Bob Tann, north-country Sam Holmes, dead-pan wise-cracker Steve Chambers, tiny Dan Fitzgerald. The last-named had sometimes a whip-lash tongue. Once, on the internal phone, he had said to the chap controlling the flow of liquors: 'How much showing on the gauge for these tanks?'

'Three foot, Dan.'

'Well, there's free foot free of effing foam all over effing floor.'

You were being watched, but kindlily. Tea began to come out of your ears, strong, highly sweetened, the kind of stuff used for curing leather. Alf Cornwall, foreman of C shift in the Press House, had a wide selection of scatological tales and usually retailed them at the witching hour of 0400. When you got home you smelt of very strong hand-rolled cigarettes and the early stages in the production of Castile soap.

As conditions eased, each shift–they all had their own persona–began to organize biennial 'socials', and great fun they were. Mick Gorst, the fastest man on two feet–he never used a lift but was reputed to be able to get round the entire Refinery in seven minutes flat–began it all, aided by the giant Harry Tree. 'Mr. Oliver's highly delighted', said Mick as he explained the arrangements for a Social. Then you were invited to boxing matches. Sam Dunlop, one of yet another large Plaistow family, a most gallant light-heavy-weight, once fought one of those desperately moving losing fights, which left the spectator feeling like an eye-witness of Thermopylae . . .

(Apologies to Thames, Love Lane and Greenock, where it was much the same but one must try to write as one knows.) At Thames they had just begun to take on Shift Managers–John Ellyatt (son of Sidney) and Jimmy Somner, both also from the Navy. Colin Lyle, Philip's son, came to Plaistow. So did George Cowpe and John Willsher.

At the behest of the Minister of Labour ('My name is Isaacs, *not* Solomon'), there was a bout of a thing called Training Within Industry, a kind of do-it-yourself personnel course. Designed for a wartime munitions factory where 6,000 people and 300 foremen, none of whom had ever met each other, had been suddenly thrown together, it may have had its points.

It seemed a little *de trop* at Tate & Lyle, where people actually knew each other already.

At Thames it was also decided to introduce a formal Works Council, probably rightly. Whereas at Plaistow, Oliver and Ian Lyle were active and Oliver's son John was a trainee Shift Manager (he would one day be Chairman), it was now nearly ten years since Vernon Tate had been continuously at Thames. At Love Lane, Geoffrey Fairrie was there and his sons, Tony and James, also back from the war, were training too, and Morton Oliphant, Ian Lyle's cousin, was a resident director. In the end the Works Council remained a Thames speciality, effective and most certainly in keeping with the spirit of the age.

There were offshoots at Plaistow. When the rather scruffy works canteen was replaced by a well appointed restaurant in what had fifty years earlier been the Chocolate Factory, a democratically elected Works Restaurant Committee was established. And when an almost insoluble problem about the rate of pay for a particular group of men threatened to get out of hand, a special committee was set up, with Tom Willis in the chair and a Shift Manager as secretary. Deadlock was near, and Tommy said uncomfortably: 'Trouble is, it's a bloody awful job and you can't do it all your life. They want a differential of 2 d. an hour and I don't think the rest will grudge it.'

Oliver and Ian, advised of this, said: 'It *is* a bloody awful job. Would they take 1½ d.?' They wouldn't, said Tommy. So it was 2 d. in the end, and was not in fact grudged by the rest. There were other similar adjustments from time to time, rapidly sorted out, and this all resulted in the general feeling that although the buck had to stop somewhere, it would never do so with a squeal of brakes and the screech of tortured metal.

This civilized, flexible, sensitive approach seemed to embrace everyone concerned, down to and including that legendary figure, 'The Boy at The Gate'. ('Who told you that'?–'The Boy at the Gate' . . . 'How am I supposed to know that?'–'Ask the Boy at The Gate').

There was, too, an indication, only slowly discerned by the New Boy, who was finding it quite enough to keep in mind the complexities of a refinery about four times the size of a battleship and ten times as complicated, that this strange Company, not entirely anachronistic, yet not entirely (what is the opposite? O.L. where is your black book?) 'katachronistic' was not blinkered. It was not just an entity involved in refining sugar. It *traded* in sugar, a dark mystery. It had once been involved in beet sugar. It had interests in what then sounded glamorous places–Trinidad and Jamaica. And it also had begun to diversify, tentatively, cautiously, into businesses at one remove from its own–lighterage and road transport.

To the newcomer these two developments were personified in two individuals, met at intervals. One was Nibs Hiscocks, who had left Thames Refinery to serve in the Army, ending up as a Major. A jolly, round-faced, affable man, and very easy to get on with, it was announced in 1947 that he was to be transferred to something called Pease Transport. It sounded like something out of a nursery rhyme – Pease Pudding Hot, Pease Pudding Cold – until you learned that it was the Company which ran Tate & Lyle's road transport fleet – all those smart-looking dark-blue vehicles with the crest of the royal warrant holder on the side.

The other was a chap – already mentioned – called Colonel Fred Sudbury, R.E. He was good-looking, clever, perhaps a bit angular – he was a little rude about the Navy, which, coming from what we naval chaps call a Pongo, seemed a bit off. (Who, after all, had extracted them from this or that place and ferried them to another during the war?) He was Managing Director of a Tate & Lyle associated company called Silvertown Services Ltd., which ran the lighterage system that supplied the London refineries with raw sugar.

Both these companies had come into the system in 1937–8, when Vernon Tate had just become Chairman, and they were the apples of his eye, for, while associated with refinery operations, they bore within them the seed of further developments. And they were also a part of Vertical Integration.

Of them and of their offshoots one would learn more later. It was now enough to be as sure as possible that one knew how the 'battery system' of cha·ring, the second and third crop in the Wharf House, and the Riddle Room worked, and to be getting to know those who worked them.

It had its drawbacks as a job, but it had its advantages too, the main one being the genuine warmth of the Company's atmosphere.

Yet all the time, in post-war Britain, there was a worm i' the bud. It became apparent during 1948 that there was something up, particularly at Plaistow Wharf. It was not overt. People were as kind to each other as ever, and showed it in the gentle way they took the mickey out of you. A shift manager, for example, on the 2 – 10 p.m. shift, having changed at 9.30 into a black tie in order to join his fiancée at a party, was on his way out of the gate, carrying his day clothes in a case. The gang from the Raw Sugar Landing seemed to be watching him darkly as they themselves checked out. Eventually one of them said: 'What sort of instrument do *you* play'? Or there was little old 'Brucie', who looked after the wash-off cocks in the Golden Syrup Department on B shift, and who seemed shocked to see one arrive by bus. 'You should be coming in more posh-like', he said severely.

There were subtle, disturbing indications. Well-established, unwritten conventions began to be challenged in long-drawn-out dialectical meetings, generally at the initiative of certain craftsmen's trade unions. Members of staff such as foremen-fitters, who, because of their trade were members of these unions, were put under pressure. When talking privately to 'The Management' they insisted genuinely that their loyalty was to the firm – many of them were second or third generation – but, they said, 'It's getting kind of awkward'.

After a good deal of independent investigation it was clearly established beyond any shadow of doubt that three, possibly four, new employees in the craftsmen's departments which were responsible for maintenance, were fully paid-up members of the Communist Party, planted on the Company in order to stir up trouble. One of them belonged to a union which at that time was openly Communist-controlled. Its Area Officer began to be a frequent visitor, clever, smooth, difficult to deal with. (He had been observed, up the Canning Town Road, changing in a pub from his smart city suit into something more like a workers' rig, before coming to the Refinery.)

After a lot of heart-searching – Oliver Lyle hated the whole business – it was agreed that the trouble-stirrers, who were all new, and, except perhaps for one, could not be expected to have any particular loyalty to the firm, must somehow go. And, over Christmas 1948 the un-Christmassy decision was taken to reduce the admittedly high allocation to maintenance. It was important not to 'victimize', so about forty new men in the maintenance departments were paid off in January, and all except four were taken back within a matter of weeks. A sharp reaction was expected from the work-force as a whole, for it seemed a brutal thing to do. But there was none.

In one case it may have been brutal. In the other three, the individuals concerned got jobs easily elsewhere and were later heard of, gaily stirring it up wherever they went. The fourth case was a member of an old Plaistow family. For weeks afterwards he would stand silent, day after day, near the bus stop outside the gate. Oliver Lyle, a man of compassion, could not bear the sight and wanted to take him back, but the man's own family were against it. 'Old – went a bit off his trolley', they said. 'Better leave things be.' In the end he went away. But it was awful at the time.

A few weeks later there was a surprise explanation of why the whole matter had taken place without a major upheaval. Bill Migliori, Tom Willis and others were at a meeting with the Personnel Manager. Cups of tea were consumed and minor matters dealt with. Then at length Bill Migliori said: 'Reckon you should have done that months ago. You were weak.'

'Done what?'

'Oh, come on. They were just as much of a bloody nuisance to us as they were to you.'

'More', said another voice with feeling.

'Now', said Bill, 'we can go on doing things *our* way'.

That chirpy old Sellers Tate, writing twenty years later, had this to say of 1946 onwards: 'After much blood, toil, tears and sweat, and a certain amount of despair, fire-watching, and Ministry Controls, there came the Piece of Luneberg Heath (or Lili Marlene) and Leonardan Vernon decided to CARRY ON AS IF NOTHING HAD HAPPENED.'

So there was a certain consensus of opinion within the Firm that things should go on more or less as before. But things never do. That same historian went on to say: 'The POWERS THAT WERE decided to nationalize sugar, mainly because it was nice and sweet and cheap and popular, and therefore a BAD THING IN THE WELFARE STATE. So several ravenous politicians, crying "Up Clem and Attlee", vigorously and verbally attacked Leonardan Vernon.'

To begin with such stuff was considered at 52 Cadogan Square – yes, we are still there, thank you, Lord – as a little akin to the crackling of thorns under the pot. 'Surely', they said to themselves as they sat in too small a boardroom in that Desirable Residence, 'It can't happen to US. Nobody' they argued, 'can be dotty enough to *want* to take on such a generally thankless and often dicey business. After all, didn't our fathers and grandfathers nearly go broke from time to time'?

But there is no knowing. There were people around who did. And what follows deserves a chapter to itself during which many a damask cheek may well go crimson with embarrassment. Or would, if their owners were still alive.

CHAPTER FOURTEEN

Mr. Cube and All That

I

'It can't happen here'
(Sinclair Lewis)

It is always unwise to say to oneself: 'It can't happen to me.' For as any philosopher will point out, that is just the moment when Fate is waiting in the wings with a sandbag.

This is the tale of how Tate & Lyle were alerted in time by deep breathing 'off stage–left', deduced that a Thing called Nationalization was loitering there with intent, and fought off a dastardly attack–aided by a champion called Mr. Cube. If occasionally the story seems biased to the right of the average reader of the *New Statesman*, kindly bear in mind that high feelings were aroused at the time. And if some of the speeches quoted appear in the late 1970s a little less than kind about bureaucrats and the like, let the reader reflect that he is by now probably so accustomed to bureaucrats that if he thinks of them at all they may seem like wasps at a picnic–a nuisance, but what can you do about them? The reader should also remind himself that 1984 is creeping up on us.

And the bureaucrats will not just go away. At least not until they are sixty-five (or sixty in the case of Les Girls), when they will receive an indexed pension for which you and I will pay unto the third and fourth generation.

Now that we seem to be in Holy Writ, it is perhaps worth noting that all this 1984 stuff can be put down to the fact that chaps like the late Marx–Karl, not Harpo–evolved a century or so ago the convenient thought that it is not merely O.K. but an act of positive virtue to break the Tenth Commandment. Few people, of course, are so literal as to covet their neighbour's manservant or his maidservant, for nowadays he hath not got one. But his ox, his ass, his income, and any shares he may own are fair game. It is all fearfully depressing and tedious, but just after the Second World War it was part of the Blue Print for Heaven.

In early 1949, a Socialist Government was still in power with a majority of 186. Coal, aviation and the Bank of England had been coveted into nationalization and gas, electricity and rail and road transport were now on the line. Keen fellows were asking for a further round of the same. One of these, a Mr. Ernest Davies M.P., had ever written two books on the subject: *National Capitalism* (1939) and *National Enterprise* (1946). Both combine a certain breathlessness with a whiff of Thomas Babington

Macaulay. Thus: '[In 1945] the floating vote had judged past governments on their failures and created a new Government for its promises. It had sold out the past and bought the future'. Or: 'Labour's case for nationalization cannot be separated from its general economic plans for the exploitation of the nation's resources in the best interests of the community'. Etc., etc., etc.

His only actual mention of sugar was a reference to the compensation paid to owners of beet sugar factories in 1936 as 'a scandal,'[1] but in a lecture early in 1949 at Ashridge College he was incautious enough to describe Tate & Lyle as 'one of the biggest rackets there is'. (He had to apologize for this slanderous statement and promise not to make it again).

Another M.P., Mr. Charles Smith, in *Britain's Food Supplies* (1940) was more specific. He gave the sugar refiners five black marks. One, the seven British refiners were 'in a monopoly position which enables them in peace and war to make very large profits'. (Come, come, Smith! A *monopoly* of *seven*? Where were you dragged up?) Two, like other industries, they had lent experts to the Government during the War and these 'might abuse their position in order to favour their companies'. (He admits, however, that this is not proven and is unlikely.) Three, Tate & Lyle had shares in the British Sugar Corporation Ltd. (We have seen why and how.) Four, Tate & Lyle 'had interests in the West Indies'. (So what?) And five, the Chairman of the Company had had the effrontery in 1938 to report 'excellent results from the manufacture of tins, packing containers, and also from its road haulage company'. (No! Did he really? The filthy Fascist swine.)

Mr. Smith concludes: 'Here is an opportunity for the extension of public control over a highly organized industry which profitably controls an article of everyday consumption'.

It should have been difficult for anyone to take him seriously, for his sense of realism is shown by his attitude to domestic beet sugar production. Bear in mind that this book came out in July 1940. Hitler's armies were twenty-two miles from Dover and his U-boats were rapidly getting into a position to cut off much of our seaborne supplies. Mr. Smith's contribution to the war effort was to suggest the abolition of home grown sugar. 'No tears should be shed over [it]. It has been exceedingly expensive and is defensible only on the ground that it is of benefit to agriculture.' But what about the war? Mr. Smith loftily says: 'There remains the defence argument, but this can be met by a policy of storage of stocks of sugar.' (In 1940? At what price? Where were the stocks to come from in a sugar-hungry world? What about the U-boats?)

If Tate & Lyle were unimpressed by such stuff, the Labour Party on the other hand began to show signs of taking it to heart. In *The Second Five Years* (1948), largely attributed to Mr. Ian Mikardo, the sugar industry was mentioned among others as 'suggesting itself for transfer to publicly owned production'. This was then apparently merely an idea.

[1] See page 106.

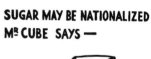

Mr. Cube at work.

VICKY'S
WEEK-END FANTASIA

'I SUPPOSE YOU'LL HAVE TO DO
THE CUBE DANCE WITH YOUR
SUGAR DADDY'

SAY "NO"
TO
NATIONALISATION

"Well, wot is it *this* time—speeding, obstruction, illegal propaganda?"

DOWNING ST.
ELEVEN DAYS

CET ANIMAL EST TRÈS MÉCHANT—
QUAND ON L'ATTAQUE IL SE DÉFEND

NATIONALISATION THREAT

LABOUR'S ZOO
MR
FRETFUL
PORCUBEPINE

Press cartoons from the
Nationalization Campaign.

Early in 1949, however, the national Press printed articles clearly based on official leaks from the inner coteries of the Labour Party. *The Times* of February 10th, for example, *The News Chronicle* of February 24th and *The Evening News* of March 19th, all mentioned sugar refining as being on the list. The Board of Tate & Lyle now become fully alerted to the danger.

The first mention of nationalization in the minutes of Board meetings of Tate & Lyle was on February 10th, which was the day when *The Times'* article was printed. The minute read: 'Every effort should be made to get the Company's name removed from any proposed list of industries to be nationalized. To this end it was considered that a considerable degree of propaganda would be necessary and Aims of Industry are prepared to submit a scheme for the consideration of the Board concerning various forms of propaganda, including the making of a film to be shown by mobile film units.'

Two of the younger members of the Board, Ian Lyle and Peter Runge, were authorized to discuss the matter further and incur any necessary expenses, but no propaganda schemes were to be started until Leonard Lyle, the President, and Vernon Tate, the Chairman, returned from a tour of inspection of the West Indies companies in early March.

The mention of Aims of Industry Ltd. is apt to raise hackles in the Hampstead homes of the trendy, where it is lumped in with grammar schools, pay beds, Mr. Ian Smith, and other Bad Things. This may at least in part be because of its anti-nationalization origins. It was formed in the mid 1940s by shareholders whose assets were being sequestered by nationalization, in an endeavour to ensure that Government paid a reasonable price for the shares. Its Director, Roger Sewill, had been in discussion with Ian Lyle in June 1948, and the latter now served on its Council. It was to be the chosen instrument in the propaganda battle which was to follow.

Writing soon after the campaign, Lord Lyle said that Mr. Cube was 'born in the Board Room of Tate & Lyle' then still at 52 Cadogan Square, since 21 Mincing Lane was still a hole in the ground, thanks to the Luftwaffe. There is, however, no record of this. Ian Lyle and Morton Oliphant, who were present, cannot now remember, and there have been claimants to Mr. Cube's genesis among members of Aims of Industry. It seems possible that either Aims of Industry or a Tate & Lyle Director may have suggested that a figure 'like Mr. Therm only made of sugar' would be useful. But in any case he did not appear for the first time in the Press until July 28th and his debut on the wrappers of sugar packets was not to be until October. By then much work had been done on propaganda, with relatively little effect. The campaign took time to get under way for the public is slow to react to an idea. And time was short. The next General Election could not be more than a year or so away.

II
'He either fears his fate too much . . .
(James Graham, First Marquis of Montrose, 1612–1650)

To win a battle you need a clear objective, but this on its own is not enough. Nor is the selection of men and equipment, important as these are. The time and place are often not of your choosing.

Once the strategy is decided and the means made available other factors become important. Swiftness in reaction is needed, and the ability to take advantage of tactical errors and strategic shortcomings on your opponent's part. Chaps like Julius Caesar, Napoleon, Nelson and Bertie Wooster will bear this out. All these factors were to be seen during what came to be known as Mr. Cube's campaign.

As we shall see, however, probably the most significant was a tactical error made by the Socialists later in 1949. Stung by the realization that the dogma which had carried them into power in 1945 – 'nationalization of the means of production and distribution' – was being queried by one of their targets, prominent and highly intelligent men in the Labour Party lost their heads and their tempers. Adopting a haughty 'How dare you?' posture, they attempted to stop the campaign by the use of threats. This was a miscalculation and it had the opposite effect to that intended, for they were by now 'the bosses'. Had not one of their number, no doubt to his everlasting subsequent regret, said: 'We are the masters now'?

In adopting the tactics of bullying, the Labour Party exposed a weak flank which the Press, who always like a news item, was quick to fall on. But first there were the preliminaries, rather like the work of a picador in a bull fight. It was necessary to annoy the bull and get him to put his head down and charge.

This has its dangers, and success in it brings a demand for another quality, courage. Under relentless pressure, abuse and menaces from an elected Government, it requires guts to continue the fight, and considerable coolness. These and a highly developed political instinct on the part of Tate & Lyle's President were then the major additional weapons.

But there were others. One was the uncovenanted if largely tacit preference, after three or four generations, of the vast majority of employees for the status quo, born of sharing of good, bad and bloody awful times experienced together. The other was the fortunate success of a disembodied, impertinent cartoon figure.

Faced with an apparently all-powerful Party, backed by a huge Parliamentary majority and able to select the most favourable timing for an Election, the chances of winning, of getting the Company's name off the list seemed slender, a bit like those of James Graham, Marquis of Montrose. As he wrote:

> He either fears his fate too much
> Or his deserts are small
> That will not put it to the touch
> To win or lose it all. . . .

But it does not do to be too solemn. The campaign depended largely on humour—notably lacking on the other side. And there was always parody to help.

As Sellers-Tateman recorded it, 'When the threat arose the Company retaliated by Aiming their Industry through a series of Specialized Committees and consulting an elderly warlock called St. John's Wood (later known as 'A lad an' his Wonderful Lump') who conjured up the UTTERLY MEMORABLE MR. CUBE during a Black Masse in Tothill Street.[2]

III

'Milton, thou shouldst be living at this hour . . .'
(William Wordsworth, 1770–1850)

In times of peril England has never lacked for a Clarion Voice, and now it was F. H. (call me Shakespeare) Tate, from whose First Folio the following is extracted. From internal evidence the work dates from the late spring of 1949, for reference is made to a meeting of the Labour Party Policy Committee which took place over Easter (April 13th) 1949 at Shanklin, Isle of Wight. (See Editor's Notes.)

Called *Henry and Abram—a lament for a threat to a Great Industry*, the Play is headed by a Dramatis Personae:[i]

HENRY ⎱ ABRAM ⎰	Honest business men
WALTER	Faithful retainer to Henry
ARTHUR	Faithful retainer to Abram
WILLIAM	A faithful scribe

---

[i] *Editor's notes*
Henry—Henry Tate ⎱ who only meet as ghosts, as they never did so when alive.
Abram—Abram Lyle ⎰
Walter—Walter King, Office Manager at Thames Refinery.
Arthur—Arthur Greene, Office Manager at Plaistow Wharf.
William—William Booth, Company Secretary.
Aneurin—Bevan.
Emmanuel—Shinwell.
Ernest—Davies.

---

[2] The Headquarters of Aims of Industry was then just off Tothill Street.

THE GIANT CONTROL

THE GIANT NATIONALIZATION   His son

ANEURIN   ⎫
EMMANUEL   ⎬   Evil Spirits employed
ERNEST   ⎭   by the Giants

Chorus of Sons, Grandsons, Relatives and Socialists.

It begins with a Prologue:

Scene: A blasted beetfield, by night
Musick: Thunder and Lightning

(Enter Three Evil Spirits)

ANEURIN: When shall we three meet again?
                            On Isle of Wight, on Shanklin's Plain [ii]

EMMANUEL: When the programme's fixed and sure,
                            Then we'll sling all our manure
                            At old Abram, honest wight,
                            And at Henry, parasite.
                            We will haunt them day and night.

ANEURIN: What is first?

ERNEST: To Ashridge I, [iii]
                            And 'racket, racket' will I cry,
                            Though I can never justify.

ALL: Fair is foul and foul is Clem, [iv]
                            We'll have their profits out of them.

(Exeunt)

Scene I takes place in a field near Mincing Lane in 1921:

(Enter, from opposite directions. Henry and Abram, attended)

HENRY: Well met, proud Lyle, my friend that is to be
                            For all our fears are gone, and vanquished quite
                            Are all those from whose nasty melt we formerly
                            Abhorred.

Editor's notes

[ii] The comrades met at Shanklin over Easter 1949. It is this which dates the manuscript.

[iii] Davies had made a speech at that well-known centre of free thinking.

[iv] Who was, of course, the First Earl Attlee (dec'd).

ABRAM: Ah friend, Great Tate, most noble Gallery,
                         This is a day that long will live and shine
                         Our fortunes twain are linked.

HENRY: Sir, I agree,
                         Long may our Prefs be cum; may bonus shares
                         Pour out in Golden flood like Syrup from the Wharf,
                         And Public Service shall our watchword be.

(Exeunt)

Scene II is in the Giants' Castle – 1948

(Enter Two Giants, attended by Three Evil Spirits)

GIANT CONTROL: I see that fortune smiles full well
                         Upon that curséd T. and L.
                         And be their margin ne'er so small
                         I cannot send them to the wall.
                         They sell their Cubes, they sell their Grans
                         They put in all the latest pans.
                         Their profits soar, yet dividends
                         Still stay as Stafford Cripps demands.
                         They pay above the general rate,
                         O, curséd Lyle, wretched Tate!

GIANT NATIONALIZATION (a growing boy):
                         Please, dear papa, leave them to me
                         I'll take their profits presently.
                         Let's buy them up so I can give
                         A well paid job to every spiv.
                         Make Konni[v] chairman, Stanley[vi] sec
                         Let's give it to 'em in the neck.
                         Just watch their assets disappear
                         When I have had them for a year.

BOTH (to their familiars):
                         Go, weave a spell and weave it strong.
                         We may not have so very long
                         Before the Voters, stupid horde,
                         Decide to throw us overboard.

(Exit two Giants)

Editor's notes
[v] Mr. K. Zilliacus, M.P. (dec'd).
[vi] Mr. Sidney Stanley.
These were two prominent people in Labour Party circles, not necessarily spivs.
Incidentally a spiv, for those who have forgotten, was a black market operator.

(A Cauldron descends. Fire, Brimstone and Lyle's Golden Syrup)

Incantation.   ANEURIN, EMMANUEL and ERNEST
        Round about the City go,
        In the poisoned stories throw –
        Tate and Lyle is a racket
        Here are the facts with which we back it –
        Directors each get fifty grand,
        In the Board Room there's a band
        Playing while each member sups
        Veuve Clicquot from golden cups.
        And the Secretaries three[vii]
        With a typist on each knee
        Just pretend to take a Minute
        In a book with nothing in it.

The incantation continued with many a local reference and ended with a refrain:

ALL: Pull the plug and once again
        Pour some money down the drain.

 The groundlings are possibly not interested in the editor's notes. And by now in any case they will have been reminded by the last couplet that before the curtain rose they had refreshed themselves at the Bar of the Globe Theatre with copious draughts of Rhenish wine, ale, sack, pommage and other fluids which soil the hands. Also, perhaps, the Play is going to be exciting. So it is time for an

INTERMISSION

IV

Months later, when the campaign had made an impact and the national Press of Britain was ringing with the name of Mr. Cube – to the extent of putting him in their crossword puzzle clues and even far-off journals like the *Tanganyika Times*, the *Omaha (Neb.) Advertiser* and *L'Echo de Tahiti* were also interested, expert P.R. men began to ask how this had come about. Leonard Lyle wrote an article for the *Financial Times* and Peter Runge one for *Forum*, an even more eclectic journal. Peter was asked to give a lecture to explain the secret to a club formed of hard-nosed ad.-men.

 Drawing on these articles and on certain internal documents – there are very few left – it is fairly easy to describe the mechanics although it seemed much harder to make them work.

[vii] In those Golden Days there were three Secretaries – one real one (Booth) and two Assistants (Tom Marshall and Tony Tate).

The first step was to get the support of fellow sugar refiners and of the Shareholders of the Company for any measures that might have to be taken, then that of the customers who bought the sugar–particularly manufacturers of sugar-containing articles and the wholesale and retail trade. Simultaneously with this the Company's own staff and workforce had to be sounded out and their views sought in such a way as to avoid embarrassing them or the trade union to which the majority belonged, the National Union of General and Municipal Workers.

There were four stages in the battle:

(i) to make the sugar-consuming public aware of the proposal to nationalize sugar refining. (As will be seen there was a certain furtiveness about the way the proposal was introduced);

(ii) to give the facts (which had been twisted by the nationalizers) and point out the probable consequences; to this end Peter Runge prepared a factual document 'The Business of Tate & Lyle' for general guidance;

(iii) to discover what people were then thinking and publish the information; and

(iv) to persuade the nationalizers to drop sugar refining from the list.

The first *official* indication of the proposal was in a Statement of Policy called 'Labour Believes in Britain', which came out immediately after the party's Policy Committee had met, in an incongruous mixture of secrecy and publicity at Shanklin over Easter. In this, under a section entitled 'Square Deal for Consumers', there appeared a sub-heading THE SUGAR MONOPOLY, which included the following paragraph.

'Sugar Refining is . . . controlled by a state-protected private monopoly which has enabled large profits to be made for private shareholders. One concern dominates the industry; it also has large interests in some of the Colonial territories which the Labour Government is pledged to develop. The sugar industry is vital both in war and peace. Labour intends to transfer to public ownership all the sugar manufacturing and refining concerns.'

This is so clear an echo of Mr. Charles Smith's and Mr. Ernest Davies' quoted works that, when the gloves were off, it was satisfying to be able to say of it and of a Labour Party Speakers Handbook, which indeed contained long quotations from these two gurus: 'the authors of these two documents had obviously gained their knowledge of sugar refining only from reading each other's books'.

At the Annual Conference of the Labour Party in Blackpool at Whitsun, there was no discussion at all of the proposal, which was introduced by Dr. Edith Summerskill in a two-minute speech and passed unanimously. The lady said that refining was subsidized by the State, and Lord Lyle corrected her in a public statement. She later withdrew this inaccuracy.

The Conference was treated to an early example of skirmishing. A rapidly prepared leaflet giving reasons why sugar refining should *not* be nationalized found its way to every delegate's place in the hall. Aims of Industry had infiltrated. It had no effect on those attending, but was good for morale at 52 Cadogan Square.

The official part of the campaign now began. Lord Lyle wrote to Mr. Morrison, Leader of the Party and Lord President of the Council asking him to receive a deputation of the British Sugar Refiners' Association to present a reasoned case. Morrison did not himself reply, but the Secretary of the Party's Policy Committee, a Mr. Michael Young, wrote curtly saying that the approach should have been made *before* the Whitsun Conference.

This patronizing rebuff had the unintended effect of liberating the refiners, and Tate & Lyle in particular, to take their case over the heads of the Labour Party to the public. An Extraordinary General Meeting of the Company was called for the autumn and the mechanics of the campaign set in motion.

Speed and quality of decisions were, as already mentioned, of paramount importance. To ensure speed it was agreed that Tate & Lyle should carry out the campaign with the full support of the other refiners. The Scottish refiners carried out a local campaign in parallel.

Concurrently with the propaganda campaign, a dignified approach to the Labour Party and to Parliament in general was initiated. This was kept entirely separate from the appeal to the public. Literature was issued by the Refiners' Association but there was no pestering of M.Ps. 'The Parliamentary Case', a carefully reasoned document, aroused no interest at all in the Labour Party, which is hardly surprising. The left wing of the Party had demanded nationalization and the remainder had to toe the line for unity's sake.

A small sub-committee of the Board of Tate & Lyle – Leonard Lyle, Ian Lyle and Peter Runge – was authorized to handle the affair and given complete freedom of action. One of the three was to be available day and night for the whole period, and in this way the Company was enabled to give an authoritative reply to any statement made about it. Usually this meant that the reply was printed alongside the remarks of Mr. Morrison or whoever else was leading the attack.

Aims of Industry were instructed to get moving. They had three main operating divisions – Editorial, Direct Relations and Research. The heads of these departments and one or two others together with Ian Lyle, Peter Runge and two other representatives of Tate & Lyle formed a Steering Committee which met once a week for an hour and a half to decide the general pattern of the campaign and to approve the expenditure of funds. (This in the event was to turn out to be much less than anyone, friend or foe, would have believed.) Sub-committees of this Steering Committee were set up to deal with matters of detail. Each had a T & L man as

Chairman and another as Secretary, with at least one man from Aims of Industry. One Tate & Lyle man sat on all the committees as liaison officer. Other members of T & L staff were co-opted to help on specific activities.

The sub-committees were:

The Distribution Committee – distributing leaflets and other material.

The Education Committee – distributing material for schools.

The Exhibition Committee – organizing stands, e.g. at the Ideal Home Exhibition.

The Magazine Committee – improving the House Magazine and arranging to keep employees advised.

The Song and Dance Committee – songs were written and dances organized, and various toys and games were evolved.

The Speakers' Committee – about 50 T & L staff volunteered to speak to local audiences by invitation. This Committee co-ordinated them.

The Mr. Cube Committee – to co-ordinate Mr. Cube's statements and activities.

These sub-committees did not all spring at once into action, but developed as the campaign grew. They were remarkably effective, the only curb on their actions being that minutes of all their meetings had to go to the Steering Committee.

Mr. Cube was soon to emerge. Warwick Charlton of Aims of Industry, who had worked on the *Daily Express,* was asked to find an artist who could design a suitable cartoon figure. Two artists were found, one the late Gerald Hoffnung, the other Bobby St. John Cooper.[3] Hoffnung's figure, a square little man with a round fuzzy head was not as flexible or expressive as Cooper's Mr. Cube, with his huge eyes and a face able to depict any kind of emotion. Bobby got the job. He is still doing it thirty years later.

Yet even before Mr. Cube there was the problem – for time was short – of carrying out the first objective, making people aware of the threat to sugar, and very difficult it proved at first. To the man in the street, or to his good lady, what *was* sugar after all? Something you put in tea or used in cooking. Was it 'refined'? Well, so what? Who did the refining? No idea. Tate & Lyle? Never 'eard of 'em. Oh, but yes, wasn't there a thing called Lyle's Golden Syrup which tasted nice on bread? But what does it matter if it *is* nationalized?

One of the major activities of Aims of Industry was their editorial service. Through a network of area officers they were able to syndicate to local newspapers up and down the country a series of articles on sugar and on Tate & Lyle. Most of these were of an entirely factual, non-propaganda nature, but they served to bring the matter to the notice of readers who

[3] It was, in fact Bobby who found Warwick. He was trying to get back £3 owed to him (he never got it but regards it as the best bad debt ever).

often pay more attention to the *Pittenweem Gazette and Chronicle* than to the national Press. Having been receptive to such articles early on, these journals later demanded and got more pungent stuff when the campaign boiled up, and many written either by Tate & Lyle men, by Aims of Industry's editorial staff or by reputable specialists were syndicated.

This formed the ground bass, to use a musical term, for a much more strident, but very simple theme: 'Sugar may be nationalized' or 'Why nationalize sugar'? with the addition of the leitmotif that under nationalization sugar would cost more, its quality would decline, and the choice would be restricted. Not very exalted thoughts, although the nub of the matter, these were to be conveyed right into the kitchen, wherever Tate & Lyle sugar was bought, by being printed on the wrappers of sugar packets. Although about two million packets a week were produced, there would of course be many households where the messages would not arrive. For one thing, only Tate & Lyle among the refiners were printing slogans. For another, under a wartime regulation still in force, sugar was zoned to save transport. This meant that the eastern part of the country, which consumed about one-third of the total sugar, would be supplied exclusively by the British Sugar Corporation, which, as a quasi-governmental body since 1936, would not be able to join any campaign, whatever the feelings of its staff.

Since the packets had to bear some print, such as 'Untouched by hand', to which could be added: 'HANDS OFF SUGAR', they were about as inexpensive a medium as could be sought. This was a major advantage, for a private firm, however well-found, cannot afford blanket P/R coverage, unlike a Government which has virtually uncontrolled used of the taxpayer's money. But, because of its volume, the use of packet panels was taken by the Labour Party as an unfair threat and it was probably the chief reason for their violent and in the end self-defeating reaction.

The messages on packets had to be simple because the paper was of low quality, designed for strength rather than legibility, and, since grocers' stocks move slowly, it would take time to get any new words of wisdom into the housewife's hands. The first few slogans were pre-Mr. Cube. A £10 prize was offered to any employee who produced one which was used. Out of the first four – HANDS OFF SUGAR, TATE NOT STATE, YOU HAVE THE BEST SUGAR – THE STATE WANTS IT and IF YOUR HOPES FOR SUGAR LIE IN STATE IT'S YOUR FUNERAL, the last came from a young clerk in the delivery department of Thames Refinery, Douglas Hall.

In retrospect they look a bit pedestrian, and they were certainly too solemn to be effective. But it was the *idea* of having a bash which counted, and out they went from late June onwards, on packets, on posters on the sides of Tate & Lyle vans, and on hoardings. With one brief exception, swiftly extinguished by trade union action, there was no objection on the part of the workforce. Simultaneously other schemes were devised, cut-out toys and a ration book holder – for sugar was still rationed – for grocers to give away, and a poker dice game 'Tate and State'. Their main impact came when Mr. Cube appeared.

He alone was able, with the appropriate expression, to impart a message without giving offence, for he was the Little Man taking on the Giant Nationalization. He could be woeful ('Sugar may be nationalized. Oh dear, dear, dearer'); determined ('Keep your key to good housekeeping'); grim ('Kill that Snake'–a serpent-shaped S on TATE); or harassed ('If they juggle with sugar they juggle with your shopping basket'). In all, during the entire campaign there were only eight Mr. Cube drawings on packets, issued at about six weeks' intervals.

Had he not caught on it was intended to introduce a family, Granny Granulated, Cousin Caster, and so forth. The imagination boggled at the sheer awfulness of this and it was lucky therefore that Mr. Cube succeeded. In the next few months, the ration book holders, the leaflets for housewives and for sugar-using manufacturers, anything to do with the campaign, bore his image.

It became not Tate & Lyle's, nor Lord Lyle's campaign, but Mr. Cube's.

V
'Let Battle Commence'
(Stanley Holloway)

The Groundlings having by now washed their hands and once more recruited their strength with Canary, Cider, and Palm Wine, the bell has gone for the next Act.

The scene is: A Battlefield near Westminster. It is a lovely day, apart from a hot air current coming from the direction of the Houses of Parliament.

(Enter Henry and Abram attended by Walter, Arthur, William and Retainers.)

HENRY:
    The fight is on! Runge with his barbéd pen
    Hath held the wing; Good William go,[i]
    Consolidate and turn to good account
    Our present credits.

WILLIAM:
    Sire, I go
    Give me as many men as there be pounds
    In half a column of our P and L. Before my face
    I throw my warlike quill. Nor overdraft
    Nor Auditors' Report can fright me now.
    Nor New Work, Buildings, nor our evil foe
    Can turn me from their present overthrow!
                       (Exit.)

Editor's notes
[i] William (Booth)

ABRAM: Great news is here, good Duff, the Thane of
                                Barrington,[ii]
                With twenty thousand pamphlets in his wake
                Bombards the public with our point of view,
                The aims of industry are true indeed –
                Old Sewill's shafts find every one a mark,
                Whilst his lieutenants, braiding up their hair[iii]
                Do dire slaughter both with lens and pen.
                The Co-op Cavalry, MacDonald's men, attack
                                their flank.[iv]
                Full of high courage and yet higher tea, they pour
                A spate of resolutions from their maw, whilst on
                The left I see the Unions standing firm, General
                                Municipal,
                Their gallant chief, restrictive practices all
                                cast aside,
                Defends free enterprise – a wondrous sight.
                Now flees Aneurin to his Jenny's side –
                Hugh to his economic fastness goes – [v]
                Their flank is turned, their programme's
                                changed, they flee!
                (Sounds of cheers and, of course, counter cheers)

    Just as Shakespeare was apt to take a little licence with time, squeezing as it were the Wars of the Roses into a few well chosen lines, so his latterday reincarnation has done the same. It did not happen as quickly as all that. Indeed for a long time nothing much happened at all.

    Perhaps this was because the telly was then a fairly rare possession, and instant news and views were not available. Not that ownership of a Box was the prerogative of the well-to-do or anything like that. It was found as often if not more so in humbler homes. Once, after a twelve-hour Sunday shift, a Plaistow Wharf Manager was waiting for a trolley-bus at 6.30 (his wife had the family car). A large secondhand Chevrolet stopped by him; it was driven by one of the men who handled bags of raw sugar on the landing wharf. A kindly man, he offered the Manager a lift.

    'Well', he said, 'Just goin' back to put me feet up in front of the telly. You got one, Mr. Er'?

Editor's notes
[ii] Duff – Ian Duff Lyle, who lives at Barrington Court.

[iii] Some of A of I's men had *very* long hair. Rare in the 1940s.

[iv] Sir Arthur MacDonald, chief executive of Co-operative Wholesale Society who were complaining of nationalization.

[v] Hugh Dalton, for part of 1949 Chancellor of the Exchequer until replaced by Sir Stafford Cripps after an indiscreet budget leak.

One of the new generation of road tankers serving food manufacturers.

Redpath Refinery — Toronto.

'No, er, can't actually afford one yet.'

'Well, its O.K. for the first three months. You're glued to it. After that it gets kind of borin'.'

So Lord Lyle's voice was not heard by the square-eyed multitude, and as the BBC steam radio then made a habit of not consulting businessmen, people will have to imagine what he sounded like.[4] The robust content of the speeches and statements would suggest a loud, confident, ponderous, prophetic bass. It was quite otherwise, almost tenor, slightly world-weary, gentle rather than menacing; a little incongruous with the burly square-set figure and the determination in the jaw inherited from Grandfather Abram. Some of his comments, for example, on government interference and Socialist incompetence may seem forced, but they were genuinely felt. He and his fellow Directors had been involved in the business for years, and in some cases their fathers, grandfathers and great-grandfathers before them. They had taken risks with their own money, had had more than once to bring the business through hard times. If they were successful it was through flair, judgment, courage and hard work. Small wonder that the assumption by the nationalizers that they were parasites, that running an enterprise is easy, aroused resentment.

Nor was it automatic, as Socialist propaganda suggested, for a member of either of the families to be taken on and given a plum job. Oliver Lyle, for example, had had to wait until 1912 and the departure of a cousin, Willie. Henry Tate, grandson of the first Henry, did not join the firm, because, according to him, his father, Sir Ernest, thought he was too thick. There have been many other members of the families since then who have opted not to join. No family man was admitted unless thought worthy of it, and even then he was subject to ruthless surveillance and the possibility of being pruned off if he wasn't found good enough. There were, even in the 1920s, a number of able non-family men on the Board, who had worked their way up. (This trend has increased over the years.)

The aspiring Director had to work in a refinery for a longish period – unspecified when he joined – on shifts, until it was known that he could take the hard work and get on with people. Only then could he expect promotion. This went for Tates, Lyles, and anyone else. Morton Oliphant spent over four years in lowly work in Head Office, thereby gaining an intimate knowledge of sales and purchases.

Almost the most important aspect was getting to know one's fellow employees, among whom, too, at all levels, there were many in the third and fourth generation. The atmosphere among those working in a refinery had in 1949 been tempered by the common experience of being bombed, of being scared, and of keeping going. And those returning from war service had that in common with men and women who came new to the company from the Forces. But it was the *family* aspect that counted most. It was a

4 He was interviewed once, later on, on television in February 1950, but the interview was entirely non-political.

little like, perhaps, those early sugar houses in the 1800s which gave employment 'to six of the family and up to nine yearly paid servants'.

It was the intimate relationship, up and down and across, that influenced the employees in their desire not to be nationalized. They might not always agree with the bosses, but they knew where they were with them, trusted them, and did not want a change.

Meetings held with the foremen, informal chats at tea-breaks, talks on the bus, all indicated this to be the genuine attitude. It was borne out most impressively when Richard Dimbleby visited one of the refineries, Plaistow, to record random interviews, in a 'Down Your Way' style, with employees. One after another they came up with similar replies. Ivy Bennett, a girl shop steward from the Small Packets department; an electrician; Sid Howlett, a chargehand from the Fill House–'What I like is the way the firm spends money on research. Old Ollie–that's what we call him–doesn't worry about money when it comes to that.' Eventually the Personnel Manager was sent to find some Labour Party supporter who would speak his mind. Harry Chaplin, shop steward on the Raw Sugar Handling, a genial, burly man, never minced his words. All right, he'd have a go. He told Dimbleby he voted Labour because he was a labouring man. 'Then you want nationalization?' 'I don't want to change my bosses.' Harry was a strong influence in the Raw Sugar Handling Department. Others thought as he did.

The Labour Party's Food Sub-Committee in the House of Commons paid a visit, led by a Mr. Ed. Porter, M.P. In the Syrup Filling Department, they watched cans being accurately and swiftly filled at ten, twelve, fifteen a minute.

'Are these girls on piece work?' asked Mr. Porter.

'No.'

(Grunt of disbelief.) 'They're working very hard.'

In the Small Packets Department, the same question, the same answer.

'They're not just putting on a show for us?' asked Mr. P.

'They always work like this.'

'It's a bloody disgrace. Slave-driving, that's what it is. Time you were nationalized and we'll put a stop to it.'

Yet these two Departments were among the happiest and smoothest-running in the place. The girls were a splendid set of people, but try to 'slave-drive' them and you would be told what to do with yourself. They actually *liked* the work.

At the time of the Labour Party Conference at Blackpool, on June 8th, William Barkley of the *Daily Express* reported a Socialist Local Councillor in Liverpool as saying bitterly that he had not had a single indication from Tate & Lyle's people at Love Lane that they were in favour of nationalization.

The National Union of General and Municipal Workers also viewed nationalization of the Company with disfavour. Captain Mark Hewitson,

M.P., the National Negotiating Officer, told Peter Runge and Ian Lyle so, privately. The Area Officer, 'Sailor' Evans, and the local branch Chairman, George Watson, who had negotiated with Oliver Lyle and his colleagues for years, regarded them with affection, referring to them as 'The Boys'. John O'Brien, Evans' assistant and eventual successor, faced with some problem in a department, would say: 'What are we going to do about this?' (*we*, not *you*). None of them wanted nationalization.

When, at the Annual Conference of the union, a delegate, not from Tate & Lyle, asked if the union would support men who refused to handle packets with slogans on them, since this was anti-Government propaganda, the Chairman, Mr. Tom Williamson,[5] said merely that the matter was being watched, but that meantime employees should carry out the instructions of their foreman.

At Question Time in the House of Commons, Mr. T. Skeffington-Lodge[6] asked the Minister of Labour, Mr. George Isaacs, if he was aware of the unrest at Tate & Lyle's refineries over the firm's propaganda, and what was he proposing to do about it? Mr. Isaacs replied that he was unaware of any unrest, and that the second question did not therefore arise.

Many rank and file Labour Members of Parliament were covertly against the proposal. One of these, indeed, asked Peter Runge and Ian Lyle to meet him in the House, and proceeded to show them the advance draft of a speech by Mr. Morrison on the subject. Just at this moment another Labour Member joined them. Peter had to read the draft like a schoolboy hiding a crib while Ian kept the newcomer in conversation.

Indeed, it seems likely that even senior members of the Party were lukewarm. Mr. Morrison's speech on nationalization at the Whitsun Conference was in general half-hearted, and Dr. Summerskill, whose job it was to speak on sugar, was laconic in the extreme. Only Mr. Aneurin Bevan raised a cheer by speaking of liberating enterprise from cartels and trusts, of how private employers kept research workers in candle-lit garrets, and suppressed their inventions, of how it was necessary to 'discipline' employers, and set up public enterprise in competition with private.

In the West Indies, Mr. Bustamante, leader of Jamaica's (then) sole trade union, and virtual Prime Minister, was sounded out for his views. His reaction was immediate and vehement. He sent telegrams. He spoke to the Press:

> 'Nationalization would not only drive foreign investment out of Jamaica, but it would debar prospective investors. The prosperity of the West Indies depends on foreign investment.
>
> 'Jamaica's future depends upon the prosperity of the staple industry–sugar. If therefore nationalization becomes a reality I shall order a general strike against the sugar industry and lead it myself.'

[5] Later Lord Williamson.
[6] Known, naturally, at 52 Cadogan Square as Sparkington-Plug.

There was more from him on the same lines. Nationalization would, by making the West Indies even poorer, destroy their hopes for the future. 'Do these statesmen [i.e. the Labour Party] want to reduce us to the same parlous state as they have reduced Britain?' etc., etc.

Bustamante spoke at that time for the bulk of ordinary people in Jamaica, as an almost mystical figure, combining a preference for private enterprise which was investing heavily (as in the new factory at Monymusk) with a deep understanding of the man in the cane-piece.

So the feelings of those directly involved in making and refining sugar, of their representatives, and even of many moderate men in the Labour Party seemed generally opposed to nationalization, or at most, lukewarm. What about the general public?

VI

'Mr. Tate Hesitates'

(The *Daily Herald*, June 23rd, 1949)

The public of Britain appeared by 1949 to be disillusioned with nationalization. Leonard Lyle was able to say repeatedly, changing the words but retaining the substance: 'Harsh reality had dispelled those Fabian dreams [of the benefits of nationalization]. The National Coal Board supplies a mixture of dust, stones and explosive cartridges at an ever-increasing price. Part of the increase is put down to increasing costs of transport on the nationalized railways who in turn charge expensive fares for journeys in shoddy carriages drawn at speeds which would have been regarded as mediocre twenty years ago and blame their increased costs on the rise in the price of coal . . .[7] Londoners shiver under the effects of a gas strike superimposed on electricity load-shedding . . .

'It is rapidly becoming obvious that one of the worst faults in the Coal, Road and the Transport Executive is over-centralization . . . Here we have towering ladders of bureaucratic organizations up and down which must pass, step by step, suggestions, instructions, and so forth.'

All very true then (as nearly three decades later), but how to harness this?

The only available large-scale medium was the panel on the sugar packets. Preparations were complete by early June for these to bear slogans, but there were doubts, not about their effectiveness, but about whether printing slogans would arouse resentment in the public. It was assumed that the Socialists would object, but would the public side with them or with the Company?

While the matter was still being discussed by the Board, a Mr. Clifford

---

[7] This was in the days of puffer-trains, before the diesel took over.

Selly of the *Daily Herald* telephoned and spoke to Tony Tate, who had been made a Director of the Company a few days before. Asked whether a decision had been taken on packet slogans, Tony replied truthfully that some colleagues were still undecided for various reasons. Mr. Selly printed next day, June 23rd, an account of this conversation under the heading: 'Mr. Tate Hesitates'. It was a clever, scornful heading, but it acted as a detonator. Its effect was to annoy the Board of Tate & Lyle and a meeting was called at once. Any doubts were swept away, and it was decided to begin issuing packets bearing slogans immediately.

The reaction of the papers of the Left was predictable. The *Daily Herald* was outraged and abusive. *The People* and *Reynolds News* spoke of impertinence and of 'using a monopoly position to force the housewife to buy Conservative and anti-Government slogans'. Polite but firm responses were made by the Company and some of these were printed.

The Ministry of Food, presumably under pressure from Mr. John Strachey, the Minister, intervened. In a telephone call to the Chairman, Vernon Tate, an official stated that as under a wartime arrangement the Ministry was paying for the cost of the board used in packet making, it could not permit its use to carry slogans.

Regrettably the Ministry had not done its homework. The wartime packets without wrappers had been so prone to leakage that the Company *at its own expense* had decided to put paper wrappers on as soon as the war was over and paper available. They were entitled to print whatever they wished on their own property and intended to do so. The official retired hurt.

This was the first Government attempt to prevent the Company from 'going to the people'. It did not become known until a few weeks later.

In the meantime on the whole the national Press was guarded in its attitude, except for the *Financial Times* and predictably the *Daily Telegraph*, and even these did not as yet find the campaign particularly newsworthy. Others were almost unfriendly. Ian Lyle and Peter Runge met Bernard Harris of the *Express*, who said that the reason for this was that the Company had in the past been unsympathetic and stand-offish to the Press. His words were taken to heart, and thenceforward a much more friendly attitude was adopted. Mr Harris, perhaps mollified, wrote an informative article 'Mr. Tate never met Mr. Lyle'. But such contributions were scarce for quite some time to come although the local and provincial newspapers continued to print syndicated articles with fair frequency. It was not the campaign which excited interest at first, but two incidents affecting supplies of sugar.

Early in July the first shipment of sugar in bulk in the hold of the S.S. *Baron Haig* arrived in London. This was an experiment, designed to reduce the cost of sugar to the housewife. By doing away with bags the cost of jute would be eliminated and the amount of labour drastically reduced. The dockers refused to handle the cargo unless paid a special rate of fantastic proportions. The union held back. The *Baron Haig* sat at her moorings, undischarged, for weeks.

Press comment, unfavourable to the dockers and to their union, the T.G.W.U., for its unwillingness to assist, linked this situation directly to nationalization.

Then there was a general dock strike in July. The army was brought in to handle the discharge of sugar and other essential commodities. But, being unused to the job, and a little thin on the ground, the soldiers only landed about 1,000 tons of sugar a day. The three Tate & Lyle Refineries needed 4,000. A press statement from the Company warned that the sugar ration was in danger.

The Ministry of Food announced loftily that ample supplies were being landed and that Tate & Lyle was only part of the Ministry's sugar organization, and could not know of stocks held in reserve. Much of the Press leaped at this. If Tate & Lyle was only a part of the system of supply of sugar, what was all this about their being a monopoly? Moreover a company of major importance would hardly issue irresponsible statements at a time like this.

It was the beginnings of an indication that Government spokesmen were not always going to be believed. And when a little later the news leaked out of the Ministry of Food's attempt to stop the use of packet wrappers for slogans, the Press pricked up its ears still further. 'Stop these slogans, Ministry tells Lord Lyle.' 'The Ministry tries to ban slogans.' What was all this? Leonard Lyle was widely quoted as saying that he rather hoped the Government *would* try to stop slogans being printed. Ministry denials were treated as unreliable.

On July 28th, Mr. Cube made his first appearance in the *Evening Standard* in a modest three column-inch feature. He was then a stripling and a little spindle-shanked, but his face showed a potential for mischief. It was now that a general instruction was issued by the President. 'Mr. Cube' he said, 'must *always* be a knight in shining armour. He must *never* be a psalm-singing little bugger'.

Then it was August, and the Silly Season. A Miss Maureen Wigger of East Ham who worked at Thames Refinery, won a beauty contest and appeared in newspaper pictures helping to paste a slogan poster on a Tate & Lyle van. Aged seventeen, she herself wrote a letter to the *Daily Worker* which had accused her of being put up to it, saying she had done it off her own bat. A Miss Patricia Triggs of the Union of Shop Distributive and Allied Workers, of Sutton, Surrey, made a slight splash by objecting to handling packets with slogans on them. The splash subsided.

And there was an early example of White-Man-Speak-With-Forked-Tongue from the then President of the Board of Trade. Mr. Harold Wilson, slim, dark-haired, and having recently shaved off a moustache, declared 'The industry is virtually a monopoly and in view of the power of a monopoly – especially when and if the people's foodstuffs is concerned – it is a thing which should be entrusted to the representatives of the people and not to a private group'.

Note the use of 'monopoly' and 'the people's foodstuffs'. We are still sixteen years away from 'The White-hot Technological Revolution' but here are keywords which, like 'privilege' and 'the forces of reaction' will be much heard in the land when the 1949 summer holidays are over.

Yet, although in a single week at the end of August, sixty-two papers had printed an account of the Ministry's attempted intervention over packets, sixteen on the question of 'monopoly', nine on rationing, and eleven on Miss Wigger, and 200 column inches of comment had occurred in the national Press, it was nothing like enough. Nearly six months' work had produced only a modest result.

VII

If sugar refining were to be nationalized, then something might be salvaged – the West Indies Companies, the transport fleet, the lighterage company and other ancillaries. It was decided to form a new company, Tate & Lyle Investments Ltd., with a nominal capital of £2,200,000 and to reorganize Silvertown Services Ltd. to own and operate these subsidiaries and use them, if the worst came to the worst, as a basis for new ventures.

This process, although less dramatic than the campaign, was equally vital, and by September 1949 after much unheralded activity, permission had been received from the Stock Exchange Capital Issues Committee for the operation of the plan.

It now remained to obtain the approval of the Shareholders to this and to all the public activities under way. It was for this that the Extraordinary General Meeting of the Company took place at Caxton Hall on September 15th.

VIII
'Clear thinking–Plain speaking'
(Financial Times. September 1949)

This was how the *Financial Times* had characterized the efforts so far of Tate & Lyle. Now was the time for a good deal more plain speaking. Preparation of the President's speech took some time. There were drafts and redrafts. The triumvirate of President, Ian Lyle and Peter Runge were the co-authors, with a bit of help from Brendan Bracken.

Just before the Great Day, Ian had said he wanted to take a copy of the latest draft home to the country and work on it. Inadvertently he picked up not only his copy but all the others, together with all the notes and drafts. This perhaps would not have mattered but he then left them in the train when he got out at Taunton and they went trundling off on their own towards Penzance. Tense telephone calls resulted in their recovery and return three hours or so later. It would just not have done for them to fall into unfriendly hands, and in any case, after all the work that had been put in, their loss would have made one member of the special sub-committee very unpopular indeed with his colleagues.

The speech was a long and closely reasoned account of the origins of the nationalization proposal and of the attempts made to obtain a hearing. It rebutted the various charges, monopoly, extravagant profits, Government subsidies. It attacked the record of nationalized industries, the woolly statements about 'sectional interests' and so forth, and repeated the statement that if nationalization came, the Board would walk out. Then there was a calculated piece of invective:

'Who do the comrades think are going to run the industry for them? Is it suggested that a more efficient Board can be found among the boys for whom jobs have got to be found? If there is a backroom boy in Bloomsbury or elsewhere who thinks he is competent to teach us our business, I am astonished that he has not already offered his valuable services to us. . . .'

The President then outlined the plan of campaign, adding: 'We have a newcomer on the staff who is employed the whole time on propaganda and who is your good friend, Mr. Cube.'

He concluded: 'If we can make sure that the public gets the facts, the Nationalizers will be forced to drop their plan to create a state monopoly in sugar'. He then put a resolution to the shareholders which would empower the Board to do all they could to meet the threats of those who 'learning nothing from the chaos, losses and labour unrest they have created in other industries, now wish to seize the assets of this Company.'[8]

The resolution was passed by 98 per cent of shareholders either present or by proxy.

In general, Press coverage of this event showed an improvement in volume and comment, with predictable exceptions—the *Herald* and the *Daily Worker,* was highly favourable. Even the *News Chronicle,* somewhat to the left of centre, said: 'The Labour Party has laid itself open to the suspicion that it is interested in nationalization for nationalization's sake—for the mere accumulation of power.'

But the public as a whole still continued to be largely unaware or disinterested. An opinion poll carried out at the beginning of November on a sample of 2,000 showed that only 51 per cent of the population knew of the threat, the majority of them by reason of the slogans on the packets. Of those who knew, 65 per cent were opposed to nationalization, 22 per cent were undecided and 13 per cent in favour.

The proximity of a General Election was indicated by the appearance in

8 This particular sentence was drafted over the telephone by Brendan Bracken.

mid-November of a Labour Party Speakers' Handbook, containing large quotes from the two Parliamentary self-styled experts, Smith and Davies, and a number of inaccurate, under-researched or snide remarks. The inaccuracies were answered, and one under-researched comment was shown up as a howler.

A Mr. Mathieson, Chairman of the Sugar Using Manufacturers' Committee in 1936, had at that time referred to the 'monopoly of refined sugar'. He had since changed his mind, although the Labour Party had not bothered to ask him, and he now said he was totally opposed to the nationalization of refined sugar, 'and you are at liberty to quote me'.

A snide comment, linking Tate & Lyle's shares in the British Sugar Corporation and the presence of Walter Johnson (as a Tate & Lyle Director) on the Board of the Corporation, suggested that this was used to influence the Corporation's policy in favour of Tate & Lyle. But Johnson had been invited, each year, by the Corporation, itself Government-controlled, to stay, and this was easy to publicize.

Yet all this would have had little effect had not the big guns of the Labour Party now begun to discharge salvos in the hope of overwhelming resistance. Mr. James Griffiths, Minister of National Insurance, fired a shot, saying: 'In the forthcoming election we shall have against us all the forces of *privilege*.[9] They are pouring out their money to try and destroy the *People's Government*.[9]. . .'

In a trenchant response, Lord Lyle, seizing on 'the People's Government', said 'What balderdash'.

Then Mr. Herbert Morrison, speaking at Birmingham on the eve of a by-election, spoke of '*vested interests*[9] throwing the full weight of their financial resources into political controversies . . . not by reasoned statements, but by *expensively publicized*[9] vote-catching slogans. . . .' He went on: 'It would be a very dangerous thing if it was allowed to become a feature of our political life that *big business*[9] could intervene in elections both by *secret subscriptions*[9] to political funds and by direct large-scale propaganda campaigns. This *pouring out of money by the forces of reaction*[9] is contrary to the *spirit of democracy*.[9]'

Containing as it did the usual catch phrases of the Left, and intended to show that he was speaking on behalf of the down-trodden masses, Mr. Morrison's speech was an unexpected flop.

'Who' asked Lord Lyle in a reply printed alongside Morrison's speech, 'does Mr. Morrison think he is? And in what country does he think he's living? He is not Chief Commissar yet. . . .

'By suggesting that democratic principles are involved, [he] is implying that Tate & Lyle's campaign is against the will of the people, and that the nation is solidly behind the Socialist plan for nationalizing sugar. In fact no such plan exists, only a blueprint for chaos.'

The Press took sides against Mr. Morrison, and, conscious of the fact

[9] Author's italics.

that the Labour Party (as pointed out by Sir David Maxwell Fyfe, M.P.) was supported by the trade unions, and had actually been given a propaganda film by the Co-op, he said lamely that he was only giving advice.

Then a keen left-winger, the late Geoffrey Bing, Q.C. asked the Attorney-General, Sir Hartley Shawcross, to advise on the legal position of such campaigns in connection with election expenditure. Sir Hartley, clearly uncomfortable, said there were no binding rules but he would watch each case. The Press sympathized with Sir Hartley, who was stonewalling on a sticky wicket, but suggested that a test case should be brought in order to avoid misunderstanding. Sir Hartley brought no test case.

Sir Stafford Cripps now put in an oar, declaring *ex cathedra:* 'Tate & Lyle will not be allowed tax relief for such expenditure. Any claim of this nature will certainly be contested by the Inland Revenue.'

The Press by now was thoroughly awakened, and day after day banner headlines and leading articles were devoted to the matter. The Labour Party mandarins, seeking to occupy the politically convenient position of the under-dog had instead begun to appear as bullies, and Mr. Cube began to be applauded for standing up to them.

During December, 1,800 column inches were devoted in the national Press alone to the campaign as compared with 200 in August. To buy such space in the form of advertising would have cost between £500,000 and £1 million. It came free, thanks to Griffiths, Morrison, Shawcross and Cripps.

The foreign Press began to take more notice, articles appearing in exotic places such as Medicine Hat (Alberta). The *Berlinske Tidende* of Copenhagen remarked thunderously, if a little obscurely: 'HR SUK-KERSTYKE ER MAASKE BESTIKKELSE'. And a Dutch reader wrote asking for Mr. Cube's poker dice: 'Dear Sir: I read in Dutch paper that you have poker stones to send at everyone. I beg you to may receive these stones.' Demands for speeches came in from the Institute of Directors, the Liverpool Chamber of Manufacturers, the Primrose League, and from dozens of small gatherings up and down the country. (It was fortunate that there existed a speakers' team of 50 volunteers from Tate & Lyle's staff.) Articles were sought by *Picture Post,* the *News Chronicle,* and numerous other journals.

Suddenly Mr. Cube *was* news, the public *were* aware. And for the most part they were on his side. Out of the thousands of letters received during the campaign, 300 were in Mr. Cube's favour to each one against.

Just to cock a snook at Mr. Morrison and his colleagues, Cube appeared on packets timed for delivery over Christmas 1949, wearing a paper cap, lifting a glass and saying: 'Whatever the Party, we wish you a Merry Christmas'.

And Leonard Lyle, at about this time, showed that Mr. Cube wasn't the only one who could cock a snook. At a large meeting in Liverpool, organized by the N.U.M. (the National Union of Manufacturers), he spoke for a while of the seriousness of the threat and then, producing a little note from his pocket, told the following story:

'Once upon a time there was a prophet called Moses and he said to the people: "Get to your feet. Saddle your asses and camels, take up your picks and shovels and let us go to the Promised Land". Several thousand years later there was another prophet called Attlee, who said to the people: "Lay down your picks and shovels, light up your Camels, and sit on your asses. This *IS* the Promised Land".'

IX
'Never glad confident morning again'
(R. Browning 1812–1889)

On January 11th Mr. Attlee announced that he was seeking Prorogation of Parliament and a General Election on February 23rd. By pure chance Tate & Lyle had arranged a Press conference that morning to launch a nationwide petition against nationalization. Although this did well, collecting over a million signatures, it was overshadowed by the announcement of the Election. A mass demonstration which had been suggested by the various housewives' leagues and associations of Britain had to be abandoned, as there would not be time to organize it before February 23rd.

The Press conference served mainly to announce that Mr. Cube was not a political figure and that he would continue to appear on packets during the Election period. Dealing with the threats from high quarters, Lord Lyle said he had challenged Mr. Morrison and his colleagues to send him to prison if he was breaking the law, but nothing had happened. He was, he said, still waiting. Peterborough summed the situation up in the *Daily Telegraph:* 'Evidently Mr. Cube refuses to be squared'.

Although the campaign cannot be claimed to have had a major effect on the General Election, it certainly had some. A cartoon by Rodger, in *The People,* showed Churchill racing Attlee on bicycles towards 10 Downing Street; Mr. Attlee was impeded by a stern Mr. Cube hanging on to his coat tails. By February 19th it was clear that the result would be a close one, and when on the 23rd the people cast their vote there was, under the grey skies and behind the inexpressive features of His Majesty King George VI's angular subjects, a great deal of excitement. People sat up all night listening to the radio, cups of tea or glasses of something stronger at hand. Early results gave Labour a massive lead, but by 10.30 on the 24th, the Conservatives were catching up, and by lunchtime the difference was down to ten. Peter Runge was observed sitting in the Boardroom alongside a portable radio, his usually sleek hair rumpled in the excitement. 'By God', he said, 'We're going to beat the buggers.'

Not quite. The final result gave Labour a majority of eight.

Nothing was said about nationalization for some weeks, despite probing by Leonard Lyle and others. Indeed the Labour Party had tried during the run-up to the Election to avoid the issue, as though aware of its growing unpopularity.

In the King's Speech of November 1950 there was a proposal to nationalize sugar, but only the British Sugar Corporation. Of this Mr. Churchill said: 'The proposal about beet sugar which was no doubt intended to keep alive the nationalization issue, however seems, while letting off both barrels, not to have hit Tate & Lyle. That was one thing they [the Labour Party] were aiming at, but they shot at a pigeon and hit a crow.'

The Socialist Government limped on until May 1951. There was no time for a measure to be introduced on sugar before they went once more to the country and were this time defeated.[10]

Mr. Cube was now relatively safe.

Now Shakespeare may be permitted his triumphal epilogue with the ghostly Henry's thanks to Leonard, Ian, Peter, the speakers' teams, the employees–and Mr. Cube:

HENRY: The David of Democracy has fought
           State ownership and snuffed his wasteful flame.
           The members owe you much–our thanks
           To each of you in Tate & Lyle's good name.

                                                  (*Exeunt Omnes.*)

X
'*Who is Mr. Cube?*'
(Mr. Justice Scarman November 1952)

True to Sir Stafford Cripps' threat, when the time came H.M. Inspector of Taxes stated that expenses occurred in the campaign were not eligible for deduction against tax. The sum involved at that time–in September 1949–was only some £47,000. A further £140,000 was forecast for the following financial year, as the major part of the expenditure was incurred after September. (In passing it may be noted that the total sum, less than £200,000, was very modest; thanks largely to the Labour Party itself.) A principle was however at stake, and the Company appealed to the General Commissioners of Inland Revenue, who found against the Inland Revenue. The Inspector appealed to the High Court. By now it was

[10] Sellers Tate puts it more colourfully. In the Election 'the pheasants were even more revolting than usual and re-instated their right wing, which meant that in the next thirteen years they went around in circles. (For pheasants read peasants).'

November 1952 and incongruously it was a Conservative Solicitor-General, Sir Reginald Manningham-Butler who led for the Revenue. Mr. Justice Scarman, commenting: 'I am, I suppose, in duty bound to ask who is Mr. Cube?', again found for the Company. The Inspector then took the case to the Court of Appeal, where judgement, delivered on May 6th, 1953 was again in the Company's favour. Finally, in an appeal to the House of Lords, their Lordships found again by a majority in favour of Mr. Cube.

And that was that. Sir Stafford had been wrong.

It is, however, poignant to report that Lord Lyle never knew this. He had died three months earlier in February 1954.

CHAPTER FIFTEEN

Post War (1)

I

'Tempora mutantur nos et mutamur in illis'
(Q. Horatius Flaccus [call me Horace] 65–8 B.C.)

Back once more at 21 Mincing Lane the Board of Tate & Lyle were faced with the need for change. Things could not, after all, go on as if nothing had happened. Mr. Cube had won the day and we were at the end of an era of what a noted sociologist[1] has described as Weeping and Wailing and Nationalization of Teeth. There were changes about. One can almost imagine the kind of dialogue:

Leonard: Times are changing and we'd better watch out, Mate–I mean Tate.

Vernon: Ah! Good old Horace![2]

Leonard: Surely you mean Leo.

Almost a century after Henry and Abram had set forth from up yonder, their descendants with their colleagues were facing the need for new thinking. From now on, in a situation more complex than ever, the development of the Company itself becomes more complex and if one is not careful, more difficult to follow.

It is perhaps as well to continue to measure history against the scale of reigns. The Monarchy has still a deeper significance in Britain than confrontation politics, and the period we are approaching is happily more or less co-terminous with the first twenty-five years of Queen Elizabeth II.

Just before it opened there had been an educational trudge over concrete called the Festival of Britain, followed soon afterwards by a General Election resulting in a Conservative Government, to be renewed at intervals for a period later referred to as Thirteen Years of Tory Misrule, during which, as already noted, 'we pheasants, having re-instated our right wing, went round in circles'. Then this aerobatic display was to cease and we were to fly into a White Hot Technological Revolution, singeing our wings and succumbing to Beatles.

In 1952, the people of Britain lost the King who had lived with them through the Second World War and into the peace, and who at Christmas time in 1939 had heartened them by telling of the Man who stood at the Gate of the Year and said: 'Put your hand into the hand of God . . .' The public grief was intense and genuine. So were the hopes that rose with the Accession and Coronation of his successor.

[1] Frank Muir. He prefers, naturally, to be known as an author and broadcaster.
[2] Vernon as a Wykehamist would recognize the quotation.

As the period is one of which any reader who has kept his TV set continuously switched on is fully aware, there is perhaps less need than heretofore to mention events external to the Company. For the spread of the telly was characteristic of the early years of the era. We have seen that it played little or no part during Mr. Cube's campaign, but now those little prickly Things began to sprout from every roof in the land and soon there would even be a commercial network.

It is convenient to split the period into two phases, coinciding more or less with two phases of central Company policy although these overlap in time. Both are characterized by expansion and diversification. As Phase I opens the Korean War is in full swing. As it closes Vietnam is about to begin. As it closes, so does Sir Winston Churchill's life. And the Establishment emerges as a target for satire.

Let us begin at the beginning. For Tate & Lyle the situation developed along these lines: the end of sugar-rationing; a heavy and expanding world-wide demand for refined sugar, requiring maximum use of existing facilities and heavy investment in new plant; a growing freedom in trading and central policy, framed in such a way as to consolidate and improve the efficiency of the refineries, in order to get away from wartime and post-war austerity and to improve the service to customers at home and abroad, housewife or manufacturer; among new techniques, the evolution of the handling in bulk of raw and refined sugar. While these activities led to improved company prosperity, there was a determined effort to share this with employees at all levels. 'Profit' was by now beginning to become a dirty word in the English language, but a profit of one-seventh of a farthing on a pound of sugar cannot be thought excessive.

Up to the present, the policy had for some twenty years and more been a conscious one of vertical expansion. The Company had taken on the capacity for delivery of its products and of its raw material. It had moved upstream to produce that raw material and had gone in for shipping to transport it across the seas. Now what?

Exporting was accompanied by a willingness to invest in countries which were importing and to make available technical know-how and also the heavy ironmongery required in sugar production and refining. For those countries would themselves want to make sugar and although this would affect export trading, it was an inevitable evolution.

There was also to be further investment in the successful raw sugar ventures in the Caribbean and in opportunities in other developing countries. The risks involved, while beginning to be visible, had to be accepted, for change was in the air.

Some of the developments fall naturally into the framework of the Company's refining activities, others are best examined on their own; the division is a little arbitrary but unavoidable. In some cases, too, they overlap into the next phase. Inevitably we shall during this phase say good-bye to people who have enlivened us. Leonard Lyle, the President, his successor, Vernon Tate, and Philip Lyle, died in the space of eighteen months. In 1955 Ian Lyle was elected Chairman and Oliver Lyle and Peter Runge became Vice-Chairman three years later. Three years after that Oliver, too, died, after a long illness born with great courage, and as Phase I came to an end his son, John, became Chairman.

But it is time to look a little deeper.

II
Sugar is Derationed

The new Conservative Government was determined to de-ration food, and in particular sugar, for increases in Commonwealth production were making this easier to obtain without dollar expenditure. Gradually the ration was increased, but there were outcries from the Left that de-rationing would mean instant shortage, that the price would rise and that The People would be unable to buy the stuff. Just to be sure, therefore, the Government, which was still purchasing all raw sugar imported into the country, ordered the refiners to build up huge stocks. When de-rationing took place in 1953 the increase in consumption was modest, for other foodstuffs, including cereals and similar carbohydrates, were freely available and meat too came off the ration. So the stocks were not needed. Leonard Lyle referred to this as a costly blunder and demanded more freedom for refiners to run their own affairs. (It took three years before this came about.)

Some rationalization of refining began. Capacity in Scotland was too large for the market and the ancient Glebe Refinery, where Abram III, the 'old pirate king', had begun his refinery interests, was closed. But Walkers' required a complete reconstruction. The plans prepared, first in 1928 by Fred Sudbury and Wellings and then revised in 1938/39, were revamped and in 1953 building permits were obtained. The work had to be carried out without interrupting refining operations. By 1958 a new Recovery House would be complete containing all the early stages of the process, and a 5,000 ton raw sugar silo.

At the same time, more capacity was needed in London, in particular to produce sugar for export. At the height of Mr. Cube's campaign in 1949/50 an investigation was made into the possibility of increasing Plaistow's capacity by adding a fifth bay at the Pan House, complete with pan, centrifugals, granulators and a new path to the packing stations. In January 1951 the decision was taken to go ahead. At the same time it was decided that all the affination and recovery, carbonatation and filtration plant should be replaced and eventually housed in a huge new building alongside the Pan House. The whole plan was meticulously worked out, and on 30th June, 1953, the first 'skipping' from the fifth bay went to market. There had been many teething problems–getting additional condenser water from the river up to the roof, ensuring that the new granulators delivered clean sugar – they didn't at first, and bullying suppliers into delivering equipment in time.

At the same time there were major new developments in the bulk handling and delivery of raw and refined sugar. At Liverpool the huge Huskisson silo, holding 100,000 tons of raw sugar, was erected. There was the installation of a new system for revivifying 'spent char', of new automatic weighing machines in the Fill House (where refined sugar was packed in 56 lb. paper packs), and the problem of fulfilling Government instructions to build up a stock against de-rationing. This was overcome by the purchase of two large buildings once used for a Franco-British exhibition at White City, and their re-erection on part of the Fison's site next door to Plaistow, which had itself been acquired. (One source of smell had now gone!)

At Thames, production was back to normal again, but there were changes in the wind. The war had made the production of the traditional Tate's wooden case for carrying 1 cwt. of cubes virtually impossible, and wood had been replaced by fiberite, much cheaper and lighter. Although the old 'diamond' cases had had many secondary uses, as the bodies of do-it-yourself hand-carts, or for standing on while orating at Speaker's Corner, they were now, like the horse-drawn carts in the Refinery, an anachronism. So the old Case-Making Plant was closed down.

There was trouble, too, with the Adant cube-making plant, the successor of the Langen, at Thames. It produced a splendid, sparkling, rather irregular cube, formed at first in moulded slabs, then centrifuged to remove excess syrup, washed with 'claircé' (supersaturated syrup), and finally cut into the familiar shape. The process was indeed, unsuitable for the second half of the twentieth century, for the moulds had to be man-handled from the centrifugals and many a lump was therefore possibly Touched by Hand even if in glove. (There was also a huge 8-foot, slow-moving conveyor band, which acted partly as intermediate storage point, partly as a feed to the Packing Department. At the height of the Mr. Cube campaign this had been photographed. Alas, just before the camera clicked, some zealous cleaner had run up it in order to remove some dust from its machine-guards. He had forgotten to cover his tracks and the photo had to be touched-up, or a fascinated public would have seen a picture of Footprints in the Cubes of Time. He was however wearing special shoes used only for this purpose.)

But the rising demand for exports included cubes, particularly for West Africa where their convenient shape and currency value had long been known – inland, and away from the alternative cowrie shell. In village shops and mammy stalls, the cube had been about five to a penny, and was given in change in small transactions. It was even said to be useful in more complicated dealings. Ten cubes would get you a goat, twenty another wife, and fifty a share in a second-hand bicycle. If, however, the Adant

Sir Ernest Tate, Bart.

Leonard Lyle, 1st Baron
Lyle of Westbourne.

George Vernon Tate,
M.C.

Sir Ian Lyle, D.S.C.

Sir Peter Runge.

John Oliver Lyle.

F. H. ('Tony') Tate.

Sir Robert Park Lyle,
Bart.

plant was beginning to wear out, it would be foolish merely to renew it. It must be replaced by something more modern. Large scale experiments in the production of a new 'crystal cube' were begun. They did not succeed for a variety of reasons, but in the meantime, there were new ready-made cube-making plants available from countries where the cube was still in higher domestic demand than in Britain; from Sweden in the shape of the Høweler, from France the Chambon. In the end the former was adopted. Even if its product was less sparkling, it produced cubes in a 'ranged' form, and these were more easily packeted than the individual Adant cubes.

Exporting was, in those days, the name of the game. Prior to 1928, and the change in duties, Tate & Lyle had never exported much; instead, they had been subject to much competition from imported beet sugar industry from continental Europe, usually still subsidized by Governments. These producers had to sell their sugar, and if they could, they did so in Britain. The 1928 duties had given some protection not only to the refiners, but to an even greater extent to the British home-grown beet sugar industry, and indirectly to the raw cane sugar producers of the Empire (about to be the Commonwealth). Stability on the home market enabled the refiners, particularly Tate & Lyle, to export sugar and between 1928 and 1939 the annual average figure of exports rose to 350,000 tons. Once the Second War was over, exports were again in demand and expanded to 650,000 tons a year, with a peak in 1954 of 800,000.

Demand was so great that little effort was required. A tiny saleroom in Mincing Lane, then led by Charles Lyle (from 1955 to 1961) and Arthur Latham – a charming man, one of whose twin sons Philip and John will be familiar to all TV viewers of the 1970s as Willy in 'The Troubleshooters', or Plantagenet in 'The Pallisers', the other still with T. & L. – arranged deals of sugar in fantastic tonnages. The sugar brokers of London – Czarnikow, E. D. & F. Man, Woodhouse, Carey & Brown, Drake and others, acted as the link. Much censured by advanced politicians ('Cut the Middle Man Out', was the cry) they serve the purpose of a buffer between seller of raw sugar and buyer, between exporter of refined sugar and purchaser. It is an ancient principle in commerce that whatever deal you may do it is better to have someone between you and the other man – if you want to avoid trouble, recrimination and legal actions and still remain on terms.

Exporting, then, seemed easy in the early 1950s. A quarter of a million tons of white sugar were exported to India, more than 100,000 tons to Russia, 40,000 to the COMECON countries, another 200,000 to Pakistan, 290,000 tons to Iraq, Saudi Arabia and the Persian Gulf States, anything from 50 to 100,000 tons to West Africa. Refineries 'worked through' many week-ends, which meant 12 hour shifts for those involved. It was well paid but tiring and one's family got fed up. There were few other refiners in the world selling outside their home markets. A little was done by the Raffineries St. Louis in Marseilles and by the Taikoo Refinery in Hong Kong. No sugar was any longer exported by the refiners of the U.S.A. Refined exports had really to be based on a firm home market.

But a new factor was emerging. In many parts of the world, notably in Russia and the COMECON countries, but also in France and other continental countries, beet sugar production was increasing again. As early as 1950, the COMECON countries were exporting white sugar from beet when it was available, while at certain times of the year they were also importing. In Poland and Czechoslovakia as well as in the U.S.S.R. enormous investments were being made in beet sugar production. Although in the U.S.S.R. productivity per acre was, and still remains, very low, the Soviet Union was determined to become the largest individual producer of sugar in the world. Later, thanks to the advent of Castro, towards the end of our Phase I, she would have to accept cane sugar from Cuba and herself export beet sugar. For, although when Stalin died, the Russian consumer was given a chance to eat more sugar, there would occasionally be surpluses in Russia in a good year for beet, when storage space for a seasonally produced commodity would be short.

Communist China, too, began to be an exporter, though her own strictly rationed people had among the smallest per capita consumptions in the world. She needed things from outside and sugar was a way of paying for these. So, in addition to *The Thoughts of Chairman Mao*, Chinese sugar came on the market, to the tune of 100,000 tons a year by 1958 and over 400,000 by the mid 1960s. India, also in need of foreign currency (and a place where a great deal of cheap if rather primitive sugar is turned out for local consumption by clever chaps using the mule or ox as motive power, and small do-it-yourself centrifugal machines driven clandestinely by electricity 'borrowed' from a local generating station), began herself to export. Pakistan began to build her own sugar mills – sometimes buying the equipment from Tate & Lyle. Mexico, Venezuela, Taiwan and others expanded, often producing fairly high quality sugar for export.

Most if not all of these, produced a free-flowing product which did not deteriorate much in storage, was usable by manufacturers not too worried about quality, and which, like coal, oil, metals, flour, or rice, can be traded on a world market. In this, sugar is unlike radio sets or motor cars. It remains the same, whereas a customer who wants a Mercedes doesn't like being told he may have to wait a year and then find he's got to take a Renault or a Marina. In other words it is a commodity.

So, during this Phase I, Tate & Lyle's export business grew, reaching a plateau, and then fell back to a respectable but unexciting level. The retention of this level depended on expert use of the great London Terminal Market, then as now the most important in the world, with contacts everywhere. It depended on providing a product to which discriminating users would be faithful, as in Norway. It would later depend also on willingness to receive raw sugar bought by customers, sent to a Tate & Lyle Refinery and delivered refined to the customer, a system called the 'Toll Contract' of which probably the first example was one of 50,000 tons for Eire in 1937/38. There would be many of these, with West Germany, Switzerland, Tunisia, Bahrein and Malaya for example. It was all a question of being flexible, watchful and willing.

III

Bulk Sugar and All That
'The greatest meliorator of the world is selfish, huckstering Trade'
(R. W. Emerson 1805–1882)

It will be recalled that during the Mr. Cube campaign in July 1949 there had arrived in London a ship, the *Baron Haig,* with some 5,250 tons raw sugar from San Domingo loaded into her holds in bulk as though it were sand, instead of in jute bags, and there had been trade union problems about her discharge.

These were not the only problems, for in those days either the unions won or the bosses did, or if you trusted each other there was a compromise. But there were also possible problems as between buyer and seller on the degrees of polarization on which payment would be made. (This is briefly explained later.[3]) And, naturally enough, since imported sugar paid a duty, there was a possible problem with H.M. Customs and Excise. England expects, after all, that every man, woman and child, will pay his/her/its/duty. But for this shipment there was no argument. The savings in cost at either end – shipment or discharge, the savings in sweat and toil of work better done by machine, were too important. For this and sundry later shipments, Tate & Lyle accepted the sellers' figures, until a proper system could be established. The seller was also accommodating. H.M. Customs had long maintained a twenty-four hour watch on samples and weights of sugar landed. It was one man for eight hours at a time, plus one supervisor over the twenty-four hours. And, completely unbribable, because they were trusted men and nobody dreamed of trying, in turn they were trusting. They even accepted in the days of hand-weighing that the Company's weigher should be allowed 'the turn of the beam'. On this *Baron Haig* shipment they agreed to accept weights and polarizations which were convenient to seller and buyer together.

This small but successful bulk sugar experiment sprang from American experience. The sugar producers of Hawaii had long had a close link with the California and Hawaii Refinery of San Francisco and just after the war had begun experimenting in bulk-handling. Geoffrey Fairrie, Fred Sudbury and a technologist from Plaistow, Frank Chapman, had seen these, and had independently formed the firm opinion that this was the way in which raw sugar would in the very near future be handled.

It also so happened that eleven years earlier in 1938 there had been that

[3] See Chapter Twenty-six.

modest incursion into vertical integration initiated by Vernon Tate which resulted in the establishment of a company called Silvertown Services Ltd. Until then, raw sugar unloaded from ocean-going ships in the London docks had been transported to the refineries by two lighterage companies, the Tilbury Contracting & Dredging Company Ltd. (to Plaistow) and W. H. J. Alexander Ltd. (to Thames). In order to ensure the smooth arrival of raw material, the tugs, barges and other equipment of these two companies had been purchased for £244,000. They numbered 6 tugs, 244 barges and sundry other equipment and the Company, beginning operations as Silvertown Services Ltd. on 3rd October, 1938, had operated ever since.

During the war many of the tugs and barges were requisitioned by the Government. Six 500-ton barges were used for balloon barrage service and moored off Tilbury. Others were used at Dunkirk and later for Operation Overlord. Some tugs were used at Fairloch on the Clyde. Others were shipped to West Africa and Ceylon. Three were lost. After the war new tugs and all-welded barges were ordered.

People have for centuries had mixed feelings about watermen and lightermen. Their attitude to the customer has always bordered on the disrespectful. Indeed, it took Dr. Johnson to silence one of them with the unanswerable remark: 'Sir, your mother, under pretence of keeping a bawdy-house, is a receiver of stolen goods', from which one may gather that lighterage is a centuries-old Thames trade. In fairness, it should also be recorded that to this day, each year, selected lightermen race from London Bridge to Putney for a prize of a coat and badge first presented in the eighteenth century by an actor named Doggett. From among the watermen, too, a number are nominated by the 400-year-old Company of Watermen & Lightermen, as Royal Watermen, and these in their magnificent livery escort the Sovereign on state occasions. Watermen have a traditional toughness and individuality and for hundreds of years father has been followed by son in the trade. When sugar began to arrive in bulk they had at first little difficulty in adapting themselves, while holding fast to their traditions. A tradition in the trade, going back to the times when the only way home was to row yourself across the wild reaches of the Thames or walk along unlit paths, was the convention that if you worked till 8.00 p.m. you were paid till midnight and if you worked till 10.00 p.m. you were paid for the whole night. These conventions persisted.

To handle bulk sugar, new equipment was needed, bucket grabs which would claw the sugar from the ships' hold and discharge it accurately into barges, and others which would discharge it from the barges when these reached the refineries. To begin with existing cranes were fitted with grabs, and existing raw sugar silos used. Then, after four further trials in 1950 with a chartered vessel, the *Hudson Deep,* bringing sugar from the West Indies, it was decided to convert Liverpool, Thames and Plaistow Wharf as rapidly as possible to bulk raw handling. The floating part of the operation was entrusted in London to Silvertown Services.

An early Lyle square-rigged vessel. The Lyles got out of sail and into steam just in time.

An early Lyle Steamer

One of the big 'uns, *Athel King* is a 59,000 tonner. Successor to the ship of the same name sunk in 1940.

Appropriately named *Sugar Carrier*. She also carries iron ore, phosphates and other materials.

Thames' storage facilities were adequate and the cranes readily converted. At Plaistow Wharf raw storage was only available for 2,000 tons, but the river frontage of the former Fison's site to the east, and the area inshore were suitable for development, and it was decided to build there a jetty at which ships of up to 5,000 tons could discharge direct. New $7\frac{1}{2}$ ton capacity cranes and conveyors were erected, and a mechanically operated coal storage area. Inshore from this was a huge 45,000 ton cylindrical silo which needed only the occasional attention of one man. Rail wagons containing raw beet sugar could also be handled with a 'tippler' which fed to the silo. The jetty was named Peruvian Wharf, for it was here that, in the early days of fertilizers, guano (or seagulls' droppings) from Peru had been landed. The whole complex, capable of handling 200 tons an hour, had been designed by Godwin Simmons, the affable but loquacious Chief Engineer at Plaistow. (He loved to describe what he was up to, but had a tendency to give one the full background, from Noah onwards, on the handling and storage of cargoes, and it was necessary to wait for the words: 'Well, it all boils down to this', before switching on.) The first direct ship-to-refinery discharge at Peruvian Wharf was made in May 1953.

At Liverpool the Refinery is at some distance from the Huskisson Dock, on the River Mersey. Ships had long been discharged by a master porterage company, the Riverside Stevedoring Company Ltd., in which the shares were owned by Tate & Lyle and by the firm of sugar brokers, C. Czarnikow Ltd., the latter managing the affair. Sugar was delivered at Love Lane refinery by another subsidiary, the Huskisson Transit Company Ltd., in 12-ton box-type road trucks. In 1952, in order to cope with bulk handling the Huskisson Dock was fitted with four special cranes discharging from the ships' hold through hoppers into the trucks which could be loaded at a rate of one a minute. Later a further four cranes were added, to enable two ships to be unloaded simultaneously, and the huge 100,000 ton concrete silo, shaped like an inverted V, constructed to act as a buffer store between seasonal arrivals. The first bulk vessel to be discharged at Huskisson Dock was the *Sugar Transporter* on 18th August, 1952.

As soon as the decision had been taken in 1951 to erect the installations at Plaistow and Liverpool, there was a further new development. Silvertown Services acquired three 4,500 ton-carrying vessels, suited for loading at smaller ports in the West Indies. The S.S. *Empire Caicos, Makena II* and *Thackeray*, they were re-christened *Sugar Transporter, Sugar Producer* and *Sugar Refiner*, and they and their eventual replacements were owned and managed at first by a subsidiary of Silvertown Services, Kentships Ltd., and were the immediate fore-runners of a still further development, that of Sugar Line Ltd. Such ventures, although regarded in orthodox financial circles as being unusual and possibly dotty, were then a necessity if full advantage was to be taken of the rapid growth of bulk sugar handling. In 1950 the total tonnage discharged in bulk was a mere 112,000 tons. Six years later it would be 1,330,000 in a year, and later still it reached 2 million.

Sugar Line Ltd. was registered on 26th July, 1951, with the purpose of running a fleet of bulk carriers which, although too large for the planned Peruvian Wharf jetty, could carry out longer ocean-going voyages and yet were of a size to be suitable at Greenock, Liverpool, Toronto and Montreal (where Tate & Lyle were becoming involved) and fifteen years later at a projected deep-water wharf at Thames Refinery. Whereas the first three 4,500-ton ships and their successors bore the prefix *Sugar*, these larger vessels had the prefix *Crystal*, and the first four, *Cube*, *Bell*, *Gem* and *Jewel* were all launched during 1955. The original plan was for ten 12,000-ton 16-knot ships, but when Sugar Line was formed, part of the equity was held by United Molasses Ltd. With their decades of experience they offered to vet the design and run the fleet through their subsidiary, Athel Line Ltd. (q.v.). The first four were still experimental and limited to 9,500 tons with a speed of $9\frac{1}{2}$ knots. Successors were larger and faster. All these bulk carriers can be used for other cargoes when sugar is not available, and carry iron ore and other minerals. Indeed they would not be commercially viable unless they did so, acting almost like tramp ships.

During the next twelve years both the *Sugar* and the *Crystal* series were improved and adapted. Silvertown Services Shipping Ltd. was formed in 1956 to acquire the smaller vessels, and the steamers were replaced by twin-engine single-shaft diesel vessels.[4] The two Lines, initially serving different producing areas, were run separately for many years. There was considerable professional rivalry between them. Eventually they were amalgamated and later still, after United Molasses Ltd. had been acquired – during the second phase of this period – the whole mixed fleet of tankers and bulk carriers were placed under single management. By then the vessels, which had at first been built by Cammell Laird and various other yards, began to achieve much larger tonnages still. Many were built by Scott Lithgow of Greenock. The two latest vessels built in Canada would be 28,000 tons deadweight.

1951 saw also what appears a somewhat anomalous acquisition in the circumstances of bulk handling, that of Thomas Boag Ltd., a company trading in jute bags, chiefly secondhand. The jute mills of Dundee were folding up for lack of outlets. Raw sugar bags, in the bad old days, had, after being cut open and emptied into silos, been collected, shaken and washed – the washings being returned for use in 'melting' the raw sugar, so that nothing should be lost. Thereafter, they had been dried, much in the same way as the baby's nappy or father's underpants were dried, before being repaired and sold (the raw sugar bags, I mean) for further use. The Bag Drying Department should have been a terrible place. In some ways it

---

[4] In 1957 its headquarters and registered office, and that of Silvertown Services Ltd. were installed at Clyde Wharf, the site of James Duncan's ill-fated refinery ninety years before. Barge repairs were also carried out here. It has since been sold.

was. Worked by women, it seemed in theory the sort of limbo into which the most difficult people would gravitate. Yet it wasn't. The girls may have been tough, and, while working, not entirely elegant, for which nobody would blame them – for eyeshadow runs and nail-varnish gets chipped. But they had, like all the girls' departments at a refinery, a character of their own, robust, cheerful, kindly, forthright. Now their day was done. Jute bags were a bygone thing. It is therefore quite inexplicable that Tate & Lyle should have acquired Thomas Boag's 'at this moment of time', as they say in Watergate. It was a little like the chocolate factory at Plaistow, though different. Let us forget it.

Since Silvertown Services Shipping Ltd.[5] and Sugar Line Ltd. were formed after the Second War, there is about them less of the drama which attended United Molasses' Athel Line fleet from 1939 to 1945, of which we shall in due course be hearing. It is through no fault of the people who man the ships, Captain Gorell, Captain Andrew Lunn, and Harry Kay, the Australian Chief Engineer and the rest. They sail their vessels round the world, arriving immaculate unless battered by the cruel sea. And when there is an emergency, they deal with it. As when in September 1955 the Chief Officer of the *Crystal Cube* fell off the Jacob's ladder into the water. A youngster of nineteen, Glasgow-born James Murphy, dived twenty feet into the sea and held the unconscious man up in the water for nearly half an hour until picked up. These things happen less frequently in peace time, but when they do, men at sea react as they always have.

Silvertown Services passed its zenith during this Phase I with the coming of bulk-handling from ship to refinery. Barges were no longer needed. This coincided with a falling-off in the export trade and the development of container shipping. In 1957 Silvertown Services handled nearly 2 million tons, using 242 barges manned by 140 lightermen. Ten years later it would have only 24 barges and employ only 19 men. Some of the men opted to accept redundancy but many were given a golden or at least silver handshake and were later found jobs elsewhere in the Company.

Geoff Collard, Manager of Silvertown Services had been an apprenticed waterman in 1933. During war service in the Royal Engineers he met Fred Sudbury and the latter took him on in 1950 as a successor to Charles Lynch who was ill. Norman Kindon and Bill Cater were his colleagues. He has seen it all happen. Now Silvertown Services has no craft except two sailing barges, *May* and *Ethel*. Rather in the same way as the horse has staged a come-back and there are more people in every walk of life than there have been for decades riding and caring for those capricious quadrupeds, so the future of the barges could be as a reminder that grace counts for something. The sight of a sailing barge, over 100 years old, comfortable, manageable, may remind us that machines are oily, smelly, and – without oil fuel – undependable, and that nature knows a thing or two.

[5] Silvertown Services Shipping became Sugar Line Terminals in 1964 and invested in a new bulk sugar handling plant at Point Lisas, Trinidad.

IV
Profit Sharing
'The good things which belong to prosperity are to be wished . . . .'
(Francis Bacon 1561–1626)

The staunch, tacit support of the people of Tate & Lyle in 1949–50 had not been bought, for it was genuine. It would be nice to say thank you. But how? An increase in pay would be clumsy and politically stupid. And in any case there was one of those perennial wage/price freezes on. These have since persisted through the thirteen years of Conservative Government and were still alive and kicking twenty-eight years later as Phase I, II and (hic) III of the Social Contract. Profit-sharing schemes had been thought up and found too difficult. Moreover, profits are subject to influences beyond the control of the man on the shop floor – indeed from time to time beyond the control of the Board of Directors. On the other hand production, productivity, and freedom from interruption are to a considerable extent things which everyone can help in.

There could be no wage increase without poking a finger in the Government's eye. But there could be a sharing in prosperity. Over a quiet glass in some pub or other Ian Lyle and Peter Runge, who at that time concerned themselves with overall personnel policy, discussed the problem with Captain Mark Hewitson M.P., the National Negotiating Officer of the N.U.G.M.W. After much examination of other companies' schemes, together they evolved a prosperity sharing scheme whereby all employees with more than a year's service would receive at three-monthly intervals, a bonus based in part on the tonnage of sugar produced over a certain minimum and in part on profits net of tax, again over a certain minimum.

It needed some explaining, and Mr. Cube was called on to do this, in an illustrated leaflet issued to all U.K. employees. This described the nuts and bolts of the scheme, at the same time pointing out that if, for example, you were suspended for calling your foreman a soppy date (or worse) you would forfeit your share for a bit. The scheme went down well, and lasted for a number of years until in between wage freezes the trade unions expressed the view that on the whole, people would prefer a rise.

A further refinement, introduced in 1959, was the offer to any employee of the chance to purchase bearer shares in the Company, carrying the full right to any dividends payable to other holders of ordinary shares. They could be purchased at share shops alongside the places where wages were paid. Although this system was fully explained, although it was regarded as a forward-looking scheme, and applauded by the forward-looking and liberal-minded, it never caught on. People were just not interested, preferring it seemed, to draw their pay, do their best, and leave all that stuff about shares to others. There were never more than about 300 holders of such shares out of a pay-roll of nearly 9,000. Perhaps the majority were right, for later the dividends would rank as unearned income and be subject to a surcharge. But at the time it was disappointing.

Even earlier than these two innovations, but following the ex-gratia pension scheme, there had been concern about what happened to an hourly-paid employee when he went sick. The new National Health Service, although at first providing what was in theory needed, was inevitably formalized and bureaucratic, and would always lack the personal touch. In 1948 a slightly ad hoc, do-it-yourself, additional sick pay scheme was introduced by Tate & Lyle. When told of it and asked for their views the unions welcomed it. Administered at each place of employment by men or women who knew their clients, and followed up by a network of pensioners who were asked to make sure that individuals were really all right, but *not* to spy on them, this was a genuinely imaginative personal service, never offered as or regarded as a 'charity'.

V

Transports of Delight

It is time for an interlude, about the highly respected, very greatly loved, but slightly awesome figure of Oliver Lyle. He (from 1922) and Ian (from 1945) had been the two Refinery Directors at Plaistow. Now he had been joined by his son John, for Ian had become Chairman. (At Thames it was Jo Whitmee and Johnny Tate, at Liverpool Geoffrey Fairrie and Morton Oliphant.)

Oliver and his brother Philip had once been interested in the production of the speedy Invicta car of the 1920s, but during the 1939 war, Oliver had become fascinated by the economic running of a motor vehicle. He had taken to driving a small 8-h.p. Standard, and trying to get as many miles per gallon as others would get miles per hour, and more. He had fitted devices to ensure this, and woe betide any garage which tuned his car up.

Of course, in order to be absolutely certain that his measurements were accurate, he had from time to time to run his tank empty. Once, coming up from his house in Kent, he did so on the Sidcup by-pass, and he had forgotten to fill his emergency can. However, he knew that his son, John, would soon be passing in a Bristol, normally driven at the speed of light, and would be able to get him petrol from the nearest garage. Instead, when John arrived on the scene, he offered to tow the little black Standard to Plaistow. The thought of a few miles at zero petrol consumption was too much – even if one had to square one's conscience later. Oliver agreed, but insisted on a speed limit, over which he would sound his horn.

Off they went, father towed by son. But then a new factor intervened. Colin Rowan, then General Manager at Plaistow, also lived in Kent and drove a Jaguar. He passed the little convoy and, seeing for once an opportunity to show John a clean pair of heels, gave him that familiar two finger sign. This was too much for John. He put his foot down and chased Colin.

A police car, parked in a side road saw them all pass a little later and reported by radio: 'We've just seen a Jaguar go by at ninety, followed by a Bristol, and behind them there's an old man in a Standard 8 blasting away on his horn and trying to pass them both.'

At 21 Mincing Lane Oliver had his own filing system, more complex than the rest. The Senior Secretary, Phyl Davies, who looked after him and sundry others, always did his first. 'He's a *poppet*', she said, by way of explanation. Poppet was, perhaps a slight misnomer, for is there such a thing as a tough poppet? But her meaning was clear and accepted.

One day, over lunch, his brother Philip was talking of wills. 'I didn't know', said someone else, 'there were different sorts of wills. I thought you just made one'. 'No', said Oliver sharply, 'There are at least two I can think of, W.D. and H.O.' No wonder he was missed when he died in 1961.

It is also endearing that the Chairman of Tate & Lyle of 1977 arrives at meetings with Ministers or other grandiose occasions in a very small car. He has a chauffeur because parking is often a problem, and the chauffeur occasionally has trouble convincing some braided functionary at the gate that it really *is* the car for the Chairman of Tate & Lyle. But that is not the point. (If this were the sequel to some epic of the screen, it might be called 'Sons of Tate & Lyle'.)

VI

Road Transport
'Hitch your wagon . . .'
(R. W. Emerson 1803–1882)

The mention of transports of delight in the foregoing is a reminder of a major element in the home trade of Tate & Lyle, and known as T.L.T. – Tate & Lyle Transport Ltd. Two passing references have been made to an early decision to develop a road transport subsidiary, and indeed the careful reader will recall a reference to Pease Transport hot, Pease Transport cold.

There must always have been ways of getting raw sugar into and refined sugar out of refineries from the word go. Indeed, Bertie Tate's fondness for the horses at Love Lane has been noted, and there were many such quadrupeds at other refineries long before the invention of the steam truck and the petrol or oil-driven box. Until 1900 there were hundreds of thousands of these creatures all over the world supplying mankind with a thing still commemorated in the initials h.p.

Also, it is sad to admit, the old refiners' bullocks' blood might often be horses' blood. For when the horse was the sole source of more than man power it was in old age given the same treatment as the dilapidated automobile 'banger' is now. Those patient creatures ended up, when written down in the books, in the knackers' yard. In some parts of the world, e.g. *La Belle France,* there were *boucheries* (butchers' shops) *de cheval* (of horse), and the decent brutes were converted into steaks. The bones ended up in places like that emporium of Messrs. J. Knight alongside Plaistow Wharf as the raw material of soap. Nothing was wasted.

Tate & Lyle ran their own transport system in Liverpool and London in the early days. There are pictures to prove this. But they needed outside contractors to cope with peak demand.

One of these, in London, was the property of a family by the name of Robert Pease and Son, Grease and Bone Merchants of Garrett Lane, Lower Tooting. For those who cannot recall Lower Tooting in 1872 it may be as well to know that it was next door to a knacker's yard, where a Mr. Atchelor 'disposed of' 25,000 horses a year.

In 1893 the Pease family moved to Wandle Wharf, Wandsworth. This move was not the result of a desire to provide their young with an élite education, for of course the Wandsworth Comprehensive did not then exist. It was merely in order to be near the River Thames up which came in barges large quantities of grain. For by now one of the family, John Robert Pease, was in charge and had diversified into the business of corn-chandling. He had also married a lady called Clementina Stacey–q.v. shortly. And he had also, during King Edward's reign, gone into the business of handling a variety of grocers' goods, dried beans and peas, canned goods. And sugar.

He was doing well but he had only a few years in which to make his fortune. In 1900 the horse was king of transport. A 'job-master' would have as many as 4,000 animals champing through nearly 50,000 tons of cereals a year and leaving in the highways and byways a similar tonnage of a deposit highly regarded by gardeners. By 1910 the same job-masters would have only cars instead.

However, Mr. J. Pease's site had by then been discovered as a suitable upstream repository for the products of H. Tate and A. Lyle. He had also found that the steam-engine could supplant the horse. It was cheap, reliable, and easy to run. If something went wrong with it you kicked it or used a hammer, and it became docile. It lived on coal and water, and if gardeners complained that it left no deposit in the streets, that was just too bad. The maker of the steam vehicles was a firm called Foden.

Tates' and Lyles' had their own fleet of 'steamers' and these all proceeded at the majestic speed of 5 m.p.h. on iron-shod wheels. But during the First War, the petrol engine really came in and the refineries used it, buying Thorneycrofts and McCurds. They were not loved. Axel von Willebrand, starting in 1917 as an apprentice in the Love Lane garage, was advised that the transport department was 'a necessary evil'.

During that First War, too, petrol-driven vehicles were often expropriated–one of the Lyles' wagons was taken over as a Red Cross vehicle–and at the same time many a man was trained in the Army to comprehend and coax these new-fangled machines. So, when the War was over, lots of them took over ex-Army vehicles and began a cut-throat competition which caused trouble to the likes of J. R. Pease. He himself, still thinking in terms of the horse as a major form of traction–when, later, his last horse was removed, he burst into tears–had unwisely ventured £60,000 in 1920s money, say about £250,000 of 1970s–in deals on the Corn Exchange.

But there now enters another figure not entirely unlike the Quiet Dane whom we shall shortly meet as founder of United Molasses. This one was an Englishman, Cyril Fisher, who had begun his career in 1904 as agent for the Cannock Chase Colliery. Now in the corn business, Cyril met John Pease in the course of a search for settlement of a bill, and lent a friendly hand. Being a shrewd chap he was aware of the future potential of the petrol lorry, and was quite undeterred by frequent breakdowns which might have renewed the hopes of any horses foolish enough to *want* to tow loads around the place.

Ernest Tate and Charles Lyle had by now inserted the Ampersand, and had gone so far as to begin the production of packeted sugar. Cyril Fisher realized that a new sort of service was needed if Pease were to retain these old customers. There were troubles, as always with a new venture, but Fisher had the wit to offer a very low-cost and extremely flexible service to Tate & Lyle, and to make Pease Transport virtually indispensable.

The refiners liked to do their own thing, and each refinery kept its own fleet of McCurds, Fords, Vulcans, Leylands and the rest, only giving Pease Transport the awkward crumbs which not only fell from the table but rolled beyond reach if you weren't careful.

However, the possession of a riverside warehouse at Wandsworth which could be fed by lighters and acted as a distribution point, helped. The tiny staff, working in a cottage at Wandle Wharf and alongside a 3,000 ton warehouse which was occasionally surrounded by uninvited growths of oats and wheat caused by spillages of seed from sacks and was not infrequently affected by leaks in rainy weather, somehow kept going.

With a wages bill of about £75 a week, the variety of goods handled kept the wolf a yard or two from the door. In 1930 Jim Coffey joined the staff as a Stock Clerk, finding there a lot of elderly men, Mr. Pease, a Miss A. Campion and eight girls, and an Office Manager called W. H. Chisholm. 'Chis' was of short stature–'Swing from the lintel, lad,' John Pease used to say, 'it should stretch you'–but he was always calm, with the peace you hope to find at the centre of any storm, and he did 50 years with the firm. It is nice to think that his daughter, Sheila, apart from being secretary to John Lyle and Tony Tate, has also found time to put this book together. Calm capability runs in the Chisholm family.

By now Cyril Fisher had become a full-time member of the firm, and had built up a close relationship with Albert Buckeridge who, at 21

Before even steam lorries. Horses were the source of a by-product much appreciated by gardeners.

A Tate 'Steamer'. The gang at work are *not* Mack Sennett & Co. There are still puddles in Liverpool.

Mincing Lane, was in charge of Tate & Lyle's deliveries. They all worked like beavers – 'Chis', Charles Gooch, the maintenance man, Bob Sly, the clerk, and Jim Farley who came from a firm of motor engineers in Balham in 1931, bringing with him a team of fitters and drivers trained by himself.

John Pease, never a business man at heart, used to fish from the windows of the cottage when he had the time. He was obviously a delightful and generous person; if someone had done well he would say: 'give the man a sovereign.' But he was still a gambler, and in 1933 he involved himself in a venture on the Stock Exchange. (It was at that tricky time just after the Great Slump of 1929–31 when things were by no means clear.)

Cyril Fisher, in order to make sure that if the worst came to the worst there would still be something left, hived off the maintenance part of the business into a separate company called Fisher & Stacey – the latter being Mrs. Pease under her maiden name. Pease Transport once more and not for the last time went into the business of general carrying – Oxo, Bovril, Whiteways' Cider, brooms, washing boards, birdcages, and anything else. They survived – just.

But if there was to be a future, Cyril Fisher had worked out that it would be with Tate & Lyle. The Pease vehicles were in good order, the staff capable, the bank balance in the black. But more long term stability was needed. So, he approached Tate & Lyle with an offer to sell. Albert Buckeridge and Robert St. Croix (his assistant) thought well of the firm, and persuaded Vernon Tate, now Chairman of Tate & Lyle, to consider the purchase. One Sunday morning the forty-seven vehicles, lovingly swept, garnished and touched up, were paraded past Messrs. Vernon Tate, Buckeridge and St. Croix. Vernon thought about it for a few days – he was not one to be bounced. Then he decided to buy the lot, old, new, touched up or not, for £22,000. At the same time Pease Transport were given the job of running the vehicles owned by the London Refineries. Vernon was the first Chairman of the new acquisition.

Pease Transport relinquished its work as a general carrier, with an A licence under the 1936 Road Transport Act, and became a C licence, specialized carrier. Depots began to be erected all over the country, at Southampton, Cardiff, Bristol and elsewhere, giving regular year round work to the vehicles. In 1939, the Government imposed a wartime restriction of sixty miles on deliveries, so more depots were established. And at the same time the vehicles were used for carrying bulk stocks of meat and other foodstuffs for the Ministry of Food. (They also carried the furniture and effects of Tate & Lyle employees in London from their bombed-out houses to safety.)

When peace came in 1946 Pease Transport, aware of the benefits of decentralized distribution, began to open depots all over the country – Caversham, Tavistock, Cheltenham and elsewhere. They invested in pallets and fork-lift trucks for ease of loading. It was now that Nibs Hiscocks, a chemist at Thames before the war, but with six years of transport experience in the Army, including the rushing of food supplies to starving Vienna, was appointed Manager. In 1949 it was decided that Pease should be geared up to do *all* Tate & Lyle's transport work. Luckily the Bill nationalizing road transport permitted C licences to continue for specialist carriers.

During the Mr. Cube campaign Pease Transport and Fisher and Stacey, now both growing rapidly, were themselves hived off from Tate & Lyle. A northern section of Pease was formed, to service the Liverpool refinery. And a further new development was the introduction of a packing station at Keynsham near Bristol which was supplied with white sugar in bulk in a new form of vehicle, a huge 13-ton tanker, at first gravity-fed and discharged, later to be operated pneumatically. There had been an attempt to interest British Rail in acting as the carrier but they put so many difficulties in the way that they were discarded and in any case the road tanker was more flexible. (It had been developed by Geoffrey Fairrie in 1948.) So, there began the daily run of 200 tons of sugar down the Bath–Bristol road from London, drivers swapping over at Theale, the Bristol drivers taking full tankers on, the London drivers returning the empties to the refinery for refilling. There were technical problems in the early days but these were soon solved.

The ladies who looked after the Hesser machines at Keynsham, under the management of Freddie Windows, were once referred to as Bristol packing mommas.[6] From Keynsham the depots in the west were fed with packeted sugar.

When British Road Services was broken up as being unmanageable, some of its fleet were sold for A licence work. Some were bought by Pease for a new venture, Silver Roadways, serving others than the Refineries. From a modest beginning with some rather dubious vehicles, Silver Roadways was to become an equal partner with Pease.

At this time it was decided to rechristen Pease Tate and Lyle Transport, in order to avoid confusion. In the early days Pease vehicles had had their own livery, red chassis and wings, two tones of brown on the sides, and pictures of sugar and syrup packs. Although the war slowed down the change, the new livery became royal blue with gold lettering.

When Vernon Tate died, Tony Tate became Chairman of T.L.T., succeeded eight years later by Colin Rowan, who handed over–but this would be in Phase II–to David, Tony's son.

A Pease Transport (Scotland) (or MacPease) was established to handle the output of the Greenock Refinery. A similar subsidiary was set up in Ulster and would one day share the vicissitudes of that unhappy province.

New depots were built. New methods of handling crystals and powders pneumatically were developed and T.L.T. found itself becoming a pioneer in this field and in the field of transport engineering generally, forming a subsidiary which–with the assistance of Fodens–provides consultant

[6] There had been a popular song in 1944 about a 'Pistol-Packing Momma.'

services to many large road transport users–Bass-Charrington, Texaco, B.I.C.C. and others. Manufacturing customers want sugar in solution and mixtures of sucrose and glucose. This has led to the development of specialist liquid tankers. Nearly 60 per cent of the sugar consumed in Britain was by the 1970s in the form of manufactured goods, and this bulk transport business is of enormous importance.

Finally, the advance of the super-market has made the existence of the scattered depots of still further importance. Mixed consignments of sugar, coffee, and other packaged goods are stored at and picked up from these depots and delivered to the huge new super-market chain stores. It is all a little like what John Pease was doing sixty or seventy years earlier. The vehicles providing the service did for a period adopt a slightly 'with-it' livery involving Dick Whittington and his cat. This was not a success. Whittington may have been no end of a chap and three times Lord Mayor of London but he is too easily thought of as some chesty lady in tights saying to the bailiff: 'Sir, you are a wotter. How dare you thweaten my Mothah!'

The vehicles have since resumed a more sober costume.

But we have run ahead of phase I and it is time to look at another set of activities.

VII

Engineering and All That
'Wit's an unruly engine, wildly striking
Sometimes a friend, sometimes the engineer.'
(George Herbert 1593–1633)

There is something odd, to be sure, about engineers. A casual visitor to any fitting shop, let us say, for example, one belonging to Tate & Lyle Engineering Services, will become aware of two things, a smell of oil, grease and hot metal, and a collection of very saucy calendars. Messrs. Slapp and Tickell Ltd. of Ashby-de-la-Zouche, purveyors of ball-bearings, encourage the shy would-be purchaser by sending him annually a calendar consisting of twelve pictures of ladies with little or nothing on, each representing a month of the year. Nor is this habit confined to England. Herren Bloch und Tackel G.m.b.H. of 20176 Neue-Gladbach-am-Blisterzee in the Federal German Republic, makers of *Kugellager*, not to be outdone, oblige with an even glossier publication showing fifty-two equally shameless hussies, one for each week. It is no wonder that your repairs at a garage fall behind schedule, for the operative, poor chap, is having trouble keeping his eyes from straying and his fancy from wandering. Indeed, there used to be a measure of time for repairs at Plaistow Wharf, the fitters' fortnight, which could mean anything up to three months.

Nevertheless the firm of Tate & Lyle had by the early 1950s, established a reputation for sugar technology, and now acquired a subsidiary, A. & W.

Smith, Ltd., of Glasgow. And, although from time to time you would hear strong men in the engineering departments muttering about male and female joints, this would merely refer – for discipline is strict in the old firm – to the pipework in some sugar factory.

We have observed the aura of intense secrecy with which Tates surrounded the mystery of cube-sugar manufacture and Lyles that of Golden Syrup production, and how this persisted even after the amalgamation. Visitors were welcome, as long as they were not too inquisitive. Few dared to ask for much in the way of information, for fear that they might disappear, feet first and neatly parcelled in a second-hand 2-cwt Cuban raw sugar bag, by way of the condenser-water outflow.

Then there was a change, after the 1945 War, in the attitude towards the progress of research in the firm.[7] Scientific data was now allowed to emerge in the form of learned treatises, so why should not technological ditto with patents attached be sold? Jim Hobbs, who was then Process Manager at Plaistow, was sent for by the Board in late 1951 and told that he was to be managing director of a new company, Tate and Lyle Technical Services Ltd. with a remit to go forth, sell techniques and bring back the berries.

But because it was considered that ideas on their own are less vendable than ideas plus ironmongery, simultaneously there came about the acquisition of a sugar-machinery manufacturing firm, A. & W. Smith Ltd., which had been established for over a century in Glasgow. The price, although not high, seems to have gratified the then boss of Smiths, a canny septuagenarian with an eye for a bawbee. Delighted with having extracted from those Sassenachs a sum rather higher than he had expected, he was reported – apocryphally no doubt – to have astonished his cronies at the club by actually standing them a round.

Why, it may be asked, Glasgow? Well, a reader who has not been long since bludgeoned into insensibility may recall that the primacy in the development of technology in sugar refining belonged for quite a time to the Clyde, largely because of strong trading ties with the West Indies. This also, in the early nineteenth century, affected the market for the newly developed steam engine. The founder of the sugar machinery industry of Glasgow seems to have been James Cook, a Fife millwright who moved to Glasgow in 1788 and is believed to have bought a Boulton and Watt steam-engine for a flour-mill, subsequently using this as a pattern for steam-powered sugar mills. At his engineering works, opened in 1805, he was at first a general engineer but by 1816 the demand for sugar mills was enough to make him specialize. Some sixty years later his company was absorbed by a relative newcomer, Peter McOnie, a man who had lost his job when his employer went bankrupt. McOnie had tried to get work on a sugar estate in Trinidad but had been advised instead to set up a repair shop for sugar machinery in Glasgow. He did so, and before long became highly successful, taking on a Mr. Mirrlees as partner. Another McOnie, Andrew,

[7] See Chapter Twenty-six.

started his own firm and between 1851 and 1876 built 820 steam engines, 1300 boilers, 1650 sugar mills and sundry other pieces of equipment for sugar producers all over the world. (There were 1600 such in Cuba alone in 1865.) As the West Indian market declined later in the century, others in the Far East and South Africa grew.

In 1851 Mirrlees set up with a Mr. Tait, and later brought in a Mr. Watson. Peter McOnie was dead. Mirrlees Watson, as it became, continued down the decades, starting offshoots, such as Watson Laidlaw, who specialized in centrifugal machines, and Pott Cassels & Williamson, who did likewise; and absorbing in due course Blair Campbell Ltd., known for their evaporators.

Five other firms developed over much the same period. In Glasgow there were A. & W. Smith Ltd., Craig & Co. Ltd., Duncan Stewart & Co. Ltd. and Fawcett Preston. George Fletcher Ltd. of London and Derby were also established at this time. (They, together with Duncan Stewart, later became subsidiaries of Booker McConnell, the West Indies sugar manufacturers.) Craig was absorbed by Blair Campbell, Fawcett Preston still exists as Metal Industries Ltd. A. & W. Smith was the company for which Tate & Lyle, after many an inquiry, paid a price which seemed to be willing-buyer/willing-seller in 1953.

It was probably the best choice for a company in general sugar engineering for many of the Clydeside companies, as things became more difficult in cane sugar production later in the nineteenth century, had again become general engineers. Some concentrated on what would now be called the turn-key job, sub-contracting specific ancillary equipment such as railways and cranes to others as the factories became larger and more complex. Smiths', whose founder had been first introduced to the sugar machinery trade by McOnie, modestly building cattle-driven mills as a sub-contractor, had moved far. By 1914 they were contracting for large mills costing £90–100,000 each–say £1 million plus nowadays.

But virtually all these firms were subject to expert criticism. For one thing, because coal was cheap in Scotland, they paid little attention to the efficient use of fuel–'after all, bagasse is a waste product, mon!' Because they were friendly and clannish, even when rivals, they certainly interchanged ideas, but these would be limited and although sound, conservative. The low cost of iron and steel in Scotland may have enabled them to capture 80 per cent of the world's sugar machinery market, but competitors have a way of coming in, and it is probable that these sensible, kindly, rather provincial folk became pawkily complacent. After all, why change, when year after year the same product, reliable but unimaginative, sold well? Intended for use in faraway places where labour was abundant but largely untrained, a piece of equipment had to be extremely simple and 100 per cent foolproof.

At the refineries, on the other hand, there had been a great deal of attention to the newest techniques. Labour was relatively more expensive, and was going up in cost. Steam was a thing to use efficiently, end-product competition was tough. So the latest types of equipment from anywhere in the world were sought for, tried out, and if accepted often manufactured for Tate & Lyle under licence in Britain.

There was, for example, the Western States centrifugal machine, developed by a Mr. Roberts in the U.S.A. Neat, small, with an ingenious system to reduce power consumption, and even in its earliest days more automated than and greatly superior to anything then available from the Clyde, this had replaced Pott Cassel's machines at Plaistow.

At first there was scepticism up north, and certainly no great enthusiasm for manufacturing Western States machines under licence. After all, although cheaper to run the capital outlay was far higher than on the older type. Here, perhaps the old Tate versus Lyle rivalry may have been of long-term use. Thames, seeing Plaistow keen on Western States, undertook the development with Watson-Laidlaw of a rival centrifugal. It was probably no better but it may have cost less, and at all events Watson-Laidlaw had entered the 1950s.

T.L.T.S. at times appeared to wonder whether their engineering bedfellows, the Smiths, would ever wish to keep up with the Joneses, but in time there was a change. Jim Hobbs and his successors, Alan James and Denis Dickinson, together with Albert Slater, now Managing Director of Smiths, and Colin Rowan, later Chairman of both, strove together and not only were most workable arrangements found, but between them the two companies began to develop a formula for providing customers all over the world with a broadly based, flexible range of services.

This began in 1967[8] when, following the disinvestment in Jamaica and Trinidad the London-based technical staff of the Caribbean companies were transferred to T.L.T.S. It coincided with the change in approach to Research and Development and the emergence of new technologies for sugar extraction and purification, with potential uses in other fields.

With this formidable collection of skills available, some traditional, some new, it seemed a matter of commonsense to use them in order to help enable Britain to make a living in a world increasingly dependent on technology. A new Company, Tate & Lyle Enterprises Ltd. was born from T.L.T.S. to undertake this.

The company offered a coordinated planning service – soils, hydrology, land clearance; farm organization – cropping programmes, livestock development; engineering and processing – roads, bridges, canals, process plant; market economics – storage, transport; finding finance; and above all training, education and transfer of technology. It had to be available not merely for sugar but for other crops – grain crops, forage crops, and industrial crops such as cotton and forestry. It involved risk, for little of the developing world offers a stable political climate. It involved adaptability, for example when, during the erection of the Rahmania

[8] See Chapter 20.

Fanji Sugar Mills in Pakistan, those involved found themselves thirty-five miles from the Indian border and fifteen from the largest West Pakistan radar station in the middle of a war between India and Pakistan. You may go out of your way to avoid taking sides in politics, but dodging mortar-shells and air-raids may even so occasionally become necessary.

All this development did not happen overnight. There were unimagined problems to meet and overcome. But from the establishment of T.L.T.S. in 1951 and the purchase of A. & W. Smith in 1953 there was, after a tentative beginning, an impressive growth, parallel to that of Tate & Lyle Transport but in an entirely different field and spreading to fifty different countries.

In the early days Smiths and T.L.T.S. were deeply involved in the provision of equipment for the developments which were taking place in East Africa and the Caribbean. As the Tate & Lyle interest in these two areas grew, they provided a user basis, friendly but critical, and the interaction between supplier and customer – as sister companies – resulted in changes and innovations beneficial to both.

It is convenient at this point to examine these overseas companies even though doing so will inevitably carry us forward well into Phase II.

CHAPTER SIXTEEN

Central Africa

'*Ex Africa semper aliquid novi.*'
(*There is always something new from Africa.*)
(Pliny A.D. 23–79)

Pliny is also responsible for the terse and probably truer statement: *In vino veritas*. For Tate & Lyle 'Africa' can have several meanings – Nigeria and Ghana in the west, where the operations are principally sales and technical assistance; Rhodesia and Zambia in the middle; and Natal in the south. There have been flurries of interest in other places, mostly ephemeral, and financial and technical consultancy has been provided in numerous African countries. Redpath, the associated Canadian Company, together with T.L.T.S. was involved at the time of writing in setting up a sugar production complex in the Ivory Coast, and people from T.L.T.S. appear from time to time by invitation in Kenya, the Cameroons, Guinea – Bissau and elsewhere. This particular chapter, however, concerns Rhodesia and Zambia.

Africa is, of course, a large place. It used to be called the Dark Continent. Size and mystery lay it open to the spirit of parody. For long, a colleague going to Central Africa would speak of being 'just off to Darkest A.', and the stern features of the one-time Finance Director would crack momentarily into a wintry smile when, on his return from some intrepid financial foray to Kilimbero, he was addressed at Mincing Lane as 'Bwana Booth'. This does not mean that those involved are not and have not been serious and effective, just that Africa adds another – and sometimes exotic – dimension.

Also a larger one. In addition to the attentions of insect pests, the sugar cane in Africa is at the mercy of elephants, and the presence of the wily baboon necessitates the employment of a guard. (Neither of these predators is easily controlled by D.D.T.) Then there is the language problem. Zulu, Swahili and others do not appear in the average English school curriculum – if they did they would probably suffer the same fate as French – and this renders it difficult to discern what is going on behind those dark, impassive and often handsome faces. Moreover, most African languages have a fairly slender technical vocabulary. An instruction in Zulu to maintain good housekeeping is: 'Keep Out Dirtee', and a chap standing by a car with a punctured tyre near the Kariba Dam may well explain his predicament in his only technological phrase, picked up goodness knows where: 'Sir. My petrol-pump is buggered, so to say.'

This all combines to give the situation the mixed air of Emperor Jones

nightmare and knockabout farce which for some observers has characterized not only such national leaders as General Amin. It is not surprising
that verse about Africa has flourished at 21 Mincing Lane.

Tate & Lyle's interest first stirred there many years ago. Then in 1950 or
so Vernon Tate renewed acquaintanceship with a fellow old Wykehamist
and Trinity man, with a similar liking for cricket and horse-racing,
Lieutenant-Colonel George Hornung. George Hornung's father John had
produced the first crop of sugar to be made in Portuguese East Africa
(Mozambique) in 1890, and George was born the same year. Trained as a
chartered accountant he went to war in 1914 and was wounded as a
gunner officer at Gallipoli, returning after 1918 to the same estates in
Mozambique, which now supplied all the sugar eaten in the two
Rhodesias. This was a 'mill white' sugar and not entirely satisfactory. So,
realizing that consumption of sugar in the Rhodesias would increase
rapidly, Hornung arranged a guarantee with the Southern Rhodesian
Government, through a Mr. Stanley Cooke, and by pledging all his
savings, obtained backing in the City of London to build a sugar refinery at
Bulawayo, with a capacity of 10,000 tons a year, the raw sugar coming by
the railway which linked Rhodesia with Laurenço Marques in Mozambique.

After service during the Second World War in the Sussex Home Guard,
he emigrated. He had allowed space in Bulawayo for doubling his plant,
and realized that potential consumption would rise rapidly, so he raised a
further £250,000 for a second refinery to be built at Salisbury.

It is worth remembering that these two towns had not existed 50 years
earlier. Salisbury, with its tall buildings, was designed like Bulawayo with
streets wide enough for a span of ox-drawn carts to do a U-turn. Much of
Africa is new as well as big. (Perhaps Pliny was right.)

Hornung realized that he needed know-how and more capital and
approached Vernon Tate. In 1953 two of Vernon's colleagues, William
Booth and Jo Whitmee, went out to look at the situation. They saw the
refineries and were taken on what William described as a Cooke's tour
(Stanley Cooke was now Vice-Chairman of Hornung's Rhodesian Sugar
Refineries Ltd.) of a proposed cane sugar estate at Chirundu on the
southern bank of the Zambesi River. Tate & Lyle acquired a 50 per cent
interest in R.S.R. and agreed to put up capital towards the development of
Chirundu and the construction of a third refinery at Ndola in what is now
Zambia.

Prior to this, sugar production had been concentrated in the Lowveld, a
huge plain in the south-eastern corner of the country. A single farmer had
cleared a modest acreage and installed a small mill and was turning out ten
tons of sugar a year by 1937. All the rest of the sugar still came in from
Mozambique at that time. The Rhodesian Government bought this small
estate (Triangle) and ran it with a Sugar Industry Board, increasing the
acreage over ten years, and then selling it back to private enterprise. It

flourished and began to become a major investment, sending its raw sugar to R.S.R.

The Lowveld is a dry area, with a rainfall of only sixteen inches a year and irrigation is needed. The natural vegetation is thorn-scrub, and in dry weather it is quite clear why lions are that colour—they fade easily into the landscape.

Chirundu was also in a dry area but could be irrigated with water from the Zambesi which, not far away at Kariba, was being dammed to provide electric power also for Northern Rhodesia (Zambia). At the time of the original T. & L. venture the Rhodesian Federation was in existence, and Chirundu's sugar would supply Ndola Refinery by rail. During the early years Chirundu had a difficult time. John Lyle and Jo Whitmee put in much time and effort, as did other members of the Tate & Lyle Board. There were the usual problems involved in clearing land and the original factory, a second-hand one from New Guelderland in Natal, needed a good deal of attention. There was the problem of finding the right cane varieties. These were at length found and an overhead irrigation system introduced. There was the problem of recruiting and training African labour, illiterate, unsophisticated—many had never even seen a wheel—and speaking only simple dialects. These had to be housed decently and fed properly, and spokesmen (Indunas), who had some English, had to be found.

Senior staff were also a problem at first. The older hands, Stanley Cooke and Cyril Martindale, had enough on their hands already. Harry Allcock, the secretary, was a tower of strength. Cultivation men came from Natal, engineers and chemists from Mauritius (adding French to the languages used). Indians and the very few Africans capable of writing became clerks. Although not always entirely accurate in their work the latter were sometimes capable of producing extremely lively prose, as the following will show. (Note the reference to the prevalent lion):

> 'Sir,
>
> On the opening of this letter you will behold the work of a dejobulated person and a very bewifed and much childrenised gentleman, who was violently dejobbed in a twinkling of your good self.
>
> For heaven's sake, Sir, consider this catastrophe as falling on your own head and remind yourself walking home at the moon's end of five savage wives and sixteen voracious children with a pocket filled with no existent £. s. d. Not a solitary sixpence, pity my horrible state.
>
> When being dejobbed I proceeded with a heart and intestines filled with misery to the den of doom myself did greedily contemplate culpable homicide, but him whom protected Daniel safely through the lion's den will protect this servant in his hour of need.
>
> As to the reason given by yourself Esquire for my dejobment the

incrimination was laziness–No Sir, it were impossible that myself who pitchforked sixteen infant children into this valley of tears can have a lazy atom in his mortal frame, and the sudden departure of £11 has left me on the verge of destitution and despair.

I hope this vision of horror will enrich your dreams this night and a good angel will meet and pulverise your heart of nether millstone so that you will waken and with as much alacrity as may be compatible with your personal safety and hasten to rejobulate your servant.

Yours despairingly,
So note it be Amen
(sgd) Daniel

The Colonial Development Finance Corporation were approached and had agreed in principle to put up a ten-year loan for the expansion of Chirundu, but being under Treasury control were subjected to considerable formalities, which made them very slow in fulfilling their commitment. When the cheque for their first instalment at last arrived, Vernon Tate and William Booth telegraphed to George Hornung, reporting it: 'Wonders will never cease. Shall we put it on a horse?'

Because the African labour recruited was totally untrained on arrival, it took three times as many of them as it would of Jamaicans to get the crop off. A measure of mechanization helped but this introduced a need for maintenance, and maintenance men were rare. Gradually productivity of soil and labour improved. Agriculturalists from Jamaica and Trinidad were brought in. John Willsher, once a Plaistow shift manager, later on the staff of T.L.T.S., became Managing Director of R.S.R. and took Chirundu under his wing. 'Rosie' du Toit, an ex-Colonel in the Air Force, who had been a great source of inspiration in the early years at Chirundu, returned to South Africa. David Hughan was brought in from Reading University and was responsible for the rapid establishment and expansion of the estate.

Staff began to settle down but there was still a considerable turnover. It was too remote a place for some, with Salisbury, the nearest big town, three and a half hours' drive away. And there were occasional health problems, notably from bilharzia, a debilitating dieseease caused by a parasite which enters the body from water through the foot. The old hands on the estate believed that water which had been through a pump had been sterilized against this, and at first people were allowed to swim in the reservoir. It was then found that the parasite survived pumping. (One of the team of headhunters who recruited staff was a distinguished retired naval officer. He evinced much concern about all this, and became known to the ribald at Mincing Lane as 'Sir Hilary Bilharzia'.)

A school and clinics were built to serve the little townships called Chigwirizano (Cooperation) and Mtendere (Peace). As the Kariba Dam had been built by Italians there was a flourishing R.C. Church nearby under the direct patronage of the Cardinal-Archbishop of Milan. (Pope Paul XI had once been to Chirundu while Archbishop.) The Catholics had also built a hospital. When the Italians left Kariba their padre approached the General Manager saying he had a spare church. This was gratefully accepted and the Manager was confronted next morning with the whole edifice, delivered at the front door on an ex-R.A.F. 'Queen Mary' trailer. By 1960 it was possible to forecast a realizable profit and a production of 15,000 tons a year for 1962, 20,000 by 1964. In fact 30,000 tons and a decent profit was achieved in 1965.

At Triangle production was increasing swiftly. It was now owned largely by the South African Sugar Company, Sir J. L. Hulett Ltd. and a new estate owned largely by Anglo-American and directed by Sir Ray Stockill, at Hippo Valley, also in the Lowveld, was coming on fast. Huletts' had persuaded the Southern Rhodesian Government to put in a dam on the River Kyle, a tributary of the Limpopo, to provide irrigation water. It was clear that Southern Rhodesia would before long produce more than enough for her own, and for Northern Rhodesia's and Nyasaland's immediate needs and would be capable of exporting raw sugar to Britain, Canada, the U.S.A. and elsewhere, shipping it the hundreds of miles by train to Laurenço Marques or Beira. A Commonwealth quota was sought and then a U.S. quota. Tate & Lyle, having provided more capital, had now a controlling interest in R.S.R. and Chirundu.

Ndola Sugar Refinery was in operation by 1960, capable of supplying 20,000 tons of refined sugar for the Copperbelt. Consumption in the territory had reached 12,500 tons a year and was rising at 16 per cent a year (compound). Erected by T.L.T.S. and A. & W. Smith, Ndola Refinery would employ 34 Europeans and 240 Africans. A number of the former came from the British refineries–Harry Rosser and John Felstead from Thames, Harry Rodwell and Charlie Stevens from Plaistow and Bill Giddings, Ted Makin and Terence Cardle from Liverpool. Relationships between the different races were good–football being a particular link. £150,000 was spent on proper housing for all employees.

But now trouble loomed. The Federation of the Rhodesias began to crack apart. Considerable efforts were made to avoid this but the views of those in power in the two Rhodesias proved irreconcilable. This is not the place to try and describe the situation, and in any case it is one which was still unresolved fifteen years later. It was an anxious period. The breakdown of the Federation took place over the next four years. U.D.I. was in 1965. (Chirundu had held an open day a few months earlier.) Peter Runge, then President of the Federation of British Industry, had led a team of businessmen to discuss the situation with the Southern Rhodesia authorities. There had been the talks between Mr. Smith and Mr. Harold Wilson, which had been fruitless. It is perhaps unkind to recall that although the latter had said that Southern Rhodesia would collapse in a matter of weeks, not months, the place was still there in 1977.

The end of the Federation did not mean the breaking of all links between the Rhodesias and Nyasaland. In particular Northern Rhodesia and Nyasaland continued to import raw sugar from Southern Rhodesia. They had to, for consumption was rising even faster than before; and it was still rising at $5\frac{1}{2}$ per cent a year in Southern Rhodesia. But it was clear that one day the new Zambia would wish to be self-supporting and it would be necessary to make major changes in raw sugar production arrangements. The Board of Tate & Lyle therefore decided to split R.S.R. and to operate separately in the two now irreconcilable countries. Ndola could be supplied with raw sugar grown in the hitherto undeveloped Kafue River basin. Rhodesia still needed more sugar. Hippo Valley needed a new factory. Capital was provided by Anglo-American, a modest equity was taken by Tate & Lyle, and A. & W. Smith erected the factory, which was a large one–grinding 250 tons of cane an hour. The impulse for this came largely from Sir Ray Stockill.

Once the decision was reached, things moved fast. On June 1st, 1965, the new Ndola Sugar Company Ltd. opened its head office in Lusaka. The Zambian Government's Industrial Development Corporation took an initial holding of 11 per cent, and plans for a £$2\frac{1}{4}$ million raw sugar factory were announced. To be in operation by 1968, this would be supplied with cane from 6,000 acres of land at Nakambala near Mazabuka, and from an initial 40,000 tons a year would eventually be capable of 80,000. Soil surveys at the estate were under way and planting would begin in 1966. At the same time a plan for training small to medium-sized farmers was instituted at Kitwe. The whole complex depended on irrigation and a new canal was excavated from the Kafue River to supply water. It had been opened in November 1964 by Mr. Mudenda, the Zambian Minister of Agriculture, who spoke warmly of future cooperation between the Government and Tate & Lyle. In the years that followed his words would be borne out. John Willsher became Managing Director of Ndola and Nakambala. Guy Hinde remained as his opposite number at R.S.R.

We are now on the fringe of Phase II. Ian Lyle retired from the chairmanship in 1964 and John Lyle was elected Chairman of Tate & Lyle. As far as Africa is concerned, this meant that Johnny Tate took over from him the responsibility for the eventual future of Chirundu, the build-up of Ndola and Nakambala and all the whips and scorns of time with which the late Hamlet gloomily associated the mere business of staying alive at all, let alone producing sugar in Central Africa.

It did not of course mean that Ian and John would cease to appear in places south-east of the Sahara from time to time. Often their visits involved problems of transport, an even more dangerous affair in Darkest A. than at Hyde Park Corner. For one thing, in Africa even more chaps who really should not be in charge of a self-driven vehicle are frequently found behind the wheel. For another equipment takes on a personality of its own in those parts, and the local rain-makers, mistrusting these new-fangled flying machines, are apt to call down an impenetrable tropical downpour while your aeroplane is surrounded by mountains. On one aerial survey Johnny Tate took Ian Lyle a little out of the way from Chirundu to Salisbury in order to photograph the Kariba Dam. There was trouble finding the way back. 'Next time,' said Ian grimly, 'I shall come by myself. Then I shall go where *I* want, instead of where *you* decide to use your camera.'

On another the car in which they were driving, with Johnny Tate at the wheel, became, as he put it, a little sluggish. A piece of fan had come off and mangled the engine's innards. John Willsher flagged down one of the rare passing vehicles and, bumming a ride to the nearest township in search of a replacement, left President and Drive-them-to-Destruction Tate plus baggage as dusk fell. 'I should stay in the car,' he advised kindly, 'because of the lions.'

And John, the new Chairman, established his reputation as a swift driver on the African roads, earning from the Muse of Mincing Lane a Piece describing the local astonishment this engendered:

> Into the Bush will disappear
> Each naked child and bare man.
> The drums beat out with the message:
> 'Look out! Here comes the Chairman.'

The varied fauna included hyenas. One night, John Lyle and Jo Whitmee, hearing one of these outside, barricaded the front door of their quarters with a heavy wardrobe. Next morning, after a sound sleep, they discovered that they had left the back door open.

At first, when the Federation split up, personal relationships were unaffected and communications between the two countries unchanged. But when Zambia wanted her own supplies Chirundu would be too far from Salisbury to be viable as a supplier of raws to that refinery. On the other hand the projected estate at Nakambala would need a mill ready to operate. So, very reluctantly, the decision was confirmed to close down the Chirundu Estate after the 1966 crop and ship the factory across the Zambesi. The 3,500 Africans, most of whom came from elsewhere, returned to their countries. Those from Zambia and Malawi took up jobs there in new sugar developments. The others went back to Mozambique, Angola or Tanzania. (The tribal system persists and overlaps the boundaries imposed from outside in the nineteenth century and jealously guarded though even more fragile in the late twentieth.) Some of the non-African staff moved with the factory to Zambia. Others went to Natal or returned to England.

Ndola and Nakambala, eventually to be metamorphosed into the Zambia Sugar Company Ltd. and gradually transferred to the Government of Zambia, would flourish, Tate & Lyle and later T.L. Enterprises having a service contract and retaining seats on the board. R.S.R. would continue to prosper amid all the ineffectual flurry of politics. But Chirundu died.

What had been truly described as an oasis in the Bushveld soon reverted to bush, and ten years later any signs of all that effort were swallowed again by lion-coloured vegetation, offering concealment once more to the lions – all except one. His skin was now on the floor of the ante-room to the Tate & Lyle Boardroom, his toothy head occasionally snarling up the trouser leg of an unwary Tate, Lyle or Other. (Bees are not allowed in the ante-room. And anyway, Samson was not involved with this lion.)

He was shot at mid-day on September 15th, 1959 near a baobab tree at Field 342, Chirundi, by a game ranger, Mr. Bredenkamp, who had been out since 4.00 a.m. nabbing a couple of elephants which had been molesting the cane. A baboon-guard reported the lion, so Bredenkamp and his gun-bearer went off in a Landrover to investigate, armed with a double-barrelled ·404 shot gun, loaded unfortunately with solid not soft nose cartridges, and a ·375 on which the safety catch was stiff. How they got the lion, being themselves mauled in the process, is related in the inevitable Calypso which concludes, after a vivid and touching blow-by-blow description:

> So now in de Anteroom we see de skin,
> Tho' dat ole lion he gets no gin.
> Dat's all for de Board of Directors
> From whom Massa Willsher protect us.
> *Chorus:*
> Ole mister lion by de baobab tree
> Don't go makin' a meal out o' me.

CHAPTER SEVENTEEN

The Spanish Main (2)

I

'Then like the wind through woods in riot,
Through him the gale of life blew high.
The tree of man is never quiet,
Then 'twas the Roman. Now, 'tis I.'
(A. E. Housman. 'A Shropshire Lad.' 1859–1936)

The Wind of Change was not officially announced until the 1960s, yet looking back to the first decade after the 1939/45 War although one perceived that it was on the way, it was not clear that it would spring up so fast. The post-war history of Tate & Lyle in the Caribbean could perhaps be written with a tinge of that autumn melancholy with which Edward Gibbon, in Rome one October evening two centuries ago, heard the barefooted friars of St. Francis chanting vespers in the Temple of Jupiter and decided to write of the decline and fall of the city. But for some fifteen years, although there was occasionally frustration, frequently disturbance, and always a sense of strain, there was usually optimism.

Investments were made, new techniques adopted, conditions for staff and work-people improved, and there was a genuine sense of contributing something to the life of the two islands, Jamaica and Trinidad. Tate & Lyle might be a large metropolitan company, might seem unimaginably rich to the man in the cane-piece, but London, Jamaica and Trinidad were parts of an Empire and that Empire still had a numinous meaning. It was not then realized, except by a few, that the Commonwealth which was to replace it would be so very different. (Maudie Littlehampton's aunt would one day say unkindly: 'I wish, dear, they were a little wealthier and not quite so common.')

It is possible that if in 1945–51 Britain's home government had been less introspective things might have been different.

Perhaps, it was thought in the 1950s, eventual independence accompanied by British parliamentary and other institutions, such as trade unions for example, would lead to a manageable, if looser system, while British experts and expertise, and the existence of London as a world trade centre would still continue to be desirable and desired. Yet parliamentary democracy is a delicate plant–even in Britain–and it would not be long before in many a newly independent African state it would come to mean one man one vote–*once*.

Although this was not envisaged in Jamaica and Trinidad, there would be problems arising from the relative newness of the populations to the area, from their small size, from the rapidity with which their numbers were expanding (thanks to the whirlwind advance of preventive medicine) and from the increasing difficulties in providing work for those numbers. Yet from the days of Belshazzar the King it has never been easy for contemporaries to read the writing on the wall, and the Roman in Housman's poem was surely not fully aware of the decline and fall of *his* empire.

Let us look at a typical Tate & Lyle estate. In the 1940s and 50s there were three; W.I.S.Co's Frome and Monymusk in Jamaica, and Caroni Ltd. in Trinidad. At the top in each case there would be a General Manager, and by 1947 in Jamaica these were Jamaicans—at Frome, Harold Cahusac, whose name indicates a Gascon ancestry, and who actually looked and behaved like a Frenchman; at Monymusk, Charlie Michelin—with a French name too, but like a calm English squire. In Trinidad it was a Trinidad-born Scot, Harold Gilbert, tall, deceptively taciturn at first, but a wickedly amusing raconteur and mimic with a gift for sharp word-pictures—so sharp they should be called vinaigrettes rather than vignettes.

At each estate there would be a Factory Manager, a Chief Engineer, an Agricultural Manager, a Transport Manager, a Chief Chemist, a Chief Electrician, a Business Manager, a Chief Accountant, and these were at the head of teams of more junior staff. Most, in Jamaica, were Jamaicans, but as there was a shortage of local men trained in certain skills such as accounting, electricity and engineering there were quite a number of expatriates. In Trinidad there were many more of these, and whereas in Jamaica the agricultural staff was virtually entirely local, in Trinidad for a decade and more the old pattern was to continue and English, Scots, Irish and Barbadians still came to the Company, and did well for it.

In particular, in both islands, expertise and devotion were also imported in the shape of research workers and medical men. The former, represented in Jamaica by Hugh Thompson and Bill Ive (himself a Jamaican trained in Canada) and in Trinidad by Frank Blackburn, brought with them a cool judgement on the techniques of cane growing and ideas of what could be done to improve productivity per acre in islands of limited space.

The second input, that of medicine, had perhaps an even deeper significance not only for the people who worked for Tate & Lyle but also, by precept, influence, and example for much of the rest of the Islands' populations. Men who would perhaps have been typical G.P.s in practice in England, instead went to Jamaica and Trinidad to cope with the harsh realities of life among the truly poor, and to introduce in a microcosmic way the new found benefits of twentieth-century medicine. They were there, men like Michael Slade, Tommy Hallinan, Dick Drennan and Maurice Judd in Jamaica, like Frank Ayrey, George McLeod, Dan Hearn and Eric Consterdine in Trinidad, to help find a path out of a morass of endemic debilitating sickness which took one child in four and reduced an average man's or woman's life expectation to forty years. The presence of these doctors on the estates, by a happy coincidence, was contemporaneous with the availability of the means of controlling the vectors of malaria and yellow fever, of the new antibiotics, and of the spread of simple hygiene and the growing knowledge of the effect of diet on health. The thousands of work-people employed on the estates benefited enormously. Whether the long term result has been entirely beneficial it is not possible to judge.

There were sparse government services for health and welfare and not much for education. Schools were overcrowded and became increasingly so as infants survived in increasing numbers. Known in Jamaica as pickneys (Spanish *pequeninos?*), these were always well turned out, smiling, attractive, but what would they do when they grew up? Ordinary housing was of desperately low quality. If you brought in an expatriate you had to provide a suitable house and all the services. If you didn't bring him in you couldn't run the estate so effectively. When you took him on you also took on his family and sometimes, although he adapted himself his wife didn't settle. (This had been found in India a century and a half before when the Memsahib turned up.) The problems were potentially considerable and it is a tribute to the Jamaican staff and to the expatriates and their wives that it all went so well, that the teams coalesced and functioned. Although earlier on there had been distinctions between the expatriate and the *indigène*, it was not long before salaries, housing, leave, and other sundries were uniform for the same jobs. An estate was a community in itself and the atmosphere was generally harmonious. It depended in the end on the General Manager, who set the stamp of his personality on the place and bore on his broad shoulders the thousand and one cares, some large, some petty, of those for whom he was responsible to an extent difficult to realize in late twentieth century, institutionalized, cradle-to-grave England.

It sounds feudal. No doubt it was, but it was feudalism with a difference, and it worked. God is known in Jamaica as Big Massa, and in a sense the General Manager was the local Big Massa. But he was not personally the owner, only the steward for an entity larger than himself. For some men in a position of such power the temptation to become an unjust steward, a bully or merely a boozy parochial version of the Almighty could be awesome; 3,000 miles away from any day-to-day controls, monarchs of all they surveyed, they could have become like this. They did not, for they were good men. There was, moreover, the fact that as air travel became easier, there were frequent visits by members of the London Boards, Chairmen, Managing Directors, Executive Directors and others. These visits were intended to be useful in sharing burdens. They must have been at times a bore, but they were also a check and balance.

Before the advance in air travel there was of course much isolation, particularly during the war, and in certain areas this led to occasional, mild *folie de grandeur*. But by 1950 visits were frequent and the General Managers themselves came regularly to London for discussions and a break.

II
'The World By The Tail.'
(Anon. 1954)

Just after the war there had been a change in Jamaica. Bobby Kirkwood had gone to the West Indies in 1936–7 to initiate the new ventures and had remained as Resident Agent in Jamaica. When the war ended he was anxious to get things moving again and had embarked on an ambitious investment programme. There were then differences of opinion and misunderstandings and he resigned, to be instantly appointed as Chairman of the Sugar Manufacturers' Association, a body representing all the Jamaican sugar estates, large and small, in dealings with cane farmers, trade unions, and Government. It was a post to which he was particularly suited by personality and by his knowledge of the people of the country. Alan Walker, who had been made Managing Director of Caroni Ltd. in 1943, became Managing Director of W.I.S.Co. in 1948.

There followed the introduction of a highly sophisticated system of communications, refined over the next decade, between London and the Estates. The telephone did not function well – you might in those days just as well try shouting across the Atlantic as talk by phone – but cables were available. For confidential matters there was a private cable code. Key figures on production, on costs of operations and so forth were cabled monthly, according to a carefully prepared schedule. Technical matters, purchasing of equipment and supplies, sales of products and so forth were organized by a series of formal minutes. Matters of policy – land purchases and sales, capital investment, relations with Government and the S.M.A., trade union affairs and so on were covered in one series of letters. More private and personal matters to do with staff, with salaries and so forth were covered by another. And each year a comprehensive report on operations in all sections of the estate was prepared. Such a system sounds onerous but, used with commonsense, it provided an effective and flexible link, and misunderstandings were rare.

The post-war world was short of sugar and producers in the West Indies and elsewhere raced to fill the gap. As long as the price remained high they could also afford to invest in factory material, in new tractors and farm equipment. At Monymusk a new factory was at last built. Operating for the first time in 1949 it stood up, clean, white and graceful in the plains of Vere. It was somewhat the victim of war, nevertheless. There had been little technical development for six years and Monymusk was almost an exact copy of Frome's factory which had been completed in 1939 and was therefore a little out of date. Well-maintained, Frome dominated likewise the plains of Westmoreland. Around the factories well-kept compounds dotted with cotton trees and ficus and hedged with bougainvillea, contained the well-built but not over-lavish staff houses.

In the old difficult days, labour had been housed in barracks, a West Indian equivalent of a mining-town back-to-back, but these were on their way out, being rapidly replaced by pleasant houses built with money from a newly introduced Sugar Labour Welfare Fund to which all manufacturers contributed, and on land made available by the Company.

The health of the workforce began to improve. There had been much malaria and occasional yellow fever. Hookworm, a debilitating complaint picked up through the bare feet and caused by shocking sanitation and filthy habits, had been endemic. There had been much venereal disease. There had been malnutrition resulting not from poverty but from ignorance, the diet lacking easily available protein and vitamin-containing foods. The Company Medical Officers had at each estate a case-book of some 18 to 20,000 a year, the patients suffering mostly from easily recognizable ailments.

In a matter of a few years malaria was eradicated. A programme of spraying with the now much-maligned D.D.T. was carried out with help from the W.H.O. In less than two years days lost from malaria fell from 500 a month to 500 a year at Frome. Hookworm treatment and improved sanitation began slowly to have an effect. V.D. was reduced – a patient only being treated if he or she brought in the partner. Dentists were employed to treat wide spread oral sepsis which resulted in all manner of internal complaints.

The then Monymusk doctor, Slade, remarked in 1950 of malaria control: 'No drug or public health measure ever devised will have such a revolutionary effect on the health of so many people throughout the world as will D.D.T. spraying. This is a fact realized as yet by but few people.' (And it is now forgotten.) And later he was to write, quite without complacency, of the six years of medical service he had given: 'More has been done in this period for the health of workers in Vere than over the past three centuries. Jamaica in 1946 was like Russia in 1920 and Britain in 1846. It is now catching up.'

The political situation in Jamaica in the late 40s and early 50s was relatively tranquil. Bustamante's Jamaica Labour Party was in power, and he himself Chief Minister. Jamaica, as a Colony, still had a Governor who, although he had considerable reserve powers, was under instructions to use them less and less, to leave it more and more to elected representatives. Bustamante believed in encouraging private enterprise and investment from abroad. His industrial arm, the Bustamante Industrial Trade Union, brought him in what is all too often known as 'grass-roots' support. It was used to call strikes but these were then fairly infrequent and of short duration, noisy but usually good-humoured. Hugh Shearer, the National Officer of the Union, then aged about thirty, was never allowed by Bustamante to go too far, and it was amusing for the Managing Director and the General Manager to listen after dinner from behind a hedge to colourful oratory about them from a man with whom they would a few days later be negotiating quite amicably. He was doing so in the safe knowledge that words were all right, but actions must be cautious.

There was a concerted move at this time by the West Indies as a whole to get the British Government to introduce a long term purchasing agreement for sugar at a fixed price, against the day when as a result of increasing world output it might again become a glut and the price on the world market become so low as to cause distress once more to the producers and their employees. Bobby Kirkwood, as Chairman of the Jamaican S.M.A., was a leading figure in this, being joined by Harold Robinson, Chairman of the homologous body in Trinidad; Archibald Cuke in Barbados; Jock Campbell, Chairman of Booker Bros. McConnell and Guy Eccles, Managing Director of Davsons, the two big producers in British Guiana. Operating as the British West Indies Sugar Association, these men were in turn later joined by representatives of producers in Mauritius, Fiji, South Africa and Australia, and in 1952 the then Minister of Food, Major Gwilym Lloyd George (Cons.) signed the Commonwealth Sugar Agreement. This, intended to provide a regular outlet for fixed quantities of sugar at 'a reasonable price to efficient producers', was to last until Britain entered the E.E.C. Political pressures would one day force out South Africa, admit and then eject Southern Rhodesia, and bring in India, which was short of sugar but even shorter of money. From 1975 it would be replaced by the Lomé Convention.

But meantime for a long period it introduced an element of stability for both producer and consumer. If surpluses forced the world price down the Commonwealth producer was protected for a large part of his crop. If shortages forced the world price up, the British housewife continued to get the bulk of her sugar at 'a reasonable price'. It had been hoped that Canada would adopt a similar measure, but while operating a Commonwealth Preference Scheme she preferred to stick to the world price.[1]

One offshoot of the Commonwealth Agreement which was of benefit to Jamaica – and to the other West Indies – was the earmarking of part of the

---

[1] The Commonwealth Sugar Agreement, as long as it was in existence, was given special recognition within the framework of successive International Sugar Agreements. Beginning in 1931 with a scheme evolved by an American lawyer and accountant, Thomas Chadbourne, attempts are made at intervals to try and regulate world production in line with demand and to stabilize the price of sugar between one year and the next. An International Sugar Council was first set up in 1932, and to this day, except for the period from 1939 to 1945, there has existed an International Sugar Organization, with a headquarters in London and an international staff of experts who provide up-to-date statistics on production and consumption world-wide. Since the war it has had, by 1977, only two Executive Directors, both British, Ralph Steadman and his successor, Ernest Jones-Parry.

price for three special funds. One, the Labour Welfare Fund, has been mentioned. The others were the Industry Rehabilitation Fund, intended to assist in long term capital investment, and the Price Stabilization Fund, intended to be used during periods of low world prices to compensate for that part of the production which had to be sold at lower prices on the world market.

Individual areas were allocated quotas for Negotiated Price sugar based on past performance, and these quotas in turn were split between individual producers. Quotas always remained a matter for considerable argument, and it would be idle to deny that down the years heated correspondence took place on the subject. All strong personalities, Kirkwood, Campbell, Robinson and others would write impassioned letters to each other. Marked Strictly Personal and Confidential these would normally receive wide and rapid circulation among an appreciative audience, for the Caribbean is not a place for secrets.

In the matter of quotas the smaller the producer the more vociferous his claims, and the Tate & Lyle interests were regarded as being quite able to afford to be generous. In 1955–6, when over-production seemed likely to affect Jamaica, W.I.S.Co., in order to keep the peace, agreed to turn some of its land over from cane to banana-growing. This was not a success. The banana walks were splendid to look at, highly productive, and offered year-round instead of seasonal employment. But the only type of banana suitable for estate production in Jamaica was the Lacatan, for the sweeter Gros Michel is attacked by Panama disease. Moreover, the banana is a greedy plant, liking the best land and a great deal of water. So, soon, some 2,500 acres of prime land, all close to the sugar factory, were in bananas. The cost of growing and transporting cane was thereby increased. At the same time the method of payment for bananas at the ports was biased against the larger producer, so that stems of bananas from W.I.S.Co. which were of better quality than much that was being sent in by smaller growers were bought at the same rate. It is no wonder that Jamaican bananas became less popular than others.

And then, of course, what with three or four years of bad sugar cane seasons coupled with intensifying union activity, the expected over-production of sugar failed to materialize and with a sigh of relief Monymusk replanted the banana areas in cane. In future quotas would be more jealously guarded.

It is true too that later the mechanisms and criteria used in arriving at the Negotiated Price which the Ministry of Food–afterwards M.A.F.F.–insisted on treating as the Law of the Medes and Persians which Altereth Not, became increasingly incapable of allowing for inflation in the costs of tractors, factory equipment and supplies. But the Agreement was in general beneficent and effective, at least during its earlier years and the Jamaican sugar scene, up to about 1955, was one of growing prosperity and relative contentment at all levels.

An elderly American was staying at Frome during this time. He had breakfasted and lunched well, had had a look at the shining, humming factory, had been driven round part of the beautifully kept cane-pieces, had paid a call on the beef herd of Brahmin-Charolais cross, and was now standing at an open window looking out over the neat parklike compound, the ice tinkling in the glass of pink gin in his hand. Evening was falling.

'Yes, sir,' he said reflectively, 'you guys sure have gotten the world by the tail.'

III

'Jamaica, de land of wood and water
Fader an' son, an' mudder an' daughter,
All you can hear de whole day long is
"Strike!   Strike!   Strike!"'
(Jamaican Popular Song. ca. 1950)

That song was written as a send-up of a new match factory recently opened in Jamaica whose products for some technical reason refused to strike. It was soon far more applicable to the scene on the sugar estates. Early in 1955 there was a General Election resulting in Bustamante's Party being defeated by his cousin Norman Manley's People's National Party. Bustamante and his colleagues had begun to be regarded as too inclined to go along with private and particularly external investors, too friendly to big business. He had, for example, recently agreed, although a little unwillingly, to the adaptation at Salt River, the port serving Monymusk factory, and Savannah-la-Mar, the port serving Frome, to the bulk-handling of sugar with, inevitably, the disappearance of many casual jobs in return for redundancy payments.

Manley's appeal was not solely based on the fact that it was time for a change. His intellectual standing attracted many prominent Jamaicans including numbers in the business community, who began to find Busta's politics a little incoherent. As part of his electioneering equipment Manley had found it desirable to establish an industrial wing to his party in the shape of the National Workers' Union, led by his son Michael, who some twenty years later would become Prime Minister of Jamaica. Unless a union can be seen to be active it loses its following. The N.W.U. celebrated the P.N.P. electoral victory by calling a strike at Frome in March 1955, Michael Manley threatening to turn the estate into 'an industrial graveyard' unless certain not very clearly specified demands were met. Now it was he instead of Shearer who was heard from behind the hedge, talking about 'a fast Englishman'. Busta and Shearer waited in the wings. If the N.W.U. demands were to be satisfied, the B.I.T.U. would become active elsewhere, perhaps at Monymusk. The Governor, Sir Hugh Foot,[2] naturally anxious that Manley's new Government should get down to work, tried to put pressure on W.I.S.Co. to concede. This was understandable, but for long-term reasons, had to be resisted. ('If once you have paid him the Danegeld you will never get rid of the Dane.') Eventually the strike ended and a solution was found which neither wholly satisfied the N.W.U. nor tempted the B.I.T.U. to have a go.

But there was still an element in it of Danegeld and from now on the pattern was set. Whichever political party was in power the other would use its trade union to cause embarrassment and disorder. The party in power would then have to engage its own industrial cohorts. And so it would go on. And Frome and Monymusk, the two largest units in the island, would be prime targets. No doubt the leaders of the unions, themselves intelligent men and agreeable on a personal level, were aware of the dangers, and they have both since had the opportunity, as Prime Ministers, to observe the end result of adversary politics.

Inevitably the ordinary employee began to develop the feeling that the unions had better do something for him, and if one union wouldn't or couldn't the other would or could–or would at least promise to. Parties and unions alike became the prisoners of their own activities and promises.

For W.I.S.Co. it was not merely a question of being a target because of size and of ownership ('we got de Tate money las' year,' said one union official genially, 'now dis year we get de Lyle money.'). As in the matter of quotas, Tate & Lyle were expected to pay a higher price for cane sold to them by cane farmers and higher rates of pay than any other estates in the island, just because they were large. At the same time, since Frome and Monymusk belonged to the same owners, they were only accorded one vote in the Sugar Manufacturers' Association, although responsible for over a third of the island's production. Looked at closely, therefore, the world's tail was far from being in their grasp. Over the years the grasp began to slip still further, though there would be times, like 1963–4, when high world sugar prices would bring in a great deal of money. (This of course inevitably led to vastly magnified demands for wage increases and crop bonuses, which even if conceded only in part meant a further erosion of profit when the price dropped back again.)

The records, year by year, make depressing reading. 1956 was fairly peaceful, but in 1957, while Frome got off its crop, it was nearing the top of its capacity and a decision would be needed on doubling the grinding capacity at a cost of £1 million or more if production was to remain feasible, for after the end of May the heavy rains come down and you can't bring in the cane. 1957 too, saw a strike of six and a half weeks at Monymusk to back vague and varying demands. The J.L.P., now in the political wilderness, wished to embarrass the Government. Busta was personally uncomfortable about it, but for political reasons was unable to

[2] Later Lord Caradon. Brother of the Right Hon. Michael Foot, M.P.

call it off. When privately urged to do so, he candidly explained this and said softly, with an unaccustomed desperation, 'So how *can* I, boy?'

In the end work was belatedly resumed without gain and without instruction from the unions. It was a bad crop. The strike had lasted longer than previous ones, ironically because of the existence of the Monymusk banana walks which provided a readily available source of food. Predial larceny was at a premium, but the Company would not call for police aid. You cannot starve people if food is there.

1958 was quieter. Tentative experiments were made at Monymusk with machines for loading cane on to trucks, to replace a back-breaking job. The unions watched these warily and bided their time. The crops were larger and factory capacities were stretched. It was decided to double up the Frome mill. The work force expected a crop bonus – after all there had been one for six years, this had been a big crop, and after the previous year's Monymusk strike there had been an increase in basic wages. But in 1958, thanks to large wage increases, there were no profits. So there would be no bonus, which led to trouble in 1959, compounded by drought and the visitation of an insect called the West Indian cane fly. Frome had a two weeks' strike before crop but then kept going. Monymusk was hit in late February. Most of the workforce would have disobeyed a strike call. Like the silent majority everywhere they were getting fed up with what is now prissily called 'industrial action'.

Strong-arm men appeared in the area, coming from Kingston. Others came, uninvited, from the hills. Some of these were probably 'Rasta-Men', a contemporary phenomenon who claimed to be the subjects of the Emperor of Ethiopia – 'Rastafari'. There were then believed to be some 20,000 in the island, many of them outlaws living in unusual squalor and smoking or chewing 'ganja' – marihuana (*Cannabis Americana*) – which grows with rude vigour like a Jamaican equivalent of garden weeds. They scared the usually reasonable majority, cowing them into a kind of helpless silence. Members of staff were stoned and injured, machines damaged, and – a new development – many cane fields set on fire. Sugar cane on fire is a terrifying natural force; the huge grass crackles and thumps and spits like fish frying on an enormous scale. Fire spreads quickly and you can, if careless, be trapped, suffocated, and burned to death. Hitherto it had not been used as a weapon. Now the Rasta-Man was introducing it. The sultry air of Vere was filled with smoke and flying ash.

The Government decided to appoint a Commission of Inquiry, headed by a Canadian Q.C., Mr. Carl Goldenberg, to investigate the sugar industry. The Rasta-Men disappeared into the hills, and work was resumed. But it was now a little late, and there was another bad crop. W.I.S.Co. was beginning to be regularly unprofitable.

In negotiating with the unions the Sugar Manufacturers' Association had used a very conservatively estimated figure for profits in 1959 and had not brought this up to date. The current figures were, of course, supplied to the Commission of Inquiry, and Mr. Goldenberg used them in reaching his conclusions. He was a man of liberal, North-American views. He had, he thought, to do something for peace and quiet. He was responsible to the Government of Jamaica, which had employed him. He made a considerable wage award, just in time for the 1960 crop.

After some heart-searching W.I.S.Co. now decided to split from the S.M.A., to accept the Goldenberg findings, and in future to negotiate by itself. It may have been the right decision, or the wrong one, but it was too late.

During 1960 throughout Jamaica, labour in the sugar industry was unsettled, vindictive, and even more convinced that from now on all that had to be done was to call a strike, and you could get what you wanted. At Monymusk the 400 or so men employed in loading the cane into trucks held things up on and off week after week. Cane cutters decided to work a day a week less, being content with what the Goldenberg awards brought in by way of additional money. Absenteeism began to be chronic at both estates, and was to get worse.

It was decided to use machines in future at Monymusk to load all the cane and to pay off the cane-loaders, a brawny, difficult, intimidating crew, as redundant. 1961 saw this innovation take place, not without difficulties. Government and Opposition objected but tacitly accepted that things had gone so far that something must be done. The machines worked day and night (mobile lighting systems were set up in the fields). Manoeuvres were controlled by local radio – a method long used for field work over the large areas of the estates. The wavelength was close enough to that of Radio Jamaica for the general population to overhear live comments on the operations. 'Number two here. De mout' de grabber sick. Him not pick up.' There were no strikes but some go-slows. Things began to settle down.

There was now a brief spell of relative peace, when the problems were mainly technical – how to overcome the fact that mechanical cane-loading introduced a lot of soil into the factory and this eroded the metal on the cane mills, how to balance the steam and power requirements of the second mill tandem at Frome, and so on. Perhaps this intermission in union and political activity came about because for a matter of three years the various West Indian territories were occupied in jockeying for position in the newly-formed and short-lived Federation of the West Indies. Inaugurated in 1958, with Lord Hailes, the Governor-General, based in Trinidad, and an additional tier of parliament and civil service on top of the existing Governors and local Island Parliaments, this creation, which would perhaps have succeeded had it been introduced ten years earlier, was, alas, doomed to perish under the force of local Jamaican, Barbadian, Trinidadian and other parish-pump pressures. A Jamaican may not have wished forever to be governed from England. He was even less content to be governed from Trinidad by a Barbadian Prime Minister. In 1961, while Iain McLeod, the Secretary of State for the Colonies, was in Jamaica,

Bustamante forced a debate in the Jamaican House on the Federation and Manley agreed that a referendum might be held on whether or not Jamaica should secede, without telling the Federal Prime Minister or the Governor-General. It was the end of the Federation. Jamaica and Trinidad and the rest would be independent from 1962 and on their own, and there would be General Elections. A considerable and potentially beneficial though belated vision had been shattered.

The pressure on W.I.S.Co. was temporarily less. Charlie Michelin went over to Trinidad to undertake a new and taxing job there, which will be described in due course. Paul Bovell, formerly Cultivation Manager at Monymusk and since 1956 General Manager of Caroni Ltd. came back to Monymusk to take over as local pro-consul for the whole of W.I.S.Co. when Harold Cahusac retired a year later. Yet the magic—although this was not yet clear—had gone forever from W.I.S.Co. Modern and independent Jamaica would never again be truly suited to large-scale operations in sugar production. It was all becoming too complicated.

The financial effects of the Goldenberg award were to some extent offset as a result of the breaking up of relations between Castro's Cuba and the U.S.A. The latter had obtained much of their sugar from Cuba, paying a price rather higher than the Commonwealth negotiated price and much higher than the normal world price. Now some U.S. supplies were purchased from the British West Indies, at first on an *ad hoc* basis, later under a quota system. Obtaining the latter was almost entirely the work of Bobby Kirkwood, who spent much time and effort in Washington.

Crops were got off, year after year, but costs continued to mount. With independence the two party-two union political structure hardened. Cane farmers began to reduce production because of costs. The Estates began to look at combine-harvesting for which machines made by Massey-Ferguson and others had begun to be available, but there was resistance from both Government and Opposition. New laws were introduced, too, demanding work permits for expatriates. These came less willingly than before and jobs were hard to fill.

And yet, when Jamaica became independent in August 1962 there was an air of hopefulness. Bustamante, re-elected after seven years in the wilderness, became the first independent Prime Minister, and married the capable, delightful Miss Longbridge. (He had been knighted in 1955.) There was goodwill all round, and as late as 1963 it was possible to be optimistic. Prices rose dramatically in the world sugar market and in order to spread the benefit a profit-sharing scheme was introduced. It was possible to look forward to a day when independent Jamaica would pay her way in the world and raise her people's living standards. To do this she had to increase her productivity, particularly in the sugar industry. If this was done, Tate & Lyle, after twenty-five years of involvement in Jamaica, could look forward to the next twenty-five 'with hope and confidence', as they said at the time.

There were good times as well as less good and some excellent seasons but alas, hope was a dupe, and confidence misplaced.

IV
'In my youth' Father William replied to his son,
'I feared it might injure the brain,
'But now that I'm perfectly sure I have none
'I do it again and again.'
(Lewis Carroll 1832–1898)

The first two or three years of Jamaican independence witnessed reasonable production, a freeze of union membership, a two-year wages agreement, productivity bonuses and certain improvements—accounting, wages and statistics were dealt with by computer. Employees became more health-conscious. Hookworm had virtually disappeared, malaria completely. But there was much absenteeism and farmers' canes fell off in quality as well as quantity. The high prices and high profits of 1963 had led to demands for even higher wages. Mechanized cropping and other economy measures were blocked by Government.

There had been further changes in management. Paul Bovell was now Chief General Manager. Frank Curtis and C. C. Murray ran the Estates. In 1966 a new Board of Directors was installed. It had a British Chairman—Jo Whitmee, and two British specialists—Bill Coupland and James Fairrie. Bill was the Finance Director and also took care of sales arrangements and negotiations. So good was he at this that all the other Jamaican Estates had for years asked him to act for them. Quiet, courteous, determined, he was quite admirable at all he did. James, younger son of Geoffrey Fairrie, and a gifted engineer, supplied the technical expertise. His light touch and wit were a great help on many sticky occasions. The Managing Director was now Paul Bovell and the two General Managers became Executive Directors. There were also two distinguished Jamaicans as non-Executives, Sir Alfred Rennie, a retired judge (Vice-Chairman) and Mr. Dick Mahfood, Q.C., who had got to know and like W.I.S.Co. during the Goldenberg Inquiry.

Over the next few years political attention turned towards the land. Why should this overseas company own so much in a land-hungry country? The question was studied carefully. Very well, the land should be sold to a Government-controlled holding company which would lease it to Jamaicans such as the W.I.S.Co. agricultural staff, people like Archie Savariau, 'Sugar' Allen and the rest, to work it as farmers. But then the Government changed, and the Jamaica Labour Party was replaced by the People's National Party, which had a liking for workers' co-operatives. Those who had been going to lease the land were held off while an experimental co-operative was set up on one of the Monymusk sections, Morelands, and later this was extended to most of the W.I.S.Co. land.

Factories elsewhere in the island began to go out of business. At the same time there was a Government desire for a national sugar company. In Tate & Lyle there were differing views. Some felt it would be wrong to withdraw altogether from Jamaica, others that the Company's presence even as owners of the factories at Frome and Monymusk was now an anachronism. In the end it was considered that under present day conditions the factories would never again be profitable, and this decided the issue. W.I.S.Co. was sold to a newly formed national sugar company.

Two elderly men sat one July day in an English garden. The sun was almost as hot, the sky as blue as on a Jamaica morning. The doves called and the thrushes and blackbirds sang. The two wondered whether sugar would continue to be produced forever in Jamaica or whether, a century and a half after the atrophy of the 1830s, it would dwindle away again. For a Government largely dependent for its revenue on sugar earnings to pay out production subsidies of $12 to 14 million–about $30 a ton, in order to keep the workers in co-operatives happy seemed to make the future perilous. But it is someone else's worry now.

> The gale it plies the saplings double.
> It blows so hard 'twill soon be gone.
> Today the Roman and his trouble
> Are ashes under Uricon. . . .

V

'Yankee gone. Sparrow take over now.'
(Calypso–ca. 1948)

Thus the Mighty Sparrow. In Trinidad, the war was over, the Americans gone. Things would be different. But how different? Certainly somewhat the same as in Jamaica, but by different routes and at different speeds.

Tate & Lyle's sole investment in Trinidad, Caroni Ltd., sprawled twenty-five miles from north to south, along a railroad on which scores of converted ex-Belgian railway cars, with a kind of cage welded on to them, carried the cane to Brechin Castle factory. The investment was potentially prosperous but, like the other six factories–Ste. Madeleine, Reform, Woodford Lodge, Orange Grove, Forres Park and Esperanza–it was bedevilled by two intractable problems. There was first of all the difficulty in obtaining staff and labour owing to the pull of employment towards the American bases. As most of these closed down people began to drift back to sugar, though at current sugar prices it was impossible to match the wages paid at the bases and for a time people preferred not to work but live on savings. Secondly there were the depredations of the frog hopper.[3] These tiny insects in their millions continued to settle on the cane–leaves, and draw their nourishment, leaving behind thousands of acres of dying cane.

By 1949 means had been found to control the insects by spraying the soil before they emerged for the first time in July from eggs laid the previous year. This demanded close control of weeds and application of Benzene Hexachloride (B.H.C.), a fairly cheap insecticide. Insects which escaped this application were later killed on the wing by blowing dust impregnated with B.H.C. over the fields. The success was considerable, and of course there were numbers of claimants for the credit for it, but there is no doubt that it had, for Caroni, been the work of Frank Blackburn and his team. By 1953 it was possible to report a year free of froghopper blight. But it was now seven years since B.H.C. had first been tried and just at the moment of success the froghopper began to exhibit signs of resistance to the insecticide. Search for an alternative had to be begun in haste.

At Caroni, as in Jamaica, it is worth noting the sterling work done by the medical department for the health of the employees and indirectly for the health of the population as a whole. In the early 1950s Caroni had about 23,000 men and women on its books.[4] The majority of these were employed in the agricultural department, nearly all being of East Indian origin. A very large proportion of the cane was then cropped by women. In the factories and on the railway and road transport, at the bulk sugar terminal at Goodrich Bay, which was opened in 1953, there were more people of Negro than of Indian origin.

Field employees in particular were not physically strong. Frank Ayrey, the company's doctor, reporting on the thousands of cases who passed through his hands each year, described them as suffering–like their brothers and sisters in Jamaica–from anaemia due to hookworm, from malaria, from oral sepsis, and from malnutrition and a-vitaminosis due, as in Jamaica, to ignorance rather than poverty. Of these complaints the worst then was hookworm. It could, he thought, be eradicated in five or six years by discipline over habits in the field, by the provision of proper latrines and by the wearing of leather footwear. Meetings with the health authorities led to the establishment of a Government Hookworm Unit, which carried out a survey and confirmed Ayrey's views, but apart from that there was no island-wide action. Propaganda was used by Caroni to spread the use of shoes on the estates. Treatment was intensified. Malaria incidence was beginning to diminish, as in Jamaica. The Indian prefers a largely vegetable diet, but this, too was being improved. Yet there was some resistance. The clinics, in order to prevent waste of time, made a small charge–three shillings, to include cost of medicine. This had a strange side effect. The employee considered that *cheap* medicine could not

---

[3] See Chapter Ten.
[4] Later the work was decasualized and the numbers fell. By 1963 there were few women working in the fields.

be *good* medicine and preferred to go to some other doctor who would charge twenty times as much for precisely the same treatment. Nevertheless, as the years went by it began to be noted that the employees of Caroni enjoyed better health than other rural Trinidadians.

The position of Government in Trinidad, and of the trade unions, was very different from what existed in Jamaica. For some ten years after the war the elected Government was provided by the Democratic Labour Party, a loose coalition of men representing varying interests, and led by the large, voluble, intelligent Albert Gomes. Divergent views meant slow progress. There were in the sugar industry two and sometimes more trade unions. These were regionally based and frequently at loggerheads with each other, their leaders being in general men who were in search of political influence but who, with one exception, lacked the quality of a Bustamante. In any case, with that one exception, they had no links with a political party.

In the south, the Ste. Madeleine area, leadership was held by a Mr. Osman Mohammed, in the north by a Mr. Oli Mohammed (no relation). Other figures were Messrs. Rampartrap Singh, Geoffroy, and above all Bhadase Maraj. The last-named was the most considerable figure, the exception to the rest. Feared by many, flamboyant, rich, with money made by the purchase and sale of war surplus goods, Bhadase was someone to reckon with. Although this would not have been admitted in India, for he had crossed the sea, he claimed to be a Twice-born, and he certainly had personal magnetism.

As far as concerned Caroni Ltd. he had a strange, individual devotion to the General Manager, Harold Gilbert. Once, when Bhadase as a youngster of eighteen had been brought before Harold, sitting as a J.P., the latter had dismissed the case for technical reasons. Waiting for him at home, later in the day, Bhadase clasped him by both hands, gazed fixedly at him with his large liquid eyes, and said: 'You have been my friend. I will always be a friend to you and your Company.' He was to keep his word. But he was selective about those with whom he would deal. When Harold Gilbert retired Bhadase insisted on being formally handed over, as it were, to the Managing Director.

A one-time all-in wrestler, huge in frame, he was regarded by many as a ruthless ruffian. Perhaps he was ruthless, but he did a great deal to help Caroni, and later Trinidad as a whole. And he had a curious gentleness. In the early 1950s, however, he disappeared from view. Following an operation in the U.S. his doctors had put him on a drug which in his case proved habit-forming and for some years he was an addict. The needle, used many times a day, damaged his splendid physique and his upper arm and shoulder muscles atrophied. Sheer determination enabled him to kick the habit, but it took time.

In his absence in 1953 the various union factions called a number of island-wide strikes. The Sugar Manufacturers' Association was not a

Farrow—makers of irrigation equipment. Part of Tate & Lyle Engineering.

Richards' Shipyard built this splendid craft.

Berger and Plate grow peas and lentils – Springdale, Idaho.

cohesive body. There was no Kirkwood and the owners and/or managers could usually be guaranteed to disagree point blank, shifting their support from one section to another of the Association. The local owners treated the general managers of Caroni and Ste. Madeleine as mere tools of far-off London, and even these two, being very different men, could not see eye to eye. Nevertheless, on this occasion they held together and the strike was broken. The unions therefore appealed to Government for help and there was a long Inquiry, carried out by a retired general secretary of the British Railway Salaried Staffs Association, Mr. Fred Dalley, who was sent out by the T.U.C. at the request of the Colonial Office. Mr. Dalley was not perhaps the best possible choice, for he was unable to adjust himself to the Trinidad scene, and in his rigid, Methodist fashion, hectored the manufacturers. But to be fair, he also considered the trade union leaders irresponsible. When his report emerged there were further troubles, but Caroni adopted a more flexible attitude than the other manufacturers—who grumbled but at length came into line—and things simmered down for a while.

On the other hand the froghopper now got out of control again, and it was only the discovery that a new insecticide, the organo-phosphate 'Malathion', was effective, which at length brought relief. The productivity of the fields, which had dropped to about half, began to recover to 28 or 30 tons of cane per acre. Medically, too, the situation continued to improve. Malaria had disappeared and hookworm was down to ten cases a year, whereas ten years previously it had been ten cases a day.

At this time, in 1956, Tate & Lyle acquired the little, locally owned Esperanza factory, a mile or so from Brechin Castle, and its estates of some 4,000 acres. Brechin Castle factory was expanded to take in the canes and the old Esperanza factory which gave the appearance of being an artefact of Tubal Cain, disappeared as scrap.

For Trinidad as a whole 1956 marked a major change. At a General election in October that year, a new political party, the People's National Movement, won a sweeping victory over the Democratic Labour Party. Albert Gomes even lost his seat. The P.N.M. was the creation of a new and perennially dominant figure, Dr. Eric Williams, a brilliant historian, an Oxford scholar, who had for some months been holding public meetings in Port-of-Spain's Woodford Square, under the trees. Calling the Square his 'University', Dr. Williams had encouraged free intellectual discussion of issues affecting Trinidad, and many influential men and women of varying origins, beliefs and backgrounds joined the movement. Twenty-one years later Dr. Williams would be re-elected for the fifth time as Trinidad's Prime Minister, standing politically head and shoulders above anyone else in the area.

Now, however, it was feared by some that he meant no good to the sugar industry. He had deeply studied the slave trade, had written books, brilliantly composed, savage, scornful. And, although there had been little or no history of slavery in Trinidad under British rule, he took the Caribbean as a whole as his scene and the sugar industry in particular as a target. In late 1955 a new Governor, Sir Edward Beetham, had been appointed, who made it his business to be on terms with Dr. Williams. The Doctor was wary at first but later cordial. Beetham had also come to know the sugar people. Some he found unforthcoming. The General Manager of Caroni, Paul Bovell, was new, but Beetham had also got to know Caroni's Managing Director and when the latter arrived in Trinidad shortly after the Election, he insisted on sending him to see Dr. Williams.

The new Premier lived in a quiet book-filled house in Mary Street. He seemed something of a solitary, his Chinese wife having died in childbirth some years earlier, and his daughter, Erica, being cared for by her mother's sister, the delightful Ursula Moyoo, who worked as a Secretary for the Caroni Ltd. trading office in Port of Spain. The first quarter of an hour of the meeting between Dr. Williams and the Caroni Managing Director was stiff and difficult. The Premier spoke at some length of the evils of the sugar industry, of slavery, and so forth. Then it was recalled that the two men had met at Oxford before the war, and Dr. Williams became less chilly. He said, with what in anyone else would have been a mild cackle of laughter: 'Well, let's see what we *can* agree on.' The interview extended to an hour, to two hours. There seemed to be much on which there was agreement. 'We must meet again,' said Dr. Williams at length. The Press were waiting back at Government House, curious to know what had happened. 'What do you think of our new Premier?' they demanded. The reply: 'He is a very remarkable man,' had the virtue of truth.

This seemed to the Press unexpected, and was given wide publicity. During the next few days there were further talks and telephone calls. Dr. Williams seemed to sense that the sugar industry was not entirely hostile, and himself became friendly. Over the years to come, although there were occasional disagreements he always remained amicable on a personal basis and extended this to Caroni Ltd. as a whole. His ministers, too, Donald Granado, Kamaluddhin Mohammed, Bert Wallace, Gerard Montano, became friends. Dr. Winston Mahabir, the Minister of Health, approved of the work initiated on hookworm by Caroni and organized a full scale campaign based on the measures taken by Frank Ayrey.

The P.N.M. did not wish to set up a trade union wing but made no secret of their concern about labour relations in the industry. Caroni and Ste. Madeleine had industrial relations officers, Pip Angel and Philip de Carteret, but while these did much good work there was still, among many in the higher echelons of the companies, perhaps justifiably, a feeling that the unions were merely there to make trouble. Back in Britain, there was criticism from the T.U.C. When Mr. George Woodcock, then General Secretary, voiced this at a meeting with directors of Caroni it was suggested that he might go and see the situation. It was true that after a recent outbreak of localized violence some employees had been dismissed for this was the kind of intimidation which could not be tolerated. The T.U.C. considered it harsh medicine. Mr. Woodcock went to Trinidad, liked the place, saw the union situation, and when he returned, arranged for a retired General Secretary of the N.U.R., Mr. Martin Pounder, to spend two years in the island, training union officials, regularizing union accounts, and in general trying to set up a workable structure.

Pounder's efforts were successful. They probably owed much to a figure who would later become much more prominent, Solomon Hochoy, the Jamaica-born Chinese who, under Colonial rule, had become Commissioner for Labour, and whose ability in solving disputes had kept the temperature far lower than it might otherwise have been. 'Solo' would one day be Deputy Governor, then Governor, and finally, as Sir Solomon, the first Governor-General of independent Trinidad and Tobago.

For some years Tate & Lyle had, through W.I.S.Co., held a considerable block of shares in the Ste. Madeleine Sugar Company. In 1957 this became a controlling interest. Coincidentally there had been a change in top management, Richard Spink replacing Eric Johnstone, while at Caroni Paul Bovell had, as we have seen, recently taken over. With the now ever more pressing concern for labour relations it was felt by Tate & Lyle that the two companies would more easily adopt common policies if both were under the same ultimate control. The Managing Director of Caroni was therefore appointed to the Board of Ste. Madeleine, and the following year Henckell du Buisson handed over the management of Ste. Madeleine to the London office of Caroni and W.I.S.Co. In May 1962 the two companies were merged, Ste. Madeleine becoming a totally owned subsidiary of Caroni.

Since industrial relations were of such importance, Charlie Michelin, with his immense experience of these in Jamaica, was now installed as a Special Representative of the Board in Trinidad, senior to the two General Managers. Paul Bovell had returned, as we have seen, to Jamaica, and Richard Spink decided that he would prefer to return to England. The same systems of communication and control between London and Trinidad had long been introduced as for Jamaica. Frank Blackburn and Graham Milner became the General Managers.

During the same period the owners of Woodford Lodge, a factory and estate producing 27,000 tons of sugar a year and contiguous with Caroni Ltd., had also sold their interest to Caroni in 1961. Tate & Lyle's investment had thus grown to include four factories—Brechin Castle, Woodford Lodge, Usine Ste. Madeleine and Reform. They now bought and processed 88 per cent of the farmers' cane in the island and produced 90 per cent of the total sugar manufactured.

This was welcomed by the Government of Trinidad. Generally speaking it was liked also by the cane farmers, a politically active body, led by Mr. Norman Girwar. In the earlier years the process had been accompanied by peaceful labour conditions and by gradually increasing production. It enabled reconstruction work to be undertaken at Usine Ste. Madeleine,[5] it permitted considerable rationalization of cane deliveries, and it justified the establishment of a Central Agricultural Research Station. The final steps coincided with the attainment of Trinidad's independence in 1962. Dr. Williams, although he had had in his time some sharp things to say about Britain, about the U.S.A. and about colonialism, regarded the situation benignly and treated the major sugar company and the major oil company, Texaco, with its huge refinery at Pointe-à-Pierre, as friends.

Yet beneath the surface there were stirrings. Mr. Pounder had come and gone. While he was there industrial relations had worked smoothly and so far as could be seen to everyone's satisfaction. But with his departure the factions began to reappear. A rival union was established by a Mr. W. W. Sutton, in competition with the All Trinidad Sugar Workers' Union and concentrated mainly in the factories. Unrest began again.

Conditions otherwise were still improving. Frank Ayrey, in particular, in his farewell report in 1961 was able to claim a vast amelioration in the health of the employees. Work was more regular, women were found jobs more physically suited to them than cane-cutting. New housing replaced the old unsightly, stinking barracks. There was a profit-sharing scheme. Long service was rewarded with extra privileges and a bonus. The majority both seemed and were content.

But from 1960 onwards there were inter-union claims and counter-claims put forward in competition for membership. The Trinidad Government set up a board of inquiry calling on Mr. Carl Goldenberg, the Canadian legal eagle, who had recently led a Commission of Inquiry in Jamaica, in order to convince everyone that justice was being done. As a result of a request to the British T.U.C. for help in putting the All Trinidad Union's case, a Mr. Lionel Murray who had spent a few weeks in Trinidad following Mr. Pounder's departure, was seconded from the T.U.C. research department. His presence was generally helpful although he did at one stage make a statement to the effect that he would give his personal assurance that the British T.U.C. would support an appeal by the Trinidad manufacturers for an increase in the retail price of sugar of 1d. per lb. as long as the money was used exclusively for the benefit of the workers. This was either unwise on the part of the future General Secretary of the T.U.C. or it was disingenuous. For the Trinidad manufacturers had themselves no control over the price negotiated with the British Government or over the price on the world market. And he knew it, or he should have done.

The Goldenberg Inquiry produced a series of recommendations which the manufacturers accepted, but certain of the recommendations were obscure and ambiguous. Unrest continued, the unions being unwilling to agree on interpretation. At length a further Commission of Inquiry was set

[5] See Chapter 30.

up, this time headed by Sir George Honeyman, a British lawyer who had a long record of coping with such affairs. It was established that only some 4,000 employees out of a total of 20,000 in Caroni as a whole belonged to any union at all. These were to be given a choice as to which they would adhere to. Unrest went on unabated. But now Mr. Bhadase Maraj reappeared, cured of his addiction and distressed at the futile scene of bickering. He seized control of the more numerous union – the All-Trinidad – at the invitation of its officers. Some of these he chastened with words, others he dismissed. Travelling with a modest bodyguard in a dazzling American car, and armed with a large revolver (christened 'Tiger') and a smaller one in an upper pocket (christened 'Baby Doll') he traversed the area and gathered considerable support. Things quietened down and he was able to negotiate a generous crop bonus for the workers. The Government was secretly relieved, although he was a political opponent.

But this tranquillity was a temporary phenomenon. Two years later in 1965 the Oil Field Workers Union, relatively wealthy and at that time opposed to Dr. Williams, made an attempt to take over, led by Mr. (now Senator) George Weekes. Bhadase Maraj did his utmost to help the company to keep going and for quite some time the majority of employees made it clear that they wished it to do so. But there was violence and intimidation on a heavy scale at the factories, particularly at Ste. Madeleine. Cane trucks and railways were attacked and a virtual siege took place. The Government became extremely disturbed. It placed no blame on the Company and indeed encouraged close liaison with the Minister for Home Affairs, Mr. Gerard Montano. But one by one the factories were closed as people were scared away by mobs of strong-arm men. The company had long maintained an auxiliary – or as it was called supplemental – police force trained by the official force and commanded by retired or seconded inspectors. Some 200 strong, it sufficed for normal troubles, for preventing malicious cane fires (in Trinidad the cane is normally burned before crop under controlled conditions) and so forth and was a steadying influence. But now it was simply not numerous enough. Peter MacIntyre, the Cultivation Manager, organized an airborne firefighting force consisting of a converted Mitchell bomber carrying two tons of water and four smaller aircraft. This was effective but such fun that people took to starting fires just to see 'The Air Force' in action.

When at last Brechin Castle came to a halt – the men in the factory had been working non-stop for forty-eight hours as their reliefs could not get in – the Government was advised at once. It had been hoped to keep one factory going as a sign. Now Government decided to declare a State of Emergency, under which all gatherings of more than six people were illegal. It did so at 10 o'clock at night. A call to the Governor-General, the splendid Solomon Hochoy, asking for news, elicited the reply 'I've just signed the State of Emergency, boy. And,' he added, 'in case anyone forgets to say it, thanks for everything.' Within a matter of two or three days people were back at work. Intimidation had ceased. Public opinion was completely behind the Government, with the exception of a few vocal elements who took care, however, to moderate their remarks.

Now there began a period of relative calm, at least in sugar. In parallel with the developments in Jamaica, it was decided to establish a Board of Trinidadian Directors similar to W.I.S.Co.'s, with only three London members, the vice-chairman being Sir Henry (Joe) Pierre, an eminent Trinidadian and the country's best surgeon, Jeffrey Stollmeyer, a businessman with considerable interests in politics and farming and one of the great West Indian cricketers of his day, and Ashford Sinanan, a prominent lawyer and Federal Minister. The latter two were both Senators. Frank Blackburn was Managing Director.

Henceforward Caroni Ltd. became more and more Trinidadian. Jo Whitmee, the Chairman, handed over both Caroni and W.I.S.Co. to Johnny Tate, who, by dint of spending many days a year in aeroplanes contrived also to be responsible for Tate & Lyle's Central African affairs, carrying these varied burdens with a deceptively dégagé air and the most entrancing sense of humour. Production was hit from time to time by drought, pest, or too much rain at the wrong time. But it continued.

At length in 1972 the Government of Trinidad made an offer for 51 per cent of the total shares. Tate & Lyle accepted and offered to assist the other, minority shareholders by buying their shares. Johnny Tate, Bill Coupland, and the London Office staff were still involved. Finally, in 1976, the Government made an offer for all the shares, acquiring the Company for itself, and in July of that year the deal was completed. The terms were acceptable to both sides. Tate & Lyle still have a service agreement with the Trinidad Company, and relationships with the Government remain cordial.

After almost exactly forty years of direct involvement in Trinidad, Tate & Lyle have, however, no longer the close and deep commitment which once bound them to the Island. It is permissible to feel a certain nostalgia.

CHAPTER EIGHTEEN

The 1950s and 1960s at Home

I
'Meanwhile, back at the Ranch . . . .'
(Any Old Horse Opera)

Back at the ranch, Phase I was a period of tidying up. Three years after the end of rationing, arrangements were at length made by the Conservative Government to restore sugar trading to private enterprise. The clear signs of a falling off in export trade were accompanied by a drop in Tate & Lyle's domestic share and by some dumping of subsidized foreign refined sugars, and there was an example of mysterious and inexplicable Government tinkering known as The Irish Hole in the Tariff.

The hiving off of sections of the Company undertaken during the threat of nationalization had to be reversed.

Steps were taken to try to contain the threat to export trade. In 1955 two graduates were recruited for the first time with a view to concentrating on trading not on manufacture. Michael Attfield and Michael Kitchin, both from Oxford, were carefully selected and thoroughly trained in sugar affairs. They both showed themselves temperamentally suited to commercial matters. It is not of course necessary to be a university graduate in order to be a good trader, but, known as Burgess and MacLean, these two were to prove that it can help.

Towards the end of the Phase a new Sales Director with wide experience in the complexities of world trading, Gordon Shemilt, formerly of Canada & Dominion Sugar, was appointed. He sought ways and means of holding the position, for example in Norway, and there were certain small acquisitions in Britain designed to increase the range of products offered. And determined steps were taken to safeguard the position in West Africa.

II
Freeing the Sugar Trade—The Sugar Board

Britain had survived the Suez crisis. Sir Anthony Eden had retired and Mr. Macmillan was Prime Minister. Some of the apparatus of Government control was being demolished, including the purchase of sugar by the Ministry of Agriculture, Fisheries and Food. The existence of the Commonwealth Sugar Agreement, with its guarantee to buy a fixed quantity of nearly 1·6 million tons a year at a price negotiated annually by the British Government, was difficult to reconcile with the freeing of trade in sugar and the re-establishment of the London Terminal Market. There was also the problem of the guaranteed payment to the producers of home-grown beet sugar. Both the Commonwealth producers and the British Sugar Corporation received a price which was usually well above that reigning in the world sugar market.

In the end, after much discussion, an instrument called The Sugar Board was evolved. Established in 1956 in Mark Lane and chaired by a distinguished former civil servant, Sir George Dunnett, K.B.E., C.B., this body bought the Commonwealth raws at the negotiated price and then sold them Free Alongside[1] to commercial buyers on a free market. The producer thus got his guaranteed price. The difference between this and the (normally) lower world price would be recovered by means of a surcharge collected by H.M. Customs. The Sugar Board was expected to operate at a loss but the Government would recover this for the taxpayer via his other hand, through H.M. Customs. The system worked well for a period of nearly twenty years. On the two occasions–in 1957 during the Suez crisis and in 1963–4, when the world price was *above* the Commonwealth price, the 'surcharge' became a 'distribution payment', a kind of surcharge in reverse. Home-grown beet sugar was similarly handled. The Sugar Board, thanks to its very competent staff, was a success.

In effect the whole of the United Kingdom sugar trade, from the point of Free Alongside onwards, was restored to private hands on a commercial basis and the facilities provided by the London market regained their former usefulness as an earner of foreign exchange.

III
'The Irish Hole in The Tariff.'

There were occasions when the system permitted the dumping of subsidized foreign refined sugar in Britain[2] and a particular thorn in the flesh was an unusual agreement arrived at between H.M. Government and that of the Irish Republic in the early 1960s. The precise diplomatic reason for it has long been forgotten, and relationships between Tate & Lyle and the Cómhlucht Siúcre Eireann, Teo, which most people even in Eire refer to as the Irish Sugar Company Ltd., were not disturbed in the long run. Although occasionally people on either side of the Irish Channel may have spoken of 'those Spalpeens', or the English equivalent, asked

---

[1] A technical term. Don't worry about it. Leave it to Burgess and MacLean.
[2] A contemporary Noel Coward Tate wrote a sharp little number, beginning:
        Mad Swiss and Maudling
        Let sugar be dumped quite free . . .

Rig of the day for Hesser girls – first Ideal Home Exhibition, 1925.

Twenty-five years on. Hesser girls at the Ideal Home Exhibition, 1950. (Mr. Cube clearly likes the change in gear.)

themselves 'phwat the divil is after happening now?' and even have threatened 'the back of me hand to them, at all', or the like, no lasting harm resulted.

At the time, however, it seemed to be an annoyance to Tate & Lyle and the other British sugar refiners who were trying to cope with an influx of dumped French sugar, imported by an Iranian gentleman who eventually welshed on his creditors. This was just when H.M. Government decided to use the Sugar Board to purchase 10,000 tons of Irish beet sugar at £50 a ton and sell it back to Ireland at £39 for the manufacture of sugar-containing goods which would end up in Ulster (part of the U.K.). At the same time the Sugar Board would sell a minimum 5,000 tons of Commonwealth sugar to Ireland for her internal requirements. The amounts were fairly small but nevertheless it complicated life and appeared to be an arrangement whereby Eire was obtaining an unfair advantage from her position as a member of the Commonwealth. Chaps talked darkly of 'The Irish Hole in the Sugar Tariff' and letters were written to *The Times* and the *Financial Times* on the subject, without much effect.

It all seemed to be one of those phenomena which are subject to Murphy's laws. Murphy was a fictional King of a part of Ireland in 650 A.D. who evolved four laws which govern any kind of activity:

(1) It's not as easy as it looks.
(2) It will take longer than you think.
(3) It will cost more than you've budgeted for.
(4) If anything can possibly go wrong, it will.

The matter was debated – and ridiculed – in the House of Commons, members of both Conservative and Labour parties remarking on its folly, one Labour member describing it as a three card trick. Perhaps the most significant statement was made by the Parliamentary Secretary to the Ministry of Agriculture (Mr. Scott-Hopkins – Conservative). Like a gramophone record, he gave the answer prepared by his civil servants: 'As far as consultation is concerned, we do not in the normal way consult with the trade interests *before* agreements are made. We consult with them *after* the agreements are made . . .'

This was 1962, not 1984 but Big Brother was already moving into Whitehall.

A leading article in the *Irish Times* said: 'Not very often does an Irish Company, whether semi-state or private, display enough commercial *nous* to get a trading advantage abroad.' They had done so with the help of the British bureaucrats at the expense of British companies.

Eventually this small but possibly unnecessary piece of High Government Thinking disappeared, but not before it had muddied the waters. Nobody knows who had engineered it. He may well have been knighted, or perhaps he was carried off by the Little People. Bad cess to him in any case, said Tate & Lyle at the time.

IV
Hiving On

At around this time the Hiving Off, which had ten years earlier been undertaken to salvage some part of Tate & Lyle should Mr. Cube not succeed, had become an embarrassing complication. It was decided to go through an operation known as regrouping, which–although felt to be a Good Thing–was probably clearly understood only by the Finance Director and his legal and financial advisers, Linklaters & Paines and Schroder Wagg. They were involved in a study of arcane mysteries which was naturally best done late at night, and called forth some mystic lines of verse:

> There's a deathly hush in the Lane to-night
> With all windows dark save one.
> Just the scratch of quill on the paper still
> For William is Hiving On! . . .
> There's Wagg and Schroder, Linklater, Paine,
> A Silk and his Junior too,
> Some bottles of coke and a stock that's broke,
> All part of the horrid crew . . .
> But never fear, for Booth is here,
> And all is put to right,
> Though if I were you I would not go through
> That Carpeted Part at night.

V
Merton Grove

The Borough of Bootle bears the motto: Aspice, Respice, Prospice (look out, look back, look forward). People looking out of a train on the Liverpool—Southport railway see a sign saying: Trade for Health, which symbolizes the existence of the Merton Grove Company Ltd. Once part of a brewing business, then owned by MacFie's and later by United Molasses Ltd., this small manufactury turns out about 10,000 tons of different grades of syrup and treacle. It has been a part of Tate & Lyle since 1957, and much of its special product goes to the makers of biscuits and those dark liquorice sweets. A good deal also goes to Norway.

VI
Tate & Lyle (Norway)

So do a number of different varieties of sugar, for Norway has no sugar industry of her own and is not a member of the E.E.C. A subsidiary called

Tate & Lyle (Norway), formed in 1962 by Gordon Shemilt when he became Director of Sales, sells the products through some 200 wholesalers in competition with Poland, Czechoslovakia and Russia, and sometimes in competition with Cuba. Some of the sugar is sold in special one-ton plastic collapsible containers and some in packets printed menacingly: *Innpakket for Norge.* The competition is fierce and the Poles for example have been known to use a sales force of attractive-looking popsies. But Gordon Shemilt's measures and the people of Tate & Lyle (Norway) have held on to the trade.

VII
Millwall Sugars

Back in 1836 a family firm of grocers, George Clark & Sons, had started up a business supplying special blends of sugar and syrup to brewers and confectionery makers. Various sugars were selected at the docks, melted and blended and sent out in barrels to customers. Clarks' headquarters at the time were at Broadway, on the site of the present London Transport headquarters, and here, in 1898 all the small 'melting pots' were collected. The usefulness of corn syrup in giving a nutty flavour to beers, and the manufacture of caramel colouring were discovered. The plant was moved to Millwall.

For a time, later on, liquid sugar was supplied by tanker by Tate & Lyle but as the demand for specialities fell, Clarks began to be pushed in the direction of high-volume, low-margin business and were a little too small to undertake it. Moreover the Clark who had consolidated the affair in 1898 had had four sons. While it was reasonable for him to draw £4,000 a year from the business, it could not stand four chaps doing the same. In 1955 the Clarks sold Millwall to Brown & Polson, a subsidiary of the large American firm Corn Products.

In 1964, as Tate & Lyle's share of the home trade was being eroded, it was decided to acquire Millwall in order to add to the range of products.

Merton Grove and Millwall represent steps taken to safeguard the home trade, Tate & Lyle (Norway) a method of servicing and improving an export market. The next chapter shows the actions taken to hold on to export markets in West Africa.

CHAPTER NINETEEN

West Africa

'While Jove's Planet rises silent, yonder over Africa.'
(R. B. Browning 1812–1889)

In the case of certain export markets continuance of the trade depended on willingness to invest locally in order to help the countries concerned to fulfil their aim to produce on the spot.

In West Africa, such a market was Nigeria. Tate & Lyle invested in two ways. First they took equity shares in a cane-sugar producing company at Bacita, installed and managed by a company called Booker McConnell with wide interests in the West Indies, of whom Tate & Lyle themselves had long been customers for raw sugar. Bacita had a difficult start. Some considerable technical help was provided by Tate & Lyle,[1] and at the same time they installed a cube-making plant at Ilorin, receiving Bacita sugar, refining it, and making cubes for local consumption. The equipment was the same as at Thames Refinery–the Høweler–and Nigerians were trained in London to operate it. In Ghana, technical assistance was given in making operational two sugar mills erected by Czech and Polish engineering companies whose experience was in beet sugar not cane. The mills did not work well.

It seems strange, but sugar production in West Africa has always, up to now, been difficult. Old hands involved in this, or indeed in other similar activities, used to say philosophically, as the sun dropped into the sea with an almost audible sizzle and the first sundowner cooled the hand that held the glass: 'Ah, well! Wa-Wa.' (West Africa Wins Again.)

The poet Browning, incidentally an almost exact contemporary of Henry and Abram, knew nothing of all this, for he was writing in the safety of a boat a long way off. He was, however, full of home-thoughts, as no doubt were those exiles in the Bay of Benin.

Is there, perhaps, some atavistic antipathy, quite irrational, resulting from the inborn but unrecognized recollection that for some three centuries until 150 years ago, one's ancestors had been traded across the seas to work in the cane piece three thousand miles to the west? Fanciful, no doubt, but the genes are strange things.

At any rate even with local production at Bacita and Ilorin in Nigeria, and the two factories in Ghana, it was unlikely that the two countries with their huge areas and large populations would be self-sufficient for many years. Of the two Nigeria was by far the bigger, with an area about that of Europe and a population of 60 million people of different religions and

[1] Including that of a brawny Monymusk estate manager, 'Sugar' Allen.

cultures. In order to ensure that Nigerian demands should be met, stocks available and distribution effective, it was decided in 1962 to establish a local trading company, Tate & Lyle Nigeria Ltd. Its first Board consisted of Tony Tate, Gordon Shemilt, Dick Oxley and Ernie Strauss. A chain of fourteen depots was set up covering the whole country and regional offices in each of Nigeria's three regions, and manned by Francis Kirkwood, Julian Bowes, and A. E. Dakoru. Nigerian sales representatives operated throughout the country, supplying sugar to traders in forty different towns.

In the years that followed Tate & Lyle (Nigeria) did well against heavy competition from many other exporters. Like many a company operating in the developing countries of the world it has had problems arising from changes in the political scene on the spot. If you are well regarded by one Government you may be mistrusted by its successor. It is a familiar dilemma and one can only do one's best as government succeeds government.

In Ghana the population in the 1970s was about eight million, occupying an area about the size of the British Isles, and consuming about 60,000 tons of sugar a year. In the old days much of this was used in the production of *akpeteshie* or bush-gin, secretly distilled, because illegal and detrimental to the health (it contained 36 per cent of alcohol). Later the Government established state distilleries, for when *akpeteshie* was legalized as a result of public pressure it was found that three-quarters of the population was drinking it anyway. Sugar is still needed for its production.[2]

Ghanaians also use sugar to sweeten their millet porridge and bake their biscuit cakes, *boflor*, *togbee*, and *nkatie*, and the large Muslim population, during the Ramadan fast when nothing is eaten from sunrise to sunset, consume sugar at night to keep up their strength. The Ghana market will always remain an important one, and, together with that of Sierra Leone and the Gambia, requires constant attention. For in these African countries, as elsewhere, as incomes rise so does the consumption of sugar, and the influence of food faddists is not felt.

---

[2] Graham Green reports another use for Tate's products. In *The Heart of the Matter*, based on a West African town, a girl is seen in a brothel 'in a dirty shift spread out on the packing-cases like a fish on a counter; her bare pink soles dangled over the words "Tate's Sugar". She lay there on duty, waiting for a customer.'

CHAPTER TWENTY

Canada

'Ye Olde Sugar Loaf of 1854.'
(A Trade Mark of Redpath Sugars, Canada)

When Tate & Lyle first became involved in sugar in Canada in 1950, they found themselves associated with a company with about as long a history as their own, Canada & Dominion Sugars. It was one of three in eastern Canada, the other two being Atlantic Sugars with a refinery at St. John, New Brunswick, not far from where Lord Beaverbrook came from, and St. Lawrence Sugars in Montreal, owned by the McConnell family who had founded the *Montreal Globe & Star*.

Caledonia, stern and wild, might in the 1850s have been losing her primacy in sugar refining in Britain, but just as we have seen Abram Lyle 'going south' so we now hear of a Mr. John Redpath who had 'gone west', as a young man of twenty to Montreal. Born in 1796 at Earlston, Berwickshire, in the south-east of Scotland, he had trained as a stonemason. His first job in Canada was building a dairy and he subsequently became a contractor on a large scale, being commissioned in 1821 to build the Lachine Canal and later a 100-mile stretch of the Rideau Canal connecting Jones' Falls and Ottawa. In Montreal he was responsible for the Church of Nôtre Dame on the Place d'Armes, the original McGill University buildings and many houses. A member of the Montreal City Council from when it was formed in 1832, he was also responsible for the fact that Sherbrooke Street was laid out as a broad and spacious thoroughfare.

His portrait, taken at forty years old, shows a vigorous and determined face framed by dark hair and short side-burns. Twelve years later the hair is grey, the whiskers longer, and there is a little fringe of white beard under the jutting chin. He has an air of benevolence but he does not look the sort of man with whom to try anything on.

By 1854 his interests included banking (the Bank of Montreal), a railway, a shipping company and a coal mine, and his many benefactions included support for McGill University and the Presbyterian church, of which he was an Elder. Montreal itself was now a major trading centre at which imports of all kinds were delivered by ocean-going ships and taken up the huge St. Lawrence River or by canal or rail to inner Canada. But it was not yet a manufacturing centre although there was plenty of money about.

John Redpath had two sons, Peter, a heavily bewhiskered replica of his father, and John James whose hair and whiskers were thinner and who sported a military moustache. Peter was in England on business for Papa when in early 1854 he wrote to his younger brother, who was learning business in Toronto:

'Father is building a sugar refinery and I suppose you and I will be involved in it. . . . It is a very great undertaking for any one man as it will require a large capital. I hope, however, it will repay Father for all the anxiety attendant upon such a serious outlay of money on a new undertaking.'

On August 12th, 1854, work began on the refinery. Five months later it was in production, turing out 30,000 pounds a day of refined sugar and with 100 employees on its payroll. It was built on the Lachine Canal which, then nine feet deep, allowed the shallow draft sailing vessels of the day to unload direct into the refinery yard. Built of stone and seven stories high, Redpath refinery was fired by wood as fuel and had ancillary workshops and storage for 8,000 barrels of refined sugar and 2,500 hogsheads of raw. Its main product was loaves of sugar produced by the same methods as Messrs. Wright and Tate were using in Liverpool. Redpath also sold dry crushed sugar, ground, extra ground and some yellows, as well as two grades of syrup.

Then the largest industrial establishment in Montreal, Redpath's 'Canada Sugar Refinery' was regarded as marking the start of Montreal's industrial development and John Redpath himself as the pioneer. Peter was taken into partnership in 1857 and John James in 1861 but the latter was more interested in the Victoria Rifles of Montreal and in 1868 withdrew to concentrate on military affairs. (He served during the Fenian Raids.)

Peter carried on when his father died in 1869. His partner was a young Scottish chemist, George Alexander Drummond, who had been brought over at the age of twenty-five from Edinburgh University to supply the technical know-how. Drummond married Helen, John Redpath's daughter, in 1857. Peter Redpath and George Drummond now ran into a period of exceptional difficulty.

Immediately after the founder's death, and after a tour of British and European refineries, Drummond added a new wing to the refinery at a cost of $150,000, in the hope of improving profits. But just as this was completed Redpath sales of sugar were undercut by white sugar coming in from England, Boston and New York. There was a tariff of a sort but not enough to protect Redpath against competition particularly from the American sugar which was under-written by a Government subsidy. By 1872 the white sugar plant had to be closed, only yellows being sold. Following the Franco-Prussian war, when Bismarck's troops entered Paris and Napoleon III fled with his Empress Eugénie to exile at Chislehurst in England, there was a world depression. The Canadian Government did nothing to protect local manufacturers and Redpath wrote to the Federal Prime Minister, McKenzie, on February 29th, 1876, saying that in the circumstances they must abandon their business. Three hundred men lost their jobs and the refinery stayed intact but idle for three years. Summoned to Ottawa to appear before a Government Committee, Drummond said tersely: 'We don't refine sugar because we cannot do it except at a loss.'

McKenzie's Government was succeeded by a Conservative Government under Sir John MacDonald (in those days Canada was a Colony and knighthoods were accepted) pledged to tariff support for Canadian industry. (The closure of Redpath had been a major issue in an election campaign of great bitterness.) MacDonald's new tariffs sufficed to enable Redpath to reopen and keep alive, and melting began again in 1879. In 1880 Peter Redpath retired and George Drummond took over.

The old plant was replaced with new; conveyor belts replaced 'buggies' manhandled by an army of men, centrifugals were installed, and an Austrian refining process, the Steffen system, introduced. By 1904 output was 420,000 lb. of refined a day and the firm employed over 500 men and paid regular dividends. George Drummond, now seventy-five, was still President, and, like his father-in-law, had been put on the Board of the Bank of Montreal. He was a lover of art and his collection was the largest in North America. In 1904 he was knighted for public services by King Edward VII. There is something of a parallel between Redpath Senior and Abram Lyle, and between George Drummond and Henry Tate.

The fiftieth anniversary of the refinery was celebrated at a ceremony involving 'band music, speeches, conjuring tricks, singing and dancing, and the consumption of meat sandwiches, cake, ice cream, ginger ale and coffee'.

A new six-storey building was erected in 1908 on the site of the old. Its capacity was 1 million lb. a day, and in 1912 a further extension was constructed for the production of cubes and icing sugar. By now Sir George had died and one of his sons, Huntly Redpath Drummond, was President, and it is time now to look at another parallel Canadian development.

The production of beet sugar in Ontario began at the end of the nineteenth century, and here we are still in touch seventy-seven years later, with someone who can actually remember it, Clarence Coyle–eighty-eight in 1977 and retired to Florida. There were four sugar beet factories by 1902, at Wallaceburg, Dresden, Kitchener (called Berlin until 1914) and Wiarton. Of these Wallaceburg was the only successful one, and that after some years of struggle. They were short of technicians and the farmers knew little of sugar beet. It was only when Hermann Wiese from Germany was taken on in 1907 as general supervisor that Wallaceburg turned the corner. He not only manufactured beet sugar but converted the plant to refine cane raws. In 1909 the Ontario Sugar Company, which owned Berlin (Kitchener) went into receivership–Dresden and Wiarton had already gone. Wallaceburg took over and the name Dominion Sugar Company was adopted. Mr. D. A. Gordon had been President of Wallaceburg during the difficult years and his successor C. H. Houson consolidated the situation.

Clarence Coyle, then thirteen years old, was taken on at Wallaceburg as an office-boy at six dollars a week, working long hours, including all day Saturday, and in his spare time, if any, playing baseball for the Crystals, a team which he persuaded his company to sponsor to the tune of $50. Three years later W. J. McGregor was taken on as a lab boy. Clarence acted as secretary and stenographer to D. A. Gordon and was encouraged to go to college. (Some of this account is based on the meticulously typed notes he sent in June 1977.)

Both Canada Sugar Refining and the Dominion Sugar Company struggled through the First War, under Government control, and then through the years that followed. The former had modernized again in 1925–6, throwing out the Steffen plant. The latter had built a new sugar factory at Chatham, Ontario, which began operating in 1916. In 1930 the two companies merged by a straight share exchange and became the Canada and Dominion Sugar Company Ltd. Houson was the first President and Huntly Drummond Vice-President. In 1942 W. J. McGregor became President. Clarence Coyle, who had moved to Montreal in 1931 as Office Manager, became Vice-President. He lived in Montreal but Bill McGregor preferred still to roost in Chatham.

In 1949 the leading sugar companies in eastern Canada were Atlantic under the Presidency of the elderly, delightful L. J. Seidensticker, St. Lawrence, and C. & D. (the biggest). Refining in Montreal had its problems. The river is closed to navigation by ice for over three months in the year from just before Christmas until April. On one occasion in the 1950s the freeze came in mid-November and ships were locked in for four and a half months. Moreover, condenser water is drawn from the Lachine Canal, and when this is drained off for repairs to walls and locks the refinery has to shut down too.

Tate & Lyle's interest in C. & D. came about when in 1949 Frank Chapman from Plaistow Wharf, on a visit, noted that the Canadian Company was employing for modernization an American engineering company with no sugar experience. The technical assistance of Tate & Lyle was offered – this was before the days of T.L.T.S. – and Geoffrey Fairrie joined the Board of C. & D. To supervise the modifications he sent his son Tony, an engineer, and Howarth Magee – also from Liverpool – to prepare specifications for new plant. These two remained in Montreal for a year, during which time Jo Whitmee also visited, to watch progress. Before Geoffrey Fairrie left he had recommended C. & D. to seek out the best talent available to run the modernized refinery. They did so, telephoning 'Mac' Magee, now back in Liverpool at his home. Geoffrey had not expected his advice to be taken so literally and was extremely put out when Mac accepted the job and moved permanently to Canada.

Apart from its climatic problems the Montreal refinery had another minor one. It was at that time next door to a distillery operated by a C. & D. subsidiary, Montreal Products Company Ltd., and numerous 'private' lines with taps on them appear to have kept some of the refinery staff supplied with potable spirit until the distillery was closed.

The newly re-equipped refinery gradually improved its performance and by the mid-1950s was very much in a leading position. All sugar for Toronto had to be shipped by lake steamers and stored. C. & D. acquired a 10-acre waterfront site at Toronto against the time when the projected St. Lawrence Seaway would be built and enable a refinery to be constructed in Toronto.

In 1950 Tate & Lyle had just come through the threat of nationalization, and recollections were still vivid. It seemed only sensible to acquire an interest in a going concern established in a fast-growing, stable Commonwealth country, among people who were friendlily disposed, and who were glad to receive technical assistance. Morton Oliphant and Ian Lyle arranged the acquisition of shares and Ian Lyle and Peter Runge were elected to the Board of C. & D. The new refinery at Toronto was erected by a joint team of C. & D. engineers led by Jim Hobbs and with such as Jack Swan and T.L.T.S. technicians like John Willsher. Initially on a small scale it was designed for increased output when demand rose, and it became almost immediately a show place.

When the Queen officially opened the St. Lawrence Seaway in 1959 she also visited the refinery. A photograph shows Her Majesty with Bill McGregor followed by Prince Philip and Mel Davidson. Mel was a newly appointed Vice-President who took care of public relations and coped with growing interference by Government bodies like the office dealing with trusts and cartels, which is even more sedulous than its homologue in the U.S.A. A sugar refiner has only to offer another a drink in the bar of the St. James's Club and next day their offices are invaded and their files impounded. Mel had the right temperament for, as he described it, snapping at the heels of Ottawa.

In the photograph colleagues were happy to point out that while the Royal Party and Bill McGregor were in step, Mel was the only one out of step, and that Bill—a prim old bachelor—appeared to be attempting to peek down the front of the Royal frock.

There is about Canada a refreshing absence of side, and an engaging immediate friendliness, as genuine as but different from what you find in the U.S. It is hard, in fact, to describe the 'feel' of the country in a brief space, the area is so large, the distances so great. It is about as far from Montreal to Vancouver as it is from London to Montreal, and the ethnic origins and customs of the 21 million Canadians are so varied. In the east, in Acadia, New Brunswick and Nova Scotia, there is outwardly a certain non-conformist Scottish dourness. The demon drink is mistrusted. Until recently in Halifax, whisky was often served from a teapot for the sake of appearances, and in St. John, New Brunswick, it was an offence to carry an opened bottle from one hotel room to another.

In Quebec Province, on the other hand, the majority of people stem from the days when Jacques Cartier discovered the area and later the armies of King Louis XIV and the Jesuit priests were dominant. The French spoken is occasionally a little like that of the seventeenth century. Montreal, apart from its rather extreme climate is—or was—an attractive city. The fact that street names are in French makes the newcomer from England feel he has just crossed the Channel, and you have to try very hard indeed to find a bad meal. The wine cellar at the Ritz Hotel is like that of the Georges V in Paris.

Further west, in Ontario, the farmers are largely descended from people of Central European origin. Ottawa is almost exclusively a Government centre, like Canberra or Brazilia. Toronto is huge, a little like Manchester, but much better planned and laid out.[1] Then there come the huge midwestern provinces and the mountains, and after them British Columbia which sometimes seems more British than Britain. There is about the whole country a spaciousness which takes some getting used to if you come from a small, overcrowded island.

Late in 1959 Tate & Lyle made an agreed offer to acquire a controlling interest. There had been problems over C. & D.'s sugar purchases and the world market would be easier to live with if use were made of direct contacts with the London market. Jo Whitmee, a member of the Tate & Lyle Board, went to Canada as Managing Director. Bill McGregor retired soon after, at nearly seventy. Bunnie Foster, a highly respected lawyer who was a Quebec senator and had been a director since before the war, became Chairman. Clarence Coyle had retired from full time work in 1955 but stayed on as a director for some years.

During his latter years Clarence had taken on two young Canadians who would later become directors of Tate & Lyle. One was Gordon Shemilt, a former fighter pilot who—although unwilling to talk about it—had flown forty combat missions before he was twenty-one. After a few years he left to become an associate of Galban Lobo, the large New York/Havana sugar brokers, coming back as Director of Sales in Tate & Lyle in 1961. The other was Neil Shaw. The two recently acquired Michaels–Burgess and McLean, otherwise Attfield and Kitchen—were sent to Canada. Neil Shaw went for a time to London. The rest of the C. & D. team, Howarth Magee, Ray Porteous, Bev Easton, Gus Hrudke and many others, continued. A new research man, the French-born Russian, Steve Stachenko, was taken on.

While the Refineries flourished the future of C. & D. was beset by two problems. One was that the factories at Chatham and Wallaceburg were perennially short of supplies of beet. Wallaceburg was closed down first and Chatham equipped and modernized to process beets from 20,000 acres. The farmers of Ontario promised again and again, but year in year

[1] Montrealers are a little unkind about it. For an essay competition in the *Montreal Star* the first prize was one week's holiday in Toronto, the second prize two weeks holiday in Toronto.

out failed to produce. In the end Chatham too was closed down. Representatives of the farmers threatened to take Tate & Lyle and the individual members of its board to law for a huge sum. Their legal advisers eventually persuaded them not to.

Chatham's equipment was sold off over a period of three years or so after 1968 and most of the land subdivided for residential purposes. Most of the factory buildings were demolished but the tall sugar silos may one day be converted to apartment blocks overlooking the Thames River.

The other problem for Canada & Dominion was that under Canadian anti-trust legislation, it would be unwise for it to increase its share of the Canadian market.

The character of C. & D. began to change with the assumption of control by Tate & Lyle and particularly when Jo Whitmee returned to London and was replaced by Saxon Tate. New policies were adopted, among them diversification into ventures far removed from sugar. But the two refineries were still the subject of particularly close attention by the C. & D. Board. Montreal was supplied with a fully integrated packing, warehousing and order-filling station, controlled by a special computer which is fed with information on the daily, weekly and cumulative annual demand for different packs. It is regarded as a model of modern materials-handling and has been made the subject of sundry learned articles. At Toronto, with technical assistance from Tate & Lyle the whole process was brought under computer control.

Much of this work was initiated by Canada & Dominion's R. & D. who also act as Tate & Lyle's development arm in French-speaking developing countries. An interesting case of this arose from a fifteen-year-old problem at the Montreal Refinery, two of whose four boilers had suddenly to be replaced with equipment fired by natural gas. The Quebec Gas Company after a while found that its supplies were insufficient. It had a ten-year contract to supply C. & D. and could have been in difficulties. The matter was amicably arranged, and when, a few years later a retired engineer from Quebec Gas was asked if he could recommend someone who could produce specifications for sugar plant translated into French, he recommended C. & D. This led eventually to a joint Redpath-T.L.T.S. project in the Ivory Coast.

Canada may have its problems but, with its huge area and relatively small population it is a place with a future, a place in which to be involved.

CHAPTER TWENTY-ONE

Towards the 1970s at Home

'"It's a poor sort of memory that only works backwards" the
Queen remarked.'
(Lewis Carroll 1832–1898)

It was relatively easy writing about Henry and Abram when, on the bonny, bonny banks of Mersey or Clyde, they were warbling their native wood notes wild—to borrow a phrase. For that was a long time ago, and there's nobody around to answer back. Even thirty years reduces the number of people liable to tell you you've got it wrong.

But now, writing of the period since 1964, which is the beginning of Phase II, one can only be sure of two things. First, that every single reader will remember, and second that every single ditto will remember differently. There is also the problem of time. In looking at the West Indies and Canada we have already trespassed well ahead of 1964. From now on we have to go back and forth like a yo-yo. For during this Phase there were to be major acquisitions which have histories of their own, and there are changes in activity sometimes resulting from historical developments within the Company. And all the while there is the broad coil of central policy, adapting itself, sometimes imperceptibly, sometimes abruptly, to the pressure of events. The only way of knitting the strands into it is to deal with them in a number of separate chapters between brief accounts of central policy and internal changes. It will no doubt seem like a piece of multi-coloured Brighton rock. Suck it and see.

The individual developments are: the new venture in Belize, the acquisition of United Molasses Ltd., the foothold in Europe, the leap in Research and Development, the incursion into South Africa, the acquisition of Manbré and Garton.

In 1964 as Phase II opened, President Kennedy had been dead a few months, and the Vietnam business had recently begun. Sir Alex Douglas-Home's Government was limping along and a General Election was not far off.

At the Tate & Lyle Annual General Meeting in March Ian Lyle announced his retirement as Chairman and was elected President. John Lyle was elected Chairman. In a family firm as long as members of the families are available and command the respect of their colleagues it is best to have one of them as Chairman. Such was the case now. Tony Tate had been appointed Vice-Chairman in 1962 and he and Peter Runge were shortly joined by an experienced non-family director, Jo Whitmee. Tony (Director of versification *inter alia*) had been Assistant Secretary in 1946–9 and Director since then. Peter had for ten years been Chairman of the West

Indies companies, and was well known in a wider sphere. He had been President of the Federation of British Industries at the time of its change to C.B.I. and had also been Chairman of the Industrial Society. Jo had a multiplicity of experience including Canada & Dominion, where he would soon be finishing a seven-year stint. The Board was equally divided between on the one hand members of the two families, and on the other 'outsiders' most of whom had worked their way up.

Central policy was changing. Operations in Jamaica and Trinidad were becoming increasingly difficult. The Rhodesian crisis was coming to a head. Investment in developing countries was therefore something to be approached more cautiously, but should not cease. The limitation in size imposed on sugar operations in Canada necessitated diversification in some new direction. As far as concerned the refineries in Britain, there were disturbing long-term trends. There was also the huge question mark over Britain's entry into the European Community. Although President de Gaulle had slammed the door in early 1963, it would one day be reopened, but meantime there might be advantages in obtaining a foothold on the Continent.

These and many other pressing matters needed close and continuous examination and the Board, although it still met fortnightly, was hard pressed to give them all the consideration they needed, since most of its members had specific duties which required frequent and repeated travel. A smaller committee, called the Policy Committee, was established, consisting of the Chairman, the Vice-Chairman and the Chairmen of various subsidiaries plus the Finance Director. Referred to by the irreverent as the Politburo, it gave close attention to long-term problems and came up with proposals to the Board. These were not always accepted but the Committee's efforts were–and still are–of the utmost value.

The position of the U.K. Refineries was not an easy one. Although the target for exports was 400,000 tons a year, there were doubts as to whether it could be achieved, for many countries, particularly in Europe, were now closed to imports and many others were increasing their own production. Home trade was stagnant. The Government had pushed through the Irish Hole in the Tariff. At almost the same time in 1962–3, it had introduced a licensing system for the importation of 200,000 tons a year of refined sugar–about 8 per cent of consumption. Although described as a measure to control imports it tacitly accepted that these should be admitted, although much was in the form of subsidized and dumped sugar. The situation called for much anxious thought. Indeed its seriousness had already led to the formation of Tate & Lyle Refineries Ltd. as the main subsidiary of what was now a group of companies. This, in effect, was a recognition that refining sugar in Britain was no longer the principal preoccupation of the main Board. It was also a recognition of the pressing need for diversification. In 1966 Peter Runge switched from the West Indies to be Chairman of T.L.R. and Jo Whitmee took on Chairmanship of the West Indies and the other subsidiaries, having been replaced in Canada by Saxon Tate.

Labour relations were becoming more complex the world over, in Britain and in the developing countries – we have seen what was happening in Jamaica and Trinidad. A further degree of instability was added by fluctuations in the world price of sugar. In 1962 it was £20 a ton at the beginning of the year, £60 at the end. In 1963 it rose to over £100 a ton, falling in 1964 to £25–30. By 1966 it was down to £12 5s. 0d.

Jamaica and Trinidad were showing deepening signs that the change from colonial childhood to independent adulthood would be more rapid than many had forecast. There would be little if any of that period in life which the otherwise tiresome Proust charmingly called '*L'ombre des jeunes filles en fleur*', and the position of a large overseas company in a small independent country might be even more tricky than expected. Sugar production there might be at some risk.

Yet production would still be needed, and the U.S.A., having broken with Castro's Cuba, was an important market for raw sugar, particularly from the Caribbean.

In these circumstances, while the situation in Jamaica and Trinidad was under continuous review, a new investment was undertaken in 1963 in British Honduras – now called Belize. In 1964, as a major diversification into a business allied to sugar, it was decided to acquire a large international company, long associated with Tate & Lyle, United Molasses Ltd.

As to Europe, before de Gaulle's ukase was issued, there had been some taking of the temperature. Peter Runge had gone with a small team to the French islands, Martinique and Guadeloupe in 1962. Unlike the independent British Caribbean islands, these were actually a part of France – *Départements d'Outre-Mer*. They are delightful places but their small factories and pocket-size estates were costly producers and seemed unlikely in the long run to be capable of supplying even the production quotas they were accorded. However, the visit led to the initiation of contacts with refining interests in France. Monsieur Clément Sorin, the representative of the *Outre-Mer* producers in Paris, arranged meetings with the owners of factories and with French refining companies. (The names of the former read like a duty rota at Versailles in the early eighteenth century:

'De la Rochefoucauld?'

'Present, Sire.')

The latter included the Raffineries St. Louis, in Marseilles, with interests in West Africa and Réunion in the Pacific, and the Compagnie Sucrière, which also had beet sugar interests. An informal Anglo-French 'Groupe de Canne' met from now on at quarterly intervals and discussed the problems of refining in Europe. These looked formidable, particularly as the common agricultural policy developed.

Tate & Lyle was also invited to send representatives to a fairly newly formed body, the Comité Européan des Fabricants de Sucre, which included sugar manufacturers from fourteen European countries, those of the Six being of course the most immediately interested. Under its able Director-General, the late Henri de Veyrac and his equally able deputy Michel de la Forest Divonne, the Comité served as a useful sounding-board and source of information. Meetings, usually in Paris, were cordial (and often accompanied by statutory gastronomic pleasures) and many friends were made—Eugène Demont, Henri d'Espies, Jean Lesaffre, Willem Lammers, Kurt Schumacher, Rudi Hiller, and a host of others. The British Sugar Corporation as fellow-members were then represented by Sheed Anderson, Campbell MacDonald and Kenneth Sinclair.

It became clear very early on that the position of cane sugar refiners and the Commonwealth producers would have to be firmly defended, while the Corporation and the British beet growers would stand to gain if and when Britain joined the Community. For some years the British refiners and the Corporation had held regular meetings at the request of Government, in the form of a Co-ordinating Committee and relationships were friendly, particularly between Ian Lyle and Peter Runge and the Chairman of the Corporation, Sir Edmund Bacon. So friendly were they that the possibility of a merger was discussed. It was regretfully rejected as being likely to encourage the nationalizing zeal of the Left.

Two modest attempts at diversification were made in the shape of Bagelle—a material for the manufacture of furniture, made by combining bagasse and certain resins under pressure, and Tendapearl, a method of rapidly 'tenderizing' meat. For a variety of reasons these, although promising, did not in the end prove satisfactory and were dropped.

On the other hand the opportunity came for a major diversification in an entirely new line of business in Canada. The Daymond Company, whose business was the extension and fabrication of plastics and aluminium, had begun operations in 1939 with headquarters at Chatham, Ontario—near one of the Canada & Dominion beet sugar factories. It had potential for vast expansion and required a larger partner. C. & D. acquired it, and in the course of two or three years established new fabrication facilities in Vancouver, Calgary, Toronto and Centralia, and storage in St. John, New Brunswick, Montreal and elsewhere. Subsidiary companies began to produce specialized equipment. A new high-speed method of continuously laying large-diameter piping, the Badger, was developed. Although initially there were problems, and times when forecast earnings were not produced, Daymond was to become a major part of the C. & D. Ltd. enterprise—later called Redpath Industries.

It is convenient at this point to examine three major ventures separately, the new Belize Sugar Industries Ltd., that huge and complex acquisition, United Molasses Ltd., which became a part of Tate & Lyle Ltd. in 1965, and the acquisition of a foothold in beet sugar production in Europe.

CHAPTER TWENTY-TWO

Belize

'Beyond the Mexique Bay.'
(Aldous Huxley 1934)

In a book of this name, Mr. Huxley suggested that British Honduras was almost the end of the world. Well, it might have been then. It is true that until recently few people had heard of the place–it is now called Belize–but it is not difficult of access and it has a charm all its own. About the size of Wales and with a population of about 130,000, it is at once innocent and sophisticated. July 1977 saw it hit the headlines not for the first time on T.V., Radio and in the Press because of a long-standing and almost insoluble disagreement between Britain and Guatemala as to whom Belize belongs to. Yet such is the ignorance about the place that a Mr. Henry Miller, reporting in the *Sunday Telegraph,* could actually say that it had had no fixed population until British sailors landed there in the 1600s. In fact it had for hundreds of years been inhabited by scores of thousands of people and these were the sparse residue of a large and civilized race of oriental origin, the Mayas. Nobody knows how they got to Central America, but it was possibly across the Behring Straits and southwards. And like the Incas, Aztecs and Toltecs they flourished. They may not have known the wheel but they made intricate astronomical observations without telescopes in difficult atmospheric conditions and sometimes separated in time by generations, *and recorded them,* on carved stone 'steles'. These, interpreted for twentieth century man, are a matter for wonder and respect, as are their temples and artefacts when released from the jungle which, as in Mexico and Guatemala, had hidden them from sight for centuries.

At about the time when William the Conqueror landed at Pevensey and changed the history of England for ever the Maya population decreased catastrophically, nobody can be quite sure why–wars, a plague, a famine? But their descendants were still there, though living unhierarchically and much more modestly, five or six centuries later when the Spanish Conquistadores arrived.

Spain brought slaves there in the sixteenth century to help search for gold and in coastal districts these absorbed or annihilated or interbred with the Maya Mopáns. To Cromwell Belize was merely an offshoot of Jamaica, and it soon became a nest of the wilder buccaneers. Sir Henry Morgan is claimed as ancestor by some present-day inhabitants. The origin of the name 'Belize' is sometimes attributed to a Scottish buccaneer called

Wallace but is more likely to be the Yucatan Maya 'Beliz' meaning muddy-watered. When piracy was officially suppressed by King William III in the 1690s the area became the source of mahogany which was much in demand in Britain for furniture, and of logwood for dyes. Piracy continued, particularly aimed at Spain. Slavery was virtually non-existent long before its abolition in the Caribbean, and there was no colour bar.

The loggers were usually British and had left behind them wide open spaces and a variety of names such as Gallon Jug, Hill Bank, or Camp Six, to compete with the Spanish Benque Viejo and Punta Gorda and the Maya Chichuanha and Kaxiluinic. In 1783 Britain was granted rights by Spain for logging. Then when Spain joined with Revolutionary France in 1798 an attempt was made to expel British settlers. A large Spanish force under the command of a general with the good old Spanish name of O'Neill, made for the cays which line the coral reef running parallel to the coast a few miles from the mangrove swamps. It was beaten off by one naval sloop, a few local ships and a motley army led by a Mr. Paslow, who, clad in a brocaded court dress which had once belonged to King George II, shouted an obscure battle cry: 'Yarborough or Fingarico.'[1] There were few casualties, if any, on either side but the Spanish fleet turned back. And the Battle of St. George's Cay was until recently celebrated by a public holiday during which a ballad was sung:

> We jooked them and poked them and drove them like fleas
> Right into salt water right up to their knees,
> And each poxy Spaniard to the other did say
> 'Vámonos, compadres, de St. George's Cay.'

After the collapse of the Spanish Empire Mexico and other central American countries claimed Belize. Mexico renounced her claims in 1850 but Guatemala continued to regard British Honduras as *irredenta*. There was a vague settlement in the mid-nineteenth century under which Britain would build a road to afford an outlet in the Gulf of Mexico for the El Petén region in return for British Honduras. The road was never built, and the claim for Belize has ever since been a convenient external target for successive Guatemalan Governments at times of internal stress. It was referred to the International Court of Justice at the Hague in 1948, but the matter is still unsettled. Guatemala wants Belize. Belize wants to be totally independent. Britain would be quite happy for her to be so but Belize does not wish to without military guarantee because of the threat from Guatemala.

For some twenty years or more Belize has been internally governed by the People's United Party led by Mr. George Price, still a youthfully handsome, articulate, dedicated man of mixed Maya, English and Spanish

---

[1] As Yarborough is the cemetery at Belize this may be a variant on Nelson's cry at St. Vincent in February 1797, 'Westminster Abbey or Victory'.

blood. The youngest of a large family, he lives simply, goes to first mass each day, and drives round the country in his Landrover. He is reputed to know almost everyone in the whole territory. There is of course, opposition to him, but it is not as yet very powerful.

The topography and climate is varied. In the north the land is flat, rising westwards to the low foothills of the Mexican mountains. In the south it is more undulating, rising to considerable mountains on the western border. At Pomona and around the southern port of Stann Creek are citrus groves. In the north around Corozal and Orange Walk, lies the sugar cane area. Wide slow rivers feed into the gulf, but the reef makes the water shallow for some miles out, and ships lie well off. Rainfall is moderate in the north, heavy in the south, and the cane ripens readily in the cool winds which blow down from the mountains of Mexico in the dry season. For the sportsman there are big fish–hammer-headed sharks can be seen basking in the water over the reef–wild hogs, pumas and a vast ant-eater called the mountain cow, as well as a myriad variety of birds. For the archaeologist there are all those temples and steles.

The Belize river is a trifle smelly because so slow-moving, but Belize city has a certain charm, a little like a Venetian version of a Wild West town with Colonial-style accretions. It can be very warm, and hurricanes followed by tidal waves cause occasional severe destruction. The network of roads in the country is primitive–largely soft limestone which turns into a clay-ey mud in the wet season.

But Belize is a nice place. After the hectic atmosphere of Jamaica or Trinidad it is positively peaceful. And it is easy of access as long as you think of approaching it via Mexico City (an hour away by air) or Miami or New Orleans (two hours).

As the situation in Jamaica and Trinidad began to pose certain possible difficulties, Tate & Lyle sought another Commonwealth country where conditions were favourable to cane sugar production and in 1963 consultations were held with the Belize Government. Mr. Price was in London for talks with the Commonwealth Office, and was encouraging, but guarded–as who would not be when faced with a large firm? There were further talks with the Minister of Trade and Commerce, the late Sir Sandy Hunter. A W.I.S.Co. director who had been there once before in 1959, paid a call on the place and returned with dengue fever–not to be recommended, for it is an ague-like complaint, known also as break-bone fever.

But, fever or no, there was so much to be said for Belize–a small population, plenty of space, sweeter cane than can be found on the islands, a helpful Government. True, it lacked quotas, for it had little record of performance, but the U.S.A. was looking for nearby sources of sugar in 1963. Labour troubles were trifling, for there was little labour. Mechanization would be encouraged. All was promising, the Government, however, asking that in due course a new factory should be built thirty miles from the existing one at Corozal, in order to receive cane from farmers in the hinterland.

Government and Company were in step. There was, of course, the problem of Guatemala. Would she, could she, invade? It was difficult to know, but there had been occasional ineffective incursions across the border which usually resulted in the invaders ending up in gaol, and an American who had lived in the area for years described the invaders as 'about as much goddam use as the Peace Corps'. (He was clearly *not* a Kennedy man.)

The history of sugar production in Belize was only three or four score years old, and had been beset by lack of capital, climatic problems, and other uncertainties. There was, in 1963, only the one small factory, rather antiquated in equipment and with a capacity of some 18,000 tons of sugar a year. Together with land it was owned by a company whose shareholders were part Jamaican, part British. In September 1963 Tate & Lyle made an offer which was accepted by the shareholders and re-established the Company (Corozal Sugar Factory Limited) under the name Belize Sugar Industries Ltd.

When Tate and Lyle took over, they found a newly appointed American, 'J. D.' Fahs, in charge. He had just arrived and was living on his own in a modest little house. His family were due to join him from New Orleans. He was experienced and he wanted to stay. He stayed until, alas, four years later he died, in his forties, of a coronary, and was replaced by Frank Curtis, from Jamaica. Volunteer staff from W.I.S.Co. and Caroni were enrolled, for, in accordance with an undertaking to the Government of Belize and in the conviction that here was a place with a future, there was to be expansion, and this required expertise in various forms.

The old factory at Corozal was to be re-equipped to a capacity of 30,000 tons a year and a new factory to be built at Tower Hill—in the Orange Walk area, where there were many cane farmers—with an initial capacity of 30,000 tons a year but capable of a phased increase to 100,000. The Government granted special development concessions, giving freedom from tax on profits for expansion and freedom from import duties on capital equipment for ten years.

In the early phases the Company cleared and planted much land and introduced mechanical harvesting, for there was little labour available and the cane farmers could not expand rapidly enough. As the farmers began to expand their cultivation rapidly once they saw evidence of a long-term development, B.S.I. proposed to Government to transfer their own land to farmers. In 1972 this was done by direct agreements between the Company and individual farmers.

The whole enterprise demanded a certain steadiness of nerve from Tate & Lyle. The period of high world prices in 1963 was followed by a period of low prices. Belize had only a modest Commonwealth quota. The U.S. Government, having considered a Sugar Act Quota for Belize of 20,000 tons, reduced it to 10,000. The costs of building the new factory, observing the same natural law as had applied to the construction of Henry Tate's and Abram Lyle's Refineries nearly a century before, overshot the estimates by a considerable margin.

Year after year, a loss resulted. But the Tates and the Lyles had been through this before, and once committed to a course they are hard to deflect. One of the earliest visitors to Belize was Ian Lyle. Living quarters were cramped. The bath in the solitary guest suite at Corozal was a wedge-shaped, war-surplus job which gripped like a vice the hind-quarters of any male of normal size. The house generator coughed and spluttered into silence when more than six bulbs were switched on. There was none of the smooth, Ritz-like staff service which could be found at Frome or Monymusk. But it was fun.

There was a *malentendu* when Ian first met the Premier in Belize. 'Ah,' said Mr. Price, 'you must be Sir Ian Tate.'

'Not quite,' said Ian. There was slight thunder in the air for no Lyle likes to be taken for a Tate (or for that matter vice versa) at any time, even after all those years. And this was at 7.45 on a very warm morning, with a long hot day ahead.

After an initial period of low world sugar prices, patience was rewarded, and between 1971 and 1977 B.S.I. made profits totalling £10 million. No dividends were paid, the money being used to finance further expansion and to pay off loans. The balance sheet of this fledgling company showed assets at the end of 1976 of nearly £18 million, and at the same time the economy of Belize had benefited enormously. Cane farmers in particular were expanding their cultivation. By 1977, although B.S.I. employed only 1,000 people, some 10,000 others, probably 25 per cent of the working population, were getting their living from sugar, which was accounting for over half the country's export earnings.

Accompanying these developments, and in fulfilment of a commitment to the Government of Belize, B.S.I. had from the beginning adopted a policy of training Belizeans to fill all technical and administrative posts in the Company. By 1977 there were only five European employees in Belize Sugar Industries, and at the same time national participation in ownership was being encouraged through the Belize Development Finance Corporation, though, since Belize is not a wealthy country, this may take time.

Nevertheless the symbiosis between a proud, stable country, with a democratically elected Government and a people of high literacy, and a sensitively disposed overseas company is full of promise for the future. From 1963 to 1977 production of sugar in Belize rose from 28,000 tons to over 90,000. Factory capacity is for 110,000 tons and in 1977 it was hoped that this figure would shortly be achieved.

CHAPTER TWENTY-THREE
United Molasses

I
'United Molasses have all gone home.'

This, of course, can never be true, because U.M.'s activities are world-wide, so someone is always beavering away somewhere. It was, in fact, the phrase used daily by the wife of Captain W. A. Meneight, retired Senior Master of the United Molasses Athel Line fleet of ships to extract him from his labours when he was writing a history of the Company in 1976. What now follows is largely based on his book, written after months of research and interviews, and on talks with him and Ted Tibbitts who spent most of his working life with U.M. Bill Meneight is an outspoken Lancastrian, who like most ships' captains, is a man who has clearly been set in authority, saying unto this man 'do this' (and he doth it).

Ted Tibbitts is typical of the tightly-knit headquarters staff who down the years looked after the Company's affairs. A quiet trouble-shooter with a dry sense of humour, perhaps he unconsciously modelled himself a little on the equally quiet founder and architect of the firm, Sir Michael Kroyer Kielberg. When Ted joined in 1933, in the aftermath of the Depression, there were many school-leavers seeking the few available jobs. Armed with a letter from his headmaster, he was determined to get this one when he arrived at Bush House for an interview and he had read up everything he could find about molasses. Others had been less thorough and one candidate, in the lift on the way up to the seventh floor, said: 'What *is* molasses, anyhow? Anyone know?' Ted told him he thought it was something to do with swamps and reflected that there, at least, was one rival less for the job, whatever it might be.

'It' turned out to be largely a matter of filling inkwells and sharpening pencils, graduating, if you were particularly industrious, to polishing the big brass knob on the front door. But you could climb to the top in time. Many, starting this way, did so, and Ted himself eventually became Finance and Administration Director.

The answer to the question put to him in the lift was: molasses is the dark treacly stuff left over when it is no longer economic to continue to extract sugar from cane or beet juice.

II
A Quiet Dane Comes to Liverpool

Almost exactly fifty years after Henry Tate had begun to think of going in

The Philip Lyle Memorial Research Laboratory–Reading.

Yonkers Refinery–Albany, U.S.A. The most recent acquisition.

for sugar refining, there arrived in Liverpool a quiet, soberly dressed young Dane. Born in 1882 he was now, at twenty-five, about to apply for a job with a modest firm of cattle-feed importers called Marquis, Clayton at 4 Chapel Street, Liverpool. A Mr. J. Clayton took him on, and within three years he was made a partner. Quite what impelled him to come in 1907 to Liverpool, the city of Liverbirds, Tates, Fairries and other fauna such as High Rippers, nobody knows. It could have been to improve his English, to learn a trade, or to start an import-export agency. Self-possessed, soft-spoken, yet expressing his views in the most decided fashion, he was to remain like that all his days.

Now Kielberg became fascinated by molasses. It was to be his life. Molasses had long been imported into Liverpool. With sugar it had once been one side of the triangle: Birmingham tin-trays to Africa–slaves to the Caribbean–sugar and molasses to Britain. It came in hogsheads borne by sailing ships (one such went aground in the Mersey in 1818). On arrival the cargo was broken down into smaller barrels. There was a thriving cooperage trade in the port.

But by 1907 the Americans had for some time been shipping molasses in bulk and no doubt Kielberg learned of this. Marquis, Clayton entered the bulk business in 1910, chartering from Lever Bros. of Port Sunlight a sailing barque, *Sunlight*, 1433 tons gross, designed to carry vegetable oil. She had just sailed from Avonmouth to carry seven cargoes of molasses from San Domingo to Boston, returning twenty-one months later to Liverpool, carrying vegetable oil. Meantime Kielberg and Clayton had built a 3,000 ton tank at Hull, in the Victoria Docks, and late in 1912 the barque *Sunlight* discharged 1,800 tons of molasses there. It was the beginning of United Molasses, though the name would not exist for another twenty-four years. July 16th, 1915, saw the incorporation of the British Molasses Company with an authorized capital of £20,000 and installations at Garston, Glasgow and Hull, together with a handful of motor lorries. A small shareholding was allocated to an American Company, Sugar Products, from whom B.M.C. purchased molasses. The shares were subsequently bought back but the two companies continued to trade together for years. By 1917, Mr. Clayton owned 1,300 and Mr. Kielberg 700 £10 shares in B.M.C.

In 1919, however, Mr. Clayton resigned. He appears to have been about as *forte* as his colleague was *piano* and an easy man to quarrel with. The break seems to have come about either because he wished to introduce an unsuitable relation into the business (Kielberg throughout his life preferred to pick an élite from wherever he found them) or because of a move he had initiated to sell the Company to an American business, the U.S. Food Products Corporation, leaving the management in Liverpool. Or both. Seven months later Kielberg bought the assets back and then the totally valueless shares in order to retain the Company's name. U.S. Food Products had over-extended itself and was a willing seller. Kielberg clearly seems to have known where he was going.

Now he formed the Pure Cane Molasses Company which henceforth would manage the trading side of his business while British Molasses would undertake the shipping. The first vessel to be bought was the *Manx Isles* of 2,642 tons gross, built in 1905 and then on charter to Kielberg. She was to remain in commission until 1929. But the true foundation of the fleet was in fact a small American vessel, the *Theodore F. Reynolds*, 2,736 tons gross, built on the Great Lakes and named after a director of U.S. Food Products. She was lying at Hull at the time (it was 1922) distrained by her crew for non-payment of wages, and cost Kielberg 7,500 $ U.S.–about £1,500 in those far-off days. Rechristened *Athelstane* after Kielberg's home in Birkenhead, she was the first-ever Athel ship. Athel and Ethel (like your Aunt) and other such names are apparently a modern version of the Saxon Aedel, meaning 'noble'.

The *Athelstane* was mortgaged soon after to help buy a Norwegian ship rechristened *Athelmere*, and then came the purchase of a string of Royal Fleet Auxiliaries, ex-Naval Service. These, called *Atheltarn*, *Athelrill*, *Athelcrest*, and so forth, demanded immense tonnages of coal a day and dozens of sweating stokers to stoke them.

The fleet continued to expand as new sources of competitively priced molasses were found. Kielberg's flair in nosing these out was probably the most important single factor in the company's advance. It had to be accompanied by the logistics of exploitation, and as the distances became greater so the type of ship and ship's engine had to be changed. All, however, were bought secondhand until the first custom-built vessel, *Athelchief*, was ordered in 1925.

While this considerable expansion was going on, Kielberg gave rein to a certain panache in terms of office accommodation. He spent little on himself but believed that having a good address helped. And in January 1923 he moved his offices to the Cunard Building, which in those days meant 'Prestige'. And he began gathering a staff round him, young men who spent much time in night schools after the day's work. An early example was George Scott, who had come to Marquis, Clayton as an office boy in 1914, lied about his age in order to join the Army, and returned to become cashier in 1919, Assistant Secretary and Office Manager in 1931, and who would one day become Chairman.

Kielberg discovered in the Dutch East Indies molasses was such a drug on the market that it was literally being ditched. He formed Pure Cane Molasses (Java) in 1924, erected tanks at ports with exotic names like Oom Poong Pong in that sunny land, and acquired longer-range, faster vessels, diesel-motored instead of steam-driven. In March the same year an installation and a company was set up in Durban, and a little later an existing plant in Georgetown, British Guiana was acquired.

All these moves were made by Kielberg himself. He had no planning staff–indeed there was very little staff altogether, only twenty-two including the office cat. All the accounts were kept in two hand-written ledgers, a green one for the ships and a brown one for the molasses trading, and one man kept the lot. Another man on his own did the victualling and storing of the ships, which then carried quite large crews. He must have been good at arithmetic for there were no computers in those days.

By 1925 Liverpool began to seem a long way from where the money was, London, and Kielberg decided to shift his headquarters to Bush House, Aldwych, then one of the smartest business addresses in the capital. This move coincided with the incorporation as a public company of United Molasses Ltd., with an issued capital of £1,000,000; branches in Liverpool, Hull, Greenock and Glasgow; subsidiaries in Holland, Germany, Italy, South Africa, the West Indies and Java; ten ships of varying age and size; and sundry other assets. U.M., the holding company for Pure Cane and British Molasses, whose combined shares were valued at £650,000, dates precisely from January 1st, 1926. Between 1926-31 sixteen ships were launched, *Athelprince, Athelking, Athelqueen, Athelmonarch,* and so on. Their interior fittings were on a slightly grand scale, more like those of a liner than a mere tanker. There was mahogany furniture, panelling in the saloons, crested china and silver plate, all giving the impression of well-founded solid worth. This was justified by the Company's growing strength, as reflected by a rise in share value to £8·15 or more by 1929/30. Towards the end of 1928 members of the staff had been offered shares at £2·50 and a Lloyds Bank loan to help pay for them. Many took the chance, and some made an immediate profit.

Euphoria was the word for it. Demand in the States for molasses for cattle-feed and industrial alcohol was unlimited. The same applied in Britain. Yeast had become a magic name in the therapeutic world. Everyone wanted molasses. There were just not enough ships. The then Lord Runciman was shortly to say that there would always be a shortage of third officers in the Merchant Navy. At the A.G.M. held in April 1929, the Chairman was able to announce a 50 per cent increase in profits to £388,000. The Board proposed to double the capital by a rights issue.

In late 1928 George Scott, who had now put in a stint in Java, was sent to New York, where a chance meeting brought information that the California & Hawaiian Sugar Refining were concerned about the disposal of surplus molasses. Seven months later, in July 1929, the Pacific Molasses Company was incorporated in San Francisco.

It was all dizzyingly successful. There seemed to be no direction in which shares could go but upwards. But just three months after Pacific Molasses came into being there occurred Black Thursday, October 29th, 1929. The American economic miracle of 1920 to 1929 was at an end. The true picture seems to have taken time to get through to London. At the U.M. Annual General Meeting of April 1930, Kielberg shrugged off the American slump as a temporary phenomenon. (Chaps might be throwing themselves out of skyscraper windows on Wall Street but Americans always tended to exaggerate, didn't they?) U.M.'s profits for the year 1929 had been well over a million pounds, nearly treble the previous year's. The Chairman forecast a further expansion in 1930.

Such optimism and self-confidence were natural. Now in his late forties, Kielberg had from very modest beginnings constructed a considerable empire with many branches and twenty subsidiaries in different countries. He had had nearly a quarter of a century of unbroken success and steadily rising profits. The impulse, the thinking and the energy had been his and he had skilfully picked men to assist him. But between self-confidence and what the Greeks called Hubris the gap is so narrow that the Furies, being blind, do not often distinguish. And now they were to fall on Kielberg, as on many other business heads, on working-people all over the world, on clerks and ships' captains alike. The export-import trade was particularly vulnerable.

By April 1931 the Great Depression was in full swing. The American slump had caused a drop in molasses imports into the States of nearly half a million tons. Stocks of molasses everywhere became unsaleable.

For United Molasses, loss piled on loss. The share value fell to 12½p per £1 share (not long before, remember, it had been over £8). Ships were laid up, orders cancelled. Kielberg at this Annual General Meeting had to eat his confident words of the year before, although he had the strength of mind to insist that one day there would be a return to normal activity and that the Company would once more prosper. This took some courage. His own personal fortunes were entirely tied up in U.M. and he would himself be losing more than the angry shareholders who assailed him.

It is known that as far as he could he reimbursed from his own pocket friends and members of staff who had invested in following his star, that he honoured his contracts with suppliers but did not hold his customers to theirs. Ship after ship was laid up. Installation after installation had to be closed. For the lucky members of shore staff there was a cut in salary of 20 per cent. For the unlucky there was no job. The shortage of third officers forecast by Lord Runciman became instead a glut. It took Bill Meneight four years to get in eighteen months' sea time towards his First Officer's ticket. He and his brother during these desperate times used to go out by night to the sand-dunes on Merseyside and call up the ships with a signalling lamp as they came in: 'What ship is that?' 'S.S. . . . . .' 'Any jobs going?' 'No.' If you went for a job to a marine superintendent in certain ports, bearing your Discharge Book, you might get one if the book had a £1 note interleaved in it. If not, no job. Anything was better than 15s. a week unemployment relief. Slowly the molasses trade, which had shrunk to a third of its 1928 volume, began to pick up. Only those subsidiaries which, like Pacific Molasses, had a good future, were retained.

Yet the cumulative financial effect of the losses had to be taken into account. By 1930 the issued capital had realized £7 million. Now the nominal value of the £1 share was reduced to 6s. 8d. and £1 preference shares became 10s. The accumulated losses of £3,230,000 was written off. The shareholders swallowed this harsh medicine on December 14th, 1933.

Kielberg was resilient. So were his picked staff, who now included Geoff Allott (joined in 1929) and Stewart J. Browne (joined in 1930)–later to become Managing Director.

The year 1934 saw the beginnings of an up-turn. U.M. made a profit of £367,000. Payment of dividends was resumed. Tanks and handling equipment began again to be installed in different parts of the world. A marketing system which helped to stabilize world prices was fashioned. There seemed to be light at the end of the tunnel.

III
'It is Great Morning, and the hour prefixt.'
(William Shakespeare 1564–1616)

The year 1934 also saw Hitler become Chancellor of the Third Reich. For U.M. the recovery continued. Dividends doubled by 1938–9. By 1937 the Athel fleet consisted of twenty-four vessels, plying to Cuba, Buenos Ayres, Shanghai, Yokohama, California, Durban, and many a port in Europe.

Once prosperity returned one of the first things Kielberg did was to introduce an excellent pension scheme (one of the earliest). The funds were placed under the control of a committee consisting of three company directors and three employees. Numbers of then unusual perks and privileges became available to the staff.

Kielberg entered the sugar refining business in 1936 with the purchase of Macfies' of Liverpool, which he later sold to Tate & Lyle. He was invited in 1937 to become a co-investor with Tate & Lyle in their newly-acquired West Indies raw sugar ventures, Caroni Ltd. in Trinidad and the West India Sugar Company in Jamaica, and U.M. took 25 per cent of the equity in each. He himself joined the Board of Tate & Lyle as an outside director.

In March 1939, recognizing that war was inevitable and that molasses would be a munition of that war when it came, U.M. and Distillers began, with Government approval, to buy and store the stuff wherever space could be found. A new installation with a capacity of 200,000 tons was built by Pacific Molasses at Port Everglades near Miami, Florida, as a collecting point for molasses near some of its major sources. When war came all the accumulated stocks in Britain and abroad were to be taken over at cost price by the Ministry of Supply. On January 1st, 1940, U.M. ceased to be a trading company and became agents for the Ministry.

For shipping purposes, U.M.'s fleet, the twenty diesel tankers, five steam tankers and two barges were transferred to a new wholly owned subsidiary, Athel Line. From the first day of war all ships came under the direction of the Ministry of Shipping. Grey paint replaced the colours, bridges were sand-bagged, somewhat ancient 4·7 inch guns were fitted where possible.

Athel Line was carrying all the molasses coming to Britain and in addition those more dangerous cargoes, oil and petrol.

Although, when Lend-Lease was introduced in 1940, Pacific Molasses was in theory in hock to the American Government, together with all British assets in the U.S.A., in practice this was to make little difference in the end. And after the fall of France there was little time to be devoted to such problems. George Scott was sent to Washington as a member of the British Raw Material and Food Mission. At home the offices at Bush House were closed, smaller quarters at Brook House, Park Lane, acquired for those who had to be in London, and the main part of the staff moved to Kielberg's estate at Leighton Buzzard.

But it was the ships which were to bear the brunt. The first casualty was the *Atheltemplar*, mined off the Tyne in September 1939, but brought in to port. Next was the *Athelprince*, torpedoed during the night in June 1940, over 500 miles from Falmouth. The crew abandoned ship for the night but reboarded her and brought her in. *Athellaird* was the next casualty and the first total loss. In those days Royal Navy escorts, having a range of only 2,000 miles, had to leave convoys at 30°W, and here the U-boats lay in wait. (Later some of the Athel ships were to be fitted for fuelling escorts at sea and extend the range. Someone in the Admiralty should have thought of this earlier.) *Athelcrest* was torpedoed; then *Athelviscount* was bombed in Birkenhead. *Athelking* was sunk 600 miles south of Mauritius on September 9th, 1940, by the raider *Atlantis* and her survivors set ashore as prisoners in Somaliland. (Captain Meneight was one of these. He was First Officer. The Master was killed.)

Athelmonarch, Athelduchess, Athelcrown, Athelfoam, the recital of the names is like the tolling of a passing bell.

In 1940 and again in 1941 4 million tons of allied shipping were sunk. The 'Big Steamers'[1] of those days were not all that big. *Queen Mary* and *Queen Elizabeth* were giants, ten to twenty times as large as the ordinary merchant ships. U.M.'s latest tankers, at 18,000 tons, were the largest in the world. So 4 million tons meant 5 to 600 ships a year. Sometimes a ship would limp into port, more often not. For many men it meant struggling in the water, or being smothered by fuel oil, or facing incalculable periods in an open boat or on a life raft.

When Pearl Harbour brought in the U.S.A. as an ally in December 1941, it meant of course that her huge resources would ensure that the war would be won. But for a time the effect on shipping was disastrous, and in 1942 sinkings of Allied ships amounted to 8 million tons. One of the worst areas was the American Atlantic coast where for three months after war was declared there was no blackout, as 'this would affect the tourist trade'. And there were, owing to U.S. lack of preparedness, few or no American escorts either. With the ships silhouetted against a background of neon-lights the lurking U-boats had a picnic. By the end of January 1942 200,000

[1] See page 88.

tons of shipping had been sunk along this coast. It was hereabouts that more Athel ships were lost, *Athelqueen, Athelempress, Athelbrae.* The air crackled with distress calls day and night.

Athel Line lost ships off Ceylon (*Athelstane*), on Russian convoys (*Athelprincess*), and in mid-Atlantic (*Athelviscount* and *Athelknight*). The crew of the latter took to the boats and at the instigation of the Second Officer, Douglas Crook, decided to make for Antigua in the West Indies, 1,100 miles to the west. Twenty-eight days later, navigating with an alarm clock and a boat compass, Crook's boat made land at St. Bartholomew, only some sixty miles off course. He had imposed strict discipline as regarded food and water. Anyone who went sick would be put on half-rations, for, said he, there was no point in wasting food on someone who might die. Nobody went sick. Two men who jumped overboard in despair were hauled back into the boat and put on half-rations until they promised not to do it again. There was still some food and water when the boat was beached at St. Bartholomew. For months afterwards, Douglas Crook had recurrent nightmares in which, sitting in the stern sheets, he saw eyes glaring at him. He was awarded the M.B.E., which seems scarcely enough.

He was to be involved in another remarkable feat later bringing the torpedoed *Scottish Heather* back to port, and was awarded the George Medal and Lloyds' Medal.

The shore staff may perhaps have had less to put up with during the war but, like their future colleagues in Tate & Lyle, not much. It is hard to recall those days, but at least then London was the centre of the civilized world, a little like Camelot in the days before the Round Table brotherhood broke up.

That brotherhood, from 1940 to 1945, included men from countries in Europe which had been over-run by the Nazis, and one of them was Denmark. Michael Kielberg was by now a British citizen, but for years before the war he had encouraged Danes to come to England to learn, to teach, to return. During the war he had become the doyen, representative, and godfather of Danes in England, kindly, welcoming, enormously generous. For this he was, when the lights went on again, to be awarded the Grand Cross of the Order of Danneberg and made a Knight Commander of the British Empire.

The tiny staff of U.M. held at their reserved occupations by national necessity, had anguish to add to all the rest, the sadness of hearing of the loss of friends in their ships. The Ministry of Supply, at one remove, seemed to care only for the arrival of cargoes, and Ted Tibbitts recalled the U.M. office being telephoned by an irate civil servant demanding to know why a certain *Athel* ship was not discharging her cargo as promised, at 10.30 that morning. That *Athel* ship would not be discharging a cargo ever again.

So it went on – *Athelmonarch, Athelviking, Athelduke* . . . the passing bells continued to toll.

By the end of the war nineteen out of the twenty-four Athel ships had been lost – about 280,000 tons, a fleabite out of the millions, but a horrible percentage for Athel. Others had been damaged but had survived. A few.

Two hundred and five men had been killed – 5 masters, 10 deck officers, 45 engineer officers, 11 radio officers, 4 apprentices, 130 ratings – rather more than one in ten of the men who had sailed in Athel Line from 1939 to 1945. Eighty-five awards and commendations were won during those four and a half years. There should probably have been many more, but 'some there be that have no memorial, and are perished as though they had never been'.

For U.M. post-war recovery was highly complicated because they had that world-wide network of installations and because so much of their fleet had been sunk.

There was, for example, Holland. Well, there, by some extraordinary chance, the liquid lolly had been transferred to London, just in time on May 9th, 1940, when the Germans arrived. No-one knows quite how. Then there had been almost exactly five years of silence, as though, just across the North Sea a huge black curtain had been drawn. Then, suddenly, in May 1945, everything changed. Too fast. And there was no boss.

Then George Scott arrived in July, said 'sort out the mess', gave some technical backing, and left for England, and within a year or two the alcohol chaps and the cattle-feed merchants were getting their molasses, and in their orderly, irresistible way, the Dutch had things in hand.

Ten thousand miles away in Java, it was more complicated. Mr. Dondorp, the Manager, who had spent four years as an unwilling guest of the Japanese, found that U.M.'s rail tankers had been removed to Siam, that the Japanese had actually floated the great storage tanks, without dismantling them, to new sites to do duty as petrol storage. Property had been damaged on an enormous scale. It was all even more complicated because the post-War Dutch Government, a socialist one, introduced new regulations which made Java molasses too costly.

All round the world, the situation was changing. The Philippines were a problem. South Africa needed a new set-up. Thailand was now an exporter, so a new terminal and a new company had to be arranged in Bangkok. Shanghai and Hongkong required a change. Then there was the replacement of all those ships lost during the war. The Government had offered £6 million in compensation. Replacements would cost £9·5 million, and the cost of building was going up every few months. But shipping produced a large proportion of the company's earnings, so ships there must be.

New tonnage was ordered and delivered, even though Geoff Allott considered that a ship had at best two good years out of ten. By 1951 there would be a virtually new fleet of twenty-three tankers, 150,000 tons gross. And earnings – or if one may use the word, profits – went on rising. By 1951 they were £8 million, and – after a bit of argument with the pundits in the Treasury – the shares had been revalued.

Athel King (the first), 1926–1940.

For Whom the Bell Tolls–*Athel King*, sunk 1940. Picture taken from her attacker, the German raider *Atlantis*.

But since the Depression U.M. had been bitten by a sense of insecurity. There *had* to be liquid assets. About £15 million was the figure to have of the ready. Banks are O.K. but there are also attractions in a piggy-bank. And here, without, one thinks, too much reflection, U.M. began to be an early example of a conglomerate. Small companies were purchased which had no direct connection with the business at hand.

The Board of U.M. cannot be blamed for hedging, but conglomerates are a dubious bet. And in due course liquidity itself can be a temptation to others, as will be seen.

More in the line of normal business was the purchase in 1949 of Anchor Line, with four passenger ships plying to the Far East, and five medium-sized cargo vessels. It was bought partly on the open market and partly from the Runciman interest for £5 a share. In a way, it was a diversion of effort, understandable but a sign of groping, for the end-use of molasses was changing. Alcohol made synthetically from oil products was becoming competitive, but this was compensated for by the increase in cattle feed usage. By shrewd dealing the Company kept abreast of the rapidly changing situation in a world that was growing smaller. Kielberg himself had been unique. New, younger men would be dominant over the next two decades, and would be joined by Jack Hoyle and Alan McGaw, but the Kielberg spark had smouldered out. In 1953 he was to retire. He had been unwell for a time, and although he lived a further five years, he was – as we all become – a shadow of the quiet, self-possessed young man who had come to 4 Chapel Street, Liverpool, nearly half a century earlier.

Reading the situation with that all too easy aid, hindsight, one can recognize some reduction of momentum following the retirement of Kielberg. The engine faltered a little. Friction began to take over. In 1953, Alan Walker, formerly Managing Director of the Tate & Lyle West Indies Subsidiaries and therefore in part a United Molasses man, became Joint Managing Director with George Scott. There was further friction, and Alan left in 1956, to become in due course Chairman of Bass-Charrington, the brewers.

When, in 1951, Tate & Lyle decided on the formation of Sugar Line, 25 per cent of its equity was offered to United Molasses, and – because that Company was then prosperous – 25 per cent to the West Indies Sugar Company Ltd. U.M. were charged with the design and running of the six bulk carriers. It was Kielberg's last major contribution, and thereafter there seems to have been a slight temporary lack of overall purpose.

Yet this perhaps is not quite fair. While molasses trading and shipping had become more complicated, clever chaps had come to the conclusion that you can alternate molasses with vegetable oil, fuel oil, alcohol, and any number of other fluids. This enables you to offer a useful transport and storage service.

Now, U.M. had, because of competition in molasses tankers, been experimenting too, with caustic for I.C.I. to the West Indies, with lubricating oil, additives and solvents for Socony Vacuum, and had begun to modify their smaller vessels to carry chemicals. This kind of trade, now called parcel tankers, was profitable. U.M. and a Dutch firm Pakhuis Meesteren formed a joint company called Paktank. Rapidly new tank installations were built, at Grays in Essex, at Eastham on the Mersey. Soon Paktank owned the largest volume of third-party tanker trade in Britain.

Prior to this, the competition of the very large crude carriers besides turning U.M. in the direction of parcel tankers suggested that it might be as well to go in also for the large tanker trade and two 59,000 tonners were bought. These were all right while long term charters could be arranged and for much of the time it was hoped that this could be managed, but their delivery came at a bad moment, late in 1964.

Molasses prices and tanker freight rates had been low for some five years by 1963, and the U.S. embargo on Cuba, the excess of tanker tonnage in the world, and other factors had resulted in a gradual erosion of U.M.'s profitability. In 1964 the net profits were at a fifteen-year low of £1,648,282. The share price fell, and—with some £15 million of liquid assets—the company was an obvious target for a take-over bid.

It is here that Tate & Lyle, long associated with United, came in, offering £30 million for the Company. It was John Lyle's first major undertaking on becoming Chairman and he had to use a lot of persuasion on some of his colleagues. He was quite right. The Board of United Molasses accepted and the operation went smoothly. There was, as is only natural, some doubt within U.M. about what might now happen, but the new owners interfered very little, and quite a number of U.M. men indeed were to benefit from the greater scope offered. Lord Runciman (Chairman of U.M.) and Lord Perth joined the Tate & Lyle Board and Jo Whitmee, a highly experienced Tate & Lyle Director, took over the U.M. chair. A new appointment to the U.M. Board was Michael Gollin, who had entered in 1959 and was to be Chief Executive in due course.

By 1965 United was already showing signs of recovery. There was some doubt about the two 59,000-ton oil tankers, *Athelking* and *Athelregent*, which had cost £5 million, and serious consideration was given to selling them. The consideration took time, and in 1967 the Israeli-Arab war obligingly broke out, which meant that on time-charters the two vessels began to earn £1 million a year, since the closure of the Suez Canal resulted in an immediate demand for tonnage. New developments followed each other, the formation of a group with the Norwegian A.N.Co. line to operate a tanker pool; more and larger parcel tankers; a blossoming of Pacific Molasses; its purchase of Berger and Plate (dealing in dried seeds and spices and various forms of vegetables); new acquisitions in Albany and on Lake Michigan.

Every now and then a clanger is dropped even by the best people, and there was a major one in Argentina when U.M. entered the alcohol industry in the late Evita's country.

All sorts of things went wrong. Businesses were acquired which did not live up to expectations. Trust was put in the untrustworthy. There was involvement in the peso which had a habit of devaluing itself at frequent intervals, and on top of all that the Argentine Government imposed export bans. Something was salvaged from the wreck, not a great deal, and this, under the name Unalco, was later flourishing under James Fairrie who had joined the U.M. Board in 1968. There was also about this time, a less awful but nonetheless tiresome contretemps with a wholly-owned subsidiary trading in oils and fats.

Then there was the Molassine venture, this one a success. This outfit, begun in Greenwich originally for the production of molassed meal for animal feed, had its product manufactured by Henry Tate & Sons in London and Liverpool, until its own factory was established in 1908. Thereafter it was supplied with raw material from the Refinery across the water at Silvertown. Over the years it had done well, and U.M. acquired it in 1971.

Now, too, Europe called. United had long been established in Holland and Belgium, and had a small installation in France. In 1970 a company, Hansa Melasse, was set up in Hamburg, and the French establishment was enlarged by the purchase of Société Européenne des Mélasses (S.E.M.) from the French sugar brokers, Louis Dreyfus, and later by a merger with Debayser and an agreement with Etablissements Legrand with distribution terminals at numerous key points. This venture was really successful, and, working in parallel with the Tate & Lyle sugar interest in Say-Beghin resulted in a huge increase in the volume of molasses profitably handled in Europe. Spain, Italy and Denmark followed.

The Chairmanship changed. Jo Whitmee switched over from U.M. to becoming Chairman of Tate & Lyle Refineries. George Scott (Junior) became Managing Director and joined the Board of Tate & Lyle. Tony Wingate-Saul succeeded Jo Whitmee and was in turn succeeded by Colin Rowan. Jack Hoyle and Alan McGaw were in turn Vice-Chairmen. The Athel Line and Sugar Line fleets were put under the same management. There was a gradual coming together between United and Tate & Lyle. A few, a very few, men left, but the rest settled into the new mould. The early and quite natural suspicions gradually disappeared, and what is more, profits continued to improve, and United maintained its share of the world market in molasses, over 40 per cent.

United Molasses in the last quarter of the twentieth century is very different from what it was when Michael Kielberg left it a generation earlier, and quite unrecognizable compared with the modest little affair which he engendered at 4 Chapel Street, Liverpool, before the first World War. The late 1970s saw a major slump in shipping, to which there had to be a well-considered reaction, in an attempt to adjust to the long-term future. But the Company still has a great deal of his dynamism.

CHAPTER TWENTY-FOUR

A Foothold in Europe

'*That Sweet Enemy, France . . .*'
(Sir Philip Sidney 1554–1586)

England and France have had a love-hate relationship for nine centuries or more, ever since in September 1066 William the Norman tripped and fell, leaping ashore at Pevensey. What might have been seen as an ill-omen he took to his advantage. Rising to his feet with two fistfuls of pebbles he cried: 'See, I hold England in both my hands.' Our Royal families inter-married for generations and there were uncountable wars and peaces.

King Edward VII, three generations ago, initiated an *Entente Cordiale* which has in spirit survived two wars, the occupation of France and the prickly régime of General de Gaulle. For many people of both sides of the Channel it is a love affair. It was therefore historically natural for Tate & Lyle to think of France as the country in which to invest while waiting for the time when Britain would join the E.E.C. There were other reasons of course in the 1960s–stable Government and a stable currency.

There are two French characteristics which one must always remember. First, more Frenchmen than Englishmen live on the land. They have, indeed, a passion for it, a Frenchman living abroad often talking seriously but quite unsentimentally about *ma France, my* France, not just France. An agricultural show in Paris draws almost as big an attendance as the Ideal Home Exhibition in London. City-dwelling Frenchmen make it their business to tend their roots in the country, and a Parisian will not infrequently be elected *maire* of a village where he has a country cottage. There was an example of this passion for the land at the funeral of that same William the Conqueror in the Cathedral of St. Etienne at Caen, which he himself had founded. The proceedings were halted by a mere vassal, one Asselin, who stood up and complained that Duke William had taken this bit of land from him by force and that he would not let the Duke be buried there. Eventually the service continued but not before Duke William's family had paid out thirty shillings for the spot in which the tomb was dug and agreed to pay an indemnity for the whole site.

The second thing is the French language. Particularly since the end of the Monarchy in France, the language has come to have an almost mystical significance, and to this day, words are only officially admitted to the French vocabulary after painstaking examination by the *Académie Française*. Of course in ordinary conversation, many English words creep in. You can be *handicappé*, you can have *un gentleman's agreement*, or insist on *le fair play*. But French is quite rightly jealously guarded, and even if as a foreigner you stumble a bit, it is appreciated when you speak it.

Good French-speakers have become commoner in Britain than they were in the 1960s and there were at that time relatively few in Tate & Lyle. On the other hand there was a long-standing connection with the Belgian Sugar Company, Raffinerie Tirlemontoise, many of whose senior people spoke good English as well as French. Accordingly, a partnership was formed, a company called European Sugars Ltd., which was to undertake the acquisition of a French sugar company. (Later it would be joined by a big French Company, F. Béghin S.A.; by the Italian Company, Eridania; and the German Süddeutscher Zucker in a Consortium [Compagnie Européenne de l'Industrie Sucrière].)

Next there was the question of which French company to approach. We had friends in St. Louis and the Compagnie Sucrière but they had problems. Béghin was large and its shares were held mainly by the Béghin family. The largest, and yet the most widely held by the public was Raffineries et Sucreries Say, S.A. with four refineries, Sermaise, Paris, Nantes and Bordeaux, and ten beet sugar factories. The original Monsieur Say had been refining sugar at Nantes when the Royal Navy's blockade cut him off from supplies of cane sugar in the first years of the nineteenth century. He had come to Paris and switched his attentions to beet sugar. The Say family had long since sold out, and the current Board of Directors were all outsiders, with very small personal holdings.

Some forty years earlier, young Peter Runge had been a trainee at the Paris refinery–through God knows what convoluted old-boy system. He went straight from Oxford, where chemical laboratories–at least at Trinity, his College–were then housed in the sort of shed where the Curies had discovered radium. (Most of the better scientific discoveries seem to be made in such places.) The laboratory at Raffineries Say in Paris came therefore as no great surprise to him.

The development of the Say beet factories had followed the historical pattern of transport and communication. The horse-drawn cart carried the first loads of beet and many factories sprang up in the north of France, where the soil was the most suitable. Later a system of *raperies,* or slicing stations, was developed, the beets being sliced near the field and the juice pumped for several miles by underground pipes to factories, for extraction. France's network of inland waterways led, too, to many factories being sited near a canal. Water transport is still cheaper than road and rail though the latter have largely taken over. In recent decades beet sugar production had spread south-eastwards into the Champagne area and beyond. The soil there had been for long thought too thin. But clusters of pine trees had been planted in the nineteenth century at the initiative of Emperor Napoleon III, and now the potash from axed and burned trees had been used to make square miles of rolling land suitable for beet-growing.

In 1967 there were seventy-eight French beet factories and Say's ten lay along a wide semi-circle starting at Pont d'Ardres near Calais in the north-west, skirting to the north of Paris, and ending up at Attigny in the east, almost in the Ardennes. They varied in size from Châlons-sur-Marne (6,500 tons of beet a day) to Sermaize (1,200 tons).

The whole region had been for centuries a scene of war. Names like Agincourt recall the 100 Years' War, and indeed one of Say's *raperies* was on the edge of the battlefield of Crécy, where in 1346 the Black Prince won his spurs and the blind King John of Bohemia rode to his death. Those ancient battlefields are peaceful places now, but even on a bright summer's day the visitor to this wide semi-circle can sense an ominous, brooding feeling, as though something terrible once happened here.

And it did, from 1914 to 1918. Every few miles one comes across a huge cemetery, with row upon heart-breaking row of trim impersonal crosses, French, British, German, American, Canadian. They mark the last resting-places of some hundreds of thousands of fellow-beings of Gavril Princip's who vicariously received the death sentence for his adolescent act of protest in June 1914. Somehow the grief of it all seems to have impregnated forever the air above those now tidy fields.

Many of the Say factories had been damaged in 1914–18, repaired, and then again *abîmé* in 1939–45 and repaired once more. For some years from 1945 on, for example, the Abbeville factory still received its beets on one side of the main road from Paris to Calais and processed them on the other. Some were too small, some, like Abbeville, too hurriedly rebuilt, some just plain old-fashioned. The Paris refinery was losing money. It was supplied with raws by a complicated system of double-handling involving rail and road, and occupied ten acres of valuable land behind the Gare d'Austerlitz. There would be much to do.

In May 1967 the Consortium made a bid for a substantial holding in Say shares held by the public. Tate & Lyle already held a number of shares, purchased for them by Schroder Wagg, the merchant bankers. The actual bid was however made by Messrs. Béghin, whose deputy President, Monsieur Jean-Marc Vernes, was also a Parisian merchant banker. Jean-Marc was what Texaco once referred to as a Tiger in the Tank. The Banque Vernes, of Swiss origin, was sometimes described a little deprecatingly as 'The Protestant Bank'. But in 1945 young Jean-Marc was a sign of the new times. Born a Swiss, he had been in the Resistance. He had learned the hard way. He had joined the Banque Vernes in 1946 and soon he was bringing in all sorts of accounts from unexpected quarters. An implacably hard worker, by 1967, he was a figure of stature. *Chez* Béghin he supplied the financial contacts which Ferdinand Béghin needed while he himself continued the enormously successful mixture of technical skill and personal leadership he gave to his vast sugar- and paper-producing company.

It is hard to describe Ferdinant Béghin. Slight, small, wiry, a keen horseman, a man who, without a word of English, liked to have four or five

English cars, in the days when there were such things, a Rolls, a Jaguar XK10 (which he drove like a demon), a Landrover and a Mini (for Paris), he was charming, impatient, sentimental and demanding – like Bustamante the sort of person one is glad to have met.

The operation for the take-over of Say was the first of its kind in many ways. (Such bids were rare in France.) It was the first for a sugar company, the first in which a European consortium was involved. There was much excitement.

The operation differed from others hitherto seen in Europe, for Jean-Marc Vernes, whose political antennae were exceptionally sensitive, recommended that the sugar beet farmers of France and their confrères in Europe should also be involved, if only on a token scale. This was wise, for it meant that not only would the *Betteraviers* be more closely involved with their inveterate adversaries the manufacturers, but also with the *Raffineurs Anglais*, particularly Tate & Lyle, and in time each would discover that the other was no Pantomine Ogre. There could be no swift demolition of the walls of suspicion, but, as Churchill said, Time is a long thing.

So the Chairman of the French *Confédération Générale des Betteraviers*, Georges Garinois, joined the Board of Say, showed his splendid qualities of warmth and common-sense, and provided a link with the scores of hundreds of French beet growers, by whom he is rightly trusted. And Henri Cayre, Chairman of the C.I.B.E., the International European Beet-Growers Confederation, gave the operation a benediction. Later, as a firm Anglophile – he set out to improve his English by a daily twenty minutes session of listening to the BBC each morning – he was to be on good terms with Lord Campbell of Eskan, Chairman of the Commonwealth Cane Sugar Producers (who incidentally speaks excellent French). While, therefore, there will no doubt always be divergence of views, at least there is understanding.

Henri and Georges are living reminders of the strength of European, particularly of Anglo-French links with the past and the future, traversing the enmities of the centuries – particularly when Napoleon made beet-sugar France's staple supply – and renewing the Entente Cordiale. There are, and will continue to be differences – notably in such matters as the production of High Fructose Corn Syrup – but in time these will be overcome.

As soon as the bid was announced the Say management reacted against it. Other French refiners, although friendly, were not involved and could not be told before but meetings were arranged as soon as possible in order to explain the situation to them. They had no complaints to make. No one said: 'Thou, species of camel, go and do something unspeakable to thyself.' But there was some understandable fear of Tate & Lyle as a very large company. And for a time the St. Louis and Bouchon interests, who had rapidly merged to form Générale Sucrière S.A. bought shares in Say, which forced up the price. This was amicably sorted out later.

With hindsight it might have been better had Tate & Lyle gone in on their own and moved more slowly. But as Britain was not yet in the E.E.C. there would have been problems with the French Ministry of Finance, and possibly political problems as well, and on balance the Consortium approach was at the time thought to be the best.

A new President of Say was appointed, Monsieur Jean Bernard, formerly a senior civil servant, and he settled down rapidly and soon became very popular with his colleagues and subordinates. A delightful retired French Naval Captain, Edouard Archambeaud, took the chair of the Consortium. (He was well known to Alan McGaw of United Molasses.) Say's own technicians, with help from people from Tate & Lyle, Tirlemont and Béghin, set to to produce a programme of modernization and rationalization. The Paris Refinery site was sold for £5 million (Monsieur Béghin, after a brief look at the place, had described it as *un cloaque*–a sewer), and the money was available to help this programme which would cost over £20 million in the course of the next few years.

Gradually the Consortium settled down to work together–most of them had never met before. Meetings were held in French at Monsieur Béghin's office in the Rue de Lübeck where he often, after meetings, hosted a most agreeable lunch. The representatives were quite an assortment–Jean Wittouck, Bob Rolin and Paul Wahl from Belgium, Giuseppe de André from Italy, Kurt Schumacher from Germany, Ferdinand Béghin, Jean-Marc Vernes, Jean Bernard, Edouard Archambeaud, a varying team from Tate & Lyle. Board meetings in France are a little like French dinner parties, the conversation flying across the table and round the room like a harassed ping-pong ball.

Annual General Meetings, too, were lively. The Directors assembled on the stage of a meeting hall in the Rue St. Dominique and sat behind the President, Jean Bernard, looking a little like the accused at the Nurenberg Trial. About 200 shareholders usually turned up. Jean Bernard, although admitting that these occasions were apt to cause a *mouvement des tripes* beforehand, nevertheless calmly took charge. ('He who holds the microphone must win,' he said reflectively.) The directors were introduced formally–the English names always giving trouble, Booth, Tate and Hugill becoming Bott, Tatt and Yoogeel–and for an hour and a half or so questions were fired, answered or parried. By 12.30 any sensible shareholder would want to get away to his lunch, so there was always a time limit.

Monsieur Béghin was not sure he cared for all those foreigners, but was hospitable and amusing. He was also outspoken. At one A.G.M. while a shareholder whose features were a little like those of a sad clown, was speaking, Monsieur Béghin's voice was heard by all in a loud aside: 'Seeing *that* Monsieur one might consider oneself to be attending a Circus.'

Say began to do well. Even *Les Evènements* of May 1968 when the students rampaged through Paris for several days and Président de Gaulle seemed temporarily to lose his grip, did not have any marked effect. The need for capital expenditure meant however that dividends were low. There was the beginning of a demand for bulk refined sugar in France, where manufacturing users had until recently been smaller and less modern than in Britain. Tate & Lyle established a small company together with a Monsieur Royer of Châlons to satisfy this demand, with bulk carriers designed in Britain *á la mode de Geoffrey Fairrie*.

The British Ambassador, Sir Patrick Reilly, aware of the potential importance of the whole affair, invited the Board of C.E.I.S. to lunch. They were thrilled, writing to Tate & Lyle to thank them enthusiastically for having 'provoked' (strange word, but better in French) such a pleasant occasion. A 1977 Think Tank on the Foreign Service would perhaps have suggested as an alternative, instead of a light meal in the erstwhile home of Napoleon's naughty little sister Pauline Borghese, a classless get-together over *un coup du Rouge* in some *Bar du Quartier*. They could be right, but this is not what is expected of H.B.M. Ambassador in Paris.

As the years went on the advantages from the French point of view of a merger between Say and Béghin came to be considered. Tate & Lyle's holding in Say was at the time only £3·5 million and Britain was still not in the E.E.C. There was much discussion, and in the end the merger took place in June 1972. Thereafter Monsieur Béghin was President of the combined Company, with a yearly production of some 800,000 tons. The composition of the Board changed, though Tate & Lyle were still fully represented. In June 1977 Ferdinand Béghin retired. He had long since reached the age, but he was so active that he hated the idea of going. As a little boy, his father and his uncle had encouraged him, sixty-five years earlier, to get to know the factory at Thumeries. Then, for a long time they had kept him out of the business while it grew. He had obeyed; but he had felt a responsibility, a *personal* responsibility, not just for the business, which was thriving, but for the people; not just for the product, but for the way it was produced. He had no sons—this was a sadness—and he left a large, efficient company which had been in his family since 1830, long before Henry and Abram got going, and which bore his own name, in the hands of 'people who were not members of his family'.

But he had at least left behind him a name, and to those who had met him, an irreplaceable warmth. If he had known Henry and Abram he would have been on the same wavelength as they, provided they had spoken French, and he would have been appreciated by them. (As a *sacré anglais* one cannot say fairer than that.)

By 1976, a year before Ferdinand Béghin retired, the French sugar industry as a whole had begun to run into trouble. It was partly because of the bureaucracy of Brussels, a small group of highly intelligent men but bureaucratic nonetheless. It was also because of domestic problems. There were two serious years of drought. (No bureaucrat, and few

Dompierre, one of the beet factories owned by Raffineries Say in northern France.

ministers ever realize that agriculture is in the hands of Someone Else.)

There was severe competition from a new sweetener, High Fructose Corn Syrup – called *Iso-glucose* in France – then produced from maize under conditions which might be described as privileged. And whereas the franc itself was devalued, the Green Franc remained, by French Government decision, at its former value. This meant that the industry was paying at one (high) rate for its supplies and receiving at another (lower) for its product. Moreover France was, in spite of droughts, producing a surplus of sugar which had to be sold abroad at a world market price below cost of production. The French manufacturers found themselves in difficulties, Générale Sucrière and Béghin-Say included. Dividends were cut or passed, cash-flow problems obtruded. Share prices fell.

This was unlikely to be a perennial problem, a solution would be found one day. But while it continued, the French sugar industry, which received no such Government assistance as is accorded by other individual European Governments to their sugar industries, faced a singularly difficult patch.

CHAPTER TWENTY-FIVE

The Seventies and Change

'Ancient and Modern Overheard.'
(Len Dow–Plaistow Wharf, 1970)

From 1967 onwards the Tate & Lyle Refineries in Britain began to adjust themselves to new kinds of change, notably, alas, to a downward movement of throughput. The export trade became the subject of even fiercer competition, and the future size of the home market share was none too certain. In accordance with its new position in the Group, T.L.R.'s Board and management structure was changed. There were still three Main Board Directors involved and a number of senior executives became members of the T.L.R. Board. But the practice of having a Director at each refinery was replaced by a system of functional Directors. Peter Runge was Chairman, Jim Hobbs and Colin Lyle were the two other Main Board members. George Payne and Norman Cullen were also Directors. Although this proved effective the disappearance of the old-established daily contact with Main Board Directors was widely regretted.

In order to accommodate the newer bulk-carriers, now 20,000 tonners, a new jetty in London was required. This could only be built at Thames Refinery, since the P.L.A.'s projected barrier would make it impossible at Plaistow Wharf. Completed early in 1968, the jetty, 440 feet long, and furnished with $12\frac{1}{2}$ ton grabbing cranes was capable of unloading 800 tons an hour direct into the Refinery–about one million tons a year. It cost £1·4 million.

With considerable sadness the conclusion was reached that henceforth all the London melt should be done at Thames, Plaistow Wharf becoming merely the producer of Golden Syrup and a packing and storage depot. It is easy to say this. It was difficult and unpleasant to carry it out, for it meant upsets for so many people. Thames went over to four shifts, running continuously through the weekends, and this absorbed quite a number of people from Plaistow Wharf. Others retired early. As people left they were not replaced. There was no abrupt dismissing. The whole exercise took over two years and each step was carefully explained to and discussed with the trade unions, who accepted the inevitability of the change. Employees adjusted themselves to working in a different place. They were philosophical but it was difficult for them. There was something quite awful about the idea that the ninety-year-old Lyles' Refinery would soon be virtually no more. It was not just that so much effort and money and ingenuity had been expended on it. It had gathered to itself a collective identity made up of the individual personalities of the thousands who, over that time, had spent their working lives there. Each corner, each station had a familiarity for scores, or even hundreds of people. In a way a sudden destruction by explosion would have been less saddening than the sight of the demolition gangs at work on the huge buildings which had stood up to the Luftwaffe.

Tommy Ormes, a Plaistow man with many years' service, settled in well at Thames but could not bring himself to come to work past Plaistow Wharf, finding it too poignant. He was one of many.

Oliver Lyle had died in 1961. Everyone was relieved that he was not there to see his Refinery go.

Perhaps it was all best summed up in some verses written in 1970 when the huge steel ball was smashing the concrete walls and the oxy-acetylene cutters were nibbling away like caterpillars at the uprights and girders. The author was Len Dow, who had once been a member of a Raw Sugar Gang and was now a Commissionaire:

'Ancient & Modern Overheard'

The young one said 'It was a shame',
The old one asks 'Well, who's to blame?'
'I've worked here for forty years',
The young one thought he saw some tears.

The young one said 'It's all this change,
You take a while to re-arrange'.
'Change for the worse', the old one cried,
'It only happened because he died'.

After a discussion on change, the old man bursts out:

'Plaistow pride built up this place.
The Governor would look you in the face,
And shake your hand, and know your name,
I tell you lad, it's not the same'.

The young man and the old have each their last word:

'And this is the end Dad, this is the end,
You've looked upon this place as a friend'.
'I know' said the old one, 'It just had to be.'
But would it have happened, I wonder, if he?'[1]

The change had barely begun when the Thames Cube House was the victim of a fire which began just after mid-night on the morning of July 3rd 1968. Although the fire brigade eventually got the blaze out by 5.00 a.m.–they had to use forty-five pumps–the damage was considerable, for there was a high wind which fanned the flames to a white heat. Two thousand tons of packed cube sugar, half of it intended for export, was destroyed. The Cube House had been rapidly but calmly evacuated, and

[1] 'He', of course, was Oliver Lyle.

thanks to close liaison over the years the Fire Brigade knew the site well. There was one casualty, a fireman who was treated for minor facial burns.

Peter Runge heard the news at 1.30 a.m. when John Ellyatt, the Thames Manager telephoned him. Peter was not at first best pleased when the telephone rang.

'All right, John,' he said testily, 'where's the fire?'

'Actually, sir, there *is* one. In the Cube House.'

Peter went straight down to the Refinery.

The organization for dealing with emergencies, dating from twenty-five years earlier, did well. The Insurance Company remarked that it had never been supplied more quickly with such a wealth of information. But it was eight months before full production of cubes was restored after major efforts by Len Agombar and his staff, who re-erected the Chambon Pressed Cube lines in the 'West Ham Depot'. In the meantime the newly associated French Company, Raffineries Say and the Belgian Raffinerie Tirlemontoise supplied cubes for the British home market.

On the Clyde, Walkers' in 1967 commissioned new storage and delivery arrangements on two acres of land which had once belonged to the old Caledonian Railway. Walkers' now handled 3,000 tons of sugar a week, about half of it going in packets to Scotland, Northern Ireland and Carlisle. They also made treacle, syrup and liquid sugar mixes. In the late 1970s, the Refinery employed 400 people, of whom 80 were girls.

Other changes were taking place. Office accommodation in Central London and the City was becoming more and more costly and the Head Office Staff dealing with Transport and Distribution were scattered in a number of different places. A new I.B.M. computer was on order. (T.L.T.S. had already moved to Bromley). It was therefore decided to lease the five top floors of a new building at Croydon, Leon House, almost on the site of the old Grand Theatre which had been opened in 1896 by Beerbohm Tree with a special performance of *Trilby*. Here a total of some 400 people were accommodated. Special tie-lines and other forms of communication linked them to the Refineries and to 21 Mincing Lane.

In order to exercise a swifter and closer control, particularly over plans for capital expenditure, and to enable priorities to be established, a new Committee of the Board was established. Called at first the BLOW group because its members were Booth, Lyle (C.), Oliphant and Whitmee, it was later referred to as the Executive Committee–or more usually by the acronym EXCO. In time it became a formidably effective body. Although EXCO themselves were relatively blameless as far as jargon was concerned the spread of new management methods, learned at courses in Business Schools and the like, began to be accompanied during the next few years by a proliferation of working documents couched in a curious form of English. This was too much for certain members of the Board, particularly 'Professor' Tony Tate, who compiled a vocabulary of verbal gems actually in use in documents circulating within the Company and provided a translation. Here are some:

Phrase in alleged English	*De-jargonized translation*
House style.	'Must you always come down to breakfast with your curlers in?'
Cross-fade slide demonstration.	'Now here we are at another edition of Come Dancing.'
Divisional in-house activities.	Wife-swapping.

Alas, no amount of ridicule will ever stem the flood.

As a Company involved in food production and one with wide contacts and commitments in developing countries, it is not surprising that Tate & Lyle were among the founder members of a new and potentially important international group which came into being in the late 1960s. The then Director-General of the Food and Agriculture Organization of the United Nations, Dr. B. R. Sen, an Indian, was pessimistic about the ability of the rapidly growing world population to produce enough to feed itself. He considered it vital to enlist the active involvement of large-scale international industrial firms—the name 'Multinational' was not then common currency. The average gross national product of the world's developing countries was increasing, according to the United Nations' Pearson Commission by 5 per cent a year—a higher rate than that of the industrial countries but scarcely enough. And far too many of the hundreds of thousands of farmers in the less developed countries—the 'Third World' is too much of a blanket term—were merely subsistence farmers.

Dr. Sen invited sixteen of the world's larger companies involved in the production of food, or of the inputs needed—agricultural equipment, fertilizers, insecticides and so forth—to form an Industry Cooperative Programme, attached to F.A.O. and therefore within the framework of the U.N. It was an unusual departure. Tycoons and international civil servants do not blend easily. They do not even use the same kind of language or apparently go through the same thought-processes. However, the Programme rapidly expanded until it had in the course of three years about one hundred member firms from over twenty countries. The Programme's activities were effective because the representatives of the Companies themselves were Chairmen or Chief Executives who could actually commit their Companies.

The Programme is unique. It is not a trade association or a sales agency or a philanthropic club. It is hard to describe. But it exists and expands.

It is, of course, the type of organization which gets a bad press from untidy young ladies with their heads full of sociology picked up at places like Vassar. But that does not detract from its value to mankind.

Tate & Lyle provided the first Englishman to be Chairman of the Programme in 1972 and have since provided the Treasurer. At the working level there has been considerable activity on the part of Tate & Lyle's Research and Development and Technical Services people.

Since food is vital to existence it is only natural that, like sex, it should involve strong and sometimes irrational subconscious emotions. The last two centuries have seen, as well as major advances in medical science, many irreversible changes in the techniques of food production. They have seen in many parts of the world, though alas still in a minority, a diminution of famine. They have seen an increase in the consumption of many foods, including sugar, for after all people have to go on eating, and over the middle and later decades of the century about a million additional members were added to the human race every week. These, like the rest of us, do not just eat a food because it is nutritious but like it to be palatable as well. No amount of nutrition, however theoretically desirable, is any good unless it is eaten, and sugar is a safe, traditional source of palatability whose workings are probably deeply embedded in some biological urge. Naturally, perhaps, it therefore became for a while the object of theorizing.

As to this, G. B. Shaw pointed out in the early years of the century in *The Doctors' Dilemma* that medical and dietary practice is, like any other human activity, subject to fads and fancies. Fifty years ago Vitamins were the New Thing. Then more recently there was The Great Protein Shortage. A score of years ago some wily fellows began to mutter darkly about fats while others damned the carbohydrates – particularly sugar. Then it was proclaimed that we should eat *more* carbohydrates. And while this book was being written it became the turn of what Grandpapa called Roughage to receive favourable mention – only it was referred to as Dietary Fibre.[2]

A sceptic would not be surprised if one day most theories at present held on diet were to find themselves in the same limbo as Sir Colenso Ridgeon's Opsonin while mankind continues to browse and sluice in order to keep alive.

Controversy is of course good but the subject of food is devilish complicated – some even go so far as to call it multifactorial. Great tomes are produced on it – the names of some recent ones are given below.[3] From these it becomes apparent that there is no harm in eating sugar – except to the teeth if you don't take care of them.

The truth being far from simple, there is a temptation to over-simplify. An example of this is the description of sugar as 'empty calories'. This is itself an empty phrase. As the classical work on human physiology of Haldane and Huxley explains, the body, in order to function properly, needs energy-producing foods, the energy being supplied by oxidation of the food, a process accompanied by the production of heat. One calorie is the quantity of heat needed to raise the temperature of one gramme of

[2] The most recently published paper on this is that of Morris, Marr and Clayton in the *British Medical Journal* of November 19th, 1977. After a twenty-year study of 337 chaps in London, whose jobs were bus-driving, bus-conducting and banking Morris et al. (as scientists like to be called) conclude: 'There was no sign of a relation between consumption of sucrose and Coronary Heart Disease.' What you are advised to do is to eat cereal fibre. Roughage.

water through 1°C. from 14·5° to 15·5°. It is *not* a space and cannot therefore be empty. Incidentally, the calories referred to in works on diet are kilo-calories, not calories, hence the capital C in those glossy magazines. And just to make it all easier the experts are considering the use of the joule as an alternative unit of measurement.

There are other over-simplifications, and few people bother to point out that gramme for gramme sugar in any case contains half as many calories or joules as fat.

And it is here to stay, anyway. About 80 million tons a year were being produced and eaten in the 1970s. And according to the Food and Agricultural Organization of the United Nations, the demand will be for 100 million tons a year in the mid 1980s, much of the increase in consumption being in the developing countries of the world. Where is it to come from?

The trouble is that between the work of scientists and the ordinary public there is a wide gulf of understanding, and often popular magazines try to fill this. Whereas a hundred years ago these would perhaps have published earnest little religious homilies castigating sin, they now publish equally earnest little pseudo-scientific ones castigating normal items of diet.

Scientific study and controversy on the subject still continues and will long do so and theories will rise and fall. Missionary zeal is therefore, to say the least, premature. Some would even call it unkind, battening as it does on mankind's innate gullibility.

Reading popular articles and the books on which they are usually based, often given Sci-Fi titles such as 'Pure, White and Deadly' or 'The Saccharine Disease', one is irresistibly reminded of earlier missionaries such as Esdras and Tobit the son of Tobiel, and we all know, don't we, where *their* works eventually ended up. In the Apocrypha.

After much thought Tate & Lyle together with the other sugar interests in Britain formed in 1967 a British Sugar Bureau, under the directorship of Michael Shersby M.P., not to feed the public with untruths but to make sure that the truth was readily available.

For some three and a half decades, too, Tate & Lyle had been staunch members of the International Sugar Research Foundation, [4] whose job it is to monitor scientific work involving sugar, to foster serious long-term studies, and to seek the truth.

---

[3] 'Evaluation of the Health Aspects of Sucrose as a Food Ingredient.' Prepared by the Life Sciences Research Office, Federation of American Societies for Experimental Biology for the U.S. Food & Drug Administration, 1976. Royal College of Physicians/British Cardiac Society. Report of a joint working party 1976.
First Report from the Expenditure Committee together with Minutes of Evidence taken before the Social Services and Employment Sub-Committee in Sessions 1976–77. H.M.S.O. 1977.
[4] Initially the Sugar Research Foundation.

CHAPTER TWENTY-SIX

Research and All That

I

*'There are those who believe in Research, those who don't,
and those who do, but only just.'*
(Professor A. J. Vlitos, 1970)

In addition, the Professor might have said (in fact he did, but it was heartlessly suppressed by the author) there are also those who feel there is too little research, or too much, or that you can turn on and off as in running a bath. There are those who think it is only a question of having an idea and hey, presto, you've got a new product that disobeys the Third Law of Thermodynamics (look up under Entropy if you must), revolutionizes space travel, and makes a delicious cake filling too. Whereas, of course, the trail from the bright idea and the laboratory bench to the customer is long, hard, expensive, and littered with the bones of lost hopes and reputations.

In the primitive, Bullocks' Blood Era, it is safe to say that the non-believers were very numerous, yet there were many chaps with bright ideas in different parts of the world, or we should still be living in that epoch. Henry Tate the First, as we have seen, owed much of his success to his willingness to adopt new ideas even if it cost money. He 'imported' Alfred Brunner, the founder of what is now I.C.I., from Switzerland as a consultant, and although not himself a researcher, is sometimes credited with the invention and perfection of that useful article, the till, which he introduced into his chain of grocers' shops. Abram Lyle III certainly had ideas of his own on ships' design, and a number of his descendants have been most inventive. Oliver Lyle was a brilliant self-made engineer and a world authority on the efficient use of steam, his brother Philip a noted statistician. Alexandre Manbré's researches were the origin of the firm that bears his name and its later success depended on the effective imagination of Albert Berry (q.v. later and don't be impatient).

Yet there is always a difficulty about judging what kind of research is needed, what its targets should be, and in knowing what the blazes those boffins are up to. Men who are immensely gifted as administrators or financiers or marketing experts can, if they have themselves no basic scientific training, too easily dismiss researchers as either mountebanks or myth-makers, conversing elliptically in a mumbo-jumbo of their own.

Even a century ago sugar refiners acknowledged a need for chemists as well as engineers, but it is only in the years since the Second World War that R. and D. has gradually become a central function. Prior to that what went on did so in small, widely separated, individual centres. There was not a great deal of it, little if anything was published, and sometimes the personalities did not harmonize. But at least there seems to have been something at each of the major refineries, and it is convenient to look separately at these and to follow the process of growth, slow to begin with, then speeding up as understanding and acceptance blossomed into positive enthusiasm.

At Plaistow Wharf the need for analysis of raw sugars for the purpose of establishing price and Duty payments was at first answered by employing a chemist, John Joseph Eastick, who had his own laboratory at Trinity Square in the City, where his brother, Charles, became his assistant. Distance–in those days when roads were un-waterproofed and the horse and the London-Southend Railway were the chief sources of movement–made this unworkable, and so a small laboratory was built in a loft over the vacuum pans, later moving to a corner of the Engineers' shop over the boilers. (A bit sweaty-hot in either case, if you ask me.) By 1888 analysis became so important that a special laboratory was built near the gate, the 'Yard Lab'. Two independent analyses of every sample were carried out for over forty years until improved techniques made this unnecessary.

One analysis was done by girls on the first floor and one by men on the ground floor. (This was probably an early example of Equal Opportunities.) And should anyone think that the girls were in any way down-trodden, they were from 1888–1896 the responsibility of Janet Lyle, who married a Mr. Carmichael and bore John Carmichael, later Chief Engineer at Plaistow Wharf. Janet lived to a great age and although diminutive, was what Alan Breck would have called a 'Bonny Fechter'. No one, but no one, would ever down-tread her gurrls–except possibly herself if they were saucy.

In 1888 Eastick took on another assistant, L. J. de Whalley, and two lab. boys, James Mann and John Watson. Watson later served for fifty-five years, chiefly as the controller of Golden Syrup–'Goldie' production. James Mann graduated to be in charge of the Yard Lab. L. J. de Whalley for a while was Chief Chemist after J. S. Eastick left to go to Australia, and his brother Charles to Martineaus' in 1890.

De Whalley lived south of the river and insisted on coming to and from work by being rowed across the river between Blackwall Point and the Raw Sugar Wharf, winter and summer. Slight, shy, and whimsical–he called one of his twelve sons Siegfried because he had been to that opera the night before his birth; it might just as well have been Parsifal–he was highly inventive and a clever designer and executant of experiments. In 1910 he was made the first Research Chemist–ever–in Tate & Lyle, and installed in Rose Cottage, a small building which had been erected in 1897 by Ian Lyle's grandfather, Arthur Lyle, as a Director's office and dining-room. Arthur insisted on having a bath put in so that he could clean up after a tour of the Refinery. By 1910 the Directors were bathing the Outer Gentleman, satisfying the Inner Gentleman, and then directing away like anything in newer quarters and Rose Cottage was available for other purposes.

John Watson was a stickler and needed to be. Goldie began in a haphazard fashion as a sort of treacle. Improvements in colour were attained but the product had to be made in batches and it varied in quality, sometimes going cloudy. The colour went on being improved until at last the customers complained that it looked like castor oil.[1] There was an argument among the Lyles and eventually a special, rigorously applied standard was agreed.

James Mann did much original work into improving the standardization of analytical methods, perfecting a polarization flask which bears his name and was later adopted by the British Standards Institution. This is not the place for a dissertation on polarization but it is an important factor in the world of sugar and the following brief note may help. One of the *savants* whom Napoleon (can't get away from the fellow) took to Egypt in 1797 was Etienne Malus, a twenty-three year old physicist. On his return to France in 1801, Malus made the discovery that light waves normally vibrate in random planes but that these planes can be brought together to the same angle–i.e. polarized. Other Frenchmen, Biot and Clerget, later found that different sugars in solution in water rotate or twist the plane of polarized light to different degrees depending on the strength of the solution and the individual sugar. Sucrose and glucose twist the plane to the right (hence glucose is sometimes called dextrose) and fructose to the left (hence levulose). This property is of immense importance in measuring the quantities of different sugars in a mixture and in determining their purity individually. The Mann flask is the means of obtaining standard strengths of solution.

In the mid-1920s there was a need for a new chief chemist and H. C. S. de Whalley (to whom his father had given that Wagnerian name of Siegfried) was recruited from the Molassine Company Ltd. in Greenwich. Oliver Lyle describes Siegfried's joining the firm as a gradual process of adsorption. He and Siegfried were to engage in a love-hate relationship down the years, each respecting the other's abilities but at the same time delighting in irritating.

Siegfried was very creative and full of new ideas, and in 1937, finding that like his Papa he was adept at research, the Board decided to appoint him Research Chemist, and Ardesco, the cottage in which the Refinery Manager had lived until the days of the telephone, was fitted out as a Research Laboratory. Here he was to produce many innovations in refining. Some of these were well ahead of their time, some were scrapped, some unsuccessful because they had not been sufficiently developed before being handled by process technicians and engineers.

[1] In those days a remedy applied with vigour to any ailment occurring below the belt.

Anything introduced into the Process had to be 100 per cent workable or someone would inevitably – usually, but not always, by accident – blow it up, burn it down or convert it to some use other than that intended.

An early idea which should have worked but didn't, was a development of the use of a phenol-formaldehyde ion-exchange resin for decolourizing sugar solutions and removing inorganic matter. This process, evolved by Holmes and Adams of the National Physical Laboratory at Teddington and now widely used in sugar factories and refineries throughout the world, was promising enough to justify a large-scale pilot plant occupying three floors with its columns and rubber-lined vessels. The type of resin used in those days, Zeocarb, was however acid and caused inversion in the raw syrup on which it was tried.

Another experimental technique, successful in the laboratory, failed on full scale. This was Gel and Tower Carbonatation, begun during the War. Involving the use of a milk of lime-sucrose gel, frozen, added to the raw liquor and then treated with flue gas in a slatted tower, this worked with raw beet sugar but not with cane raws because the presence of cane fibres (bagasse) clogged the tower. Temperatures were critical, too, and a new research chemist, Denis Dickinson, recalls how, just arrived at Plaistow, he was watching a run on the plant. He found himself being questioned by two men he did not know, one short and one tall. 'I'm sorry' he said at length, because the temperature of the 'Gel' mixture had to be kept below $4°C$ or it went solid, and he did not want to spend a hot afternoon digging out 10 tons of it, 'but I can't answer any more of your questions. I'm supposed to be in charge of *this* bloody thing.' The two men were Oliver and Ian Lyle.

The Tower at last caught fire one day and the refrigerators burned out too. And that was the end of Gel and Tower Carbonatation. But it led to an overdue conversion to continuous instead of batch carbonatation.

By the end of the war de Whalley had a staff of about eight people of different disciplines including Messrs. Stan Hill, Bull, Austin, Rayner, Jackson, Barratt, Runeckles and Dickinson, and Dr. Pamela Scarr, an extremely capable micro-biologist, and work was being undertaken on vacuum-oven drying for analysis, bauxite coated with carbon as an alternative to charcoal, steam regeneration of charcoal, and numerous improvements in control in the process, as well as into the sex life of various micro-organisms.

At Thames the early days of research took a different route, starting before the 1914 war when Hugh Main was Chief Chemist, with the study of Refractive Index measurements of syrup as a means of establishing the percentage of solid matter present and the measurement of 'ash' (see above) in sugar solutions by the use of electric resistance. A notable entomologist (expert on bugs, to you) in his spare time, he met a young fellow naturalist, Harold Powers, in the summer of 1914 pursuing butterflies in Essex and took him on as an assistant. Harold at once became involved in

A.R.D.E.S.C.O.–home of Plaistow Wharf's Manager before the telephone. Later the Research Laboratory. Jimmy Lyle at the gate.

The first laboratory at Liverpool.

research, and began to make a considerable contribution to sugar refining techniques, applying, for example, the pH system which had been developed in Sweden to sugar solutions of all kinds.

There was little opportunity for research in the inter-war period, as Thames Refinery was engaged in raising its throughput–between 1924 and 1939 it increased nearly five-fold–and all laboratory efforts were directed to normal day-to-day controls. There was little or no contact between the three Refineries until after 1945, and virtually no research results were allowed to be published. An exception was a paper by Hugh Main, printed in the Journal of the Society of Chemical Industry on June 16th, 1919, on 'The Refractometer in the Sugar Industry', outlining work he had done from 1910–1914. In the later 1930s occasional papers were given to the International Commission for Uniform Methods of Sugar Analysis (I.C.U.M.S.A.), by de Whalley, Powers and others. Even Powers' work on pH in the 1920s was unpublished for years and, when communicated to the sister refinery at Love Lane, was disbelieved. During the 1939/45 war virtually the only research was into the measurement of water in dehydrated vegetables.

Harold Powers became local Chemical Warfare Officer for the area in 1939 and between whiles found a means of controlling a particularly malignant mosquito, Culex Molestus, which bred in the dark and attacked men working in the Boiler House. It was rather a long way from Research and Development, yet the search for truth did not cease altogether. Alarmed by the amount of sugar lost in the Refineries, the Directors ordered an investigation into suspected causes such as leaks to the sewer or petty thieving. The latter was probably the more important in days of rationing but the former was not neglected, and a special system of control was set up. The searcher never found what caused the loss, but it wasn't the sewer.

At Liverpool, all this time, there had been a strong tradition of what is more properly called sugar technology rather than research, no doubt stemming from Henry Tate's predilection for well-established new methods. This was carried out for some twenty-seven years by J. W. MacDonald,[2] who had done some classical work on sulphated ash in cane and beet. A successor, Percy Chantrell, carried out experimental work in the laboratory, recording his results in intense secrecy and a small black book which was never seen by anybody but the Manager.

These men usually became Managers of a Refinery in time, taking responsibility for all aspects of the work, including chemical control, and working through Shift Foremen. Technical control was therefore of the most rudimentary kind. Eventually a Chief Chemist and Shift Chemists were appointed, but the former's instructions often conflicted with those of the Manager. So that, although there had been a laboratory of a kind at Love Lane probably since the beginning of time, there was always friction,

[2] See Chapter Two.

and production, although efficiently managed, was something of a mystery of its own, without too much benefit of chemical clergy.

The laboratory at Liverpool seems still to have been a proving ground for makey-learns in the 1920s and 1930s. Among those who had served in it were Sam Gee, Louis Tate, eldest of Bertie Tate's sons, and brother of Tony and Johnnie, and Tom Storey his cousin.

Carrying on the Liverpool tradition of technology rather than research was Alf Potter, who, coming from the Fairrie Refinery at Vauxhall Road in the 1930s, was chief chemist at Liverpool until 1952, thus bringing us through to the end of the Second War and the beginnings of the formal establishment on a Company-wide basis of Research. Potter was very gifted as a technologist but not an easy man, and no lover of the Process Management, or of Shift Chemists. When one of these reported in his log that some material might be contaminated by rain water, Potter wrote in red ink in the same log: 'I fear the acts of the Almighty rather less than I fear the acts of his Shift Chemists.'

Alf Potter could normally be relied on to be at loggerheads, too, with Siegfried de Whalley and with a new acquisition, Frank Chapman, an able, self-taught sugar technologist taken on at Plaistow by Oliver Lyle. Frank, at times eccentric, was inclined to appear without warning in the middle of the night, make some adjustment with his own bare hands to a feed valve deep in the bosom of the process in order to check one of his theories, and forget to tell the Shift Manager. His delightful assistant, Bill Gibbard, often bore the brunt of the Shift Manager's displeasure. (He was unkindly referred to as the Sorcerer's Apprentice.)

Clearly this piecemeal approach to scientific research would be unsuited to the future and if the efforts of de Whalley and his team were to be generally acceptable rather than merely of potential use to the Refineries as a whole, everyone must be involved. It was here that, as the War drew to its close, Philip Lyle brought to bear the clout which can only be provided by a senior Director. He established a small Research Committee with himself in the Chair and Bill North from Thames as Convenor and Secretary. This Committee met monthly, and very early on it was agreed that the old convention of secrecy should be relaxed.

Harold Powers, who had from his earliest days been interested in the mechanics of the formation of sugar crystals, was encouraged to pursue this line of research, begun, before 1914, by Young in the U.S.A. and the Earl of Berkeley in Britain, but then dropped. For Tate & Lyle, and later for the industry as a whole, this led to a method of expressing the sizes of crystal or 'grain' by a new and simple system. Instead of using a series of sieves and characterizing caster sugar, fine, granulated and so forth, by the percentage passing through them, crystals henceforth were classified by the Mean Aperture through which they would pass and the Coefficient of Variation on either side of the Mean. Three decades later Harold is still a world authority on crystallography.

II
'Science moves but slowly, slowly, creeping on from point to point.'
(Alfred, Lord Tennyson, 1809–1892)

Well, Alf (not *you*, Potter. The other chap, Tennyson), I must disagree. You might have been right in the 1870s, but nowadays the damned thing's moving much too swiftly, swiftly, hopping along like an agitated prawn, you might almost say.

But not quite yet. In 1947 it was realized that Ardesco was not really large enough for a proper Research Laboratory. Also the Oliver-Siegfried Idyll was becoming a little less than idyllic. So the Board decided to set up A Research Establishment Elsewhere. Anywhere, in fact, but at Plaistow Wharf.

After some house-hunting a suitable site was found at Ravensbourne in the one-time village of Keston, between Bromley and Biggin Hill, in Kent. The late Charles Darwin had lived nearby at Down, pondering on the Origin of the Species. Ravensbourne was a spacious Victorian house in some thirty-five acres of parkland. For what seemed a lot of money, about £22,000, the property was bought, and later a neighbouring one, Forest Lodge. And the move took place.

There was a farewell party at Plaistow Wharf, and Oliver Lyle spoke a little sharply about the bits of magic which were *supposed* to come from Research. Siegfried de Whalley retorted that one thing the Research Department had learned at Plaistow was to suffer fools gladly, adding, for good measure, in connection with one of Oliver's recollections: 'You're wrong. My memory is better than yours. A woman remembers. An elephant never forgets. I am a female elephant'.

In those days, the Research budget for Tate & Lyle was £80,000 a year – multiply by about four for present day figures. But Research was still on something of a trial basis. After all, sugar refining was a fairly simple process, technically well advanced. Was there much point in Research?

As if to establish the answer to this, it was decided to hold each year a Technical (*not* a Research) Conference, to which were invited all the senior engineering staff and the many younger men with degrees who had since the War joined as trainee and junior managers.

There was progress, even if the aims were limited. And the regularity of the meetings gradually resulted in more communication between the hitherto independent-minded Refineries. When Denis Dickinson was looking for a suitable site for experiments in the hydraulic handling of char, Alf Potter affably suggested using the Vauxhall Road Char House in Liverpool. The first full-scale hydraulic char-handling system later went in at Thames. A comprehensive series of Abstracts, collecting and collating all published scientific data on sugar, was begun. Publication of results, unless patents were under negotiation, was at last officially encouraged, and technical papers began to appear in the *International Sugar Journal*,

Sugar y Azucar, and elsewhere.

The faces inevitably changed. Alf Potter retired in 1952 and was suceeded by Murray Hutson, another Oxford chemist like Jim Hobbs and Bill North. Haworth Magee, Alf's chief assistant, was seconded to Montreal to help with problems at the newly acquired Canadian Refinery,[3] and later decided to stay there. Murray Hutson moved south to London and another John Watson–no relation of the Golden Syrup maestro but the author of *One Hundred Years of Sugar Refining* took over. Siegfried de Whalley, now full of years, retired in 1957 and was succeeded by Bill North, Process Manager at Thames. Philip Lyle was joined by Jo Whitmee as representative of the Board on the Research Committee in 1954. Then, alas, Philip died in the summer of 1955 and Kenneth Brown replaced him. Colin Lyle replaced Jo. He had early shown an interest in Research. As a trainee at Plaistow he had wickedly been set by his Uncle Oliver to write a thesis on the amount of sucrose inverted at each stage of refining–an impossible job. At Ravensbourne he had been introduced to David Gross, who knew much about this. (Colin found The Natives friendly.) Kenneth Brown retired and Saxon Tate, youthful and enthusiastic, replaced him.

But Bill North's remit from the Board and his range of actions were limited. Only such problems as bore directly on sugar refining were studied. His budget was set at first at £120,000 p.a. which is not a great sum. He managed nevertheless to recruit two new highly qualified men, Ken Parker, a D.Phil. from Oxford, and Mike Bennett, who had graduated from Imperial College of Tropical Agriculture in Trinidad, the former in January, the latter in October 1959.

III
'The pith of an Indian Cane.'
(Joseph Addison, 1672–1719)

Although the Tate & Lyle interests in the Antilles never produced more than some 20 per cent of the total sugar refined by the parent Company in Britain, it is worth remembering that it requires anything from 8 to 10 tons of cane (and 10 is far too much) to provide 1 ton of sugar. In scale, therefore, in tonnages of material handled, in numbers of employees, the West Indian companies were comparable in size and in many ways larger. The pith of the whole matter is in the growing of the sugar cane, the selection of varieties, the proper application of fertilizer, the correct forms of irrigation and drainage, the protection of the crop from insect and virus attacks.

The arrival of Tate & Lyle in Jamaica had been accompanied by an intense study of these matters, and the intensity increased after 1945.

[3] See Chapter Twenty.

Encouraged by Bobby Kirkwood, the other sugar manufacturers joined in a cooperative research programme based at Mandeville, up in the hills, and led by Bob Innes, a brilliant Welshman. The West Indies Sugar Company had a strong research team at each of its estates, led at Monymusk by Hugh Thompson, an Ulsterman, and at Frome by Bill Ive, a Jamaican trained in Canada.

In Trinidad research had for long been principally directed at the cure for froghopper attacks. Much of the success in this was owed to the young Caroni Ltd. Research Officer, Frank Blackburn. It was not just a matter of finding the necessary chemical insecticides, for these were known, thanks to work by the World Health Organization on mosquitoes. It was a matter of applying them at the right moment and in the optimal manner. This had been solved, and now Blackburn had been made Cultivation Manager.

In Jamaica insects gave much less trouble. In both islands there were intense arguments about the best lay-out for fields. A system known as Louisiana Banks found favour in some places. Specialists being only human, that system found disfavour elsewhere. Tony Tate, visiting the West Indies for the first time, and, not being an agriculturist, wondered whether this Louisiana Banks they were all getting so passionate about was some sultry, langorous Belle in lil' ol' Noo Orleans.

The two West Indies companies had come under the same London management team, and in the mid-fifties had the same Chairman, Peter Runge, and the same Executive Directors. The large St. Madeleine factory and estate had been acquired.[4] While the research effort in Jamaica was satisfactory, Trinidad lagged, and began to suffer for it. The froghopper was still active and a new type of pest, the jumping borer (*Elasmopalpus*) began to devastate the canefields, particularly at Ste. Madeleine. A young entomologist, Dr. Derek Fewkes, was taken on to research into this insect and had some considerable success on this front. Yet the problems were deeper-seated and a crop worth from £10 to £15 million a year justified a more extensive research effort than hitherto.

It was accordingly decided that the two companies–Caroni Ltd. and Ste. Madeleine–should jointly support such an effort. The Research Station was to be established as a separate entity, called the Tate & Lyle Central Agricultural Research Station, and was responsible direct to the Managing Director.

It was also decided that an attempt must be made to find a scientist of the highest calibre as Director of Research, and an advertisement was placed in *Nature,* which brought in over 200 replies. By far the most attractive was one from Dr. A. J. Vlitos, a U.S. citizen working for the Boyce-Thompson Institute at Yonkers, New York. Interviews elicited the fact that he was of Greek origin, was American-born, had a French wife, and wished to work in the British Commonwealth.

The Research Station was established in a converted school at Waterloo

[4] See Chapter Seventeen.

near Carapichaima (remember that Carib-Indian name?), houses were built for the Vlitos family and for the cadre of specialists recruited by the new Director, and by 1958 the Station had begun to take a grip on some of the problems. The Station was encouraged to publish its results at regular intervals, quarterly and annually and in special papers. It began to make a name for itself not only in Trinidad and the West Indies but in the scientific world generally.

But externally things were changing as pressure grew for the break-up of large estates, particularly those held by non-nationals.

IV

'A subtle chain of countless rings
The next unto the farthest brings.'
(R. W. Emerson, 1805–1882)

Countless rings should not imply ever-decreasing circles whose end result is unpleasant. And by coincidence there were now quite a few members of the Tate & Lyle Board who had begun to question the balance of the Company's research effort. Was it right to do fundamental research in a largely rural area and yet confine work in the metropolitan country to rather more limited studies? What about new uses for sugar, substances which could be derived from that potentially versatile sucrose molecule?

At the same time it was known that Chuck Vlitos, as an American citizen, was a little uncertain about his long term future in independent Trinidad. It was at length decided that there must be a shuffle, that the central research effort would be concentrated in Britain, and that the job of organizing this should be done by Vlitos.

It was not an easy decision for it would disappoint senior men of long service with the company, but it commanded general acceptance. A number of research specialists, chiefly expatriates with the required scientific disciplines, accompanied Vlitos from Trinidad to Ravensbourne. Others, nearly all Trinidadians, stayed behind to continue the agricultural research effort in the island. At Ravensbourne there began the long, intricate business of integration, of grafting new lines of research on to existing branches, or changing of direction and of building multi-disciplinary teams to tackle a whole range of projects.

The development was begun of new sucrose-based materials as surfactants, as intermediates for making resin polymers, as agricultural chemicals, pharmaceuticals and food additives. Some of them might one day become competitive with similar substances based on petroleum, if that raw material became costlier. It was to begin to do so in 1973, quite suddenly and unexpectedly, as a result of O.P.E.C. and it is in any case limited, because it is a fossil fuel whereas sucrose is renewable annually since it is the product of solar energy trapped by plants.

Gums, such as the alginates and xanthans, which are used extensively in the paper, food and pharmaceutical industries, were until recently extracted from natural but limited sources such as seaweed. Microbial fermentation can not only produce the existing ones but can offer new areas for exploitation.

There is a demand for high-intensity sweeteners, many times as sweet as sugar, for special purposes. Some of these were reported to occur in certain plants growing wild in West Africa of which little was known. They might be of use as replacements for chemical sweeteners such as cyclamates, but they would need extraction, and toxicological testing for side effects, and the plants themselves were timid creatures. The study of the basic process of photosynthesis, if continued, might yield great benefit to companies in the Tate & Lyle group engaged in agro-industrial development. Natural substances called enzymes are involved as catalysts essential to the metabolic processes in man, animals and plants. Enzymes can also be used in industry. Their production and separation is economically desirable but presents complex problems.

Food manufacturers use much sugar, and may use new forms of mix and new products associated with it. Their doing so depends on precise and dependable formulations. At the same time sugar technology, highly developed as it already is, needs constant study.

All these and many other new possibilities require highly sophisticated analytical techniques. Analysis in the past has been a slow, laborious business. It could be made rapid and reliable and the results could be collated by the use of mini-computers.

These kinds of work demand time and demand 'patient' money, i.e. they cannot be expected to pay for themselves rapidly. They begin in the laboratory but in order to establish their economic potential, they must be further studied under pilot-scale industrial conditions.

On average it takes seven to ten years from the genesis of an idea or the discovery of a phenomenon to its exploitation on an industrial scale, and if three projects out of ten are successful it is surprising. Pharmaceutical firms are accustomed to examining thousands of products a year without finding one that is of use. (Hence the high cost of new preparations.)

A promising early discovery under Bill North's regime in 1967 was a new process for decolourizing sugar solutions, which could be easily incorporated into existing refinery processes. Its development was led by Mike Bennett, and it involved the addition of a special substance christened 'Talofloc' which–just as bullocks' blood did a century and more ago–precipitates impurities and colouring matter. From this, whole new systems of clarification and a series of new clarifying agents were developed–all given names beginning with Tal–from Tate & Lyle. The technology was later to be applied to the recovery of sugar from waste confectionery and from citrus waste and to the treatment of effluent from fruit, vegetable and fish-processing plants.

It seemed desirable that the discovery should be carried through to development and marketing by its originator and Mike Bennett was given the job of doing so. If he succeeded he would provide an indication of how Research and Development could, instead of being some back-room, inexplicable Thing, bring in the berries. There was little doubt that Mike would succeed, and he and his team had by 1977 done so. Talo systems are in use all over the world, and are a considerable profit-centre.

His replacement was Fraser Imrie, a Scot, built on the Large Economy Size, who joined from Manbré and Garton.

While the Talo processes were already in a position to advance rapidly, the new research teams began work on seven of the projects mentioned above, selected after much rigorous examination. It soon became clear that, useful as Ravensbourne had been, it was not ideal as a Research Centre. There is, moreover, a psychological factor which affects many research scientists. They may feel that unless they are in some way associated with the academic world, they are cut off from their natural habitat.

For these two reasons Vlitos, together with the two Board members responsible, decided to see whether some University with strong science faculties would be prepared to agree to the establishment of the Tate & Lyle Research function as an adjunct. Numerous Universities were visited. Most were friendly, but few had suitable space. In the end it was Reading which seemed to offer the best possibilities.

The Vice-Chancellor and the Council of the University were most helpful. They would erect a building to the requirements of Tate & Lyle and lease it to the Company, for their statutes would not permit ownership of property on the Campus by an outsider. But they would need backing from the Company for a loan of £500,000 or so to cover the cost. Those who believed in research on the board of Tate & Lyle decided they must go ahead. But the firm was having one of those difficult years. Those who did not believe, or believed but only just, were against. There were also those who believed you could turn research on and off as in running a bath and that now it was time to turn off.

The University authorities had their own problems. It was during that period when the hirsute young were squeaking and gibbering and demonstrating and sitting-in everywhere. (A connoisseur might have thought it like a little e'er the mightiest Julius fell. Ah, it seems like yesterday, but it is, of course, to-day.) At Reading, a drop-out undergraduate was leading a sit-in in the Vice-Chancellor's office.

But even with such sundry tiresomenesses well inside the doorstep, the University kept its word. It went further. This was among the first, if not *the* first example of a University seeking to cooperate with an Industrial Company for the benefit of all. The Bursar, the late John Carpenter, persuaded the Senior Common Room to offer membership to Tate & Lyle Research Staff.

The non-believers on the Board accepted that the company was committed and the Finance Director's conscience was assuaged by the discovery that the Ravensbourne site, purchased for £22,000 in 1947, could now, with planning permission for housing on about half its 35 acres, be sold for ten times that.

After much time-consuming argument, the move went ahead. The new building, called the Philip Lyle Memorial Research Laboratory after one who had been a believer, was officially opened by the Chancellor of Reading University, Lord Sherfield, in June 1969. It was not too long before the Ranks of Tuscany began to dilate on what wisdom they had shown in pushing through the move to Reading of Tate & Lyle Group Research.

Now for Development, which was still embryonic. By 1974 the need for premises for pilot scale production for the first new projects was recognized and a 40,000 square foot factory in the industrial zone of Reading was purchased and equipped. By 1977 it had a staff of forty. Success with the Talo series of products–now bringing in £1 million a year–was being followed by success with the surfactant based on sugar, 'TAL', which had been tested on the market. The production of Xanthan and Alginate gums was being developed in partnership with the Hercules Company, of the U.S.A. The manufacture of microbial protein from waste for animal feed was being tested in Belize and interest in the process, designed for village-scale low-technology use was becoming widespread, particularly in countries dependent on low-cost protein feed. On a more sophisticated plane and in cooperation with one of the Group's subsidiaries, Farrow Effluent Engineering and a confectionery manufacturing company, George Barrett of Sheffield, a commercial plant was being erected to produce 3–400 tons of protein a year from the factory's carbohydrate waste which was causing a pollution problem.

It all seems a long way from sugar production and refining. Yet there is a link. The result for sugar refining of the entry of Britain into the E.E.C. was a surplus of capacity and by the early 1980s, this would affect Liverpool, the place where Henry Tate began over a century ago and an area of chronic high unemployment. The loss of jobs in refining might be to some extent mitigated by the decision to construct a £12 million plant for the manufacture of new products.

At a time when Tate & Lyle is faced by consolidation and adjustment, the commercial exploitation of the results of R. & D. can yield clues as to the future. It can of course only provide some of the answers but it does offer the policy-makers a degree of flexibility and it is dangerous to neglect it.

It is not, however, merely the direct results of the work and their potential which count, important as these are. The 'image' of the Company, if that is the correct P/R word, is improved. It is observed to be not just a slightly stuffy old Sugar Firm but one also concerned with All That.

CHAPTER TWENTY-SEVEN

The E.E.C. and After
—Manbré & Garton

I

'True wisdom lies in masterful administration of the unforeseen.'
(Robert Bridges, 1844–1930)

That doesn't sound like poetry, although it came from the pen of a Poet Laureate. Of course, one sees what the fellow meant, though it reads rather like a local electricity board's version of 'The Charge of the Light Brigade'. It has a bearing, however, on what follows, for the beginning of the decade 1970–80 saw Britain about to enter the E.E.C. President de Gaulle's long dominance of France and of the Community of the Six was drawing to its close. At a General Election in July 1970 a Conservative Government committed to Britain's entry was elected and the British Prime Minister and de Gaulle's successor, Monsieur Pompidou, had reached at least a tacit understanding.

For Tate & Lyle and Manbré and Garton,[1] now the only sugar refiners in Britain, the fact of Britain's entry would mean considerable changes. Membership of the *Comité Européen des Fabricants de Sucre* and association in the Say venture had provided Tate & Lyle with a considerable insight into the workings of the E.E.C.'s Common Agricultural Policy as it evolved. Designed to suit countries whose agricultural populations were proportionately much higher than that of Britain—13 per cent, in France, for example, as against 3 per cent in Britain—the C.A.P. would mean that home grown sugar production would increase at the expense of the refining of imported raw cane sugar. Owing moreover to the fact that the Community's calculations were based on home-grown beet sugar, the margin permitted for refining seemed likely to be seriously eroded for most forms of sugar other than cubes, for which the market in Britain is tiny. There were many other lesser but still difficult technical and semi-political problems.

For some two years, in 1970, Tate & Lyle had had a special Standing Committee, set up under the Chairmanship of Peter Runge. Meeting informally twice a month or more frequently if required, it included two other members of the Main Board and members of staff with special knowledge, Norman Cullen, the Secretary and Director of T.L.R.; Michael Attfield who was responsible for the purchases of raw sugar; John

[1] See page 302.

Graham, a specialist on E.E.C. Regulations, and others.

In the summer of 1970 Peter Runge died. He was only just over sixty and, although he had been ill for some months, he had not allowed it to prevent him working. Then, one July day, he rang to say he wouldn't be in to meet some French visitors for lunch as he was 'feeling a little ropey'. A few days later he was dead. A most influential figure in the Company for nearly forty years his sudden going was difficult to believe. Hard-working, sometimes nervous because a perfectionist, kindly, amusing, it was ages before one could get used to going past that well-known door and not hearing that well-known voice calling one in – for a chat, for some information, to share some bit of news or a story. He was marvellous at letting his hair down while never letting himself be shifted from the job in hand, whether it was the problems at a Refinery, the Mr. Cube Campaign, organizing a Limbo dance on some beach in Trinidad, or persuading the Company to subscribe to the University of the West Indies and thereafter helping to smooth out local problems. He touched life at so many points and illuminated them all. It is good to think that besides being remembered so well in Tate & Lyle, one of his many activities external to the Company is commemorated by the naming of the Industrial Society's[2] Headquarters House after him, and that one of his sons, Charles, has created for himself in Tate & Lyle the sort of niche his father would have wanted for him.

What had been the Peter-Tony Committee was now most ably chaired by another Vice-Chairman, Tony Tate, the Bard, and it became known henceforth as the T.T. Committee.

The discussions in Brussels were on a Government to Commission level, and the British principal in sugar matters was the Ministry of Agriculture, Fisheries and Food. Tate & Lyle Directors and specialists of course had access to the sugar division of the E.E.C. Secretariat at Berleymont and to individual Commissioners, but could not themselves negotiate on matters of high policy, but merely advise. It became clear that after accession Britain would no longer be able to import raw sugar from Australia (350,000 tons a year) for the Ministry had early conceded that Australia, as an independent, highly developed country, could not expect the same treatment as the developing countries of the Commonwealth.

Contacts with the Ministry were kept up. These seemed to find the unrelenting pressure from the Refiners somewhat irksome, and they were also under extreme pressure from the Commonwealth Producers who regarded as insufficient a pledge by the E.E.C. that it would *avoir à coeur* (keep in its heart) the needs of the developing countries whose economies were so largely dependent on sugar.

For the Refiners the reduction in imports – even if the tonnages from the developing countries were ensured – would mean over-capacity. Tate & Lyle had already begun to demolish Plaistow Wharf. But still the Refineries in Scotland and in Liverpool would be over-capacity, and these two areas

[2] Formerly the Industrial Welfare Society.

were politically sensitive and suffered normally from unemployment above the national average. Unions representing Tate & Lyle employees formed an Action Committee which made independent representations to the Commission in Brussels. (This was a curious historical parallel to a Liverpool working-men's Anti-Sugar-Bounty Committee of the 1880s and 90s.)

In the end the E.E.C. recognized what was, as it were, an appeal *ad misericordiam* and accepted that as 'The Rich' they could not deprive 'The Poor' of an outlet. Quotas for the importation of raw cane sugar into the enlarged Community were proposed for some forty-two developing African, Caribbean and Pacific countries, including certain former French and other European colonies, and this decision was embodied, with others, in a Convention signed at Lomé in February 1975.

When the time came, Britain was accorded a Transition Period during which to adjust her supply arrangements, from Accession in early 1974 until 1975. During this time there were two General Elections. After the first, in February 1974, the Labour Party formed a minority Government. Then in October at a further slightly opportunist Election, they achieved a small overall majority.

From the point of view simply of sugar, the political situation was if anything improved. Mr. Fred Peart[3] (Lab.) became Minister instead of Mr. Joseph Godber (Cons.). Peart had been in the job before and knew it. He was sensitive to the needs of both the Commonwealth Producers and the Refiners and their employees. Indeed, before going to some particularly difficult negotiations, he received a personal message from Mr. Cube saying: 'Good Luck, Fred.'

The end of the Transition Period coincided, as luck would have it, with a sudden and acute world shortage of sugar. For some fourteen years, thanks to a steady tendency for average world consumption to exceed average production, world stocks were low. There was then a fall in production not only of cane sugar but also of beet sugar–particularly in the U.S.S.R.–due to climates throughout the world. Amongst other effects this tempted the A.C.P. and particularly the Commonwealth Producers, now liberated from the Commonwealth Sugar Agreement, to demand for their sugar the equivalent of the temporarily high price prevailing in the tiny World Market–it reached over £600 a ton for a brief period. They even threatened to withold supplies unless their demands were met.

Faced by a situation in which Britain might apparently be without sugar–housewives were beginning to hoard it in desperation–with the Community bound by its Regulations, and with Britain half-in and half-out of the E.E.C., the Minister had an appalling time. Legally and politically he was the person responsible for the procurement of supplies, but his Ministry was neither equipped nor staffed to obtain them. Both Commonwealth and home-grown sugars were short. Some refined sugar was imported from the E.E.C. but the price was higher than the

[3] Now Lord Peart.

customer was used to. After much consideration the Government, with the agreement of the European Commission, decided to buy African-Caribbean-Pacific sugar at £250 per ton and make it available under subsidy to the home trade consumers for the period April 1975 to March 1976. The Refiners, under competition from E.E.C. sugars, and with their normal supply arrangements distorted, had to work at below capacity and, within the limits imposed by the Price Code, could not recover their full costs.

Later they had, in order to obtain guaranteed supplies of A.C.P. sugar, to negotiate–at their own cost–special five-year contracts at premium prices. It was a nightmare period. It was found by Tate & Lyle that strict adherence to the Price Code would automatically give them an undeserved advantage of about £6 million. They pointed this out to the Ministry, who quite rightly withheld payment–and this sum has never been paid.

The tangle was still incompletely resolved a year later when the House of Commons Public Accounts Committee went into the matter.[4] The Ministry was vulnerable to criticisms for vast amounts of public money were involved. Both they and Tate & Lyle had done their best, and the two parties had cooperated in trying to ensure that payments were due and proper. The Ministry did not carry sufficient staff to deal with the matter and made use of the staff of the Raw Sugar Purchasing Department of Tate & Lyle when they needed outside help in what was a most complex affair.

It is probably best to leave the whole issue to be investigated and reported on by some future Edward Gibbon. But there was, associated with it, a most unusual lapse by *The Times*, which in its turn awakened in the Deep Left a Pavlovian reaction. Mr. Maurice Corina, whose articles in the Thunderer one usually reads with respect, published early in 1977 a piece based on the report of the Public Accounts Committee, appearing to suggest that during this intensely complicated period, Tate & Lyle had kept two sets of books and had unreasonably made money thereby.[5] The imputation was later withdrawn with an apology and it need not be further pursued.

In a strange way this was cosy. It meant that that old battle long ago has been worth while. In general, the country seemed by the late 1970s to have had enough of nationalization and the extremists were feeling their position a little. Mr. Cube, nearly thirty years of age, was still a youthful, vigorous figure.

Which leads us conveniently to the next 'Epi' as people say of T.V. soap opera.

[4] See Report–Appropriated Accounts 1975–76. Class II Vote 4 paras 127 onwards.

[5] Other newspapers, finding the business a little too complex were more cautious. *The Economist* carried a query 'A large gift to Mr. Cube?' but was otherwise careful to print the facts.

II
'Thrice MacBreath hath T.V. time,
Thrice and once MacPuff hath blown.'
(Shakespeare Tate, c. 1974)

Unable any longer to stand the Second Best Bed at Stratford-upon-Avon, F. H. (Shakespeare) Tate was once more on hand with a new Historical-Pastoral-Comical Piece from his 2nd Folio. The manuscript is, like the earlier one, undated but internal evidence indicates composition during the Period of National Staggers between spring 1974 and ditto 1975.

The Dramatis Personae had changed since 1949, and now included such people as John and Saxon–successors to Henry and Abram, and Wedgie, Footie and Healie–'three whorelocks with one left wing between them'. There was also a Kearn or Gallowglass (a Ministry warrior apt to use strong language) and a crowned Scilly islander with his tongue in his cheek. The last, an apparition, leaves the stage with the injunction: 'I pray you, let not noble Marcia starve', which effectively dates the piece.

A Monarch (unseen), commenting on the successful outcome of a battle between John and Saxon and the Powers of Darkness, concludes after offering Saxon four Windsor Greys to drag his bicycle, with the words:

'A great day too, for Philip and for me.

At last we can have sugar in our tea.'

We are, as the original Shakespeare has pointed out, such stuff as dreams are made on, but reality at last began to take over in 1975, as it must occasionally even in Whitehall. There was going to be too much sugar-refining capacity in Britain, it was whispered, then mentioned over the cups of tea, in the loo, and occasionally, perhaps, in the intervals of other discussions.

Well someone has to refine the stuff, but who? Ah!

There had been discussions, friendly or otherwise. The Government were now about to collar, all undeserving, the benefit of Mr. Philip Snowden's 1922 decision and that of Major Walter Elliott in 1936 on home-grown sugar production. Of the two Refiners left, Manbré's were largely, though not of course entirely, dependent on Tate & Lyle facilities for their raw material. In Liverpool the Sankey refinery received most of its raw sugar via the Tate & Lyle Huskisson Dock. In London, Hammersmith, well up-river, could not accommodate ocean-going bulk-carriers. In Greenock, Westburn used Walkers' facilities.

All kinds of solutions were thought of. The Ministry, either trying to be helpful or hoping to dodge the issue, arranged for a specialist firm of consultants to go into the matter confidentially. The consultants came. They stayed, they left with the information, and, of course, a fee–paid by the Companies–but with no solution.

In the end, the only workable one was for Tate & Lyle to acquire
Manbré & Garton and do their best to sort the matter out. But there were
three impediments. First, who wanted any more refining capacity,
particularly when other opportunities were offering for diversification into
businesses that would bear fruit in the 1980s? Second, what about
Monopoly and all that–in a sense a true monopoly, not one of seven à la
Charles Smith (c. 1940)? Third, what would Manbré and Garton say?

The first question answered itself. There was nothing else to be done.
After very delicate discussions between Tate & Lyle, the Ministry of
Agriculture Fisheries & Food and sundry other new and not entirely
necessary Government bodies, H.M.G. tacitly accepted that this was one
of those cases of 'when is a monopoly not a monopoly'?

That left question number three, which was in most ways the most
difficult. What would Manbré & Garton say? Relationships for years had
been cordial. The older families in Manbré's had gone, but there were
many people, Kerrs, Martineaus and others, who were involved now in
Manbré and were family friends. It was pretty awful. Understandably the
Chairman of Manbré, Frank Smith, and the Chief Executive, Alastair
Annand, were not disposed to give way without a fight. At length terms
satisfactory to the shareholders and undertakings satisfactory to the
Manbré employees were agreed and late in 1976 the merger took place.

Of course there were misgivings. There always are when there is a
merger. At the time of writing these are still being resolved. As to the
customers, the Associations representing the chief sugar-using industries
also had misgivings about losing choice of supplier.

Tate & Lyle were anxious to reassure them, and the Government, early
in September 1976, endeavoured to appease these bodies, for they wished,
again with varying degrees of enthusiasm, to refer the merger to the
Monopolies and Mergers Commission, and the Government wished to
avoid this. A Customer Relations Unit was established inside the enlarged
Tate & Lyle, and an independent committee formed by the Government
to look into such complaints as might be referred to it by the Company's
customers.

It is time to look briefly at Messrs. Manbré & Garton. High time.

III
Monsieur Manbré and Mr. Garton (and don't forget Mr. Berry).

Why, it may be asked, leave it so late? Why have they not up to now
been mentioned? Who was Manbré? What about Garton? Why this
neglect? All right, relax. There is a sound reason. Distinguished as these
gents were they were not fully associated with crystalline sucrose, sugar if
you prefer it, *until just before the Second World War.*

The Firm has a long and interesting history, associated with three
names–Manbré, Garton (of course) and Berry.

The Manbré family–also spelt Membré, Membrez and even Membrer (c. 1506)–hailed from Valenciennes in the old, northern French province of Hainaut. The East London district of Hainault to which this gave its name, is spelt differently. It was called after Queen Philippa of Hainault, the plump little wife of King Edward III and mother of the Black Prince, who also came from those parts. But her arrival in England ante-dated that of Alexandre Manbré the First by five centuries. Hence the different spelling.

Alexandre, born on February 19th, 1825, was the son of a *cultivateur* (a long French word for farmer), Paul Ignace Manbré who, like many farmers (or *cultivateurs*) in those days, was probably a maltster and brewer of beer. Alexandre seems to have been an inventive chap, and this is probably why, some time between 1855 and 1857, he came to England. Tradition used to have it that he did so because, France being a wine-drinking country, there was no scope for his ideas, which had to do with the production of brewers' sugar–maltose–from starch. But tradition, as so often, is probably mistaken, for this is not true of Hainaut, where the inhabitants tend to tuck into the beer and there have always been plenty of breweries. The more likely explanation is that in early nineteenth-century France patents were hard to protect, whereas in England the Law–for some obscure reason known perhaps to people like the Master of the Rolls–was on the side of the inventor. And Alexandre needed protection for his patents, for he was by no means a financial whizz-kid.

Certainly he applied for two patents in London in 1858: 'for the manufacturing of colouring spirits from the sugar of potatoes, known as glucose', and 'for the extracting of the saccharine matter in malt . . . for the purpose of brewing and distilling'. His name was spelt Mambré in the Census of 1861. No doubt this was his fault for being a Foreigner and having a difficult name. However he was a tenacious character and continued to insist on 'Manbré'.

On January 1st, 1854, just about when Henry T. and Abram L. were getting under way, Glucose Sugar and Colouring Ltd. was registered as a Company, with A. Manbré as a Director, a nominal capital of £75,000 and a mixed and unlikely bag of shareholders including three army Captains, a dentist, a foreman and 'a servant in Cheltenham'. It produced glucose, starch, gum and, of course, colouring matter, and bought patents from A. Manbré. The factory was at 9 Booth Street, Spitalfields, which is not as rude as it sounds, spital being cockney for hospital. Within two years the Company was in financial trouble and had to be rescued by men of good will.

By now Alexandre Manbré (Jr.), son of the above, had arrived with wife and little ones, followed at intervals by brothers Paul, Ernest and Alfred, of whom we do not hear much, for Paul eventually returned to France and the other two went to Liverpool and set up the Liverpool Saccharine Co. (which later failed).

The two chief backers of Manbré Saccharine were a Mr. William McNeill of Manchester and a Mr. Theodore Andreas of Lime Street, London. The latter owned a site at Hammersmith which he leased to the company at £400 p.a. To this then relatively idyllic spot, early in 1876, the Booth Street plant, valued at £30,000, was transferred. Most of the shareholders were brewers–among others, members of the Courage family–and the nominal capital was £100,000. The Hammersmith site was on a farm belonging to Brandenburgh House (shades of that old German Archduke for whom J. S. Bach composed all those Concertos).

There were by then some 300 British companies making brewing sugar, most of them, like, for example, Garton's, attached to a brewery. The Lyles were also among these companies and their product, called Saccharum, a nearly solid 'fondant', was apparently profitable but it was given up, according to John Lyle (father of Oliver, and grandfather of John Oliver), because in order to sell it, the competition had to be bought off by lavishly entertaining the sons of brewers with hunting, shooting and fishing.

The Lyles may have found Saccharum a profitable but philosophically distasteful product, and abandoned it, but during the same period, from 1875 on, another of the 298 Companies, Johnson's Saccharum Co. Ltd. had been undergoing, at Carpenter's Road, Stratford, E., just up the way from Plaistow Wharf and Silvertown, a somewhat bumpy development, similar to Manbré's. By 1905 it had likewise run into difficulties.

This year saw the death of Alexandre Manbré and the appearance of Mr. Albert Berry on the glucose scene. Born on April 4th, 1875 the latter had been trained in the laboratories of United Alkali (now part of I.C.I.) Berry had done well for himself and was, in 1905, looking for a business of his own. He was then only thirty.

In 1906 he bought Johnson's Saccharum and founded Sugar & Malt Products Ltd., which prospered thereafter. By 1916 he was serving on a Ministry of Food Committee formed during the War to ration sugar to the brewers. It was thus that he met people from Manbré, who eventually offered him a job as Managing Director, when in 1919 a Committee of Manbré shareholders was endeavouring to salvage the Hammersmith Company. He refused the offer and instead proposed purchasing Manbré Saccharum himself. His proposal was accepted and with a bridging loan from the Midland Bank, he founded Manbré Saccharine and Sugar & Malt Products Ltd., beginning a new era at Hammersmith.

The Manbré's had begun by now to fade out of the picture and Albert Berry became the driving force. Under his highly competent leadership the new Company did well. In 1922 Eustace, his eldest son, joined the Company, followed in 1928 by the younger, Derbe. In some ways, with his flair, tenacity and toughness, Albert seems to have been rather like Abram Lyle III. He had taken up the Manbré inventions, used some and discarded others, such as Karamello for preventing fogginess in photographic plates. He had invented Candy Sugar, made by pouring partly inverted sugar into trays to crystallize, or by letting the crystals form on strings. It was like sugar candy but quicker to produce and was found to taste nice in coffee. Coffee crystals indeed are still supplied inter alia for Buckingham Palace, By Order of Her Majesty the Queen.

All this, however, availed little when the Depression came in 1931, and the Company like so many others faced a cutback in production and the need to lay people off. Mr. Snowden, then Chancellor again, had just put another penny on the pint of beer and brewers would use less brewing sugar. But, musing one day on the banks of the Thames, Albert Berry observed Mauritius Plantation Whites being delivered in sacks to a newly opened jam factory belonging to some people called J. Lyons, alongside his works. Anxious to keep going and save jobs, he approached Lyons' with the idea that he could pump liquid sugar in from next door, thus saving the customer the cost of dissolving and heating. His offer was accepted and in a short while he built up a special service to this nearby client, and later expanded it to suit others further afield.

Berry's successes had already made an impression on the Garton family, brewers who had a brewing-sugar factory at Battersea, known to its more snobbish inhabitants as 'South Chelsea'. The Chairman, Sir Richard Garton had been ill in 1926, and offered 'little Berry', as he called him, the business of brewing-sugar production for £2·3 million. The firm became Manbré & Garton Ltd. Sir Richard retired in 1927 and after a brief spell the Gartons withdrew from active participation.

During the late 1930s expansion continued and an increasing range of products was made available to sugar-using industries. There was an attempt to produce cane sugar in Kenya but this failed, owing to drought and to the attentions of plagues of locusts, attracted like any sensible creature to something sweet, but a confounded nuisance. At this time a South African Company, African Products Manufacturing Co., Ltd. at Germiston in the Transvaal, processing maize into starch and liquid glucose, had run into difficulties and appealed for help. Eustace Berry went and undertook a successful reorganization, for which service Manbré & Garton were given shares in lieu of a fee. Eventually the Transvaal company became a wholly owned subsidiary of Manbré's. In 1935 the Sankey Sugar Company of Earlstown, Lancashire, was acquired, and Manbré & Garton at last became sugar refiners proper.

During the Second World War the Hammersmith site was less knocked about by Hitler than the Tate & Lyle Refineries down-river or in Scotland. The only damage suffered was the result of blast from a stick of bombs falling nearby, which blew out windows.

After the War, further expansion in refining took place. Martineaus' Refinery in Whitechapel was acquired in 1961. The remaining starch conversion plant at Hammersmith was dismantled, part being scrapped and part shifted to Garton's at Battersea, where starch operations were concentrated. This made room for the installation of sugar refinery equipment to accommodate the Martineaus' output.

The venture into the production of maize starch in Africa led to technical developments and in 1962 to the acquisition of James Laing, Sons & Co. of Manchester, who were well-established producers of dextrines and, to an agreement with the National Starch and Chemical Corporation of the U.S.A. for the use of their patents and knowhow for the production and sale of starch specialities in the U.K. and elsewhere. 1962 also saw the acquisition of one of the two remaining sugar refineries on the Clyde, Westburn at Greenock, and by the 1970s Manbré & Garton were refining over 400,000 tons of sugar a year, thus becoming the third of Britain's sugar companies after Tate & Lyle and the British Sugar Corporation.

Manbré & Garton was now the holding company for sixteen subsidiaries, with a range of products, solid and liquid, from starch to packeted refined sugars, and Candy Sugar to liquid glucose.

The Company had changed much over the years. The inventive but never entirely successful Manbré's had gone. The Gartons had briefly contributed their influence and left. Albert Berry had been followed by his sons, but Derbe Berry had retired in 1968.

With the acquisition of Westburn, the Kerr family, descendants of John Kerr, Abram Lyle's friend and partner, had become part of Manbré's. David became Managing Director of Manbré Sugars and his cousin Walter Director of the Manbré Scottish transport fleet. Both had been trained at Plaistow Wharf Refinery. When Martineaus' was acquired, William Martineau, a descendant of Gaston Martineau, the refugee Huguenot surgeon of 1686, joined Manbré's, becoming Brewing Sales Manager and a Director of a number of the Companies in the Group.

In 1976 Manbré & Garton had acquired Fowler Limited, a small compact cane sugar refinery, on the banks of the River Lea at Bow Creek, Blackwall, London. Fowler's was established by two brothers, James and Alexander, in 1871 in Glasgow as commission agents specializing in molasses imports. Moving to London in 1875 they closed their Glasgow office in 1877, acquiring the present site in 1881 and erecting buildings, plant, and a wharf for £3,200.

In 1899, when it was making a profit of about £1,750 per annum, it was incorporated as a Limited Liability Company, three large brewing Companies taking substantial shareholdings. Over the years thereafter it established a range of products – Invert Sugars, Caramel, Treacle, Golden Syrup etc., the best known being 'West Indies' Treacle which was popular in the retail trade.

Like Tate & Lyle, Manbré & Garton have a record of long service among their employees. Families like Bose, Mayer, Kennedy, Streamer and many others have served at Hammersmith and Battersea for generations and the refineries at Greenock and Earlstown retain a similar family atmosphere.

CHAPTER TWENTY-EIGHT

South Africa and All That

A Home on the Range
(Song of the Middle West 0000–1890)

Pliny was nearly right about Africa. A new possibility presented itself in 1967, this time in Natal, which as the clued-up reader will be aware, is a part of the Union of South Africa – the most English part. Sugar cane has been grown there since the early 1850s,[1] on the gently undulating country which extends north and south, 'looking lazy at the sea', like the dusky lady by the Old Moulmein Pagoda. The soil is good, and the climate favourable. There are well-marked seasons and in the cold period – from April/May onwards, for this is the Southern Hemisphere – the night temperature falls obediently to ripen the cane.

About 70 per cent of total sugar production is split between two major groups, the Hulett-Tongaat interest in the north and the C. & G. Smith group in the south. The rest in 1967 was looked after by smaller sugar-millers, of whom the largest, with about 10 per cent, was the Illovo Sugar Company.

Tate & Lyle had for a long time had somewhat tenuous connections in South Africa. Since 1907 Lyle's Golden Syrup had been sold by J. Solomon & Sons. The chief customers were the Kaffirs who in some cases had found means of converting it into beer. Leonard Lyle was on the Board of Sir John L. Hulett & Co., Ltd., being for a time succeeded there by his son Charles. T.L.T.S. had been called upon by Hulett's for technical advice on a new sugar refinery in Durban. Douglas Saunders, Chairman of Tongaat, and his son Chris were old friends. Chris, indeed, had spent a year at Plaistow as a trainee.

The Illovo Company had three sugar mills, largely supplied by cane farmers, one at Illovo itself near the coast just south of Durban, the other two, Noodsberg and Doornkop, inland. There had been pessimistic and optimistic periods during the history of South African sugar. During a recent period of optimism (1963–64) Noodsberg, capable of producing 100,000 tons of sugar a year, had been built with finance largely from bank loans. Illovo was older – indeed a little old-fashioned. Doornkop was a Shangri-la of a place, in a charming valley, but, because of its situation, it could not expand. After 1964 the price of sugar fell from £100 a ton on the world market to £12. Illovo Sugar owed 18 million Rand to sundry banks,

[1] David Livingstone, the explorer and missionary, ordered a mill from Mirrlees Tait in 1858 as a present for a Chief in the Makololo district of Natal.

equivalent then to £9 million, and could see no immediate way out of the impasse. Taking the children away from school, as Henry Tate had once had to do, or ceasing to buy an evening paper, as John Lyle the First had done, would not have contributed much towards servicing the loan. Even increasing the years of ratooning the cane and thereby avoiding the cost of replanting was only a temporary expedient and could not be continued for ever.

David Haysom, the Chairman of Illovo, a former R.A.F. pilot with a splendid war record, and Olliver Pearce, decided to approach Tate & Lyle. The majority shareholders of Illovo were the General Mining Corporation of South Africa. Themselves not sugar men, they were disenchanted with an investment which had not for some time even paid its preference shareholders and seemed unlikely to. They were relieved at Haysom's initiative.

The offer was tempting to Tate & Lyle in some ways, less so in others. The shares were cheap. The other two main production groups would welcome an outside interest which would demonstrate to Government that there was no cartel. Potentially the Company was profitable. Domestic demand was high and world demand would one day recover.

On the other hand there were negative considerations. There was that enormous loan. There had been the difficulties in sorting out the pieces when the Rhodesian Federation broke up. There had been the long-drawn-out saga in Jamaica. There was the burden of being associated with Apartheid and all that. Sterling was going through its problems. (This was the 'Pound-in-your-Pocket' epoch.) At the practical level the acquisition would consist of Illovo—in need of modernization; Noodsberg—short of cane supplies because the farmers were not sure it was a going concern; and Doornkop—incapable of expansion at a time when either you expanded or went under.

Tate & Lyle's financial advisers were dubious. 'Go into *that*' they said in effect, 'and you'll have to sink even more money. You'd be off your Collegiate trolley.' No doubt much the same had been said in the 1880s, to Abram Lyle and Henry Tate. Nevertheless, discussions took place during 1967 and 1968. Influential voices in the Tate & Lyle Politburo and on the Board were against. It was probably Ian Lyle who swung opinion in favour. He had a long track-record of being right.

So in early 1969 it was finally decided that Illovo Sugars should be acquired. William Booth, the Finance Director of Tate & Lyle, was asked to be the new Chairman, and Jim Hobbs was to go on the Board of Illovo. And it was decided that John Willsher, tempered by many a problem in Zambia and Rhodesia, should be Managing Director. This inevitably meant some departures from the existing Illovo Board, painful, horrid for those who go and for those who have to insist. All behaved very well under considerable personal strain.

That left four major things to sort out. First there was the enormous sum owed to the banks. Barclays', the Standard Bank, and the rest insisted that these should now be covered by a Tate & Lyle guarantee. Second, there was the required injection of a further 3 million Rand by Tate & Lyle and how it was to be recouped. Third, there was the fundamental need to improve performance in production. Fourth, there was the rule under which the Reserve Bank of South Africa was not allowed to permit an overseas investor to hold more than 50 per cent of the shares in a South African company which was heavily in debt to local banks.

One and two were dependent on three being solved. The Reserve Bank gave a five year dispensation, during which time most of the loans must be paid off.

Gradually productivity improved. On the financial side the Reserve Bank trusted Tate & Lyle. At a time when share prices justified it, a Rights issue was made which would in due course ensure dividends to both preference and ordinary shareholders. It also left Tate & Lyle with just less than a 50 per cent holding which satisfied the Reserve Bank. The local loans were paid off in three years, and Tate & Lyle's in another three.

By 1975 Illovo Sugars were producing about 180,000 tons a year, and paying shareholders a reasonable dividend. At the same time they were taking better than average care of the ordinary, silent majority of employees. In 1972–3 there was a great deal of emotive outcry about British firms in South Africa who were alleged to be paying their African employees at a rate below what was described as a Poverty Datum Line. It is always easy to be in the wrong when pilloried by some academic think-tank. As a result of the outcry a House of Commons Sub-Committee sent for data and for individuals. Tate and Lyle were found to be good employers.

In any case, the Company is no longer involved, for in September 1977 an offer was received and accepted for Illovo Sugar Limited. Tate & Lyle no longer produce sugar in South Africa.

CHAPTER TWENTY-NINE

Where Are We Now?

We are the pilgrims, Master. We shall go
Always a little further. It may be
Beyond that last blue mountain bathed with snow,
Across that angry or the glimmering sea,
High on a throne or guarded in a cave
There lives some prophet who can understand
Why man were born. But, surely we are brave
That take the Golden Road to Smarkand.
(James Elroy Flecker, 1884–1915)

Samarkand is a not particularly attractive town somewhere in the middle of the south east of the U.S.S.R. It could as easily be Silvertown, E.16, Cartdyke Street (Greenock), Chisenhale Street (Liverpool), Monymusk (Jamaica), Orange Walk (Belize), Ndola (Zambia), Bulawayo (Rhodesia), Chalons-sur-Marne (France), Chatham (Ontario), or many other places. And the Road is by no means Golden.

But it is the road that was taken by Henry Tate and Abram Lyle. They could not have known the verses quoted above, for they had died before Flecker wrote them. By the way they lived their lives, however, they seem to have been pilgrims as well as the 'Merchant Princes' the contemporary Press called them. The modern Press does not speak in such terms and Henry's and Abram's descendants would laugh at the idea of being pilgrims. Nevertheless they do follow a trail. The mountains and the seas are different, but obstacles are still there to be overcome. The old 'paternalistic' days, for example, have been replaced by an era of co-determination, or *Mit-bestimmung* as it is called in the Fatherland. Decisions are, therefore, more difficult and slower to reach. But they still must be made.

In the course of Phase II we have lost many people, none of them Tates or Lyles, but people from among the other families on that same trail. Jo Whitmee, who went on working after two coronaries, Kenneth Brown, who died soon after retirement (the first Shift-Managers); George Rutty, Ernie Jones, Mick Gorst, Arthur Greene, Bill Strickett–the kindly Commissionaire at 21 Mincing Lane. Too many, alas.

And as Phase II ends the world changes even more rapidly and a new Phase begins in the Jubilee Year of Queen Elizabeth II. For Tate & Lyle as for anyone it has become an even more complex world than it was twenty-five years ago. The development of the central policy of the Company has been adapted to change during those two phases. Sugar refining in Britain has for over ten years been only a part of the Company's activities, though perhaps this is not realized by the general public. At the same time there has been an adjustment to the effects of the Wind of Change, and activities in raw sugar production have been modified. Fifteen years ago it was normal in the Annual Reports of raw sugar producing companies to refer to 'The Hazards of Tropical Agriculture'. These still exist.

An American, once chance-met in Belize – he later left apparently to avoid paying taxes he didn't think he owed – produced a tale to illustrate this:

A young man once established a fruit farm in Canada and from the sale of apples made a million dollars or two. Then a nearby forest fire spread and engulfed the lot. So, being of a determined nature, he went to Florida where in a few years, he had built up a large and flourishing citrus plantation and was smiling all the way to the bank. But then a hurricane wiped it out, smile and all. With a few dollars left and a stiff upper lip he started up again, this time with a rubber plantation, up the Amazon in Brazil. Great initial success was unfortunately followed this time by a flash flood on the Mighty River, which left him sitting in the mud surrounded by the broken stumps of rubber trees.

His head in his hands, he muttered: 'God! Three Times! Why do You *do* this to me?'

At which the Heavens opened, there was a blinding light, and a puzzled Voice from Above said: 'I dunno, George. There must be something about you that cheeses me off.'

A reduction in the involvement in sugar production and refining has been accompanied by new ventures, for it is after all silly to sit in the mud with your head in your hands. (That is why this book is called *Sugar and All That*.)

Looking back over a century it is easy to see occasions when matters might have been otherwise arranged. There have however been relatively few mistakes. The Chocolate Factory in the 1890s at Plaistow was one. It is difficult to explain why the investment was made in Thomas Boag Ltd. when bulk sugar handling was being introduced. With hindsight it might have been better to disengage earlier from Jamaica and Trinidad but this would at the time have been difficult. Perhaps it would have been a good idea to have expanded R. & D. activities a little earlier but again, although they were late on the scene these have produced some excellent results in a short space of time. Tendapearl and Bagelle were other innovations which failed. There were the U.M. difficulties in the Argentine.

Recently, trading has become an increasingly important part of the Company's activities. It is a long time since 1882 when Abram Lyle's possession of six cargoes of Java sugar coincided with a bumper beet harvest in Europe. Tate & Lyle, International (Ltd.) has established itself as one of the foremost houses operating on the world sugar market, either on its own or in joint ventures with other international sugar houses. (The vital role of the Middle Man is beginning to be better understood by people generally.) This activity will be considerably assisted by the possession of Yonkers Sugar Refinery in the U.S.A., which was acquired late in 1976 and is being operated by Redpath.

Then there are other commodities. Trading in molasses is different from trading in sugar. Tea is traded world-wide by auction and there is as yet no Terminal tea market, but it is an interesting commodity. Moreover it needs packeting, and since jobs are difficult to come by in Liverpool, Ridgeways' has become part of Tate & Lyle and a packing operation is established there. Coffee and cocoa are traded, too.

It is agreeable to report that while the great buildings at Plaistow Wharf had all gone by 1977, the place is still alive. The Harlequin Packing Station is a model of its kind, and the 'White City' Stores are as busy as ever. Even more important, great improvements have been made in the method of production of Golden Syrup and new syrup-filling machines introduced. The new techniques involve the use of a special type of charcoal and the process is far more attractive to look at than the old one. The whole business has begun, at the time of writing, to take on something of the freshness that, a century earlier, made Lyle's Golden Syrup so popular.

There may be only 600 people on the site now, compared with four times that number a generation earlier, but they are in the vanguard of modern food technology.

The splendid old Lyle Refinery, so far from being as it were a candidate for the knackers' yard, like those poor old horses of whom Mr. Atchelor of Lower Tooting 'disposed', has, by some kind of genius loci, become more like a phoenix arising from the ashes.

Pure trading, although reputable, is not enough on its own for a firm which has always moved from trading to involvement in pro-duction–Abram Lyle from shipping and trading in sugar and herrings, and Henry Tate from groceries, into sugar refining. The arrival on the scene of new sweeteners based on starch demands that this be investigated. Production of these was held up by E.E.C. regulations in 1977 but it may one day be worth while if the need for it develops.

There is, too, the furthering of technologies developed by R. & D. which will come to fruition in the 1980s in much the same way as Henry and Abram in the 1870s were looking forward to the 1880s. One is the range of Talo products which are being sold by Tate & Lyle Engineering Ltd., forming a major part of T.L.E.'s own range.

Shipping has its problems.

Henry and Abram lived through difficult times–Bounties and the like. Times are nearly always difficult. In the fourth quarter of the twentieth century a phenomenon called inflation which used to be associated with toy balloons and water-wings has taken a grip on life in general. To cope with this it is necessary to Take a Long View and pay attention to

Discounted Cash Flows. (What would Henry and Abram have made of that?) The situation demands a readiness to look further ahead than tomorrow or next week or the next General Election. What, for example, might happen if sugar became too valuable to be merely eaten? It is a carbohydrate and man could, one day, find other uses for it.

So it is as well that as the 1970s draw to an unlamented close (the 1940s were interesting, the 1950s rather nice, the 1960s not so agreeable, and 1984 isn't here yet) at least the Old Firm has a number of very bright chaps having a dekko (or Indian look) at what to do in the 1980s.

This is really the end of this book, and yet it is difficult to stop, for Tate & Lyle do not seem to be in the mood to come to a halt.[1] One can feel a certain sympathy with the late Ludwig van Beethoven when, in Old Vienna, he was getting towards the end of his Fifth Symphony.

All that V-sign stuff (Ta-ta-taTum) had been properly scored, so had the magical transition from the third to the last movement. But now, how to bring it all to a close? Dominant. Tonic. Dominant. Tonic. Tonic. Tonic. Tonic. (Where's that blue pencil?) Tonic. Tonic. Tonic. *TONIC*. (Ah, at last. Where's the gin?)

There is still, however, one unsolved Dominant (or Tonic). Henry Tate and Abram Lyle, as has been said as nauseam (or rather, come to think of it, I hope not as far as that) never met. Even by the late 1970s Tates and Lyles had never interbred. There were sons of Tate and sons of Lyle (and certainly S.O.B.'s) but never, so far, *Sons of Tate (Ampersand) Lyle*. It seemed worth asking why. The best answer came from Saxon Tate. Himself the Chairman of the acronymic EXCO, he happens also to have been one of England's top jockeys until he had broken an awful lot of bones and in any case had been advised to take up something relaxing, perhaps like Tate & Lyle. As an expert he gave the matter a good deal of consideration. 'No', he said gravely at length, 'It wouldn't do. It would be like crossing a runner with a stayer. You'd get a slow horse which wouldn't last the course.'

There's genes for you.

Perhaps, however, the last word should rest with that constant source of fun: Shakespeare-Holloway-Sellers and Yateman-Mighty Sparrow-Chevalier-Professor F. H. (Tony) Tate:

'*A Tucket Sounds.*
The shades of H. Tate and A. Lyle are seen hand in hand tip-toeing away (Stage left). (Do you really mean left, *Tate?)*
The Band plays: In a Monastery Garton.
The Curtain Descends.'

---

[1] Indeed, as this book goes to print they are moving from 21 Mincing Lane, after nearly a century, to a new site called Sugar Quay, overlooking the Thames.

After Thoughts

No. Sorry. Parting that curtain and dashing off the dust from my lapels, I want to say Thank you to John Lyle[1] who asked me to write this book, perhaps because I spent half my life in the Firm. I am truly grateful. It has been a labour of love.

Now that it is finished I can see all the defects of such a labour; defects in organization of material, in composition, even in grammar. It is far too long, but it could have been longer if only there were not limits to what people will read. It will never have the *succès fou* of *Lady Chatterley's Lover* for, although Tate & Lyle for long maintained a farm in Norfolk for training young agriculturists, they never seemed to employ that sort of game-keeper.

It should, I know, have included more facts, more incidents–*not*, I think more figures, but above all more about individual people. There is probably too much verse in it, but poetry is a part of people, or should be. There are so many names I have omitted or barely mentioned, partly from ignorance, partly for that hoary old reason, lack of space. But because they are not mentioned it does not mean that they are, or have been, of less importance than those whose names occur in the book. I hope the living will forgive me. As to the dead, I shall have (I hope) to wait for a bit to hear.

John Donne wrote:

'All mankinde is of one Authour and is one volume. When one manne dyes one chapter is not torne out of the booke but translated into a better language and everye chapter must be soe translated. God employes several translators. Some pieces are translated by age, some by sicknesse, some by warre, some by justice. But God's hande is in everye translation and His hande shall binde up all our scattered leaves again for that librarye where everye booke shall lye open one to another . . .'

And I like to think he was right.

---

[1] As this book went to press, on January 19th, 1978 he was elected President in succession to Ian and Lord Jellicoe, the first non-family man to do so, became Chairman in his stead. This does not of course mean the end of the tradition that family members become Chairmen.

Bibliography

I
Published Works

Agricultural Enterprise Studies: *Economic Report No. 7, Britain's Sugar Dilemma*, 1949
Aims of Industry Ltd.: Sundry articles, 1949–1950
Anon: *Manual of Sugar Companies*, 1929
Anon: *Workshop of the British Empire*
Aspinall, Algernon: *Pocket Guide to the West Indies*, (West India Committee) 1954
British Sugar Bureau: *A Study of Sugar*, 1977
Canadian Sugar Institute: *The Story of Sugar*, 1976
Davies, Ernest: *National Capitalism*, (Gollancz) 1939
Davies, Ernest: *National Enterprise*, (Gollancz) 1946
Deerr, Noel: *History of Sugar*, (Chapman & Hall) 1949
Fairrie, Geoffrey: *Sugar*, (Tate & Lyle Ltd.) 1925
Fairrie, Geoffrey: *The Sugar Refining Families of Great Britain*, (Tate & Lyle Ltd.) 1951
von Hagen, Victor Wolfgang: *Maya Explorer* (University of Oklahoma', 1949
Hampshire, Cyril: *The British in the Caribbean* (Weidenfeld & Nicholson', 1972
Harris, Simon. & Ian Smith: *World Markets in a State of Flux* (University of Newcastle-upon-Tyne)
H.M.S.O.: *Report on the Sugar Beet Industry at Home and Abroad*, May 1931
H.M.S.O.: *Report of the U.K. Sugar Industry Inquiry Committee Cmd. 4871*, April 1935
H.M.S.O.: *Sugar Policy. Proposals of H.M. Government. Cmd. 4964*, July 1935
Hughes, Richard: *A High Wind in Jamaica*, 1929
Hugill, J. A. C.: *Sugar* (Cosmo Publications), 1949
Hugill, J. A. C.: *WISCO in Jamaica*, 1963
Hugill, J. A. C.: *Caroni in Trinidad*, 1963
Hutcheson, John M.: *Notes on the Sugar Industry of the United Kingdom* (James M'Kelvie & Son), 1901
International Sugar Journal: passim
James, Hurford and St. J. Sayers: *Story of Czarnikow* (Harley Publishing Co.), 1967
Jones, Tom: *Henry Tate 1819–1899*, (Tate & Lyle Ltd.) 1952
Labour Party: *Labour Believes in Britain*, 1949
Leigh Fermor, Patrick: *The Travellers' Tree* (John Murray), 1950
Lewis, Frank: *Essex and Sugar*, 1974
Lyle, Alexander Park: *Family Notes* (MacLehose & Jackson), 1922
Lyle Oliver: *Technology for Sugar Refinery Workers* (Chapman & Hall), 1950
Lyle Oliver: *The Plaistow Story* (privately published) 1954
Lyle of Westbourne: *Mr. Cube's Fight against Nationalisation* (Hollis & Carter), 1954
Martineau, George: *Sugar, (1910)* (Pitman), 1932
Meneight, W. A.: *A History of the United Molasses Company (Seal* (Xal House Press), 1977
Prinsen-Geerligs, H. C.: *The World's Cane Sugar Industry, Past and Present* (Amsterdam), 1912
Smith, Charles: *Britain's Food Supplies*, (Fabian Society) 1940
Smith, Ian *see* Harris, Simon
Stoddard, Jeanne: *Manbré–A Hundred Years of Sugar Refining in Hammersmith and Fulham* (Hammersmith Historical Society), 1974
Tate & Lyle Transport Ltd.: *Pease Progress*, 1974
Tate & Lyle Times: passim, 1949–1977
Thompson, J. Eric S.: *Maya Archaeologist* (University of Oklahoma), 1963
Watson, John A.: *100 Years of Sugar Refining*, (Tate & Lyle Refineries Ltd.) 1974

II
Manuscripts and Unpublished Sources

(N.B. These are being sorted out. At present some are at Head Office, some at Thames Refinery some at Plaistow Wharf, some in Greenock, and some at Liverpool.)

Henry Tate & Sons: Dividend book (Ordinary Shares) 1903–1921
Henry Tate & Sons: Private Ledger 1903–1921

Henry Tate: Book of photographs of the Tate Collection 1895

Henry Tate: Catalogue of collection of pictures at Park Hill, Streatham

Henry Tate: Prospectus for sale by auction on May 5th 1920 of Park Hill

Henry Tate: Illuminated address to–from the Friends of the Tate Institute, February 1895

Henry Tate: Printed letter from, dated December 31st 1861

Henry Tate: Transcript of programme by John Cotterell, Radio Blackburn, September 26th, 1976

Henry Tate: Book of press cuttings following death of Sir Henry Tate 1897

William Henry Tate: Family tree of Tates, March 1904

William Tate (The Rev.): Debit note from A. Crompton, June 20th 1811 for teaching Ellen Gent.

Oliver Lyle: Personal notebook containing statistics on Abram Lyle & Sons, Tate & Lyle Ltd. etc. 1912–1961

John Orbell: *History of the Lyle Shipping Company* (awaiting publication, 1977)

John Russell: *The Growth of Thames Refinery* (typescript), 1966

John Russell: *Early Days of Sugar Refining (1576–1640)* (typescript)

John Russell: *Clyde Wharf Sugar Refinery (1864–1887)* (typescript)

John Russell: *James Blake: Biographical notes* (typescript)

John Russell: *J. P. Muir: Biographical notes* (typescript)

John Russell: *J. W. MacDonald: Biographical notes* (typescript)

John Russell: *Henry Tate (Jnr.): Biographical notes* (typescript)

John Russell: *Sugar Refining 70 years ago* (typescript)

John Russell: *Sugar Bounties 1879* (typescript)

James Blake: Diary December 31st 1875 to November 16th 1876 (original and typed copy)

Walter M. Stern. B.Sc.: *The London Sugar Refiners around 1800* (Reprint from the *Guildhall Miscellany* No. 7, February 1954)

A. P. Crouch: *Silvertown–the Neighbourhood* (typescript), 1900

C. L. Anderson: *A History of Thames Refinery* (typescript), 1973

W. A. Coupland: *Belize Sugar Industries Ltd.* (typescript), 1977

George F. Chalmers: *Caroni Ltd. and its Predecessors* (typescript), 1970

Peter Clark: *Background to Broadway Works, Millwall* (typescript), 1977

Reginald Gower: *Note on Fowlers' Refinery* (typescript), 1977

N. F. Kindon: *A Short History of Silvertown Services* (typescript), April 1965

J. A. Watson: Correspondence re *100 Years of Sugar Refining*, 1971–74

John Wright & Co.: 3 packets of letters (1858–62)

R. F. Wall: Book of technical formulae, 1910

J. F. P. Tate: *Wandsworth Packing Station* (typescript), 1955

H. E. C. Powers: *Notes on Research at Thames Refinery* (typescript), 1977

F. A. Sudbury: *Notes on Thames Refinery, John Walkers' and Shippers* (manuscript) 1977

Anon: *The War years. Historical record at Thames Refinery*, September 1939–43 (incomplete)

W. R. Booth: *History of Tate & Lyle Ltd.* (typescript), February 1949

F. H. Tate: *History of Tate & Lyle Ltd. (Labour Relations)* (typescript), February 1949

Richard Dimbleby: Transcript of recordings at Plaistow Wharf, July 1949

Anon: *Sugar Refining in Great Britain. A Fifty years' record 1859–1909* (Reprinted from the *Gentleman's Journal and Gentlewoman's Court Review*), 1949

W. N. Walker: *Walkers' 1795–1950* (typescript), 1950

W. N. Walker: *Centenary of John Walker & Company 1850–1950*, 1950

J. A. C. Hugill: *A History of the British Sugar Corporation* (typescript) 1975

Press Cuttings: *Anti-Nationalisation Campaign*, Books 1–5, 1949–50

Various: Papers & documents on sugar refining and on speakers' teams, 1949–50

Various: Correspondence on nationalisation, 1949–50

Various: Copies of posters, wrappers and slogans, 1949–50

Various: Sundry campaign booklets & other literature, 1949–50

Various: Notes on Refinery meetings, 1949–50

Various: Survey of public opinion on the nationalisation of sugar, November 1949

P. F. Runge: *The Business of Tate & Lyle Ltd.* (typescript), 1949

Tate & Lyle Ltd.: Board minutes (passim), 1921–1977

Tate & Lyle Ltd.: Director's Meetings, Plaistow Wharf 1936–65, Manager's Meetings, Plaistow Wharf 1936–65

Various: Correspondence & Reports, WISCO, Caroni Ltd. and Belize Sugar Industries, 1948–1967

Various: Central African Investments, 1953 onwards

Anon: *Survey of the Position of the South African Sugar Industry*, April 1964

Index

Achard, Franz Carl, *22*
Adams, Norman, *92*
Adant process, *40, 63, 177*
Africa, *201–8, 238–9*
Allan, Jimmy, *38*
Allcock, Harry, *203*
Allen, Charlie, *139*
Allott, Geoff, *261, 264*
Anderson, C. L., *92*
Andrews, David, *124*
Anglo-Dutch Sugar Corp., *87, 90, 106*
Anglo-Scottish Group, *90, 92–3*
Arnold, Ada, *136*
Arnold, Nell, *98*
Athel Line Ltd, *186, 256, 260, 262–4, 268*
Attfield, Michael, *231, 245, 297*
Auger, Harry, *100*
Austin, Henry, *92*

Banana-growing, *215*
Barbados, *17*
Bartlett, Bill, *131*
Beet, *20–3, 25, 87–91, 94, 146*
   assets taken over, *105–6, 111*
   Communist bloc production, *180*
   refining, *25–6*
   subsidy, *89, 92–3*
   Sugar Beet Committee, *87*
Belize, *251–5*
Bennett, Henry, *127*
Bennett, Bill, *127*
Bennett, Ivy, *162*
Bennett, Mike, *291, 295*
Berry, Albert, *283, 304–6*
Blackburn, F., *210, 223, 227, 230, 292*
Blake, James, *37–8, 40–3, 61, 63*
Blanchard, Walter, *91, 112, 115, 124*
Boag, Thomas, Ltd, *186–7, 311*
Booth, William, *202, 204, 308*
Bounties, *57–9*
Bovell, Paul, *220, 221, 226*
Bowes, Julian, *239*
Boyle, Jimmie, *127*
Bracken, Brendan, *167, 168*
British Sugar Corp., *105, 146, 169, 172*
British Sugar Refiners' Association, *29*
Brown, Kenneth, *92, 99, 100, 129, 138–9, 291, 310*
Browne, Stewart J., *261*
Brussels Convention (1903), *59, 66*
Buckeridge, Albert, *192*
Bulk shipments, *181–7*
Bull, George, *70, 100*
Burns, J., *133*
Burrows, Peggy, *136*
Bury Group, *91, 106*
Bustamante, W. A., *116–18, 163, 213, 216, 220*

Cahusac, Harold, *210, 220*

Caine, Sydney, *102*
Campion, A., *192*
Canada, *240–6, 250*
Cane, *15–20, 24, 120, 124*
   refining, *24–5*
Canteen facilities, *101, 141*
Cantley, *23, 87–8, 90*
Cardle, Terence, *205*
Carmichael, John, *92, 139, 284*
Caroni Ltd, *122–3, 210, 222–30, 261*
Carr, Matt, *101*
Carter, Leonard, *124*
Cary, Jim, *133*
Cater, Bill, *187*
Chalmers, George, *124*
Chambers, Steve, *140*
Chantrell, Percy, *288*
Chaplin, Harry, *162*
Chapman, Frank, *181, 243, 289*
Charley family, *114*
Charlton, Warwick, *157*
Chisholm, Sheila, *192*
Chisholm, W. H., *192*
Clacher, Dan, *38*
Clark, George, & Sons, *237*
Coffey, Jim, *192*
Collard, Geoff, *187*
Colwick, *89, 90*
Commonwealth Sugar Agreement, *214, 231, 299*
Confectionery business, *54, 311*
Cooke, Stanley, *203*
Cornwall, Alf, *140*
Coupland, Bill, *125, 221, 230*
Cowpe, George, *140*
Coyle, Clarence, *242–3, 245*
Crispin, J. B., *75*
Crook, Douglas, *263*
Cubes, *63, 131, 177, 179*
Cullen, Norman, *277, 297*
Curtis, Frank, *221, 254*
Customs duties, *57–9, 103, 181*

Dakoru, A. E., *239*
Darlow, Dan, *100*
Davidson, Mel, *244*
Davies, Phyl, *190*
Delessert, Benjamin, *21–2*
de Whalley, L. J., *284*
de Whalley, Siegfried, *133, 285, 290–1*
Dickinson, Denis, *199, 286, 290*
Dillon, Bill, *96*
Dobson, Rose, *81*
Drummond, George Alexander, *241*
Drummond, Huntley Redpath, *242*
Duggan, Tim, *139*
Duncan, James, *23, 29–30, 49, 186*
Dunlop, Sam, *140*
Dyke, John, *81*

Eastick family, *284*
Easton, Bev, *245*
'Electrical refining', *56–7*
Ellyatt, John, *78, 140, 279*
Ellyatt, Sidney, *78*
Engineering, *196–200*
European Economic Community, *297–300*
Executive Committee, *279*
Export trade, *179, 231*

Fahs, J. D., *254*
Fairrie family, *30, 31, 33*
Fairrie, Geoffrey, *99, 141, 181, 189, 195, 243*
Fairrie, James, *57, 221*
Fairrie, Leslie, *93–4*
Fairrie, Tony, *243*
Farley, Jim, *194*
Felstead, John, *205*
Fewkes, Derek, *292*
Fisher, Cyril, *192*
Fitzgerald, Dan, *140*
Food and Agriculture Organization, *280, 282*
Fowlers Ltd, *306*
France, *269–76*
Freestone, *77*
Friend, Henry C., *56–7*
Frog-hoppers, *124, 223, 225, 292*
Frome (Jamaica), *115–16, 210, 212, 216, 217*

Galloway, Wally, *138*
Garton, family, *305–6*
Gee, Sam, *126, 289*
Ghana, *238–9*
Giddings, Bill, *205*
Gilbert, Harold, *123, 125, 210, 224*
Gilbey, Bob, *100*
Gillies, Archibald, *124*
Glebe refinery, *48, 176*
Golden Syrup, *48, 53, 64, 81, 97–8, 131–2*
Gollin, Michael, *267*
Gooch, Charles, *194*
Gorst, Mick, *140, 310*
Graduate employees, *92, 99, 231*
Graham, John, *92, 298*
Greene, Arthur, *92, 139, 310*
Greene Committee, *95, 102–7*
Greene, Wilfred, *102*
Greenock refinery, *48–9*
Grieve family, *48*
Gross, David, *291*
Guile, Ivy, *136*

Hale, Rose, *98, 136*
Harrison, Arthur, *43, 63*
Hesser machines, *96–7, 195*
Hildrup, George, *77*
Hinde, Guy, *206*
Hiscocks, Nibs, *129, 141–2, 194*
Hobbs, Jim, *126, 129, 139, 197, 199, 244, 277, 291, 308*
Holmes, Sam, *140*
Home Guard, *133*
Hornton, Alf, *81*
Hornung, George, *202, 204*
Howlett, Sid, *162*

Hoyle, Jack, *266, 268*
Hrudke, Gus, *245*
Hughan, David, *204*
Hungarian sugar beet, *91*
Hunt, Harry, *78*
Hutson, Murray, *291*

Imports of sugar, *16, 28–9*
Imrie, Fraser, *295*
Industrial relations, *84, 142–3*
Innes, Bob, *292*
Irish Republic, *232–5*
Ive, Bill, *210, 292*

Jacques, Emmy, *68*
Jamaica, *112–19, 199, 209–22, 247–9, 291–2*
James, Alan, *199*
Jenkinson, Tom, *75*
Jervis family, *114–15*
Johnson, Lottie, *136*
Johnson, Walter, *69, 82, 92, 94, 139, 169*
Johnstone, Eric, *227*
Jones, Ernie, *310*
Jones, Jack, *84*
Jorisch, Robert, *91*

Kay, Harry, *187*
Kebbell, Mabel, *136*
Kelham, *88–90*
Kerr family, *30, 34–5, 302, 306*
Kerr, John, *47*
Keynsham, *195*
Kielberg, Sir Michael Kroyer, *256–66*
Kindon, Norman, *187*
King, Christopher, *127*
King, Walter, *82*
Kinnison, W., *133*
Kirkwood, Francis, *239*
Kirkwood, Robert Lucian Morrison, *80, 91, 106, 111–12, 118, 123, 212, 214, 220*
Kitchin, Michael, *231, 245*

Latham family, *179*
Laurie, Alex, *139*
Lavenham, *23, 29, 40, 49, 63*
Lee, Sir Kenneth, *102*
Lennox-Boyd, Alan, *131*
Lenz, Alf, *78*
Lessware, W. H., *134*
Lewis, Daisy, *136*
Lewis, Gladys, *136*
Lewis, Ivy, *136*
Lighterage, *141, 167*
Lincolnshire Group, *90*
Liverpool refinery, *35–6, 44, 61–2, 177*
    handling bulk cargoes, *185*
    modernizing procedures, *63*
    new building, *126*
Lloyd, Cyril, *102*
Longbridge, Lladys, *117, 118, 220*
Lunn, Andrew, *187*
Lyle family, *46–56*
Lyle, Abram (I), *29, 35, 46, 310*
Lyle, Abram (II), *46*
Lyle, Abram (III), *46–55*

Lyle, Abram (IV), *49, 64*
Lyle, (Abram) Arthur, *64, 75*
Lyle, Alexander, *48, 49, 54, 78, 80, 134*
Lyle, Charles, *49, 64, 69, 74, 75, 76, 179*
Lyle, Colin, *140, 277, 291*
Lyle, Ian, *64, 82, 98, 129, 137, 139, 149, 156, 163,*
   165, 167–8, 188–9, 206–7, 244, 247, 255, 308
Lyle, Ian Archie, *98, 126*
Lyle, Janet, *284*
Lyle, John, *54, 64, 75, 141, 176, 189, 203, 206,*
   247, 267
Lyle, Leonard, *64, 69, 75, 83, 98, 149, 154, 156,*
   164, 166, 170–1, 175, 307
Lyle, Oliver, *53, 55, 64, 69, 74, 75, 80, 83, 89,*
   139, 161, 176, 189–90, 278, 290
Lyle, Philip, *64, 69, 75, 80, 83, 139, 176, 189, 291*
Lyle, Robert Park, *49, 54, 56, 64, 68, 74, 75*
Lyle, William, *54, 64, 75*
Lyle Shipping Company, *47, 54*
Lynch, Charles, *187*

MacDonald, John W., *38, 40, 61, 75, 81, 288*
MacFie family, *31*
McGaw, Alan, *266, 268*
McGlone, Mick, *86*
McGregor, W. J., *243–5*
MacIntyre, Peter, *229*
McPhail, Charles, *56*
Magee, Howarth, *243, 245, 291*
Main, Hugh, *43, 81–2, 286*
Makin, Ted, *205*
Manbré & Garton, *34, 297, 301–6*
Manbré family, *303–4*
Manbré, Alexander, *283*
Manley, Norman, *116, 118, 216*
Mann, James, *284–5*
Maraj, Bhadase, *224, 229*
Marshall, Tom, *154*
Martin, L. A., *61*
Martin, Lionel, *75*
Martindale, Cyril, *203*
Martineau family, *30, 33–4, 302, 306*
Martineau, David, *30*
Martineau, Doris, *132*
Meneight, Bill, *256, 260, 262*
Merton Grove Company, *236*
Michelin, Charlie, *210, 220, 227*
Migliori, Amelia, *136*
Migliori, Bill, *74, 143*
Miller, Gordon, *124*
Milner, Graham, *227*
Mr. Cube, *145, 149–51, 154–73, 188*
Monymusk, *113, 164, 210, 212, 217, 222*
Morris, Jack, *124*
Mountjoy, Charlie, *77*
Moyoo, Ursula, *226*
Muir, John Patrick, *38, 40, 43, 61, 63, 81*
Murphy, James, *187*
Murray, C. C., *221*

Nationalization plans, *143–73*
Newstead, Charles, *92*
Nigeria, *238–9*
North, Bill, *78, 126, 129, 291*
Norway, *236–7*
Nyasaland, *206*

O'Connell, Mark, *133, 140*
Oliphant, Morton, *64, 98, 129, 141, 149, 161,*
   189, 244
Oxley, Dick, *239*

Packaging, *96*
Palache, Albert, *90, 94*
Parker, Ken, *291*
Payne, George, *139, 277*
Pease, John Robert, *191, 194*
Pease Transport, *142, 191*
Plaistow refinery, *53, 127, 176, 277*
Porteous, Ray, *245*
Potter, Alf, *99, 289–91*
Potter, C. V., *99*
Potter, Charles, *75, 80*
Potter, Vernon, *92*
Powers, Harold, *81, 286, 289*
Profit sharing, *175, 188*
Pullen, Bob, *100*
Pullen, Len, *100*
Purifiers, *30, 31*

Raffineries et Sucreries Say, *270–6*
Rationing, *131–2, 175, 176*
Raymond, Steve, *44*
Reading University, *295–6*
Redpath family, *240–2, 312*
Reed, Albert, *140*
Research, *283–96*
Rhodesia, *202–8*
Rhodesian Sugar Refineries Ltd, *202*
Ricketts family, *114–15*
Road transport, *141–167, 197–6*
Robinson, Claude, *63*
Rodwell, Harry, *205*
Rogers, Jennie, *68*
Roof, Harry, *77*
Rosser, Harry, *205*
Rowan, Colin, *99, 127, 129, 189, 195, 199, 268*
Rowan, Donald, *99, 127, 129*
Royal Commission on Sugar, *68, 78, 105*
Runge, John Julius, *68, 75, 78*
Runge, Peter, *75, 82, 92, 129, 137, 139, 149, 154,*
   156, 163, 165, 167, 171, 176, 188, 205,
   244, 247, 270, 277, 279, 292, 297–8
Rutty, George, *100, 139, 310*

St Croix, Robert, *194*
St John Cooper, Bobby, *157*
Sands, Ivy, *136*
Scott, George, *264, 268*
Sewill, Roger, *149*
Shaw, Neil, *245*
Shemilt, Gordon, *231, 237, 239, 245*
Shift managers, *99–100*
Ship ownership, *47*
Sick pay scheme, *189*
Silver, Samuel Winkworth, *62*
Silver Roadways, *195*
Silvertown, 1917 explosion, *70*
   refinery, *62*
Silvertown Services Ltd, *142, 167, 182, 185–7*
Silvertown Services Shipping Ltd, *186–7*
Simmons, Godwin, *185*

Slater, Albert, *199*
Slave trade, *17–19, 111*
Sly, Bob, *194*
Small Packets Departments, *97*
Smith, A. & W., Ltd, *91, 197, 205*
Smith, Florrie, *98*
Society of Sugar Refiners of London, *28*
Somner, Jimmy, *140*
South Africa, *307–9*
Spink, Richard, *227*
Stacey, Clementina, *191, 194*
Stachenko, Steve, *245*
Stevens, Charlie, *205*
Storey, Tom, *289*
Strauss, Ernie, *239*
Strickett, Bill, *310*
Strike action, *85*
Subsidy on beet, *89, 92–3*
Sudbury, Fred, *81–2, 111–12, 126, 129, 142, 176, 181*
Sugar Board, *232*
Sugar Line Ltd, *185–7, 268*
Sugar Line Terminals Ld, *187*
Sugar machinery industry, *197–8*
Sutherland, D. W., *99*
Swann, Jack, *244*

Tann, Bob, *140*
Tate family, *35*
Tate, Alfred, *61, 75*
Tate, Alfred Herbert, *61*
Tate, Bertie, *75*
Tate, David, *195*
Tate, Edwin, *43, 61, 63, 75*
Tate, Ernest, *61, 74, 75, 83, 98, 161*
Tate, F. H. (Tony), *9, 151, 154, 165, 195, 239, 247, 298, 313*
Tate, George, *61*
Tate, George Booth, *61, 63*
Tate, G. V. (Vernon), *69, 75, 81–2, 83, 98, 126, 134, 141, 149, 165, 176, 182, 194, 204*
Tate, Henry, *30, 35, 38, 45–6, 310*
Tate, Henry Jr., *61, 161*
Tate, Johnny, *189, 206-7, 230*
Tate, Louis, *78, 289*
Tate, Saxon, *246, 291, 313*
Tate, William, *75*
Tate, Sir William Henry, *61*
Tate & Lyle Ltd
　acquire Fairries, *33, 99*
　acquire Trinidad businesses, *122*
　amalgamation, early mistrust, *78–9*
　share exchange, *76*
　between wars, *80–6, 96–101*
　early merger negotiations, *74–6*
　interest in MacFies, *31*
Tate & Lyle Enterprises Ltd, *199*
Tate & Lyle Investments Ltd, *167*
Tate & Lyle (Nigeria) Ltd, *239*
Tate & Lyle (Norway) A/S, *236–7*
Tate & Lyle Technical Services Ltd, *197, 199–200, 201, 205*
Tate & Lyle Transport Ltd, *190, 195–6*
Tate Gallery, *45*

Tate Institute, *45–6*
Taylor, Tommy, *131*
Thames Refinery, *38, 43, 177, 277*
Theakston, Bill, *131*
Thomas, Wally, *96*
Thompson, Hugh, *210, 292*
Tibbitts, Ted, *256, 263*
Tobago, *122*
Trade union recognition, *84*
Transport & General Workers' Union, *84*
Tree, Harry, *140*
Trinidad, *119–25, 199, 209–10, 220, 222–30, 247–9, 292*
Trinidad Shipping & Trading Co. Ltd, *121–2*
Tyrell, Joe, *140*
Tyzack, Bill, *127*

Unemployment, *126*
United Molasses Co. Ltd, *31, 112, 186, 256–68*

Van Rossum, Johannes Petrus, *87, 106*
Vlitos, Chuck, *292–3, 295*

Walker family, *30, 34*
Walker, Alan, *123, 125, 212, 266*
Walker, Claud (Johnnie), *81*
Wall, Bob, *81*
Wall, Dudley, *81, 82*
Wall, R. F., *43, 75, 81*
Waterman, *182*
Watson, Captain, *123, 125*
Watson, Charlie, *92*
Watson, John, *284–5, 291*
Watson, Maud, *68*
West Indies, *17, 108–25, 146*
　medical improvements, *210, 213, 223–4*
　naval warfare, *19*
　Tate & Lyle involvement, *111–12*
　see also Jamaica; Trinidad
West Indies Sugar Company, *114–19, 167, 215, 261*
Wetherall, Bill, *92*
Whitmee, Jo, *92, 99–100, 129, 139, 189, 202–3, 207, 221, 230, 243, 245–7, 267–8, 291, 310*
Wigger, Maureen, *166–7*
Williams, Lil, *98*
Willis, Tilly, *136*
Willis, Tom, *140, 141, 143*
Willmott, Amelia, *81*
Willsher, John, *140, 204, 206–7, 244, 308*
Wilson, Sandy, *81*
Wiltshire, Jessie, *135*
Windows, Freddie, *195*
Wingate-Saul, Tony, *268*
Wissington, *90, 91*
Woodward, Herbert, *60*
Works Council, *141*
World War I, *67–73*
World War II, *129–37, 261–4*
Wright, John, *35–6*

'Yellows sugar', *44*
Yetman, Joe, *43*

Zambia, *202, 206–7*